# mother panic

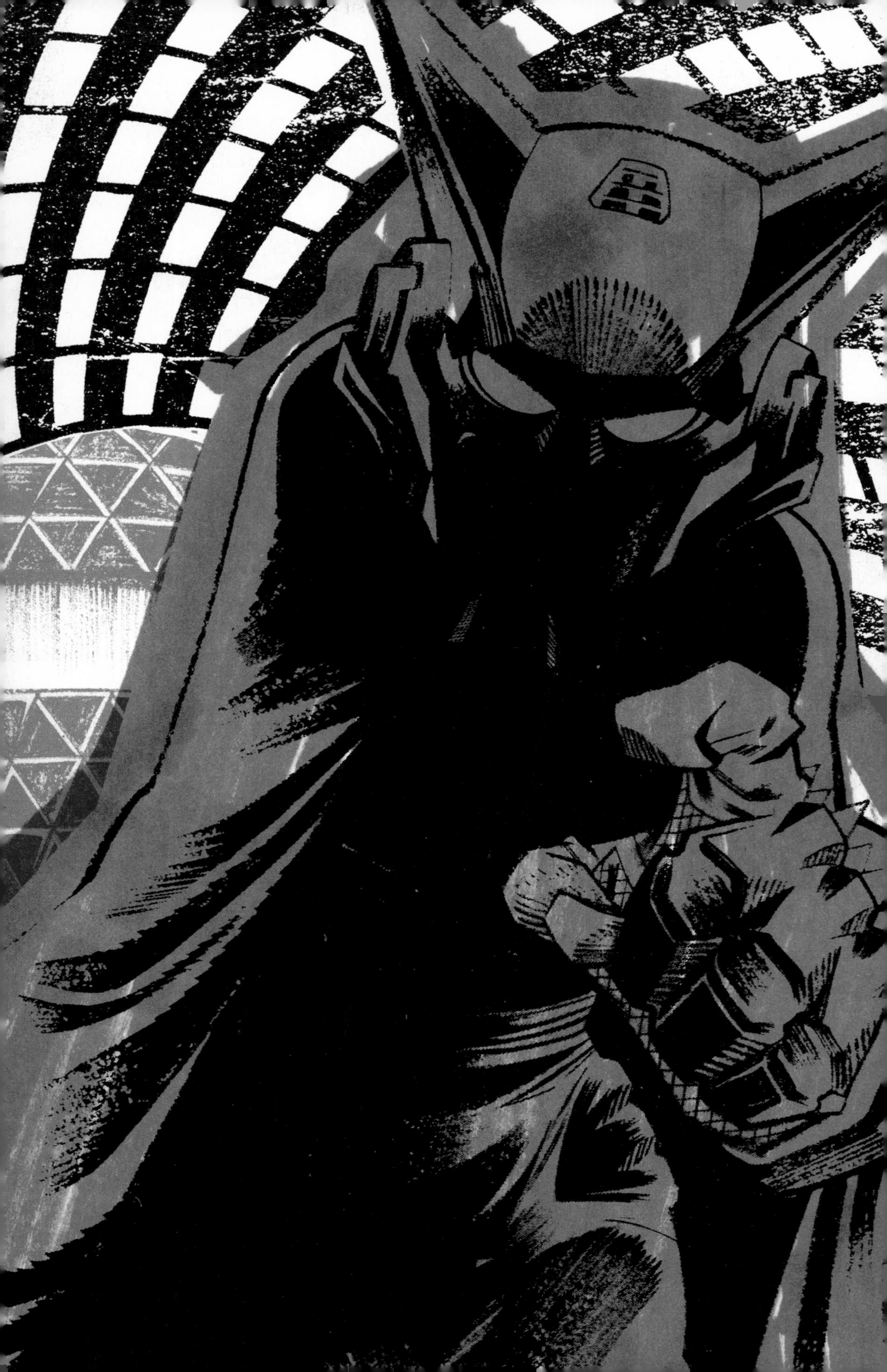

# mother panic

## VOL. 1: A WORK IN PROGRESS

**JODY HOUSER** Writer
**TOMMY LEE EDWARDS**
**SHAWN CRYSTAL** Artists

TOMMY LEE EDWARDS   JEAN-FRANCOIS BEAULIEU Colorists
JOHN WORKMAN   SHAWN CRYSTAL Letterers
TOMMY LEE EDWARDS Cover Art and Original Series Covers
GERARD WAY DC's Young Animal Curator

MOTHER PANIC CREATED BY GERARD WAY,
JODY HOUSER AND TOMMY LEE EDWARDS

Molly Mahan Editor – Original Series
Jeb Woodard Group Editor – Collected Editions
Scott Nybakken Editor – Collected Edition
Steve Cook Design Director – Books
Louis Prandi Publication Design

Bob Harras Senior VP – Editor-in-Chief, DC Comics

Diane Nelson President
Dan DiDio Publisher
Jim Lee Publisher
Geoff Johns President & Chief Creative Officer
Amit Desai Executive VP – Business & Marketing Strategy,
Direct to Consumer & Global Franchise Management
Sam Ades Senior VP – Direct to Consumer
Bobbie Chase VP – Talent Development
Mark Chiarello Senior VP – Art, Design & Collected Editions
John Cunningham Senior VP – Sales & Trade Marketing
Anne DePies Senior VP – Business Strategy, Finance & Administration
Don Falletti VP – Manufacturing Operations
Lawrence Ganem VP – Editorial Administration & Talent Relations
Alison Gill Senior VP – Manufacturing & Operations
Hank Kanalz Senior VP – Editorial Strategy & Administration
Jay Kogan VP – Legal Affairs
Thomas Loftus VP – Business Affairs
Jack Mahan VP – Business Affairs
Nick J. Napolitano VP – Manufacturing Administration
Eddie Scannell VP – Consumer Marketing
Courtney Simmons Senior VP – Publicity & Communications
Jim (Ski) Sokolowski VP – Comic Book Specialty Sales & Trade Marketing
Nancy Spears VP – Mass, Book, Digital Sales & Trade Marketing

**MOTHER PANIC VOL. 1: A WORK IN PROGRESS**

DC Comics
2900 West Alameda Avenue
Burbank, CA 91505
Printed by LSC Communications, Salem, VA, USA. 5/19/17. First Printing.
ISBN: 978-1-4012-7111-4

Library of Congress Cataloging-in-Publication Data is available.

MIX
Paper from
responsible sources
FSC® C132124

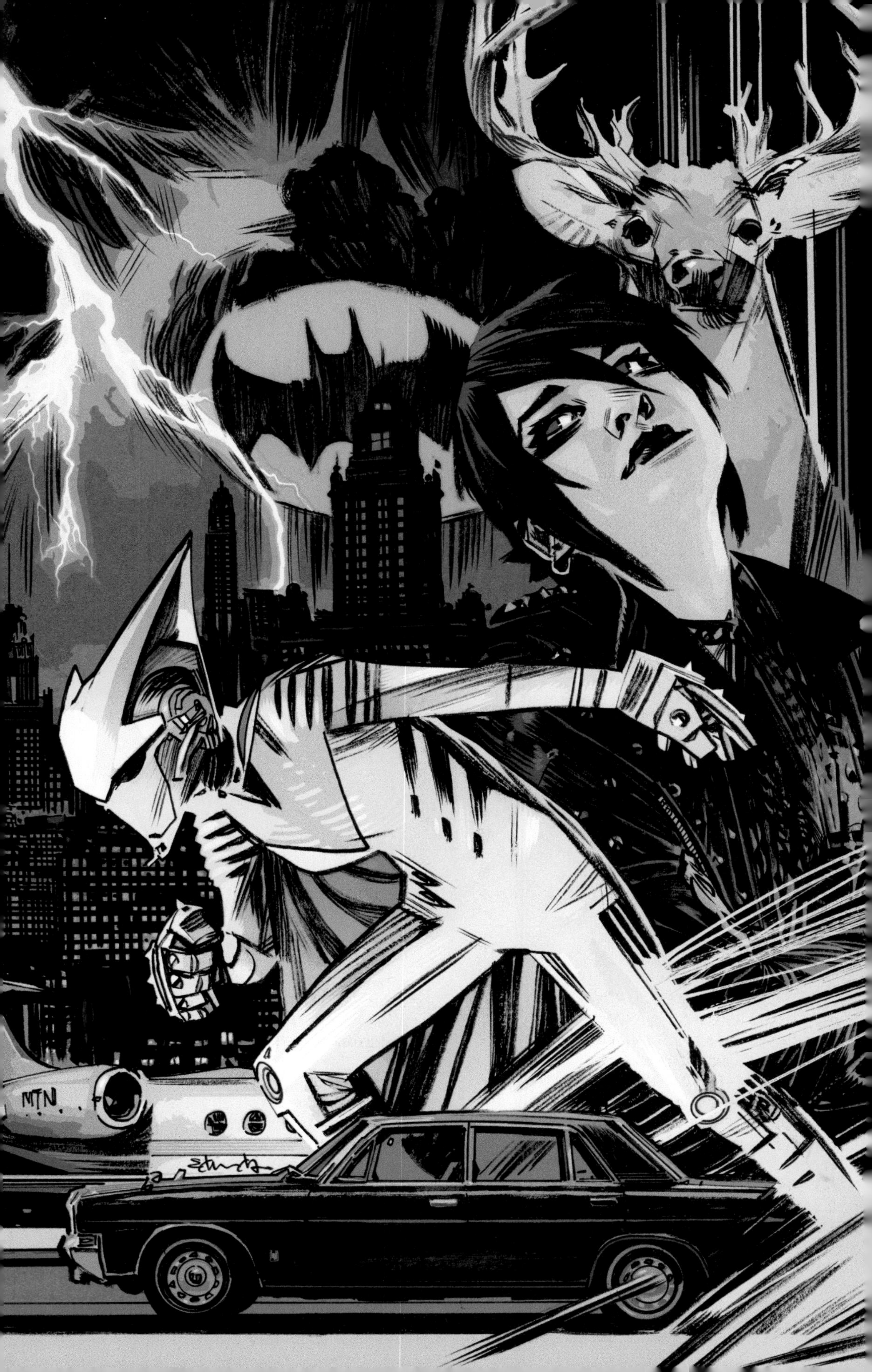

Variant cover art by Bengal

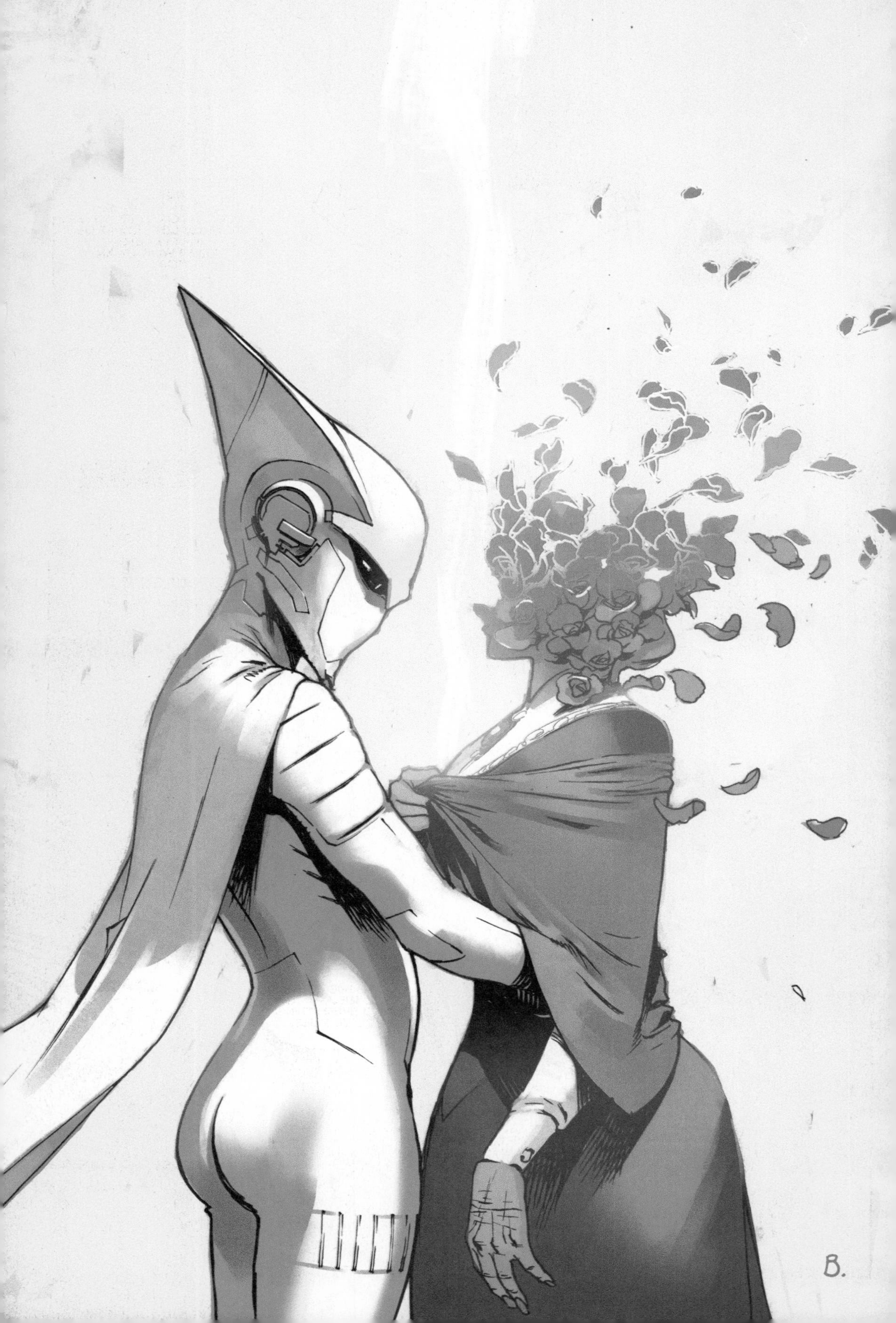

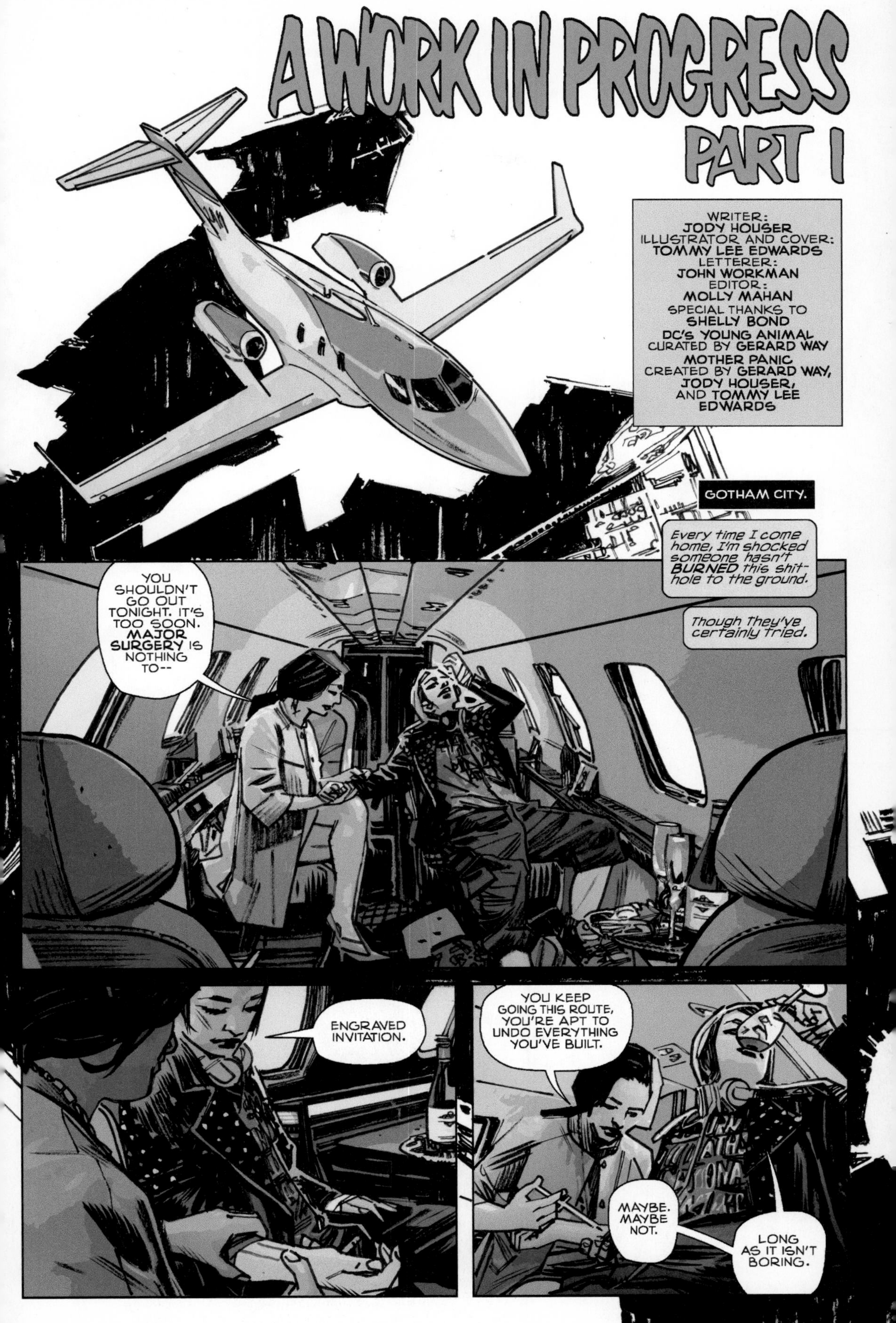
A WORK IN PROGRESS
PART 1
WRITER: JODY HOUSER
ILLUSTRATOR AND COVER: TOMMY LEE EDWARDS
LETTERER: JOHN WORKMAN
EDITOR: MOLLY MAHAN
SPECIAL THANKS TO SHELLY BOND
DC'S YOUNG ANIMAL CURATED BY GERARD WAY
MOTHER PANIC CREATED BY GERARD WAY, JODY HOUSER, AND TOMMY LEE EDWARDS
GOTHAM CITY.
Every time I come home, I'm shocked someone hasn't BURNED this shit-hole to the ground.
Though They've certainly tried.
YOU SHOULDN'T GO OUT TONIGHT. IT'S TOO SOON. MAJOR SURGERY IS NOTHING TO--
ENGRAVED INVITATION.
YOU KEEP GOING THIS ROUTE, YOU'RE APT TO UNDO EVERYTHING YOU'VE BUILT.
MAYBE. MAYBE NOT.
LONG AS IT ISN'T BORING.

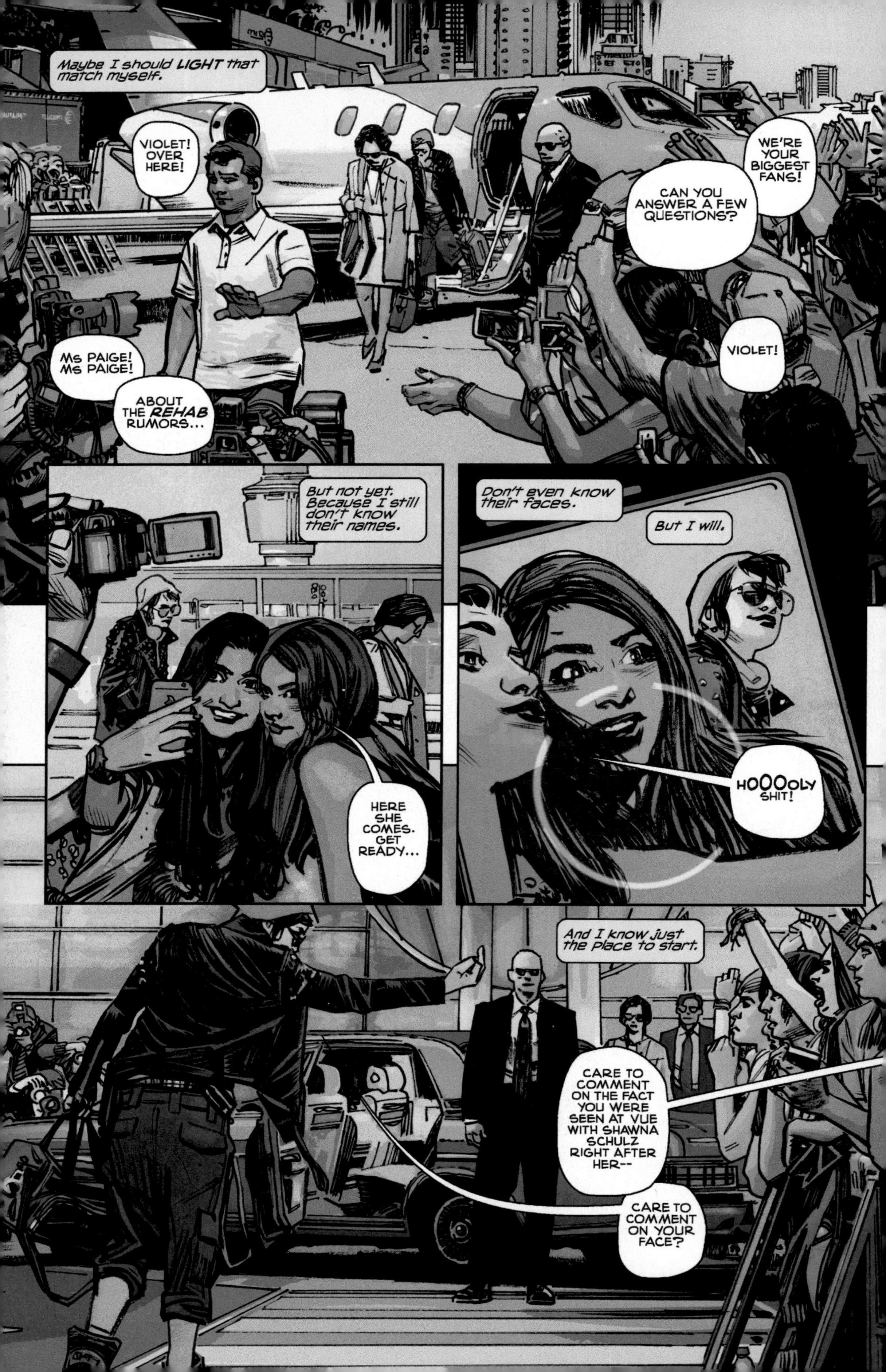
Maybe I should LIGHT that match myself.
VIOLET! OVER HERE!
WE'RE YOUR BIGGEST FANS!
CAN YOU ANSWER A FEW QUESTIONS?
VIOLET!
Ms PAIGE! Ms PAIGE!
ABOUT THE REHAB RUMORS...
But not yet. Because I still don't know their names.
HERE SHE COMES. GET READY...
Don't even know their faces.
But I will.
HOOOOLY SHIT!
And I know just the place to start.
CARE TO COMMENT ON THE FACT YOU WERE SEEN AT VUE WITH SHAWNA SCHULZ RIGHT AFTER HER--
CARE TO COMMENT ON YOUR FACE?

*Back at the very beginning.*

15 YEARS AGO.

THINK I'VE GOT EVERY-THING.

DID YOU SAY GOODBYE TO YOUR MOTHER?

IT'S A BAD DAY. SHE DOESN'T REMEMBER ME.

BUT SHE WILL TOMORROW. OR THE NEXT DAY. AND SHE MIGHT REMEMBER YOU DIDN'T SAY GOOD-BYE.

THAT'S A GOOD GIRL.

MAMA?

I HEARD THEM SINGING. REBECCA, REBECCA, REBECCA, REBECCA, REBECCA...

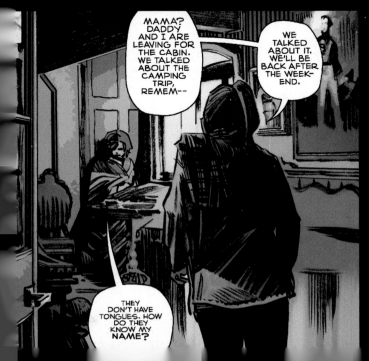

MAMA? DADDY AND I ARE LEAVING FOR THE CABIN. WE TALKED ABOUT THE CAMPING TRIP, REMEM--

WE TALKED ABOUT IT. WE'LL BE BACK AFTER THE WEEK-END.

THEY DON'T HAVE TONGUES. HOW DO THEY KNOW MY NAME?

YOU'LL BE BETTER WHEN WE GET BACK. I KNOW IT.

YOU CAN'T TRUST THEM. YOU CAN'T LET THEM TELL.

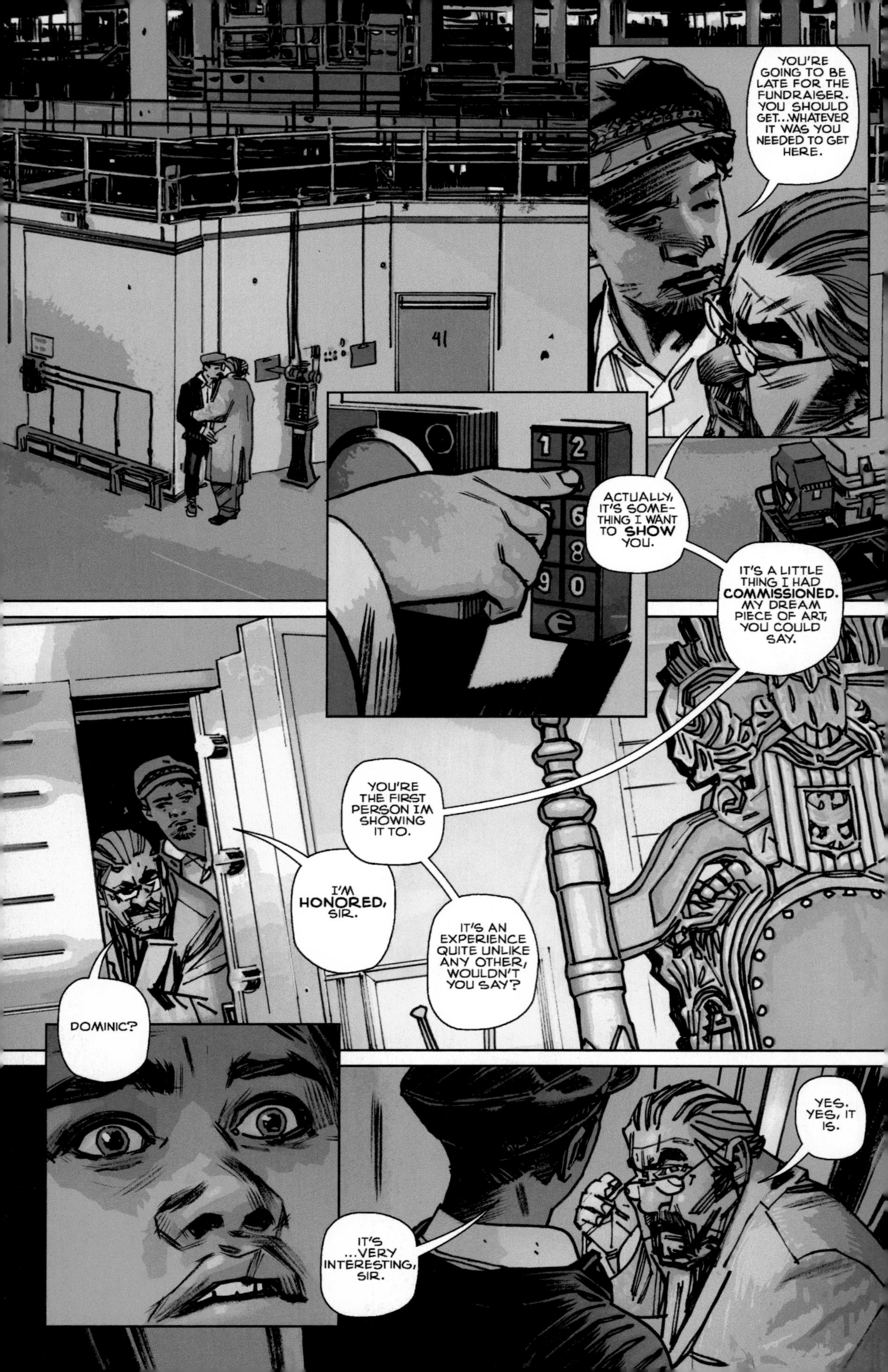
YOU'RE GOING TO BE LATE FOR THE FUNDRAISER. YOU SHOULD GET...WHATEVER IT WAS YOU NEEDED TO GET HERE.
ACTUALLY, IT'S SOMETHING I WANT TO SHOW YOU.
IT'S A LITTLE THING I HAD COMMISSIONED. MY DREAM PIECE OF ART, YOU COULD SAY.
YOU'RE THE FIRST PERSON IM SHOWING IT TO.
I'M HONORED, SIR.
IT'S AN EXPERIENCE QUITE UNLIKE ANY OTHER, WOULDN'T YOU SAY?
DOMINIC?
IT'S ...VERY INTERESTING, SIR.
YES. YES, IT IS.

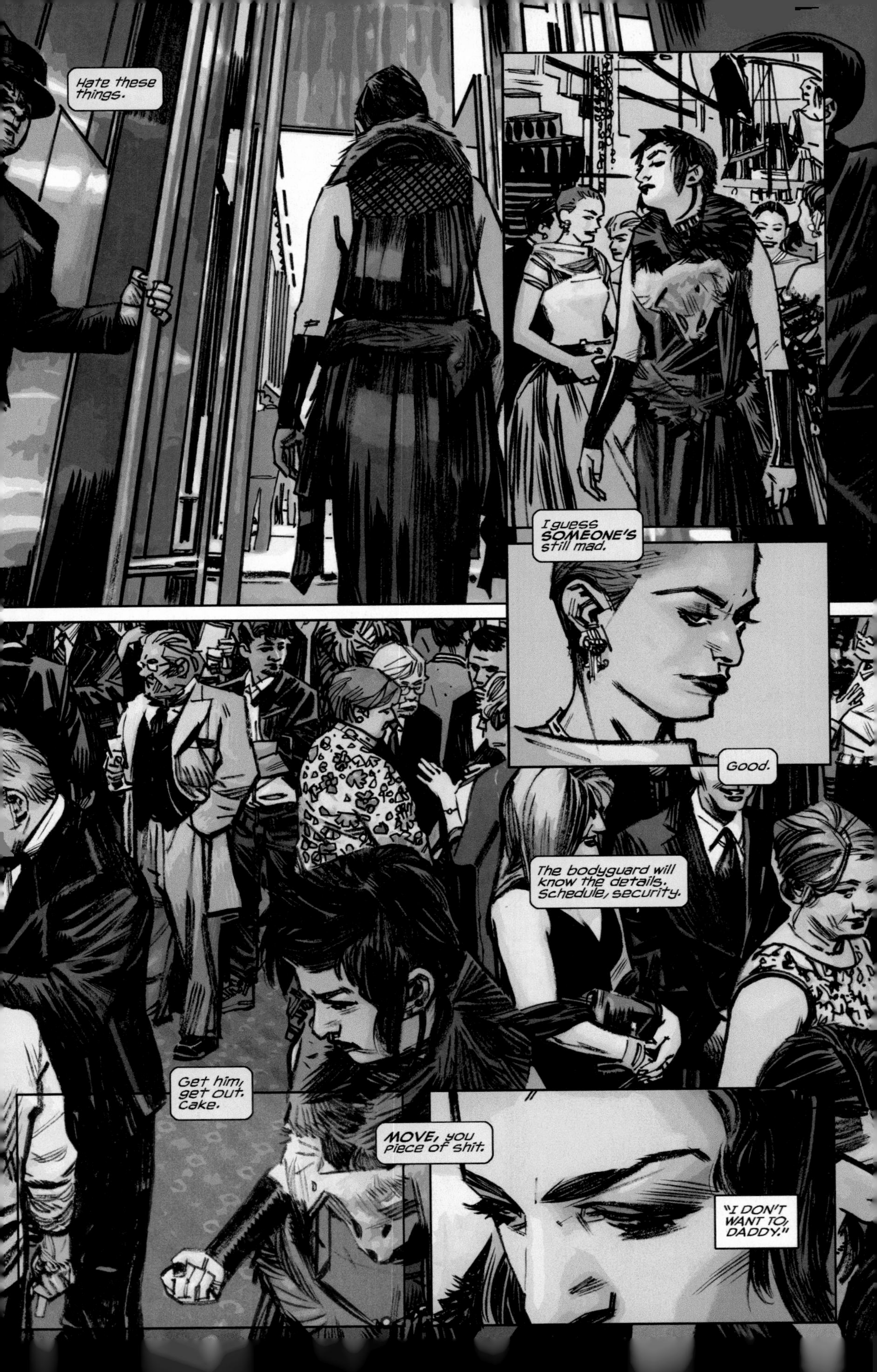
Hate these things.
I guess SOMEONE'S still mad.
Good.
The bodyguard will know the details. Schedule, security.
Get him, get out. Cake.
MOVE, you piece of shit.
"I DON'T WANT TO, DADDY."

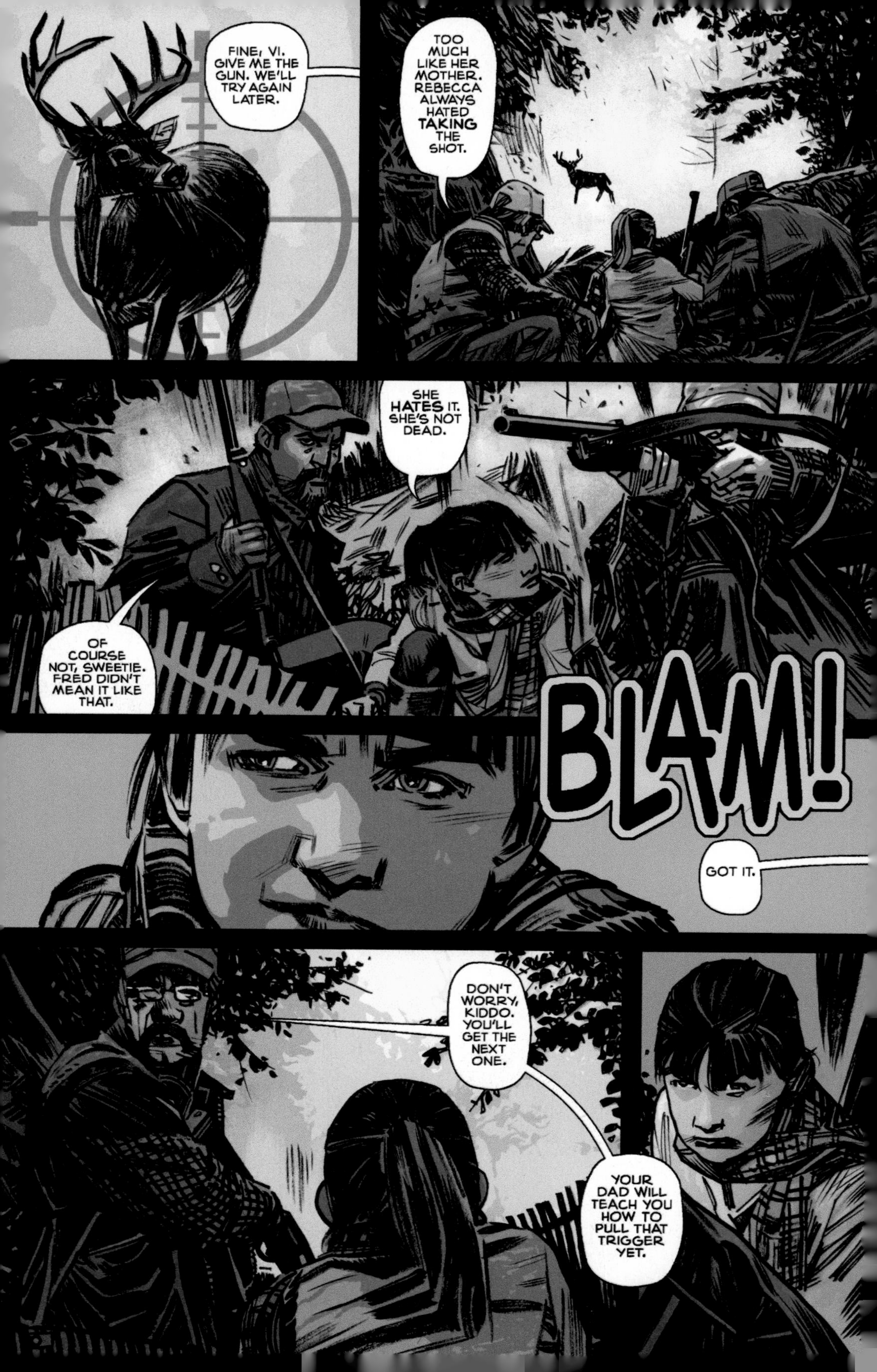
FINE, VI. GIVE ME THE GUN. WE'LL TRY AGAIN LATER.
TOO MUCH LIKE HER MOTHER. REBECCA ALWAYS HATED TAKING THE SHOT.
SHE HATES IT. SHE'S NOT DEAD.
OF COURSE NOT, SWEETIE. FRED DIDN'T MEAN IT LIKE THAT.
BLAM!
GOT IT.
DON'T WORRY, KIDDO. YOU'LL GET THE NEXT ONE.
YOUR DAD WILL TEACH YOU HOW TO PULL THAT TRIGGER YET.

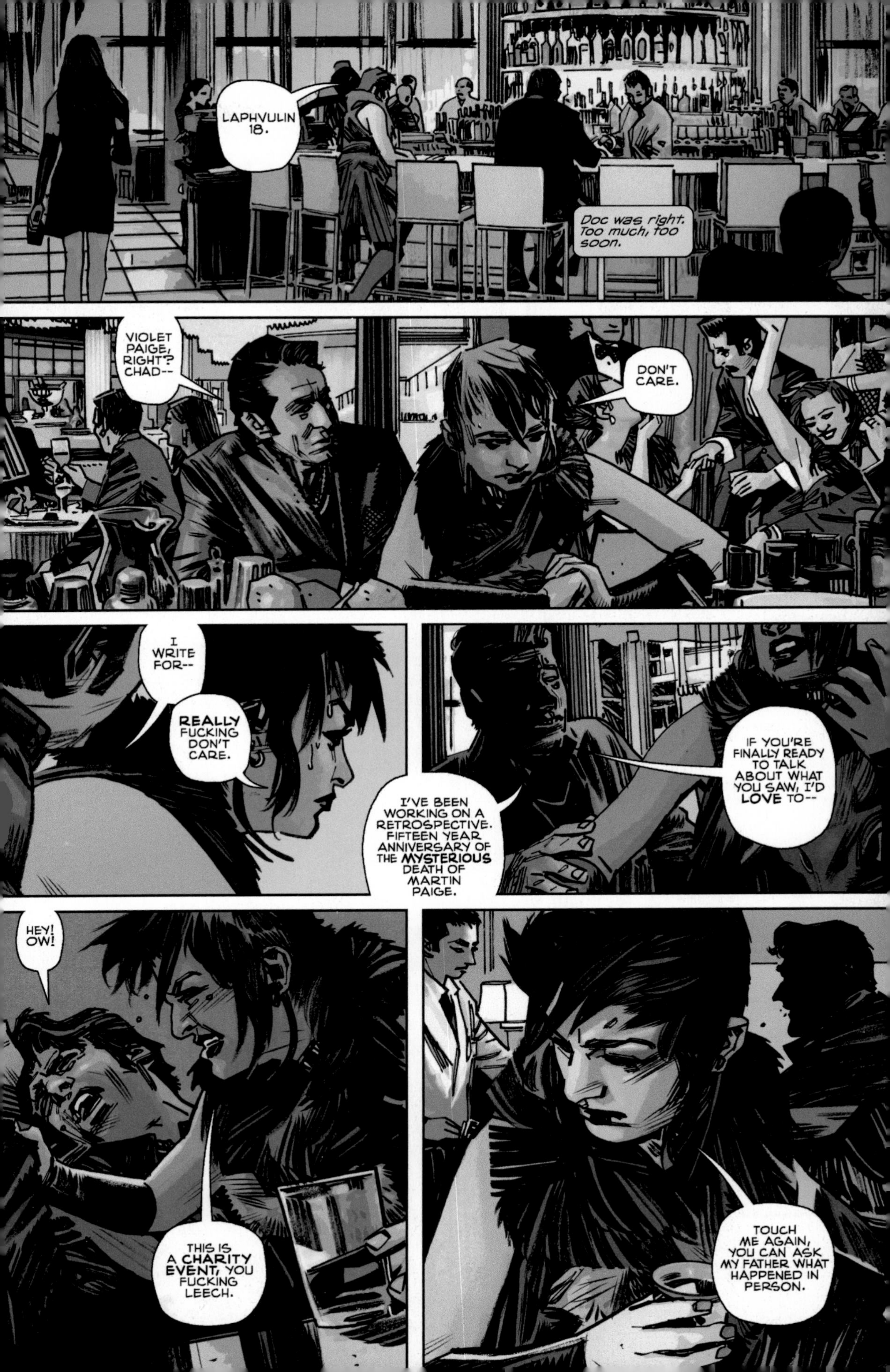
LAPHVULIN 18.
Doc was right. Too much, too soon.
VIOLET PAIGE, RIGHT? CHAD--
DON'T CARE.
I WRITE FOR--
REALLY FUCKING DON'T CARE.
I'VE BEEN WORKING ON A RETROSPECTIVE. FIFTEEN YEAR ANNIVERSARY OF THE MYSTERIOUS DEATH OF MARTIN PAIGE.
IF YOU'RE FINALLY READY TO TALK ABOUT WHAT YOU SAW, I'D LOVE TO--
HEY! OW!
THIS IS A CHARITY EVENT, YOU FUCKING LEECH.
TOUCH ME AGAIN, YOU CAN ASK MY FATHER WHAT HAPPENED IN PERSON.

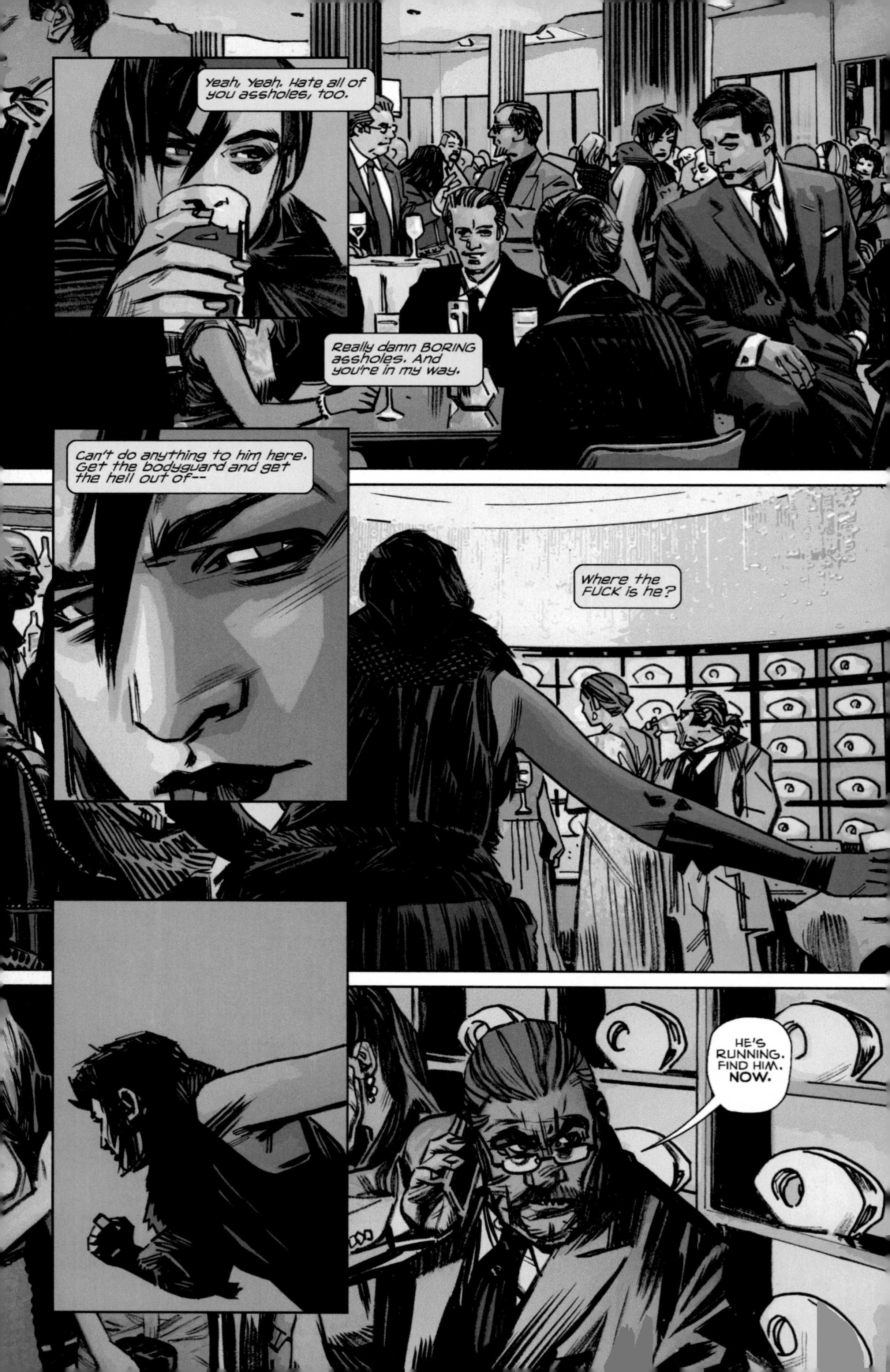
Yeah, Yeah. Hate all of you assholes, too.
Really damn BORING assholes. And you're in my way.
Can't do anything to him here. Get the bodyguard and get the hell out of--
Where the FUCK is he?
HE'S RUNNING. FIND HIM. NOW.

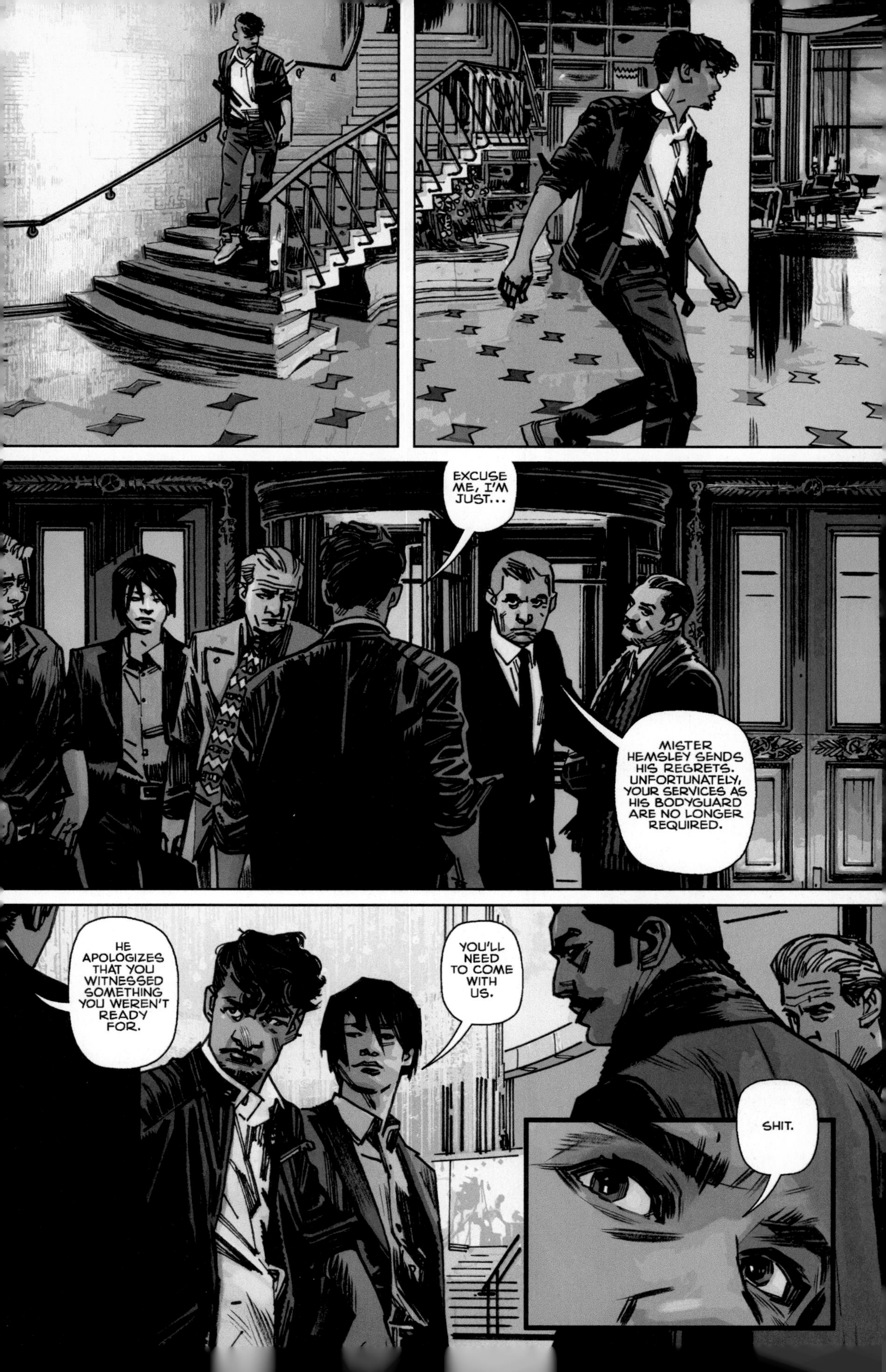
EXCUSE ME, I'M JUST...
MISTER HEMSLEY SENDS HIS REGRETS. UNFORTUNATELY, YOUR SERVICES AS HIS BODYGUARD ARE NO LONGER REQUIRED.
HE APOLOGIZES THAT YOU WITNESSED SOMETHING YOU WEREN'T READY FOR.
YOU'LL NEED TO COME WITH US.
SHIT.

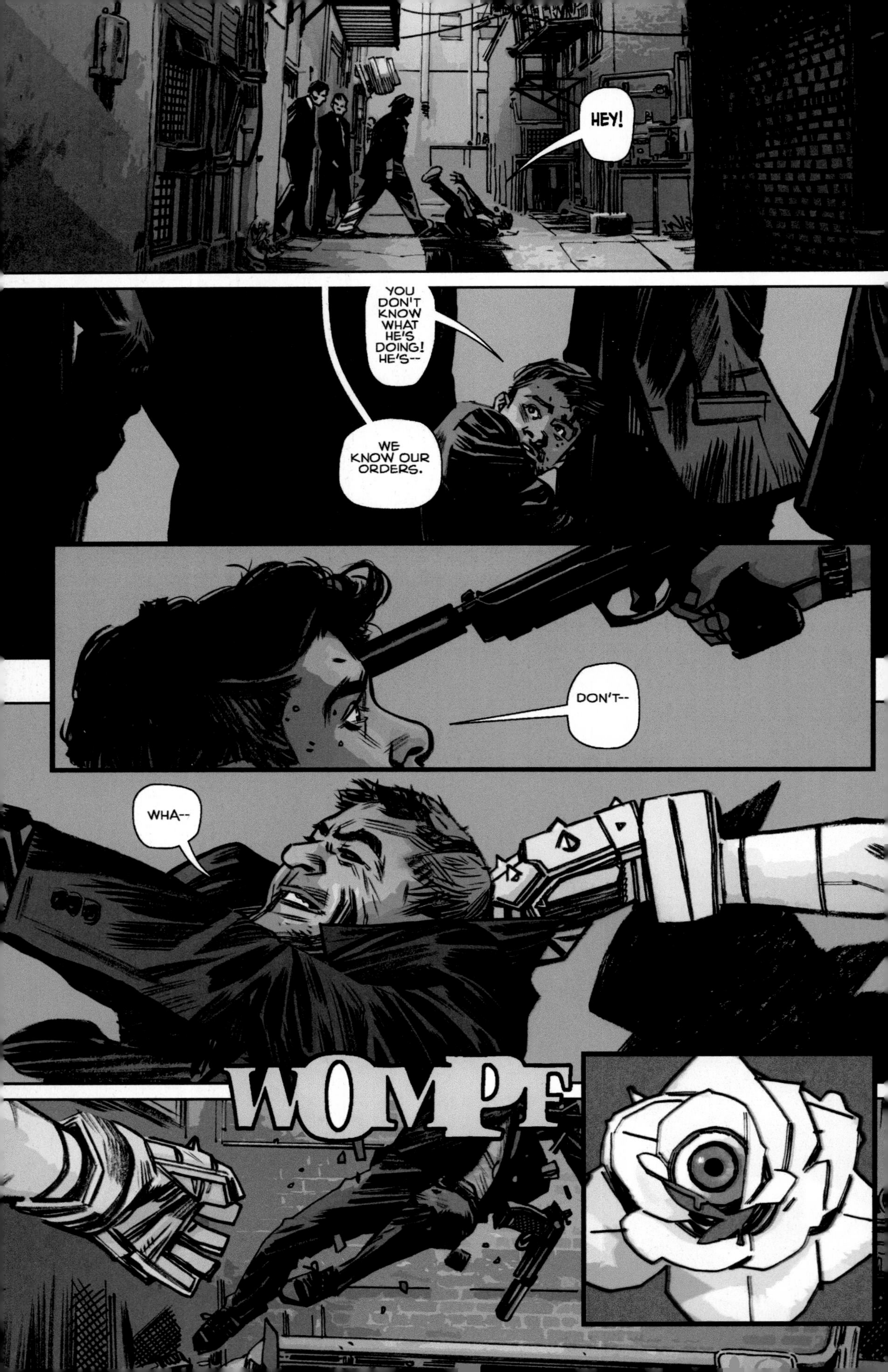
HEY!
YOU DON'T KNOW WHAT HE'S DOING! HE'S--
WE KNOW OUR ORDERS.
DON'T--
WHA--
WOMPF

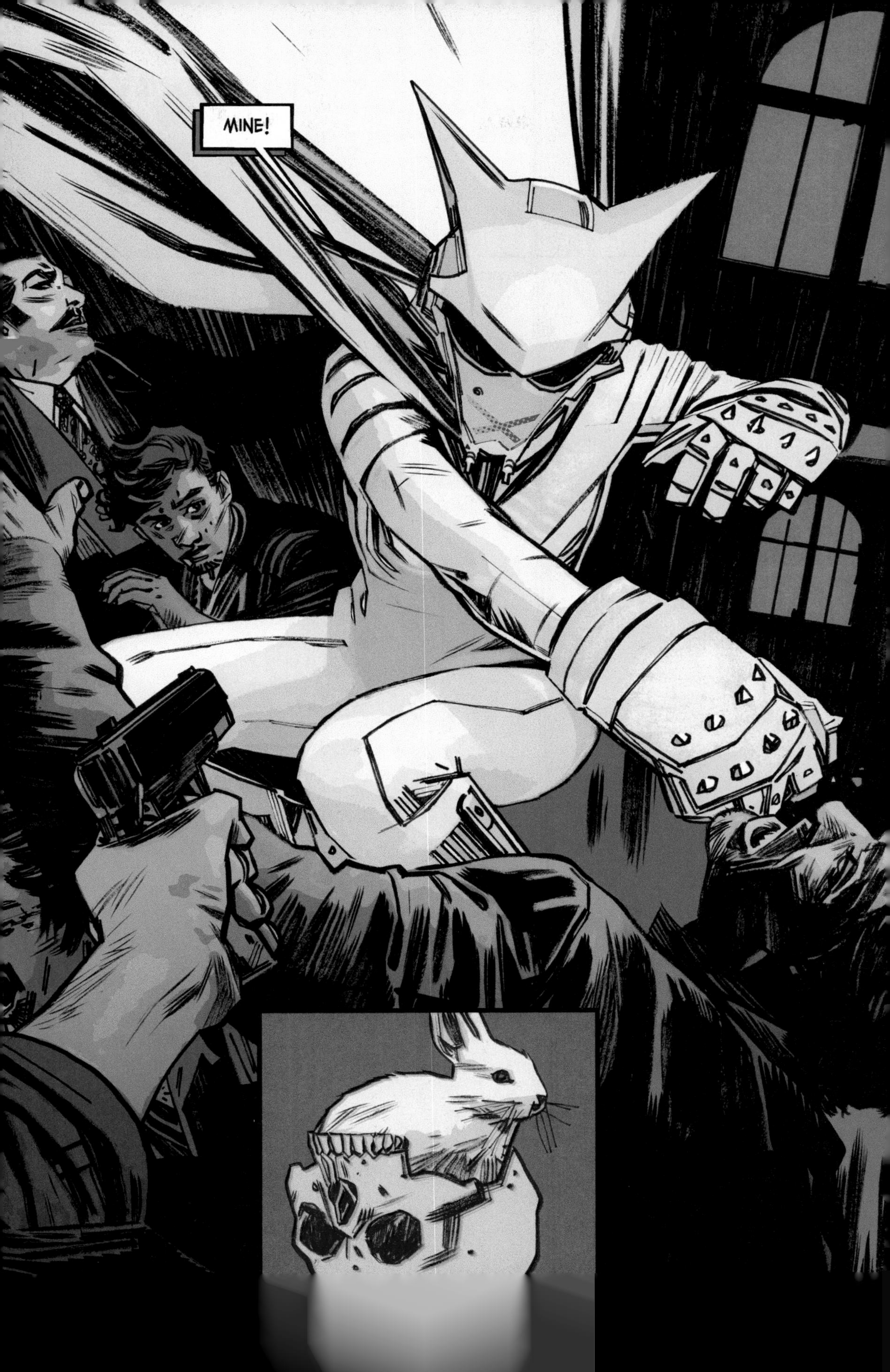
MINE!

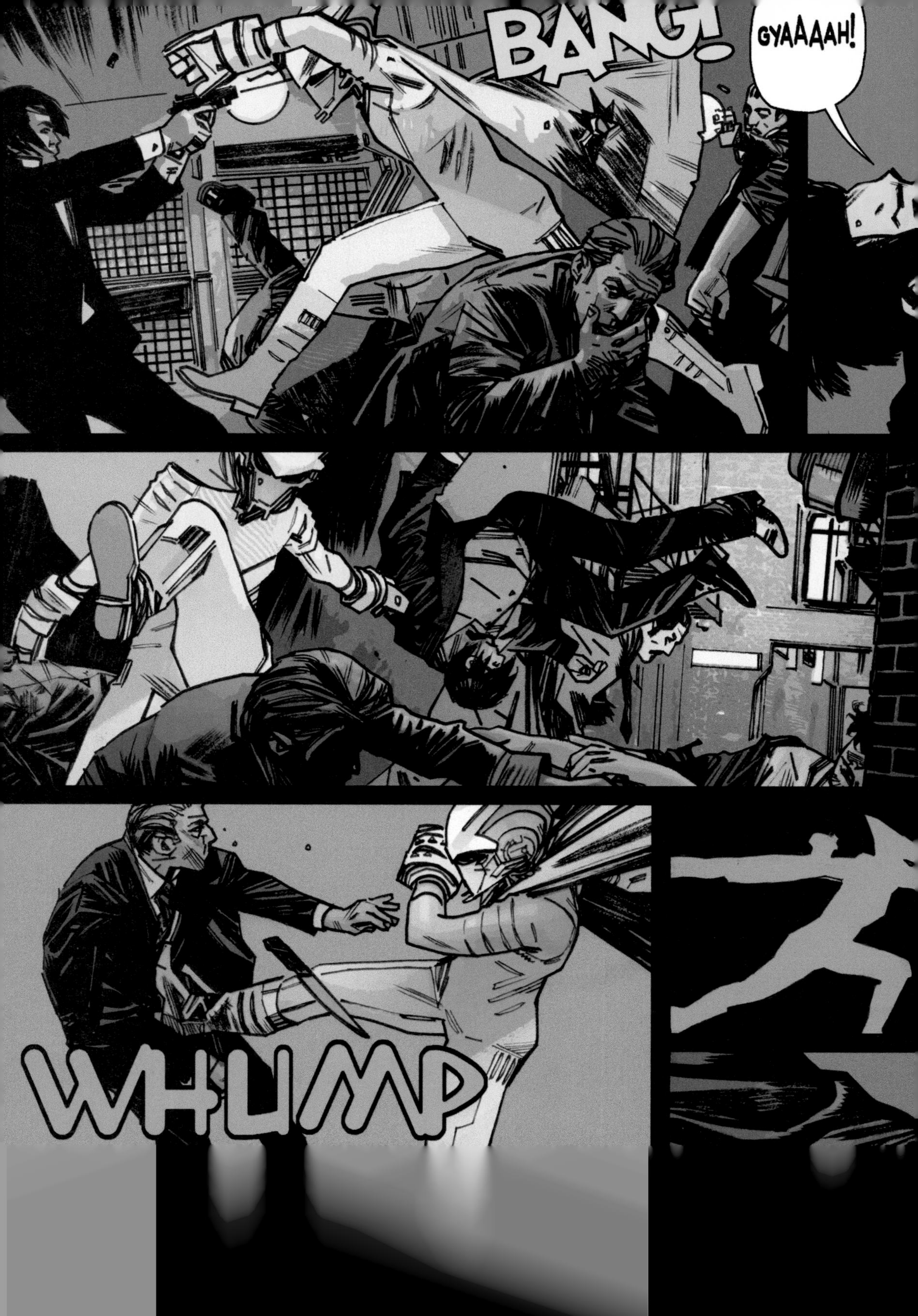
BANG!
GYAAAAH!
WHUMP

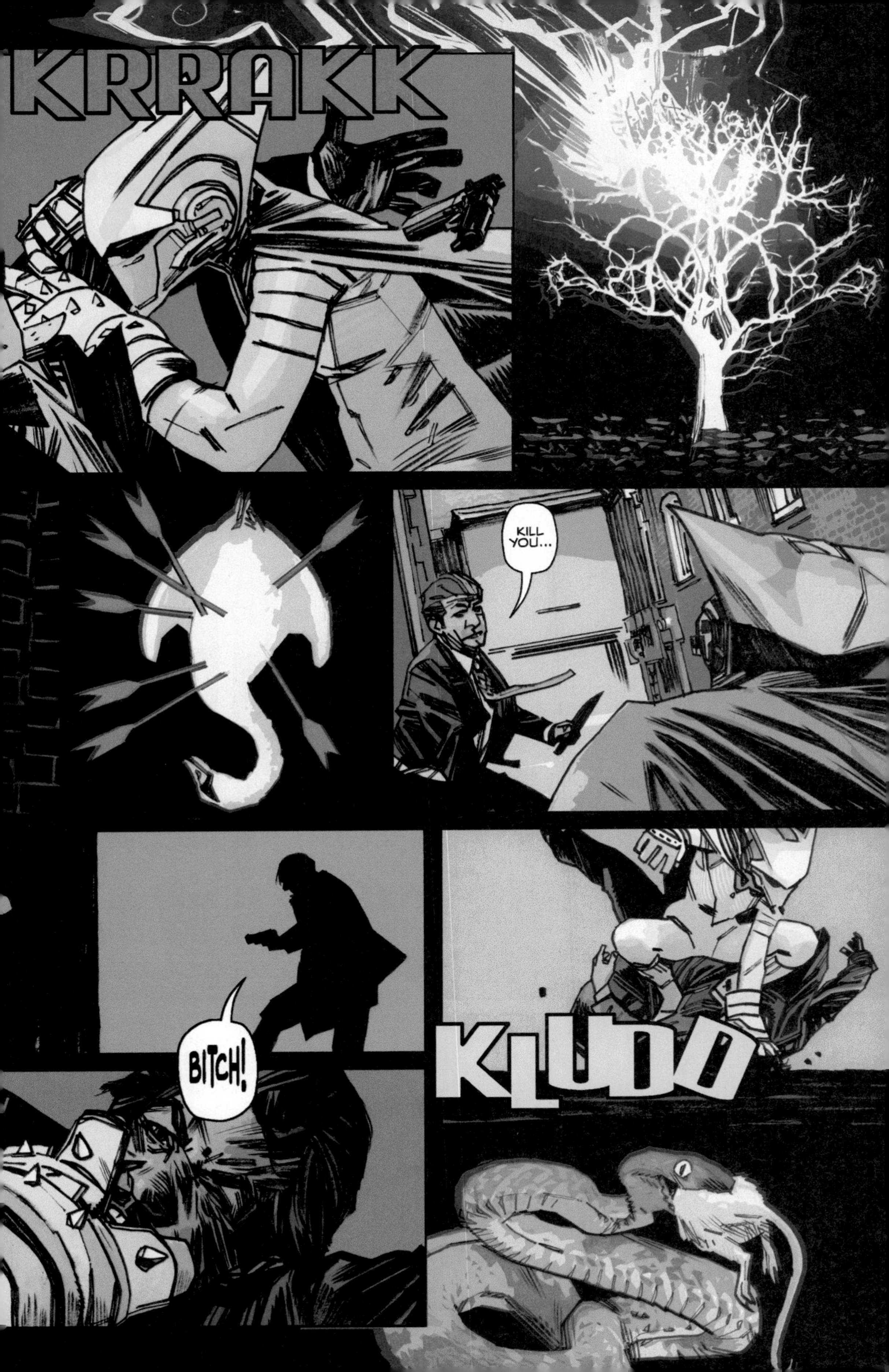
KRRAKK
KILL YOU...
BITCH!
KLUDD

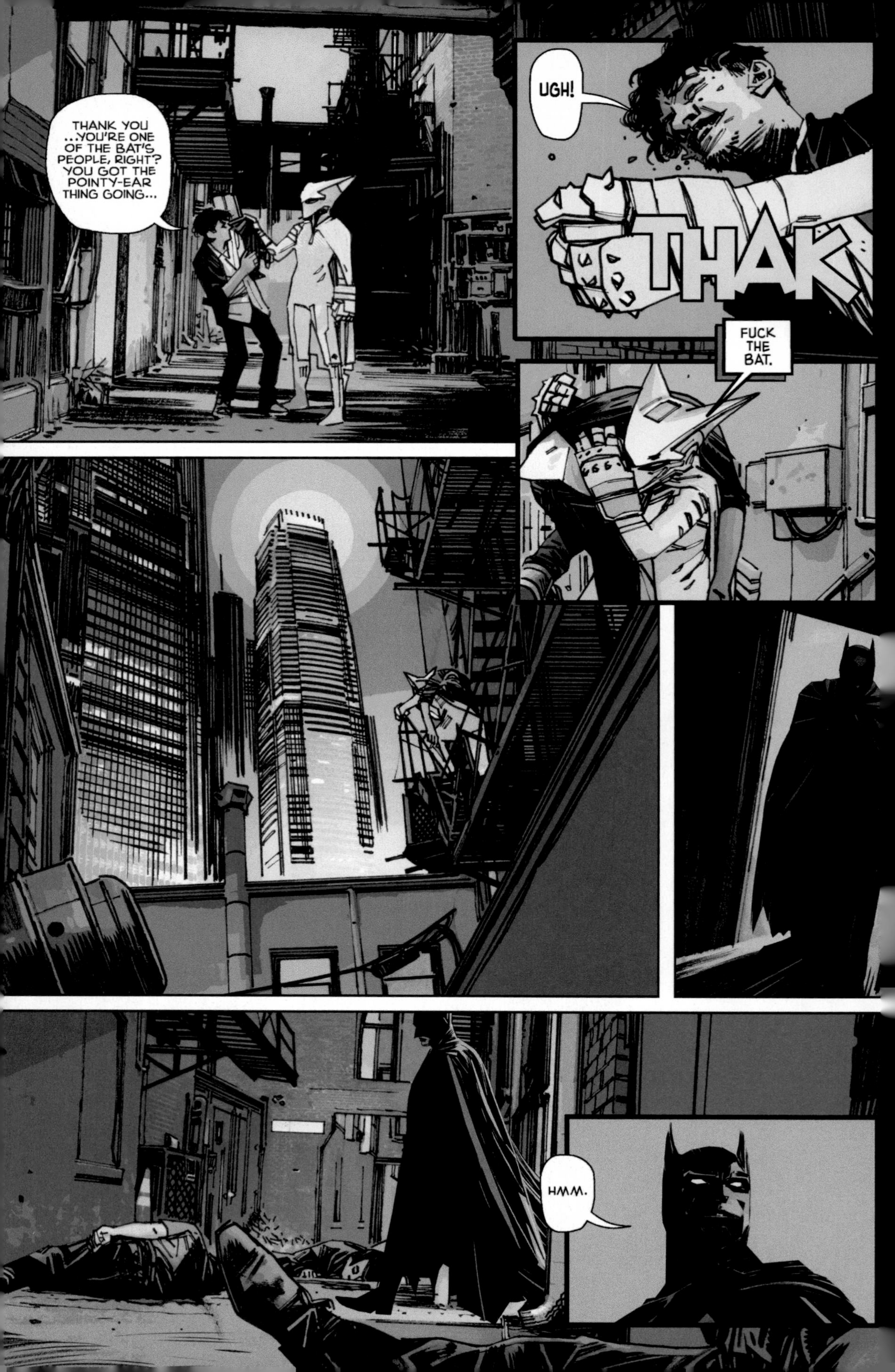
THANK YOU ...YOU'RE ONE OF THE BAT'S PEOPLE, RIGHT? YOU GOT THE POINTY-EAR THING GOING...
UGH!
THAK
FUCK THE BAT.
HMM.

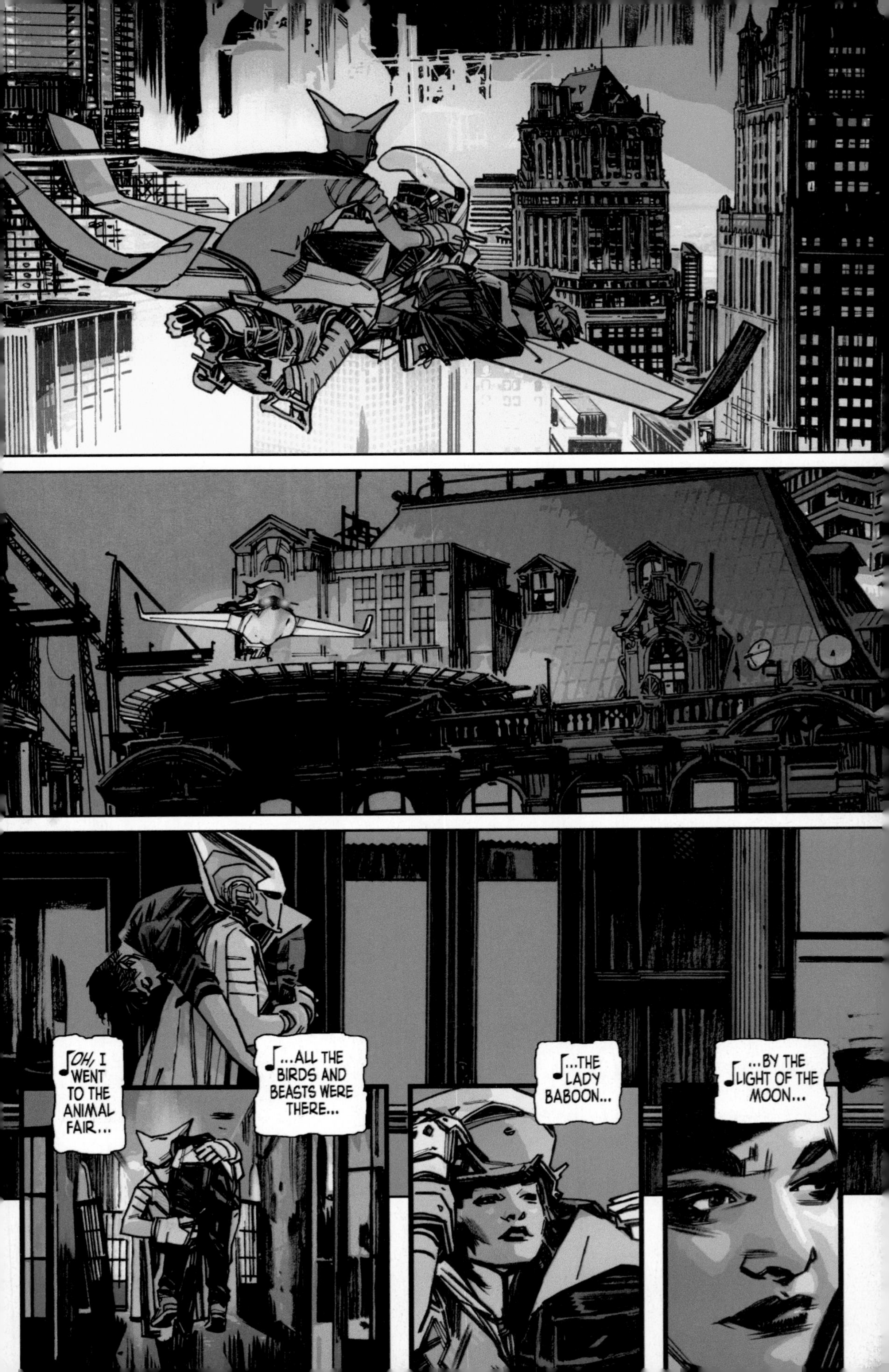
♪OH, I WENT TO THE ANIMAL FAIR...
♪...ALL THE BIRDS AND BEASTS WERE THERE...
♪...THE LADY BABOON...
...BY THE ♪LIGHT OF THE MOON...

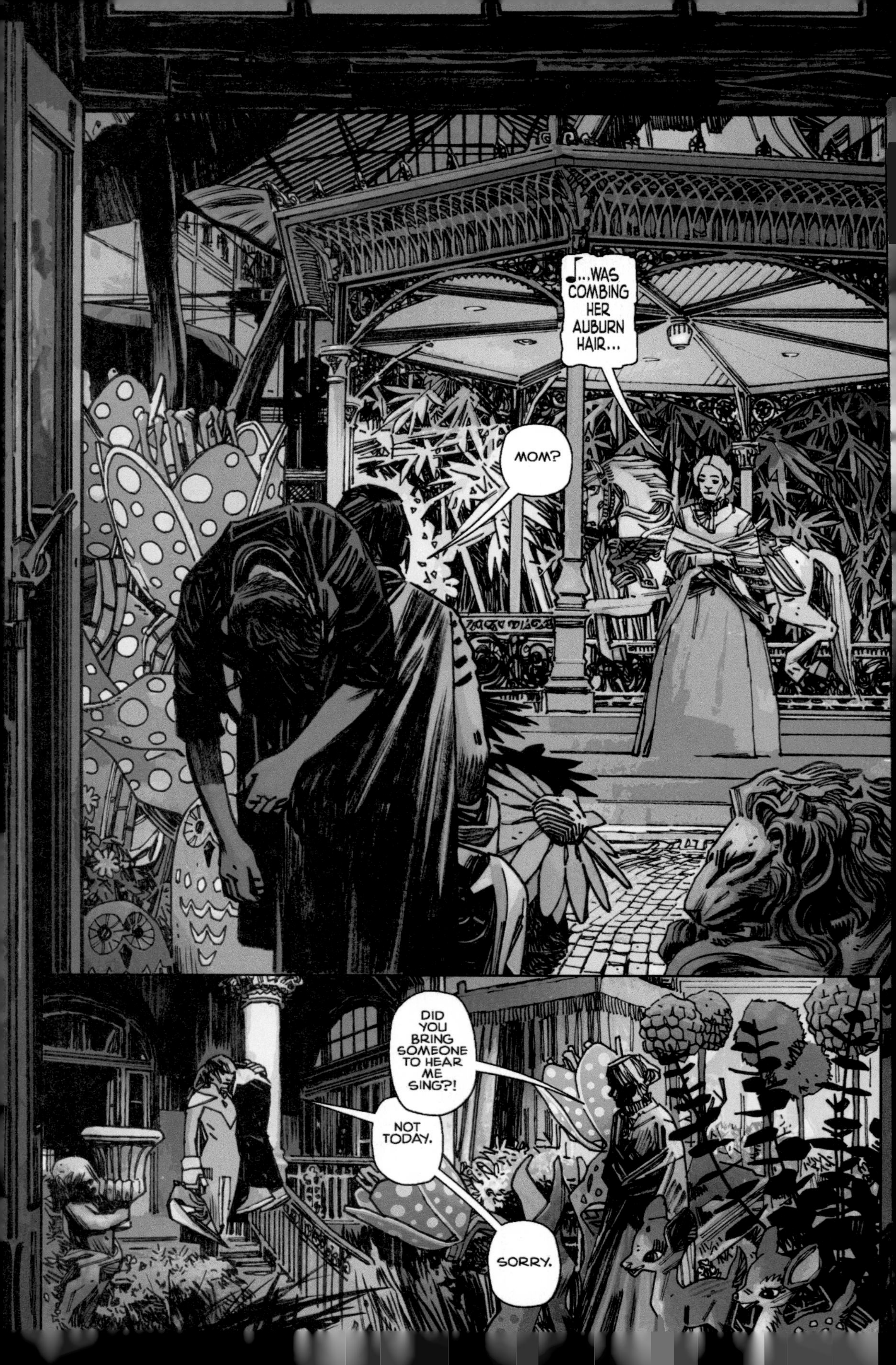
♩...WAS COMBING HER AUBURN HAIR...
MOM?
DID YOU BRING SOMEONE TO HEAR ME SING?!
NOT TODAY.
SORRY.

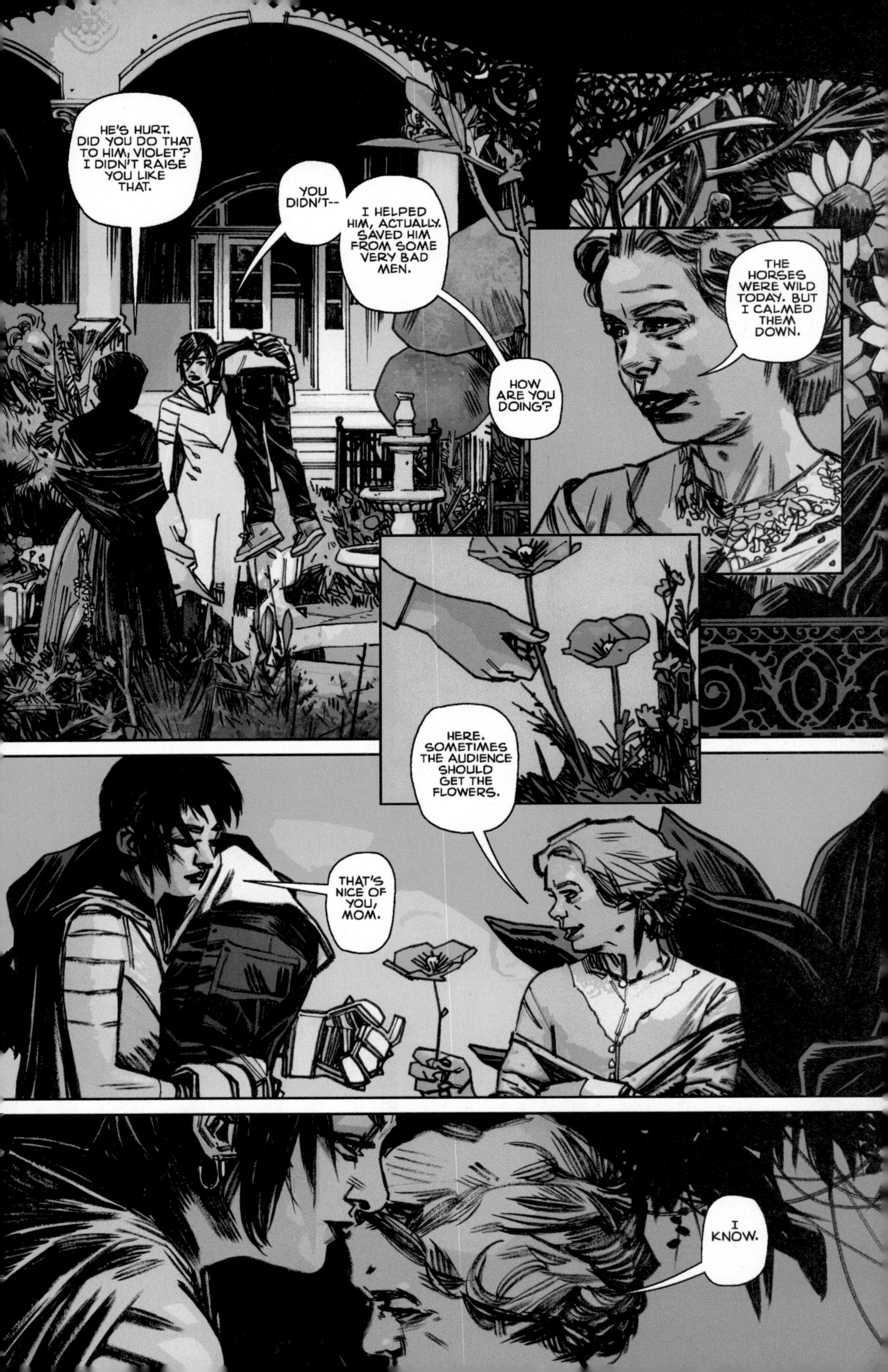
HE'S HURT. DID YOU DO THAT TO HIM, VIOLET? I DIDN'T RAISE YOU LIKE THAT.
YOU DIDN'T--
I HELPED HIM, ACTUALLY. SAVED HIM FROM SOME VERY BAD MEN.
HOW ARE YOU DOING?
THE HORSES WERE WILD TODAY. BUT I CALMED THEM DOWN.
HERE. SOMETIMES THE AUDIENCE SHOULD GET THE FLOWERS.
THAT'S NICE OF YOU, MOM.
I KNOW.

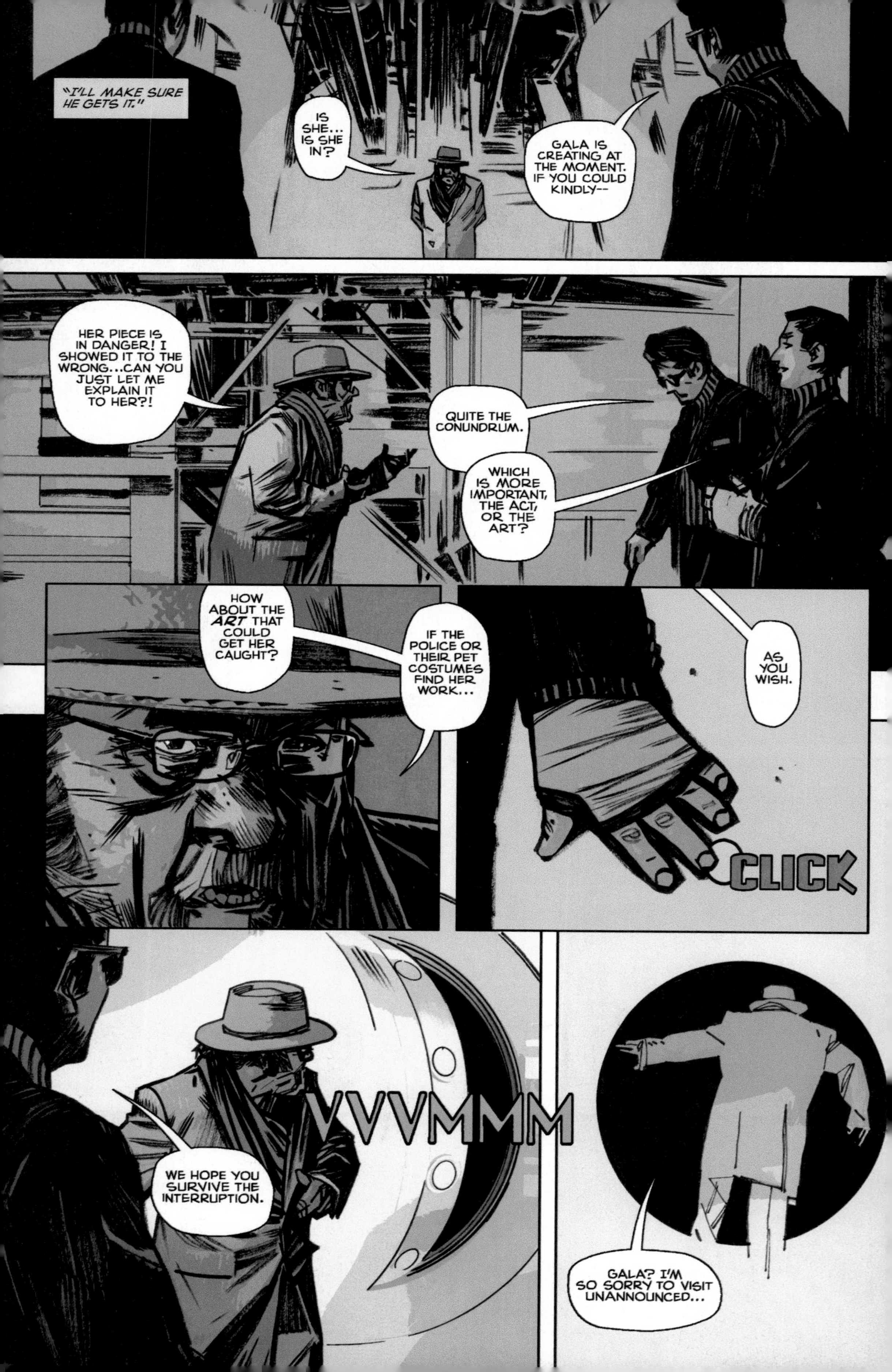
"I'LL MAKE SURE HE GETS IT."
IS SHE... IS SHE IN?
GALA IS CREATING AT THE MOMENT. IF YOU COULD KINDLY--
HER PIECE IS IN DANGER! I SHOWED IT TO THE WRONG...CAN YOU JUST LET ME EXPLAIN IT TO HER?!
QUITE THE CONUNDRUM.
WHICH IS MORE IMPORTANT, THE ACT, OR THE ART?
HOW ABOUT THE ART THAT COULD GET HER CAUGHT?
IF THE POLICE OR THEIR PET COSTUMES FIND HER WORK...
AS YOU WISH.
CLICK
VVVMMM
WE HOPE YOU SURVIVE THE INTERRUPTION.
GALA? I'M SO SORRY TO VISIT UNANNOUNCED...

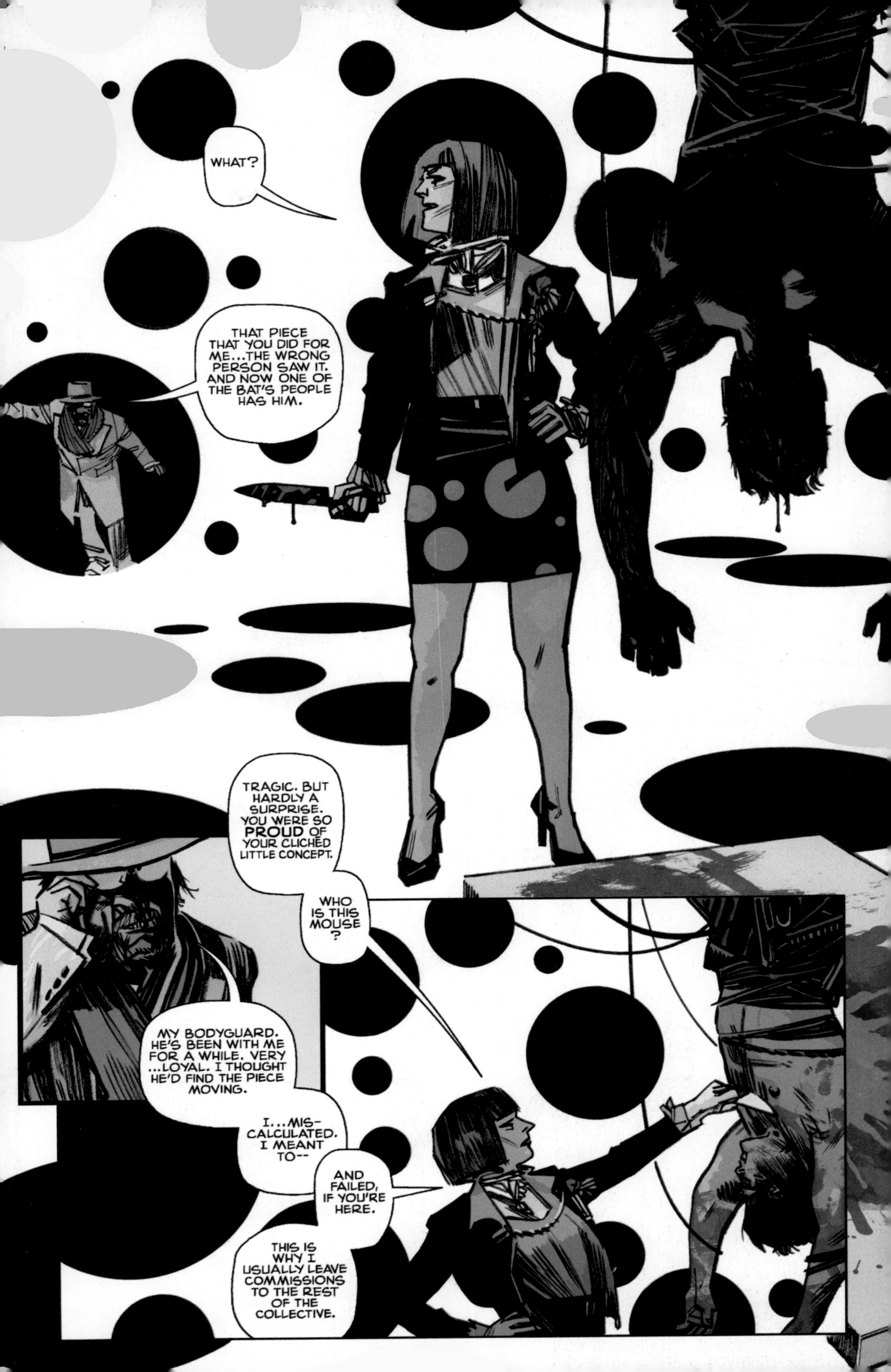
WHAT?
THAT PIECE THAT YOU DID FOR ME...THE WRONG PERSON SAW IT. AND NOW ONE OF THE BAT'S PEOPLE HAS HIM.
TRAGIC. BUT HARDLY A SURPRISE. YOU WERE SO PROUD OF YOUR CLICHÉD LITTLE CONCEPT.
WHO IS THIS MOUSE?
MY BODYGUARD. HE'S BEEN WITH ME FOR A WHILE. VERY ...LOYAL. I THOUGHT HE'D FIND THE PIECE MOVING.
I...MIS-CALCULATED. I MEANT TO--
AND FAILED, IF YOU'RE HERE.
THIS IS WHY I USUALLY LEAVE COMMISSIONS TO THE REST OF THE COLLECTIVE.

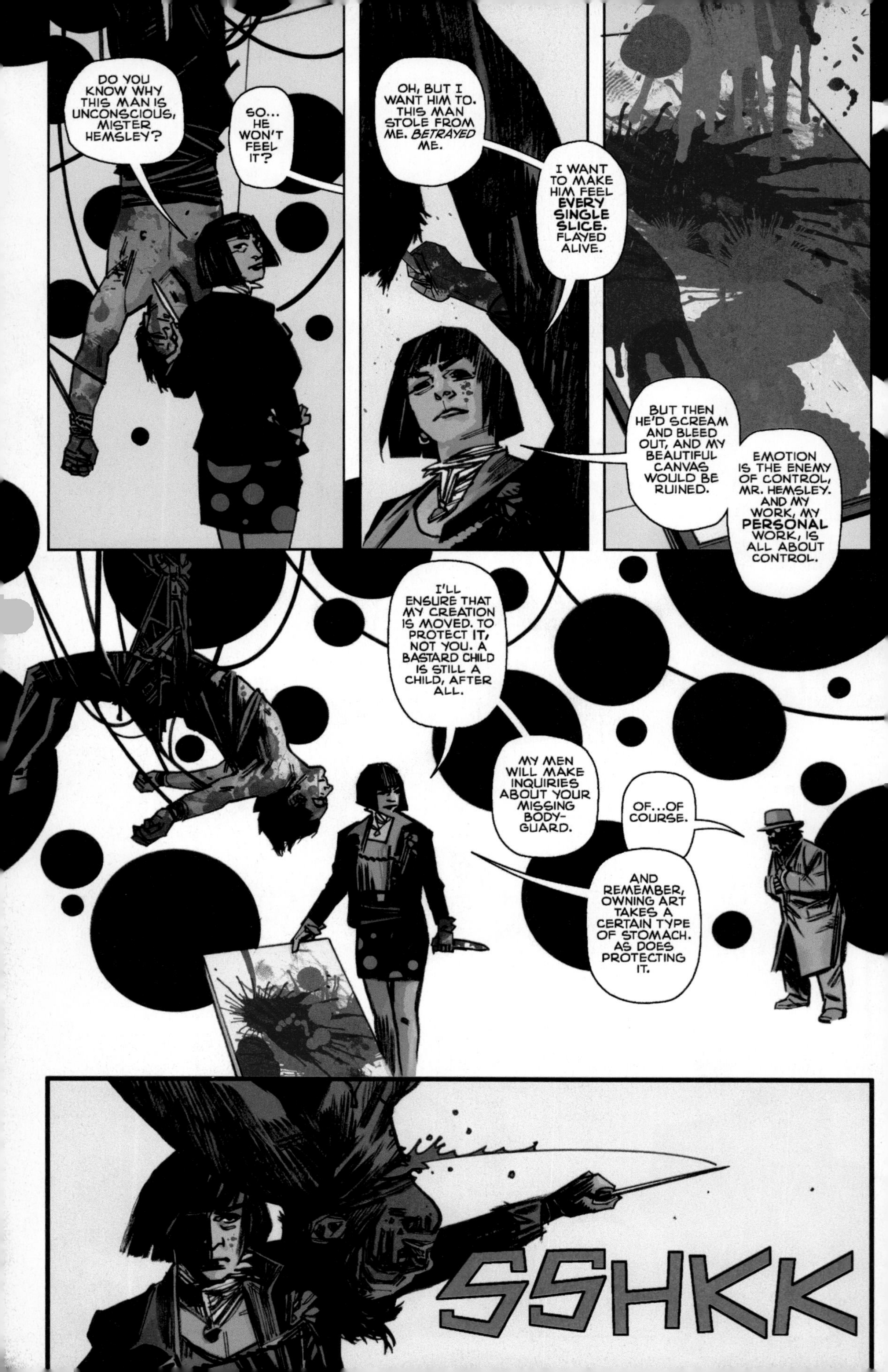
DO YOU KNOW WHY THIS MAN IS UNCONSCIOUS, MISTER HEMSLEY?
SO... HE WON'T FEEL IT?
OH, BUT I WANT HIM TO. THIS MAN STOLE FROM ME. *BETRAYED* ME.
I WANT TO MAKE HIM FEEL **EVERY SINGLE SLICE.** FLAYED ALIVE.
BUT THEN HE'D SCREAM AND BLEED OUT, AND MY BEAUTIFUL CANVAS WOULD BE RUINED.
EMOTION IS THE ENEMY OF CONTROL, MR. HEMSLEY. AND MY WORK, MY **PERSONAL** WORK, IS ALL ABOUT CONTROL.
I'LL ENSURE THAT MY CREATION IS MOVED. TO PROTECT IT, NOT YOU. A BASTARD CHILD IS STILL A CHILD, AFTER ALL.
MY MEN WILL MAKE INQUIRIES ABOUT YOUR MISSING BODY-GUARD.
OF...OF COURSE.
AND REMEMBER, OWNING ART TAKES A CERTAIN TYPE OF STOMACH. AS DOES PROTECTING IT.
SSHKK

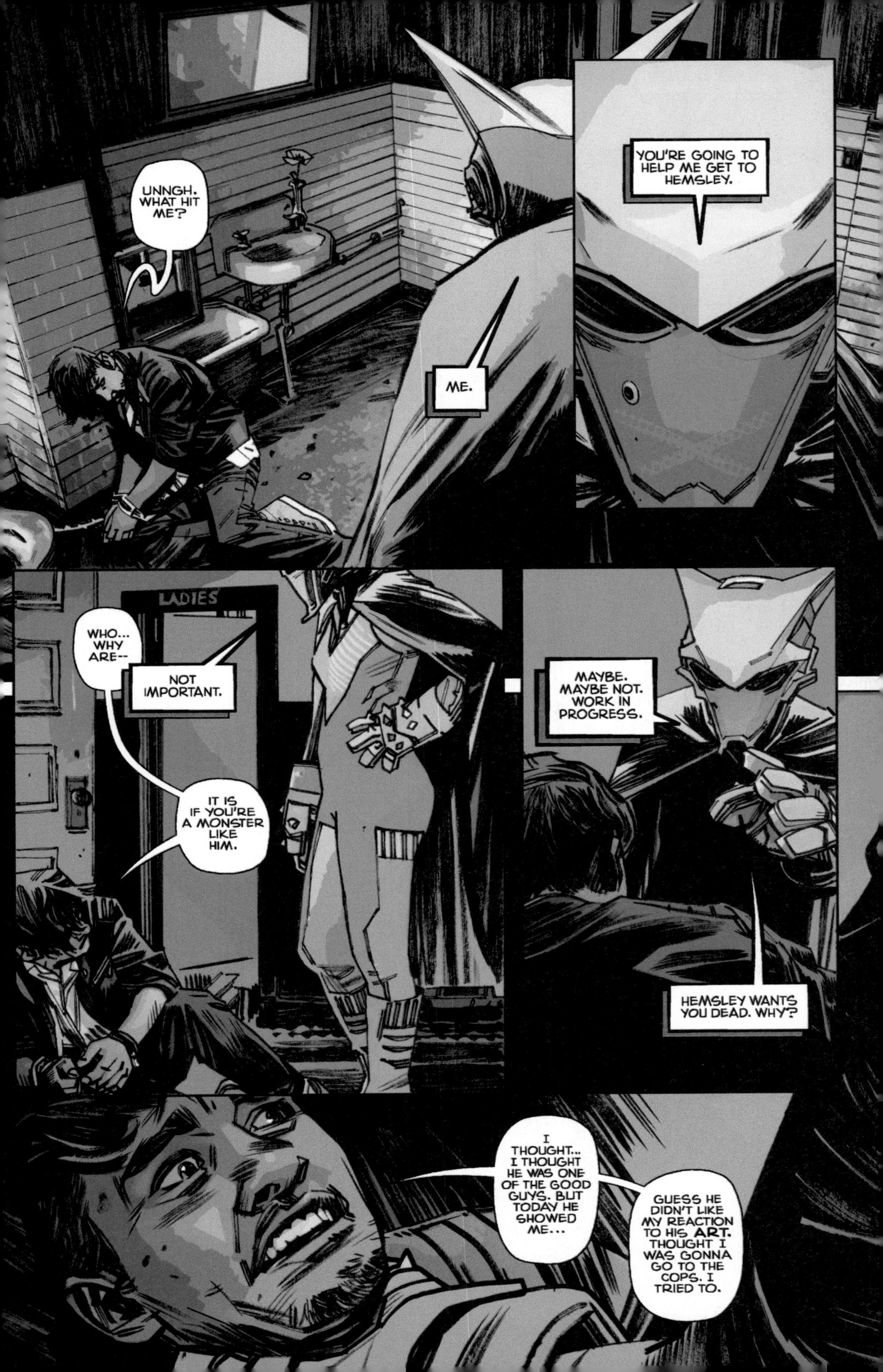

UNNGH. WHAT HIT ME?
ME.
YOU'RE GOING TO HELP ME GET TO HEMSLEY.
LADIES
WHO... WHY ARE--
NOT IMPORTANT.
IT IS IF YOU'RE A MONSTER LIKE HIM.
MAYBE. MAYBE NOT. WORK IN PROGRESS.
HEMSLEY WANTS YOU DEAD. WHY?
I THOUGHT... I THOUGHT HE WAS ONE OF THE GOOD GUYS. BUT TODAY HE SHOWED ME...
GUESS HE DIDN'T LIKE MY REACTION TO HIS ART. THOUGHT I WAS GONNA GO TO THE COPS. I TRIED TO.

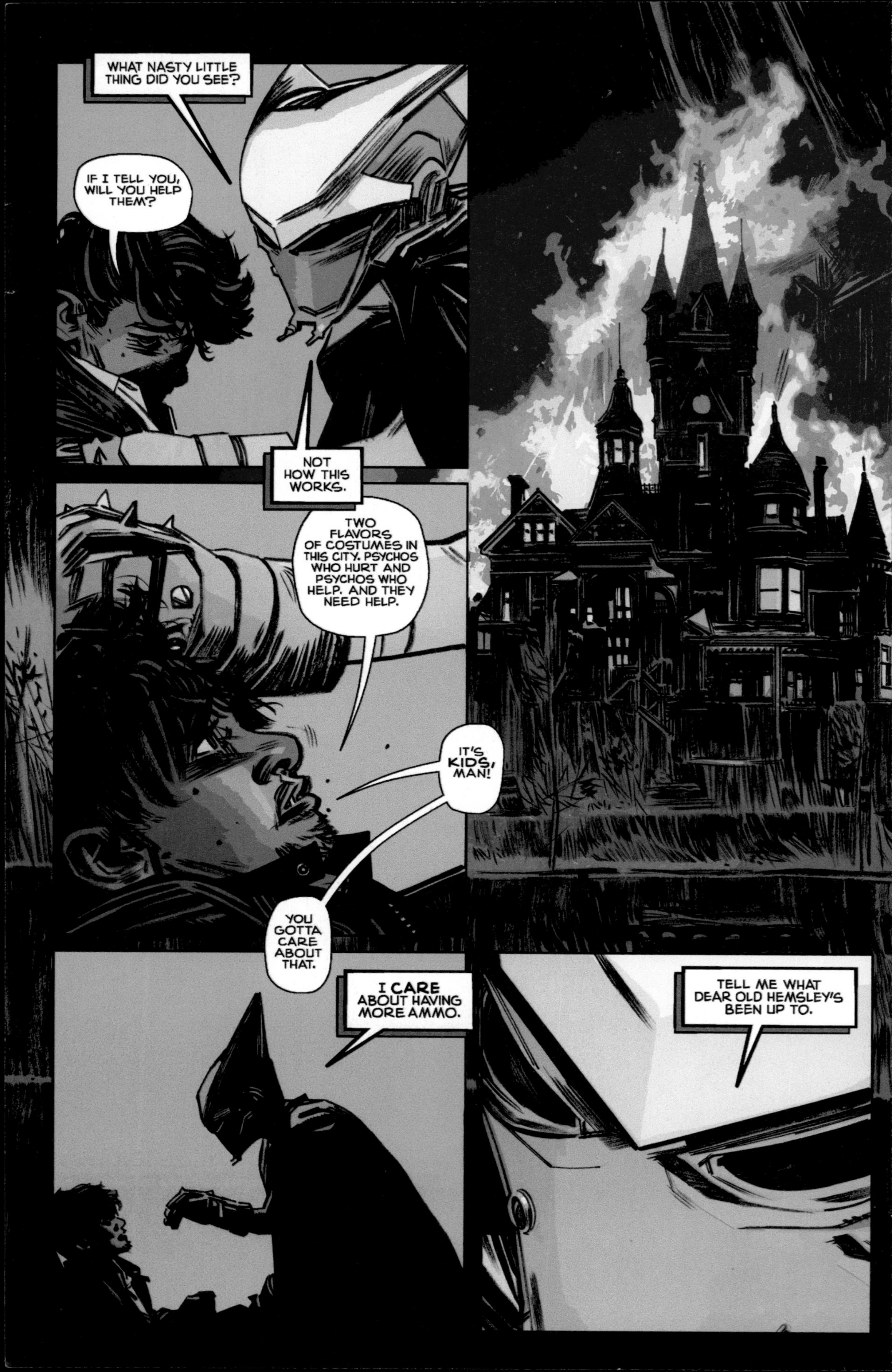
WHAT NASTY LITTLE THING DID YOU SEE?
IF I TELL YOU, WILL YOU HELP THEM?
NOT HOW THIS WORKS.
TWO FLAVORS OF COSTUMES IN THIS CITY. PSYCHOS WHO HURT AND PSYCHOS WHO HELP. AND THEY NEED HELP.
IT'S KIDS, MAN!
YOU GOTTA CARE ABOUT THAT.
I CARE ABOUT HAVING MORE AMMO.
TELL ME WHAT DEAR OLD HEMSLEY'S BEEN UP TO.

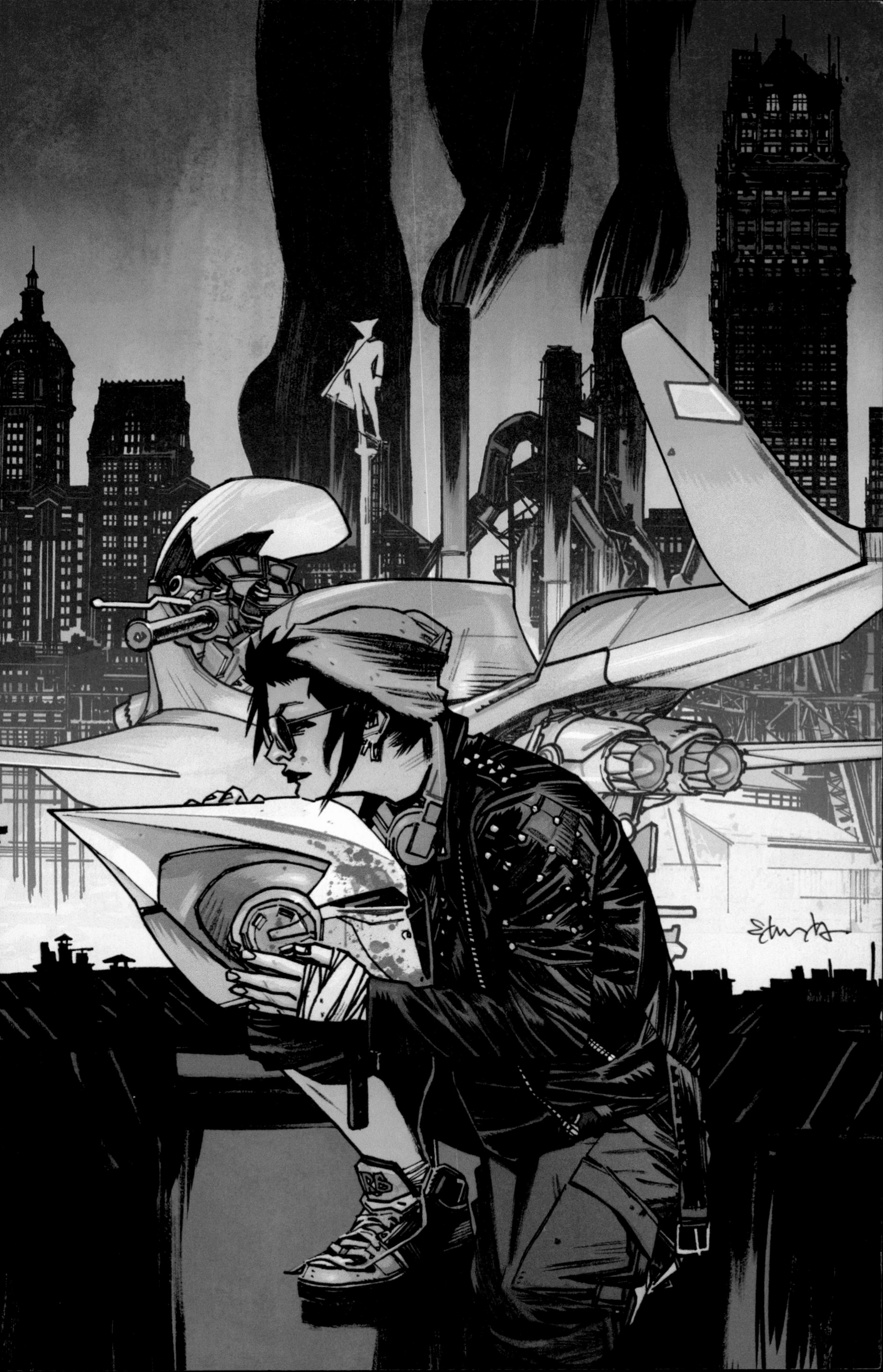

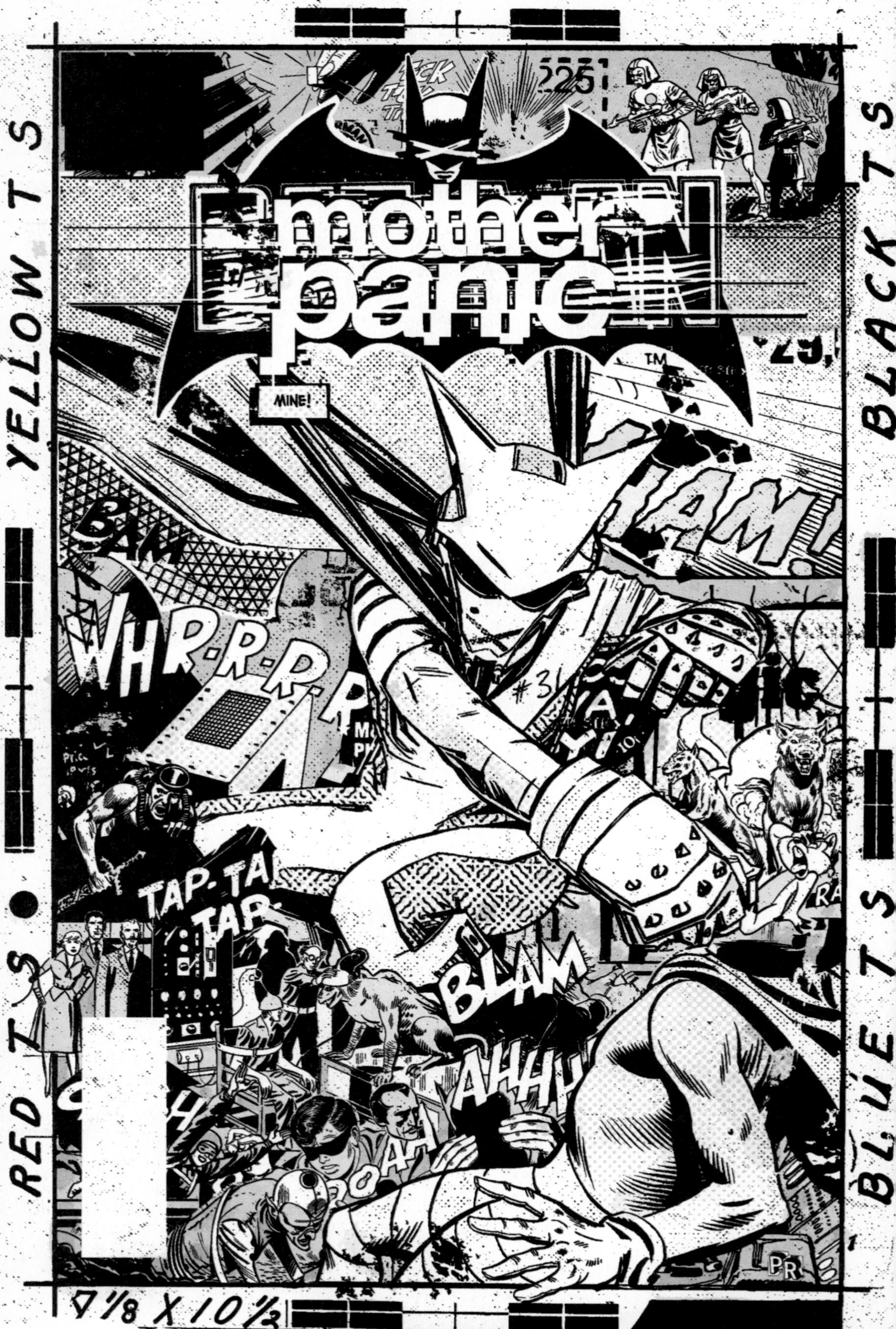
YELLOW TS
BLACK TS
225
mother panic
TM
MINE!
BAM
WHR-R-R
TAP-TA TAP-
BLAM
RED TS
BLUE TS
PR
7 1/8 X 10 1/2
Variant cover art by Paul Rentler

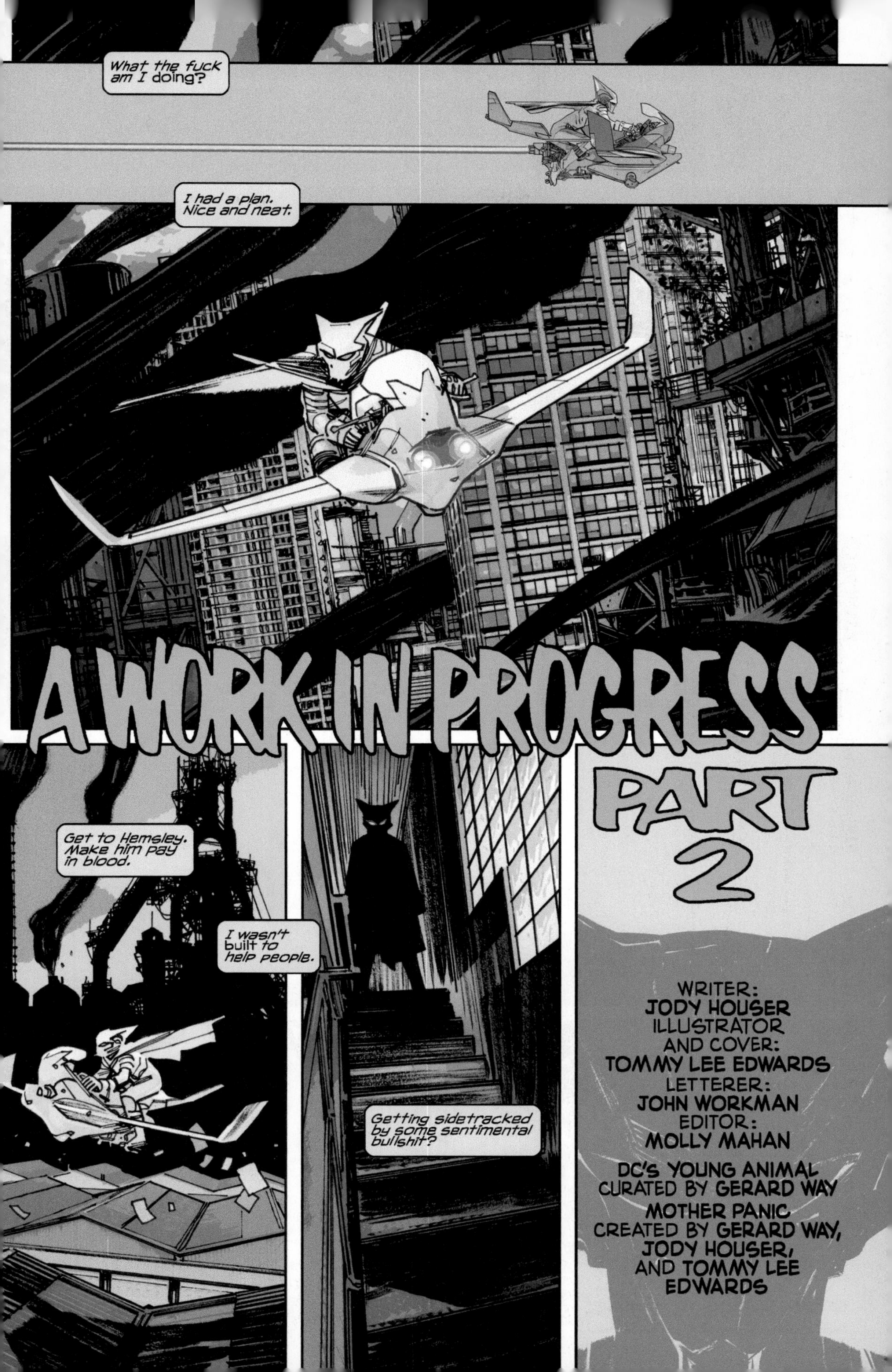
What the fuck am I doing?
I had a plan. Nice and neat.
A WORK IN PROGRESS
PART 2
Get to Hemsley. Make him pay in blood.
I wasn't built to help people.
Getting sidetracked by some sentimental bullshit?
WRITER: JODY HOUSER
ILLUSTRATOR AND COVER: TOMMY LEE EDWARDS
LETTERER: JOHN WORKMAN
EDITOR: MOLLY MAHAN
DC'S YOUNG ANIMAL CURATED BY GERARD WAY
MOTHER PANIC CREATED BY GERARD WAY, JODY HOUSER, AND TOMMY LEE EDWARDS

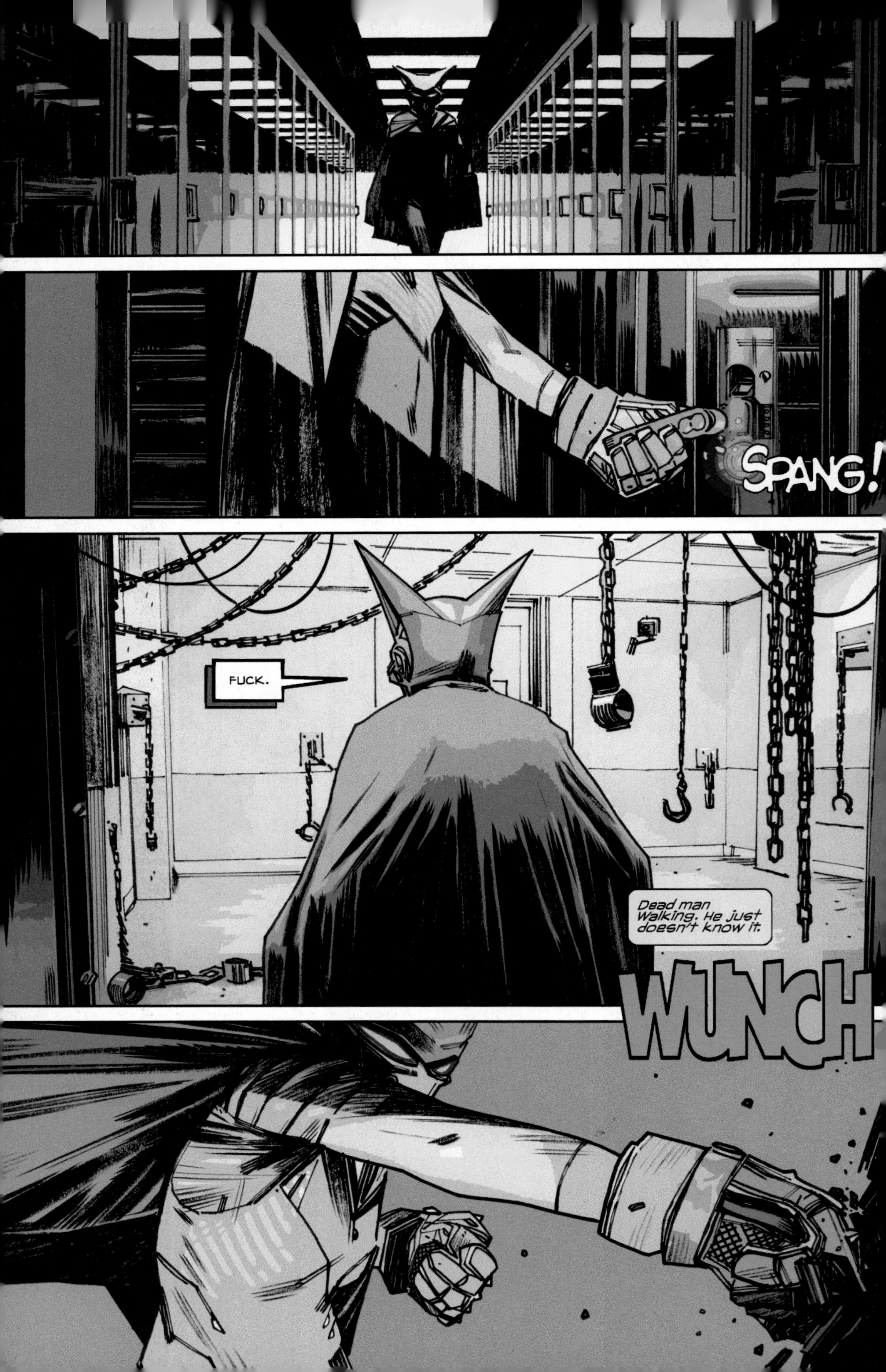
SPANG!
FUCK.
Dead man Walking. He just doesn't know it.
WUNCH

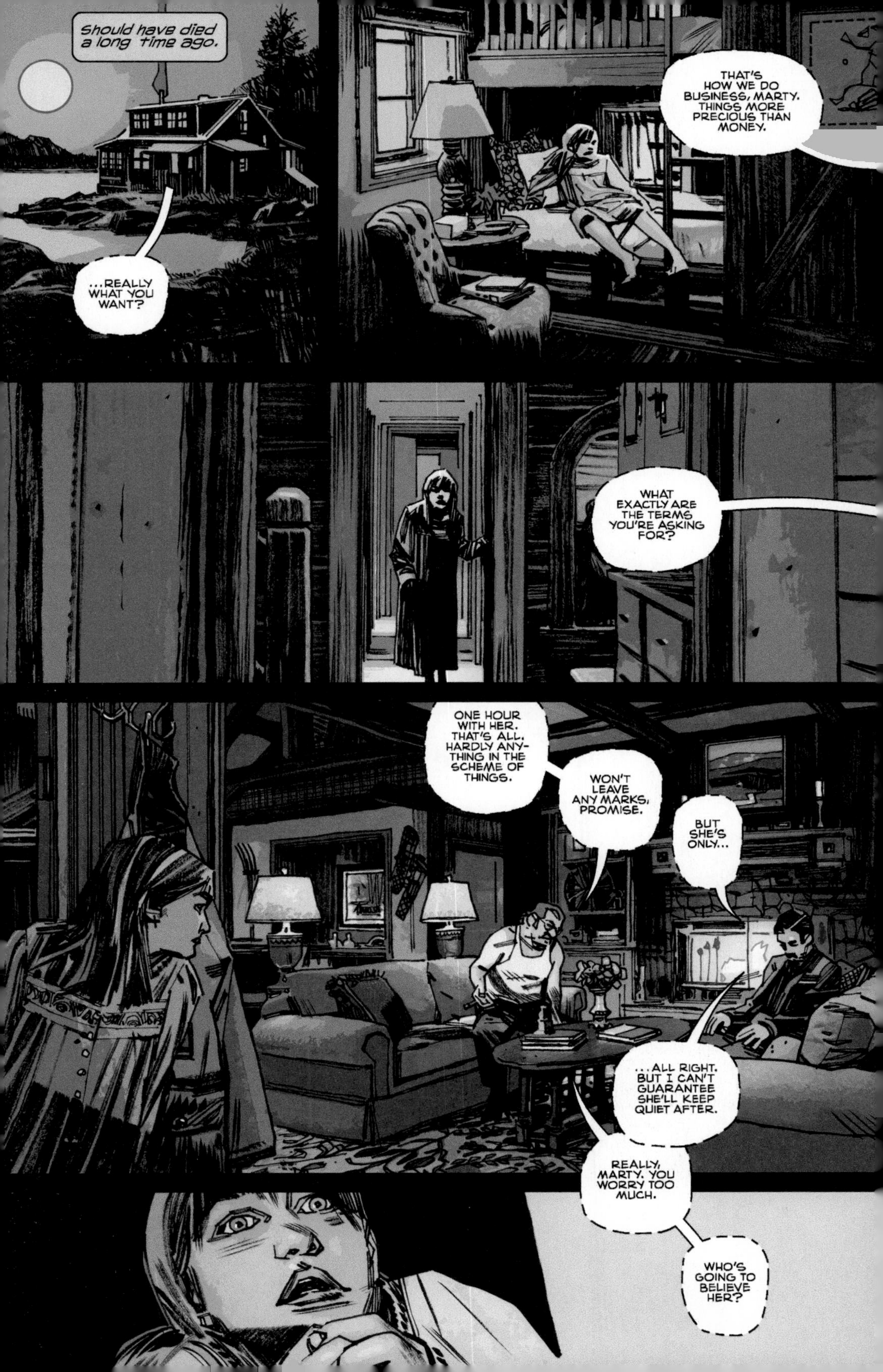
Should have died a long time ago.
...REALLY WHAT YOU WANT?
THAT'S HOW WE DO BUSINESS, MARTY. THINGS MORE PRECIOUS THAN MONEY.
WHAT EXACTLY ARE THE TERMS YOU'RE ASKING FOR?
ONE HOUR WITH HER. THAT'S ALL. HARDLY ANY-THING IN THE SCHEME OF THINGS.
WON'T LEAVE ANY MARKS, PROMISE.
BUT SHE'S ONLY...
...ALL RIGHT. BUT I CAN'T GUARANTEE SHE'LL KEEP QUIET AFTER.
REALLY, MARTY. YOU WORRY TOO MUCH.
WHO'S GOING TO BELIEVE HER?

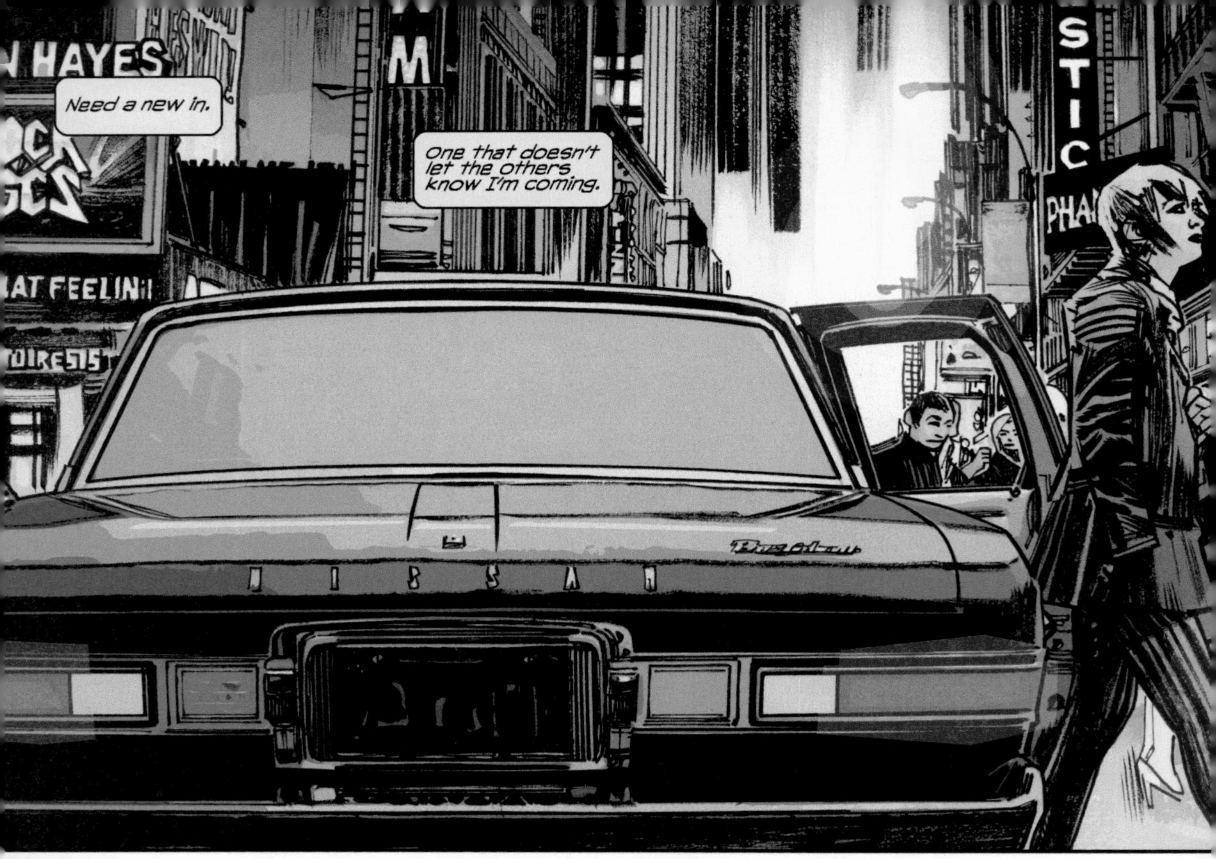
Need a new in.
One that doesn't let the others know I'm coming.
N HAYES
M
STIC
AT FEELIN


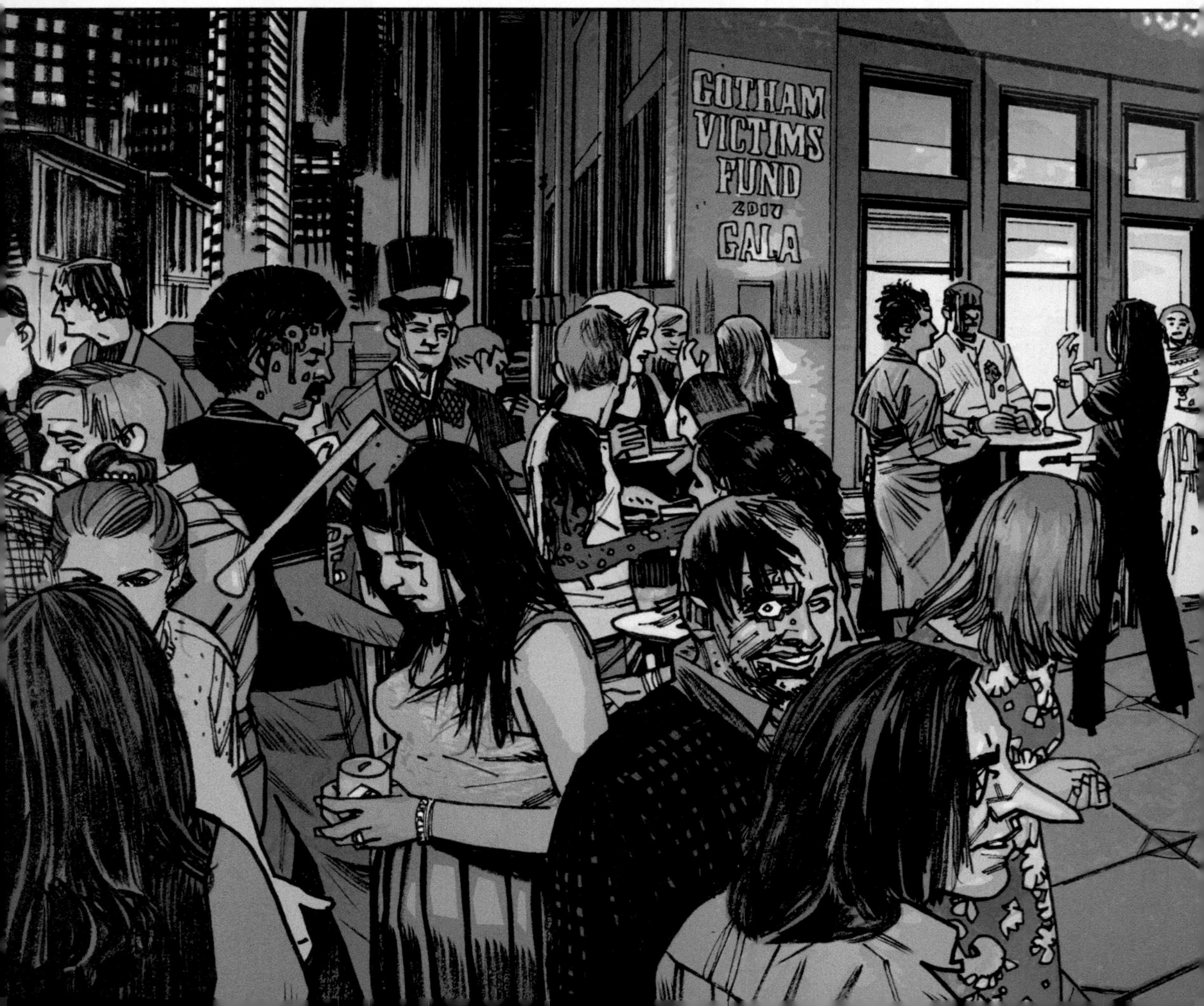
GOTHAM VICTIMS FUND 2017 GALA

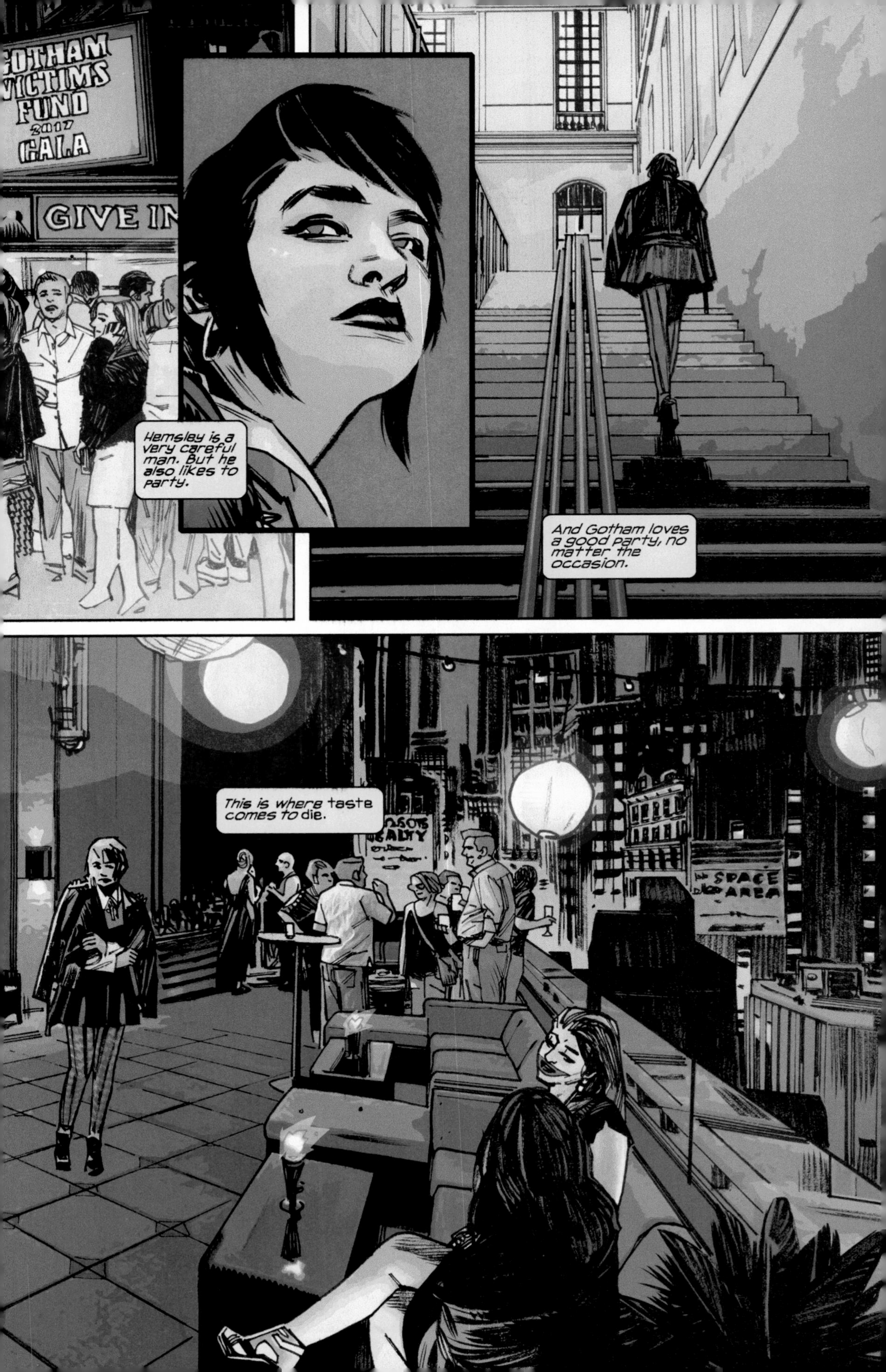
GOTHAM VICTIMS FUND 2017 GALA
GIVE IN
Hemsley is a very careful man. But he also likes to party.
And Gotham loves a good party, no matter the occasion.
This is where taste comes to die.
SPACE AREA

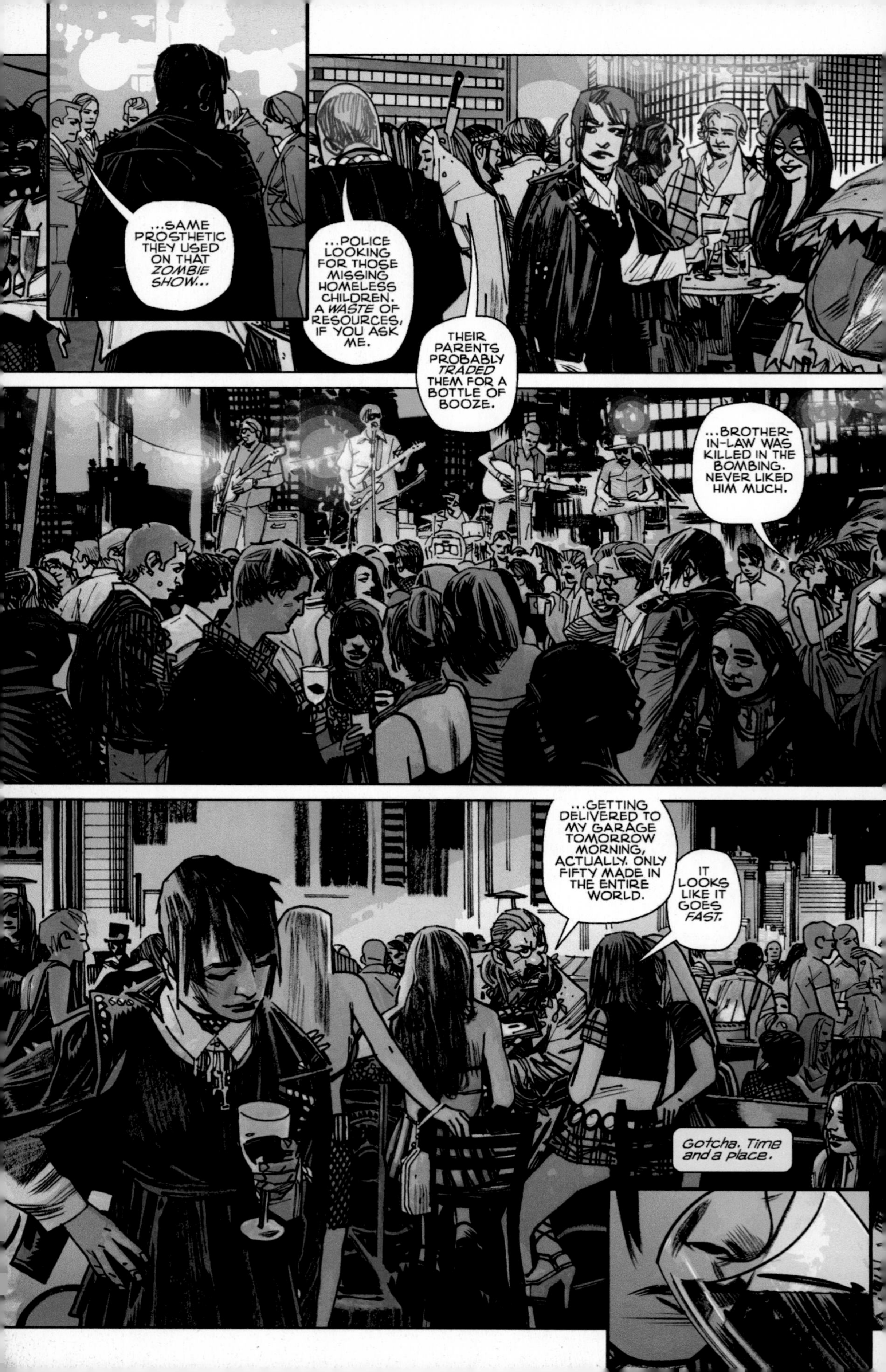
...SAME PROSTHETIC THEY USED ON THAT *ZOMBIE SHOW*...
...POLICE LOOKING FOR THOSE MISSING HOMELESS CHILDREN. A *WASTE* OF RESOURCES, IF YOU ASK ME.
THEIR PARENTS PROBABLY *TRADED* THEM FOR A BOTTLE OF BOOZE.
...BROTHER-IN-LAW WAS KILLED IN THE BOMBING. NEVER LIKED HIM MUCH.
...GETTING DELIVERED TO MY GARAGE TOMORROW MORNING, ACTUALLY. ONLY FIFTY MADE IN THE ENTIRE WORLD.
IT LOOKS LIKE IT GOES *FAST*.
*Gotcha. Time and a place.*

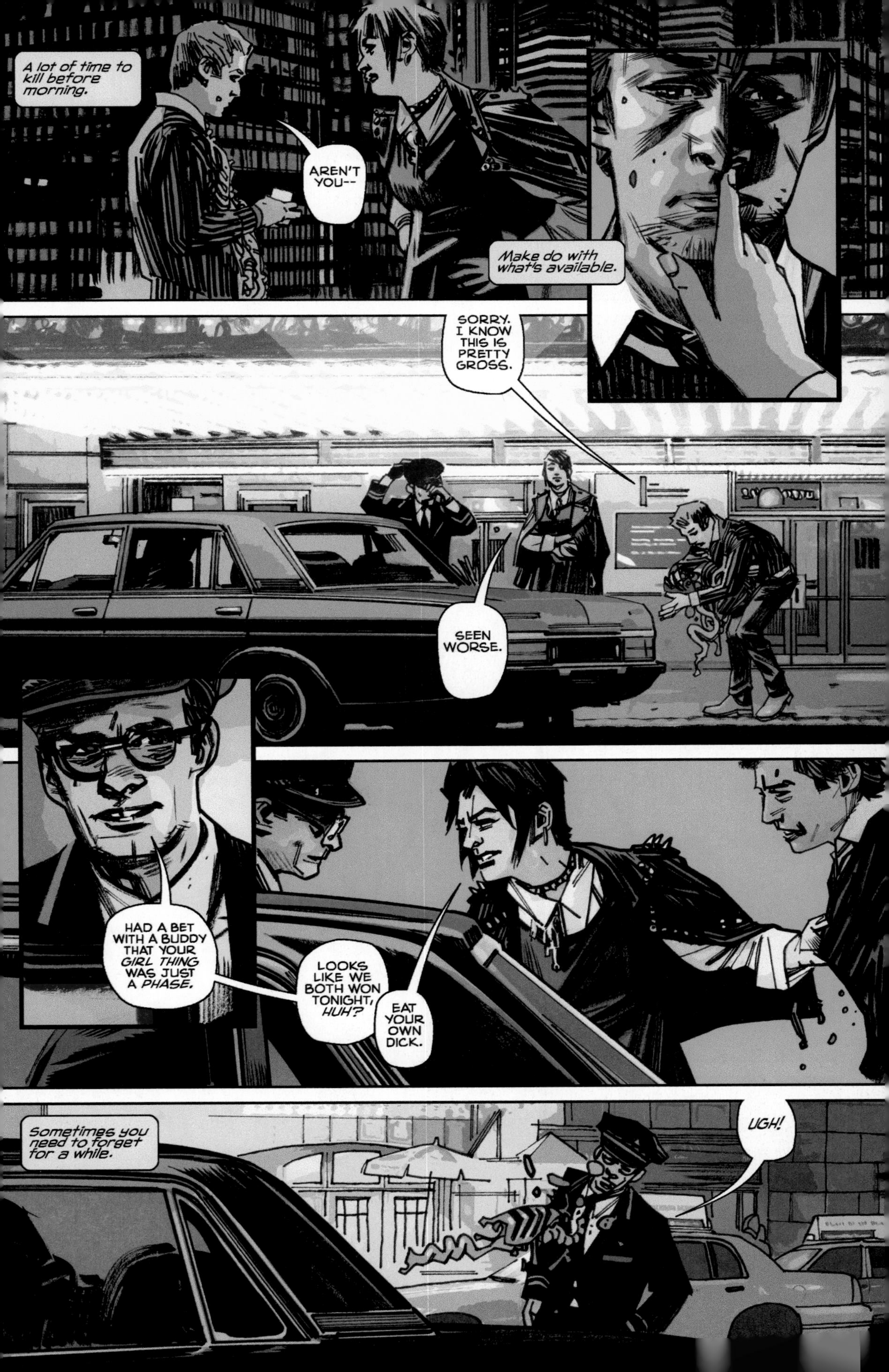
A lot of time to kill before morning.
AREN'T YOU--
Make do with what's available.
SORRY. I KNOW THIS IS PRETTY GROSS.
SEEN WORSE.
HAD A BET WITH A BUDDY THAT YOUR GIRL THING WAS JUST A PHASE.
LOOKS LIKE WE BOTH WON TONIGHT, HUH?
EAT YOUR OWN DICK.
Sometimes you need to forget for a while.
UGH!

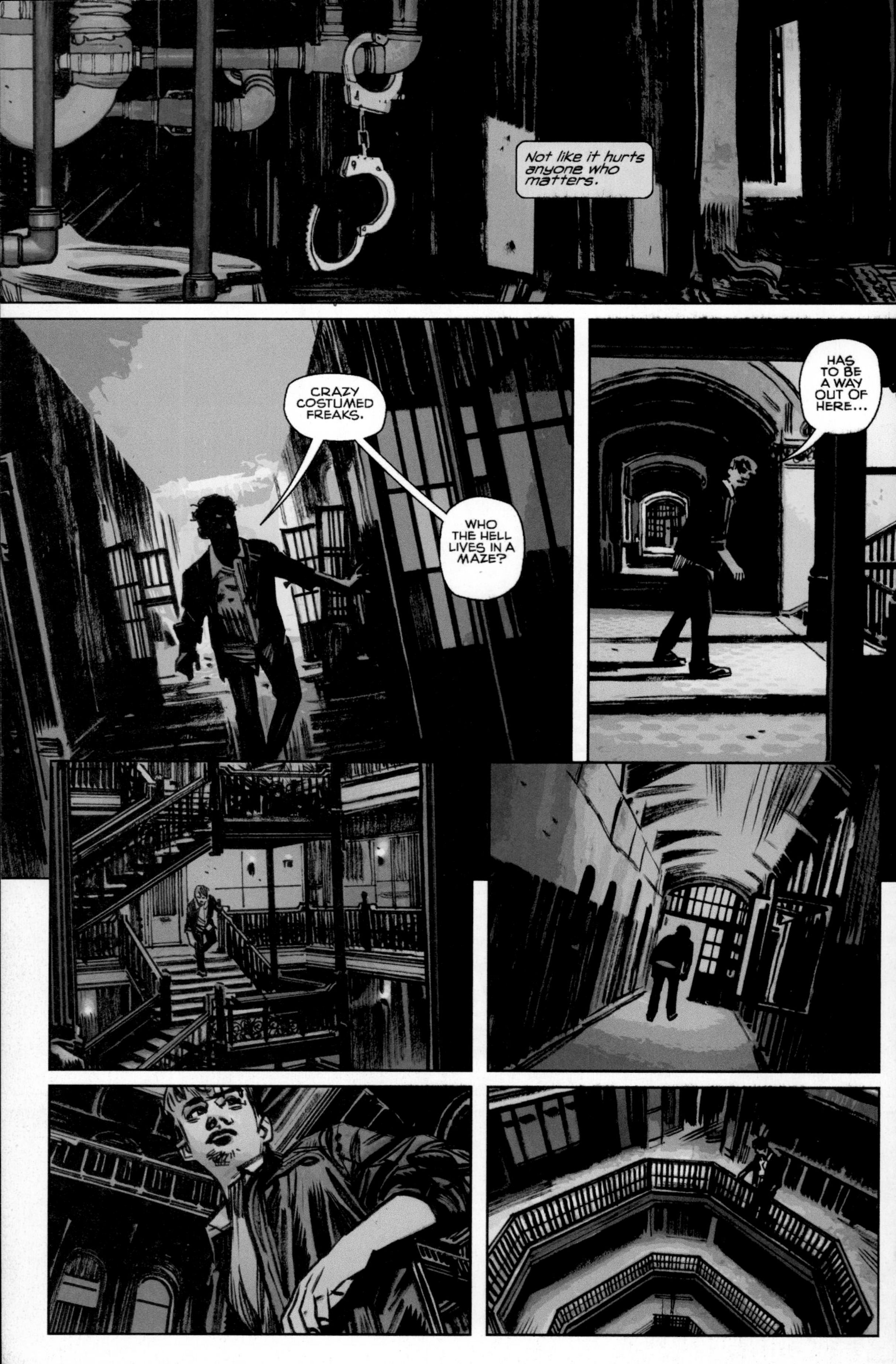
Not like it hurts anyone who matters.
CRAZY COSTUMED FREAKS.
WHO THE HELL LIVES IN A MAZE?
HAS TO BE A WAY OUT OF HERE...

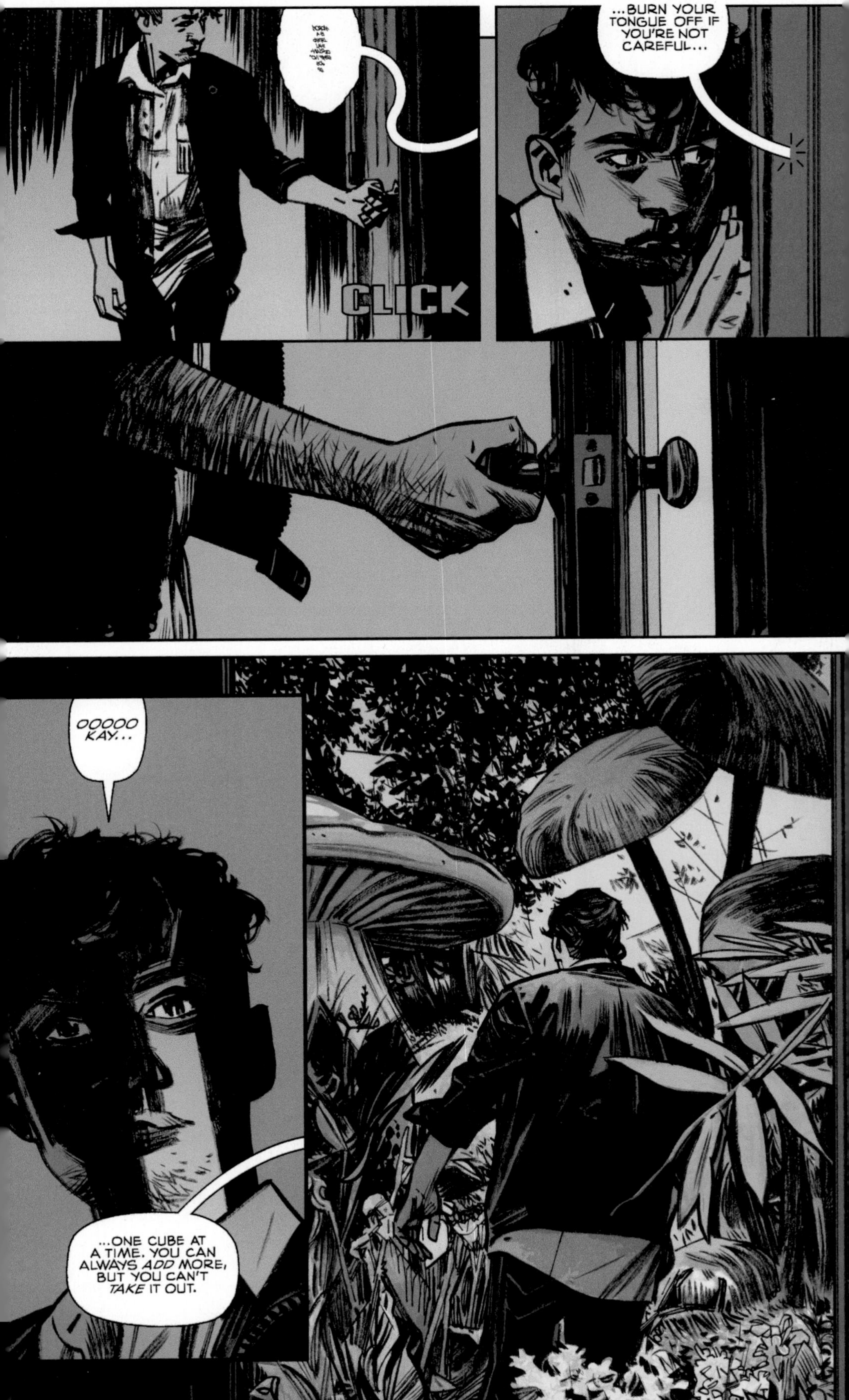
CLICK
...BURN YOUR TONGUE OFF IF YOU'RE NOT CAREFUL...
OOOOO KAY...
...ONE CUBE AT A TIME. YOU CAN ALWAYS *ADD* MORE, BUT YOU CAN'T *TAKE* IT OUT.

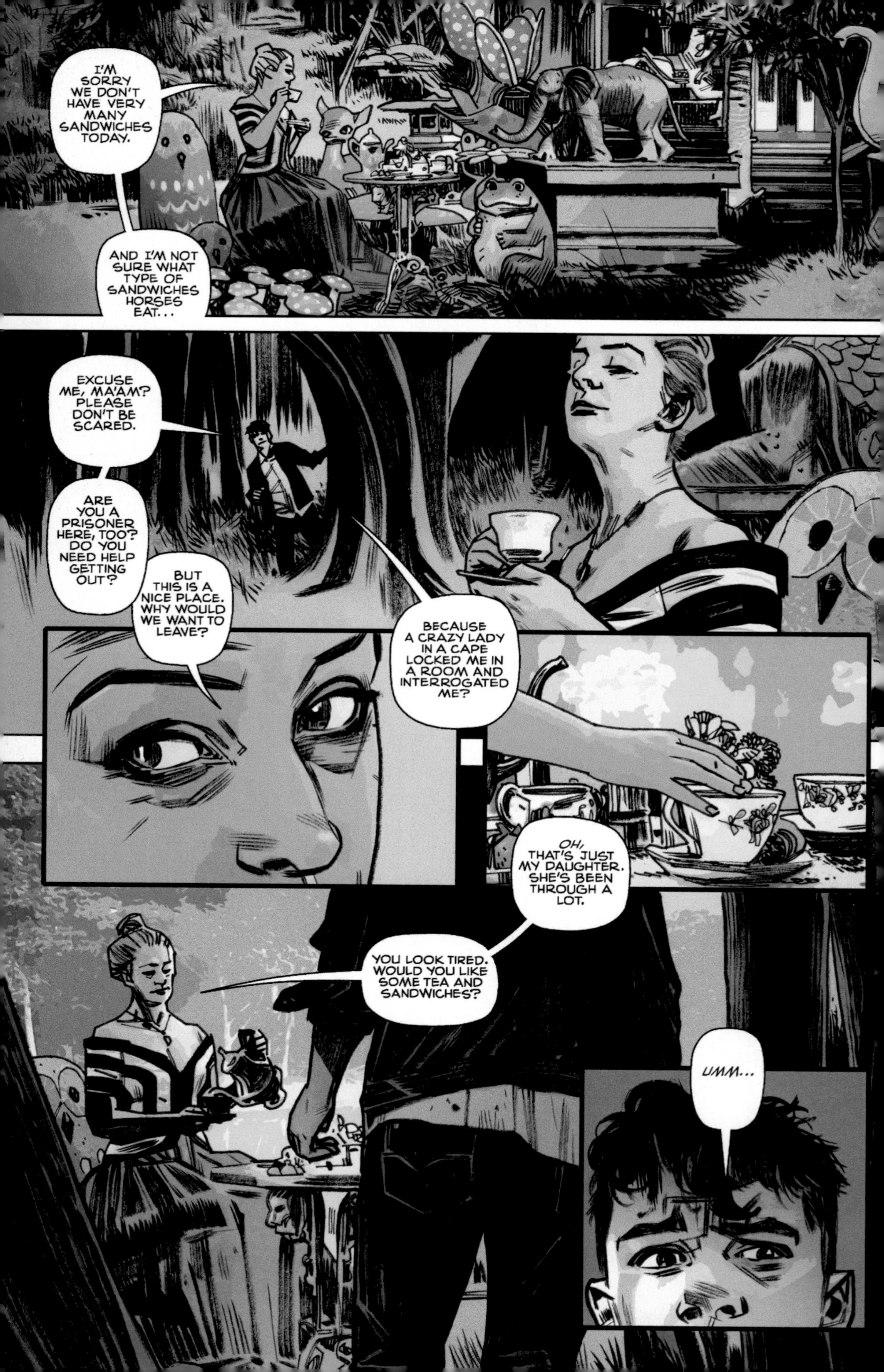
I'M SORRY WE DON'T HAVE VERY MANY SANDWICHES TODAY.
AND I'M NOT SURE WHAT TYPE OF SANDWICHES HORSES EAT...
EXCUSE ME, MA'AM? PLEASE DON'T BE SCARED.
ARE YOU A PRISONER HERE, TOO? DO YOU NEED HELP GETTING OUT?
BUT THIS IS A NICE PLACE. WHY WOULD WE WANT TO LEAVE?
BECAUSE A CRAZY LADY IN A CAPE LOCKED ME IN A ROOM AND INTERROGATED ME?
OH, THAT'S JUST MY DAUGHTER. SHE'S BEEN THROUGH A LOT.
YOU LOOK TIRED. WOULD YOU LIKE SOME TEA AND SANDWICHES?
UMM...

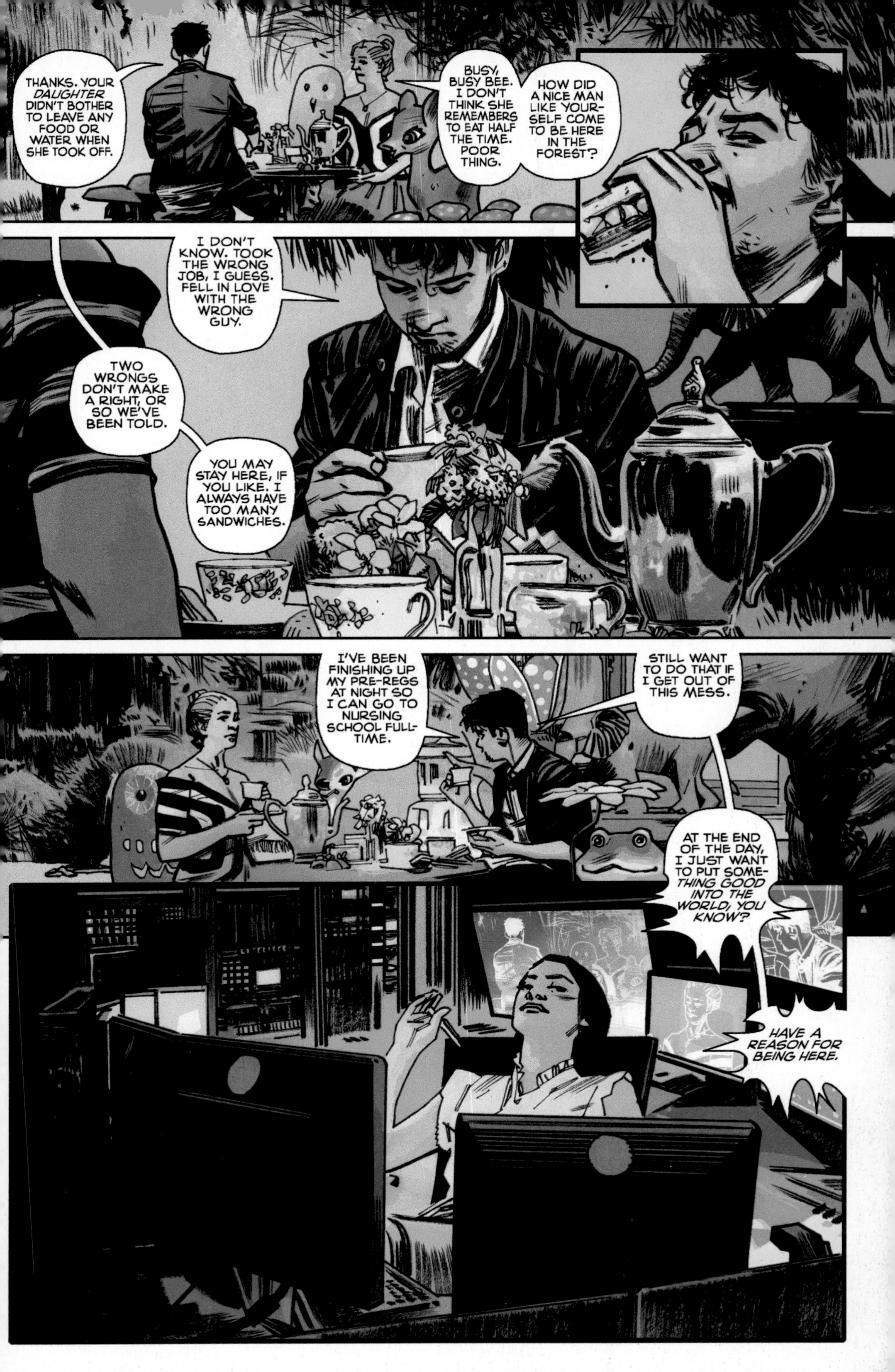
THANKS. YOUR *DAUGHTER* DIDN'T BOTHER TO LEAVE ANY FOOD OR WATER WHEN SHE TOOK OFF.
BUSY, BUSY BEE. I DON'T THINK SHE REMEMBERS TO EAT HALF THE TIME. POOR THING.
HOW DID A NICE MAN LIKE YOURSELF COME TO BE HERE IN THE FOREST?
I DON'T KNOW. TOOK THE WRONG JOB, I GUESS. FELL IN LOVE WITH THE WRONG GUY.
TWO WRONGS DON'T MAKE A RIGHT, OR SO WE'VE BEEN TOLD.
YOU MAY STAY HERE, IF YOU LIKE. I ALWAYS HAVE TOO MANY SANDWICHES.
I'VE BEEN FINISHING UP MY PRE-REGS AT NIGHT SO I CAN GO TO NURSING SCHOOL FULL-TIME.
STILL WANT TO DO THAT IF I GET OUT OF THIS MESS.
AT THE END OF THE DAY, I JUST WANT TO PUT SOME-*THING GOOD INTO THE WORLD, YOU KNOW?*
*HAVE A REASON FOR BEING HERE.*

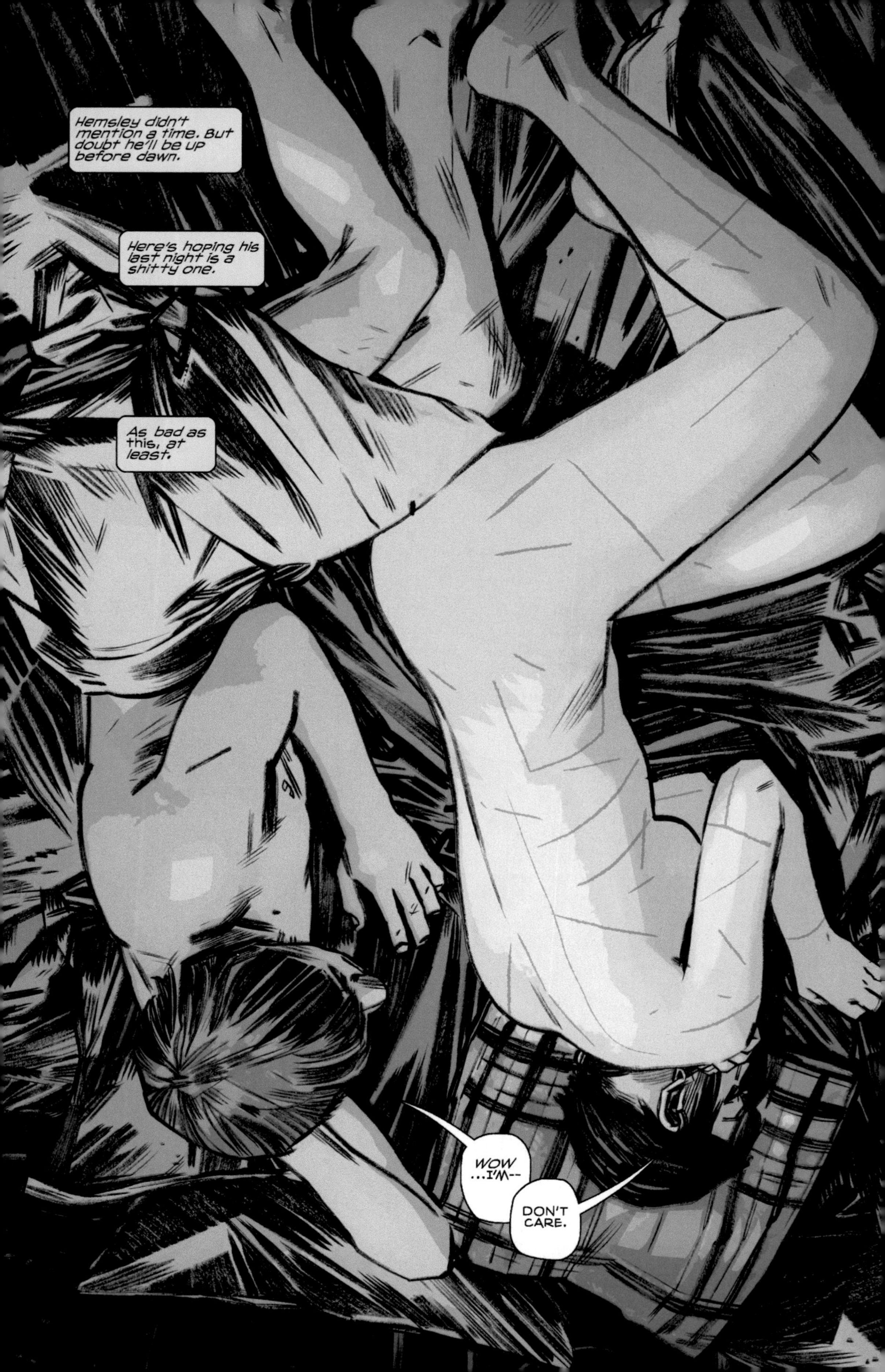
Hemsley didn't mention a time. But doubt he'll be up before dawn.
Here's hoping his last night is a shitty one.
As bad as this, at least.
WOW ...I'M--
DON'T CARE.

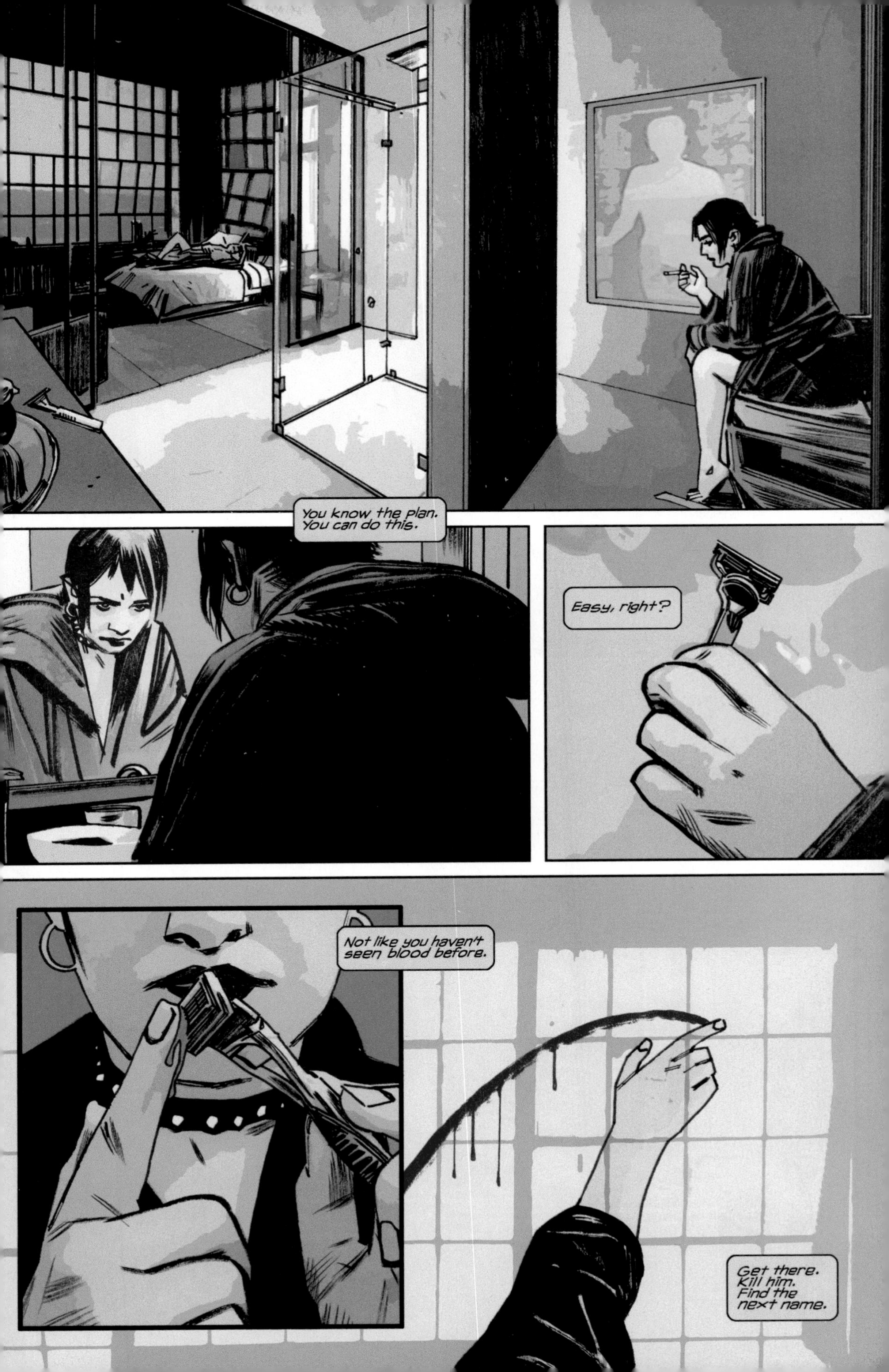
You know the plan. You can do this.
Easy, right?
Not like you haven't seen blood before.
Get there. Kill him. Find the next name.

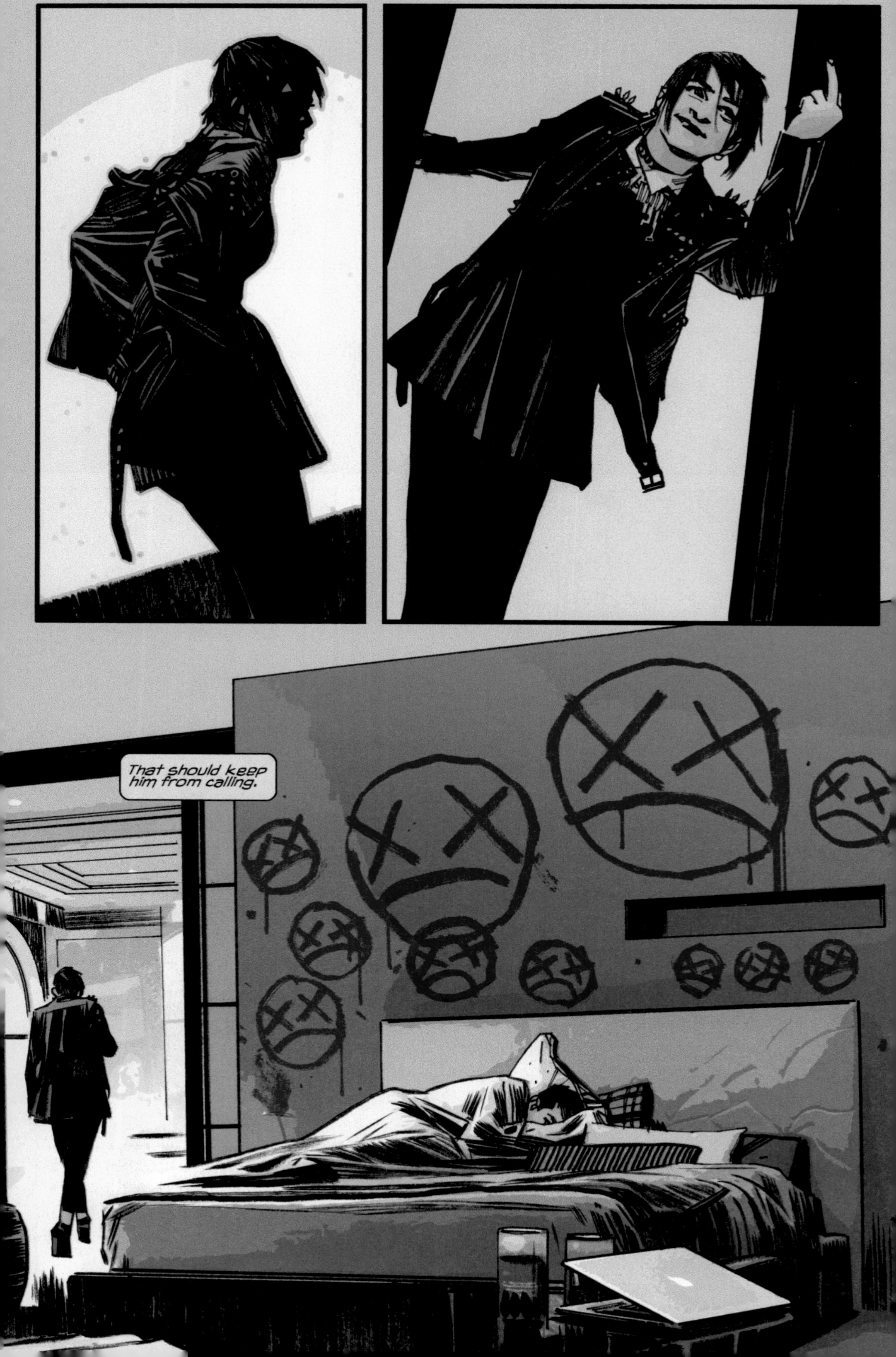
That should keep him from calling.

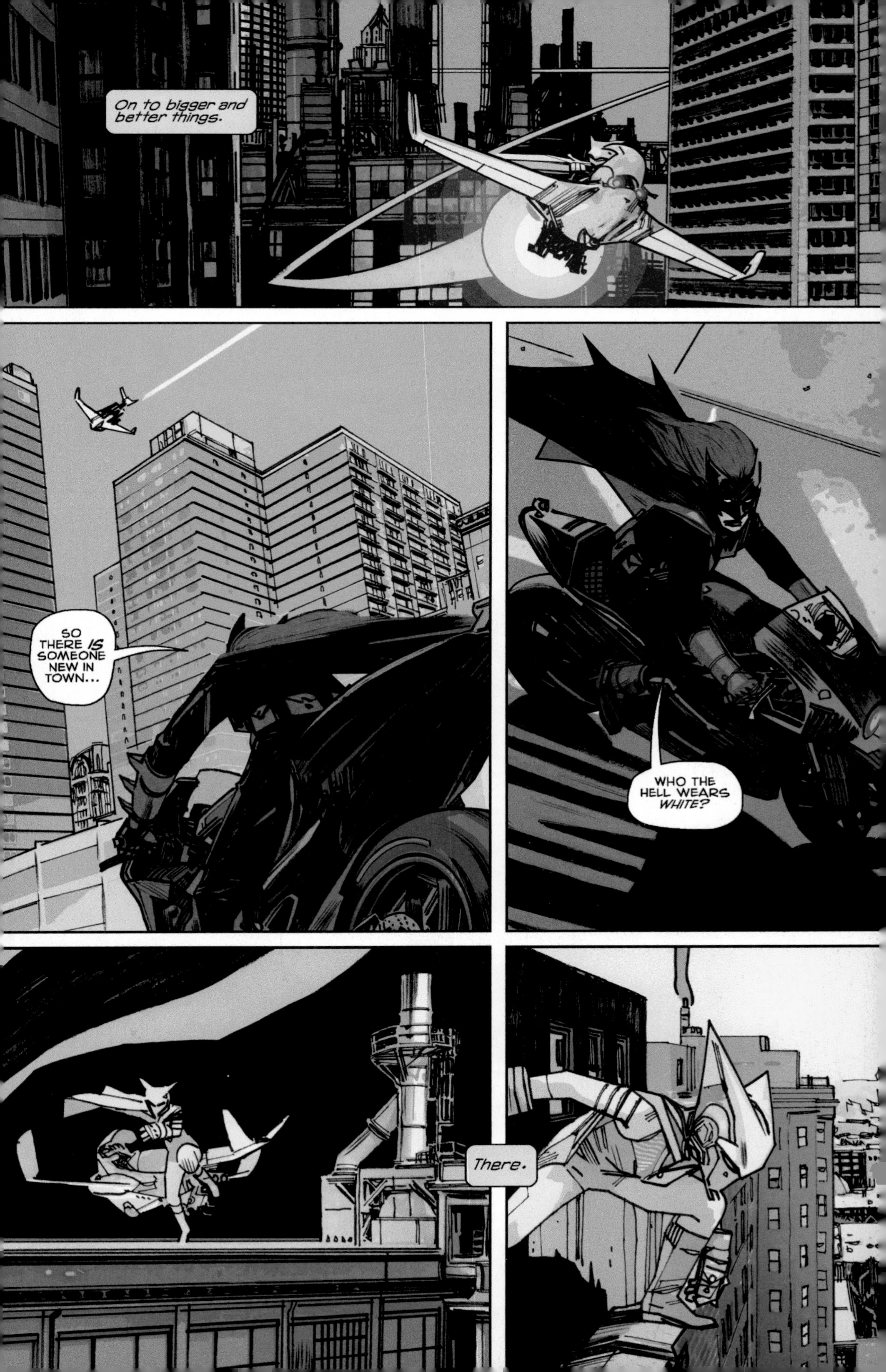
On to bigger and better things.
SO THERE *IS* SOMEONE NEW IN TOWN...
WHO THE HELL WEARS *WHITE?*
There.

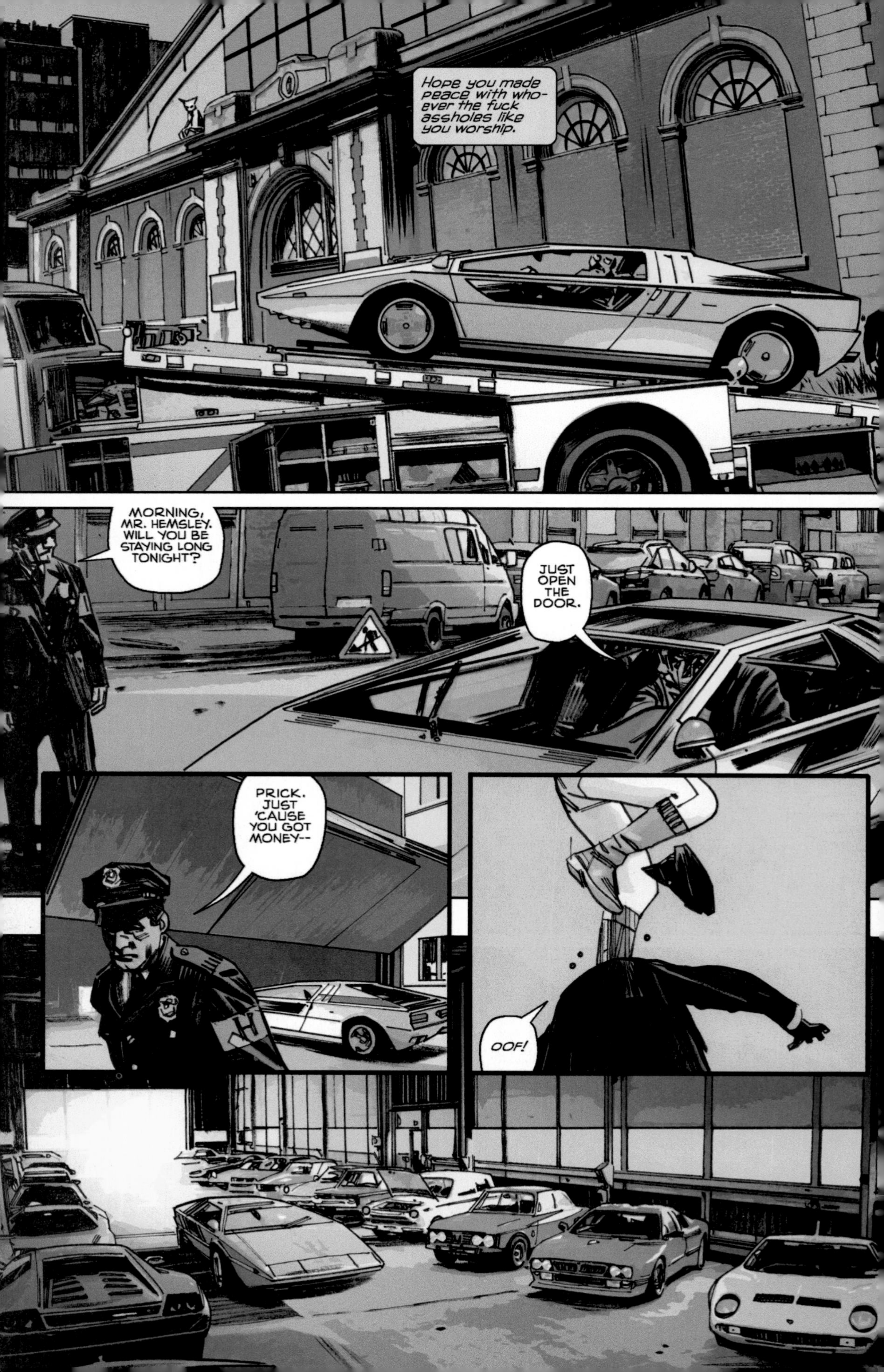
Hope you made peace with whoever the fuck assholes like you worship.
MORNING, MR. HEMSLEY. WILL YOU BE STAYING LONG TONIGHT?
JUST OPEN THE DOOR.
PRICK. JUST 'CAUSE YOU GOT MONEY--
OOF!

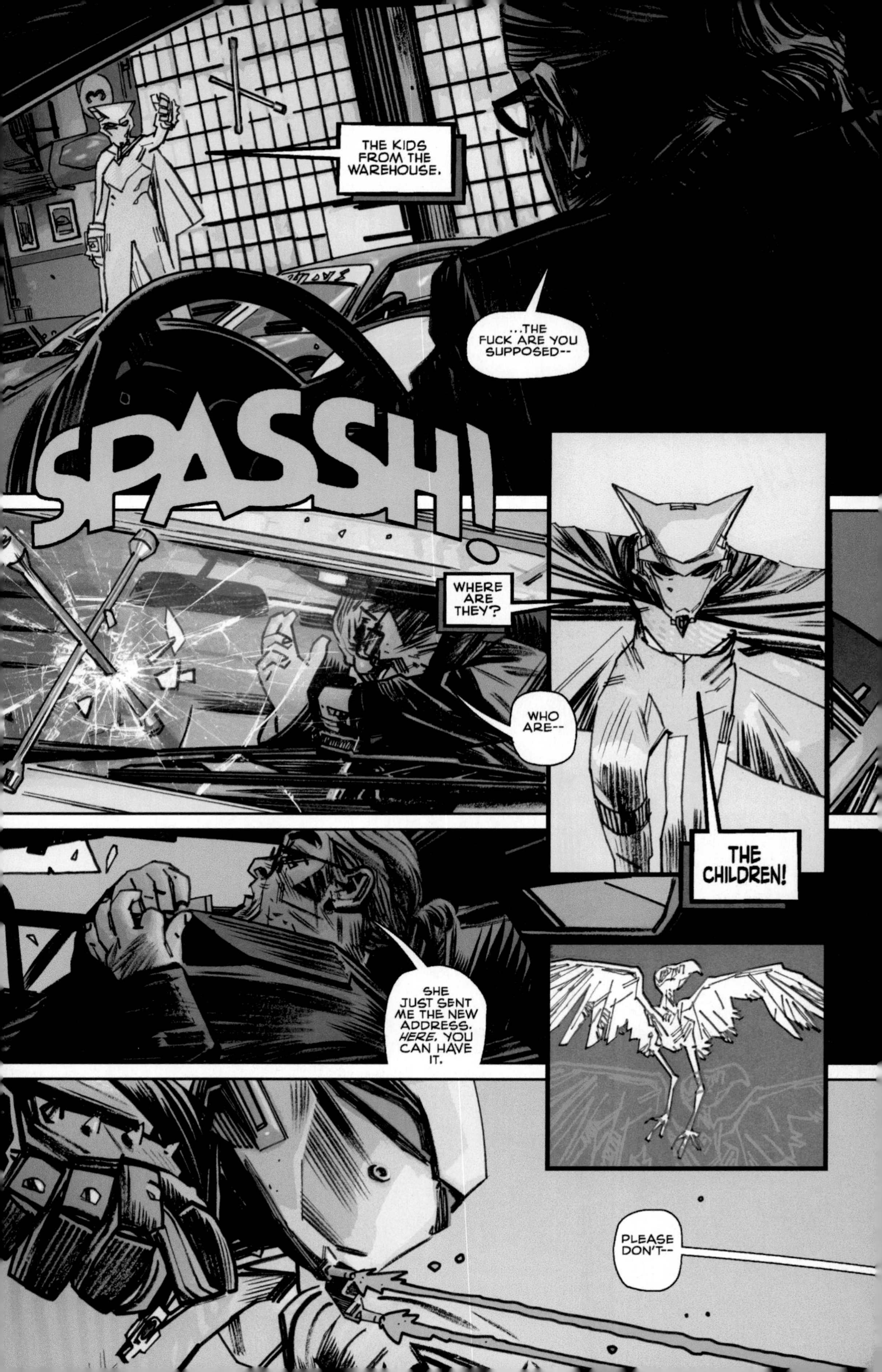
THE KIDS FROM THE WAREHOUSE.
...THE FUCK ARE YOU SUPPOSED--
SPASSH!
WHERE ARE THEY?
WHO ARE--
THE CHILDREN!
SHE JUST SENT ME THE NEW ADDRESS. HERE. YOU CAN HAVE IT.
PLEASE DON'T--

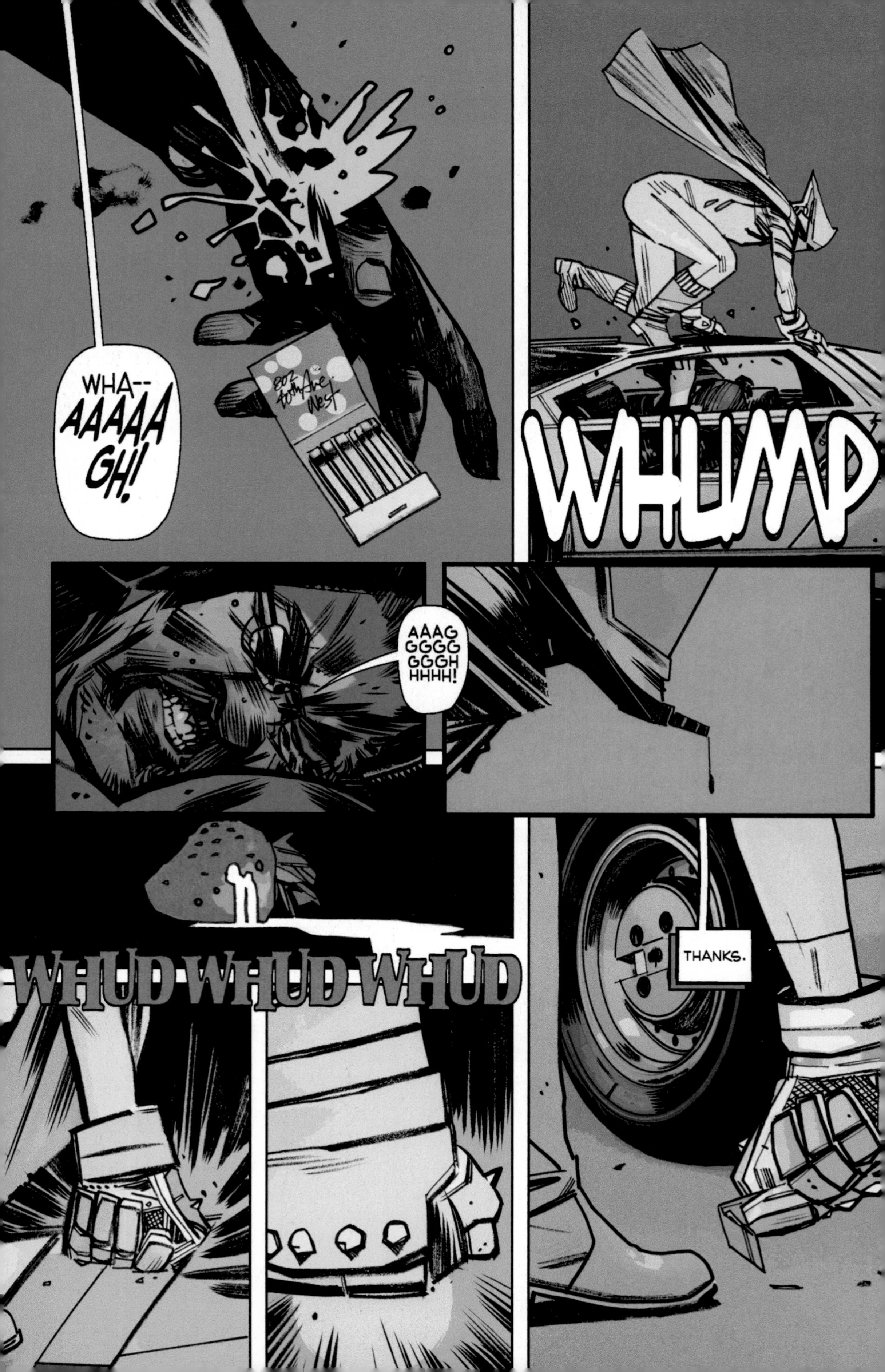
WHA-- AAAAAGH!
802 40th Ave West
WHUMP
AAAGGGGGGGGHHHHH!
WHUD WHUD WHUD
THANKS.

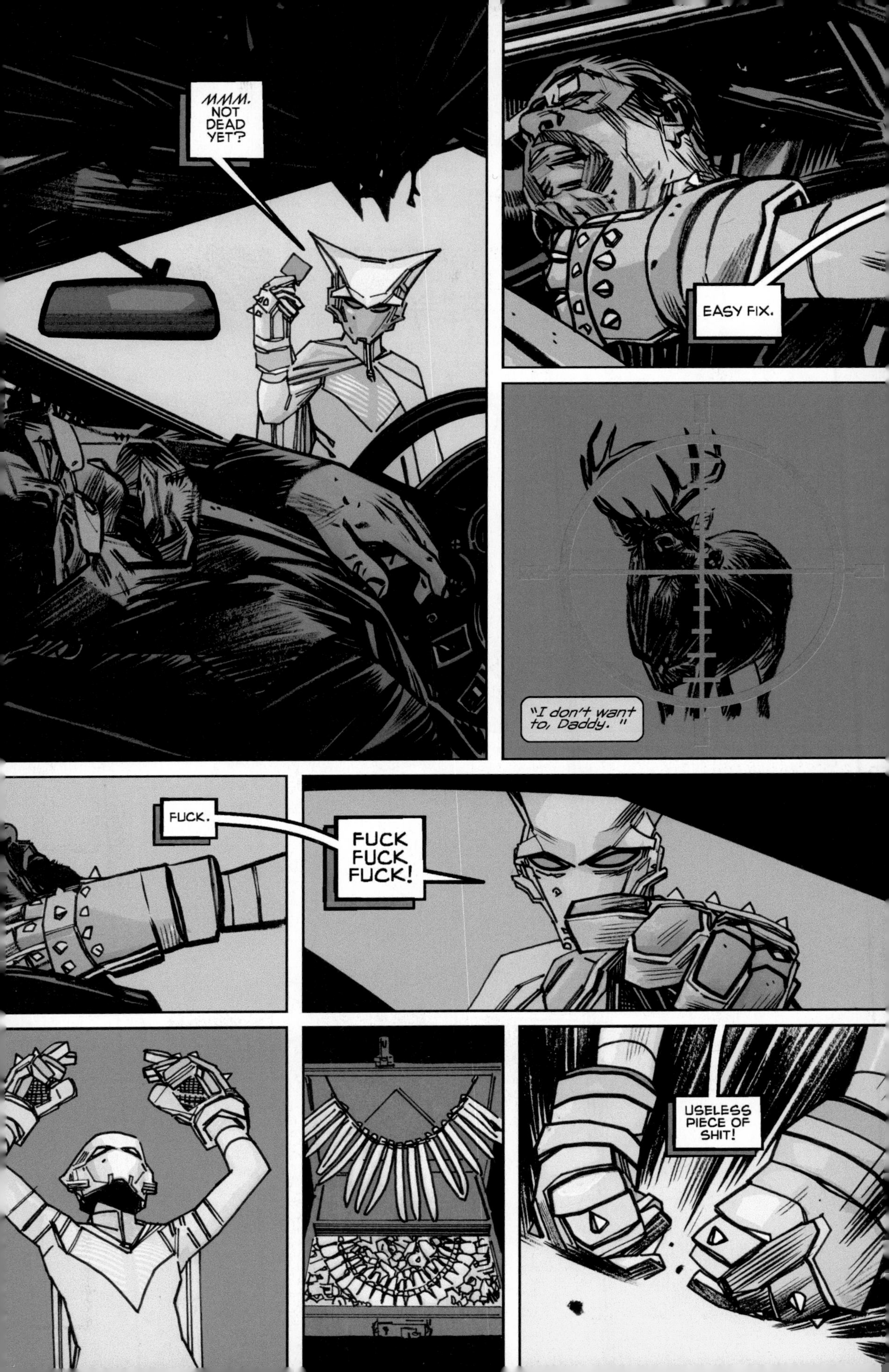
MMM. NOT DEAD YET?
EASY FIX.
"I don't want to, Daddy."
FUCK.
FUCK FUCK FUCK!
USELESS PIECE OF SHIT!

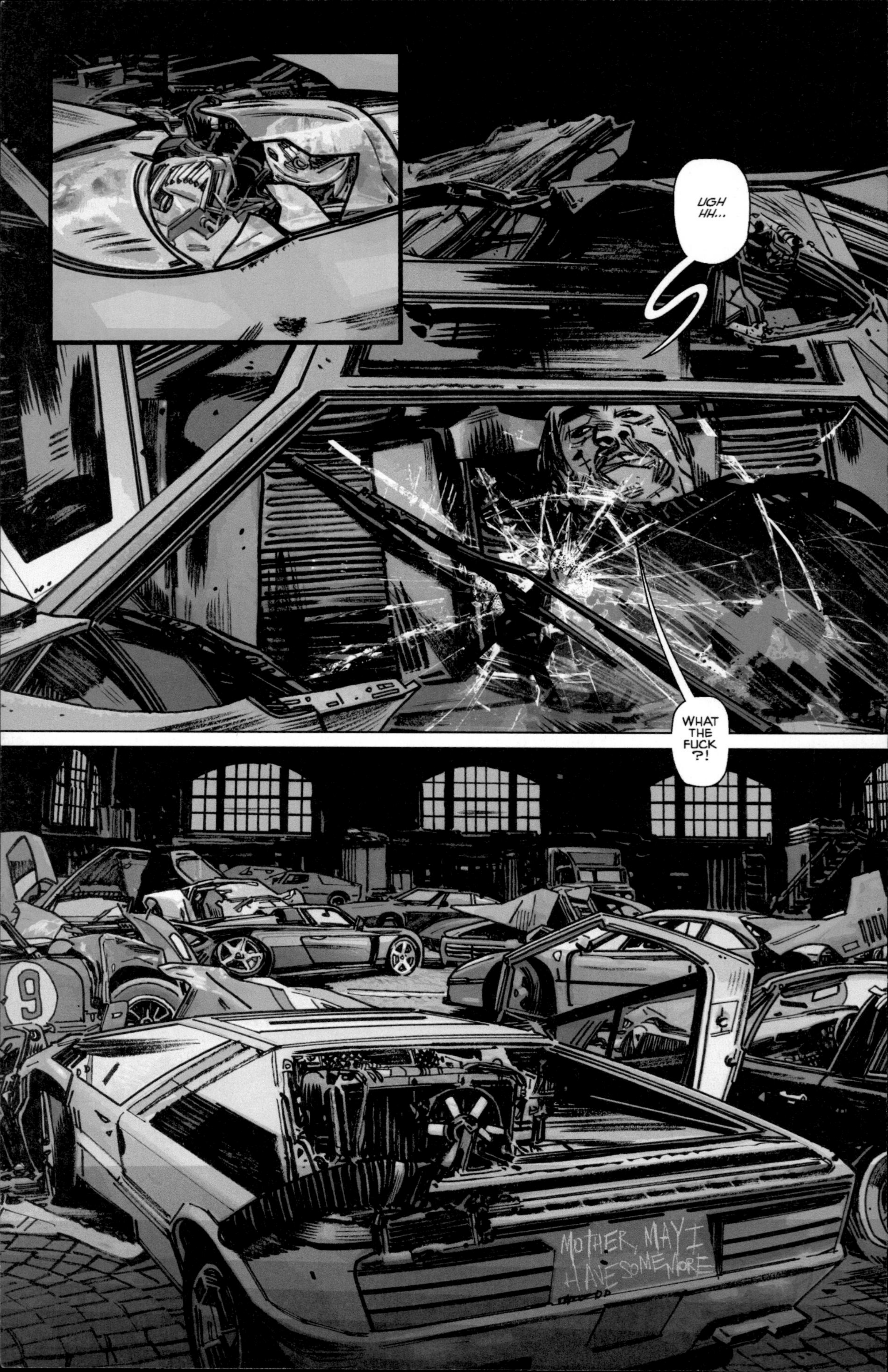
UGH HH...
WHAT THE FUCK ?!
MOTHER, MAY I HAVE SOME MORE

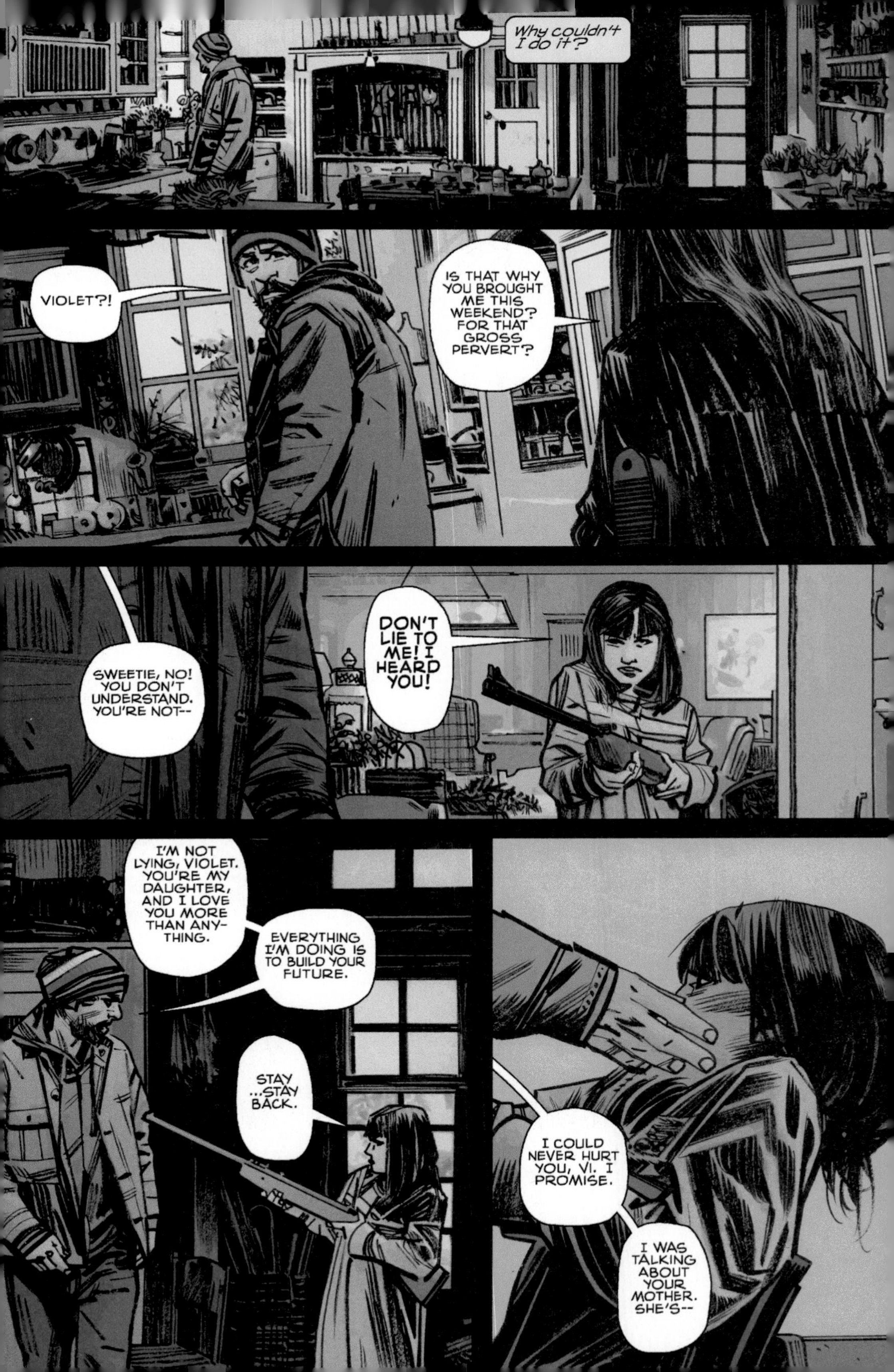
Why couldn't I do it?
VIOLET?!
IS THAT WHY YOU BROUGHT ME THIS WEEKEND? FOR THAT GROSS PERVERT?
SWEETIE, NO! YOU DON'T UNDERSTAND. YOU'RE NOT--
DON'T LIE TO ME! I HEARD YOU!
I'M NOT LYING, VIOLET. YOU'RE MY DAUGHTER, AND I LOVE YOU MORE THAN ANY-THING.
EVERYTHING I'M DOING IS TO BUILD YOUR FUTURE.
STAY ...STAY BACK.
I COULD NEVER HURT YOU, VI. I PROMISE.
I WAS TALKING ABOUT YOUR MOTHER. SHE'S--

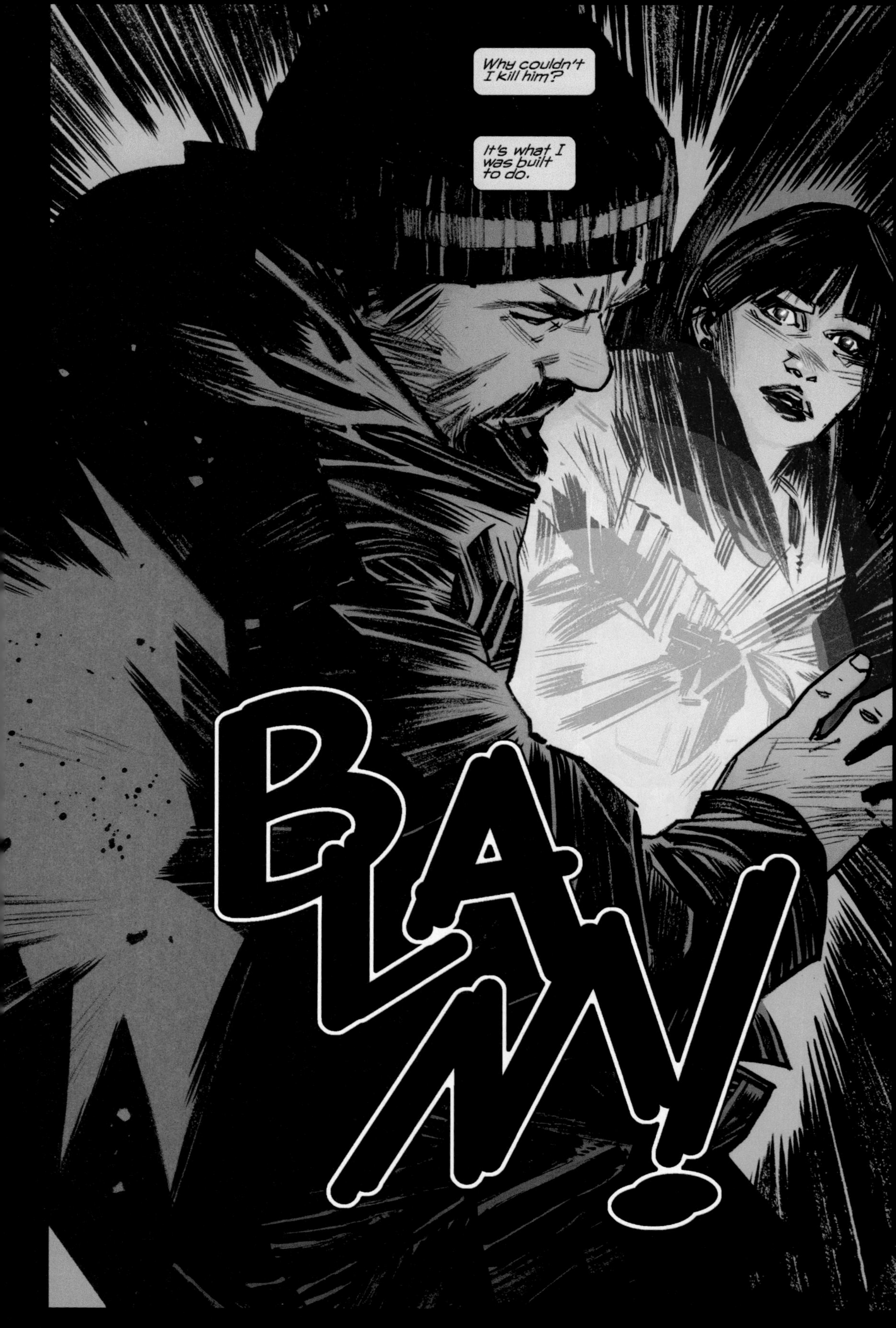
Why couldn't I kill him?
It's what I was built to do.
BLAM!

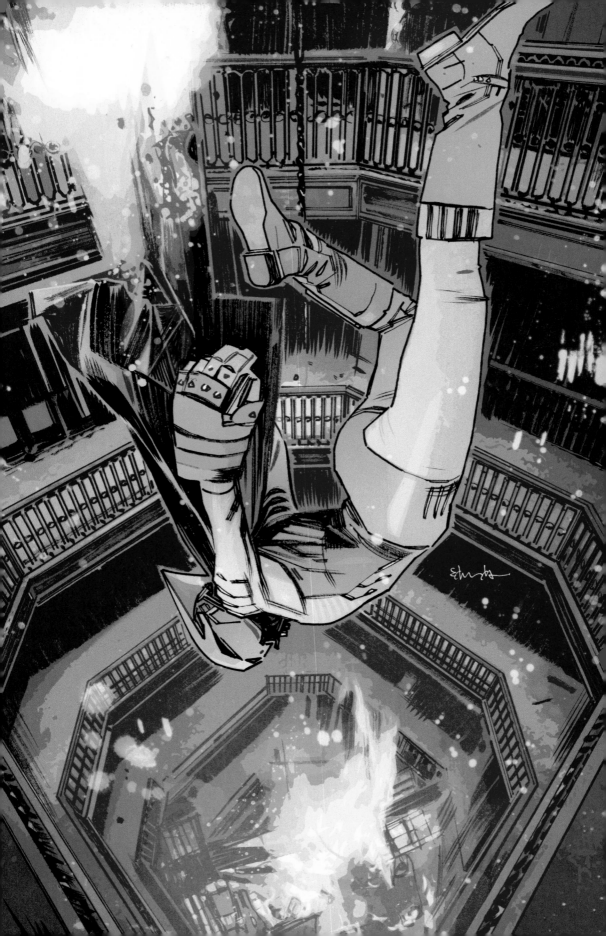

Variant cover art by Mingjue Chen

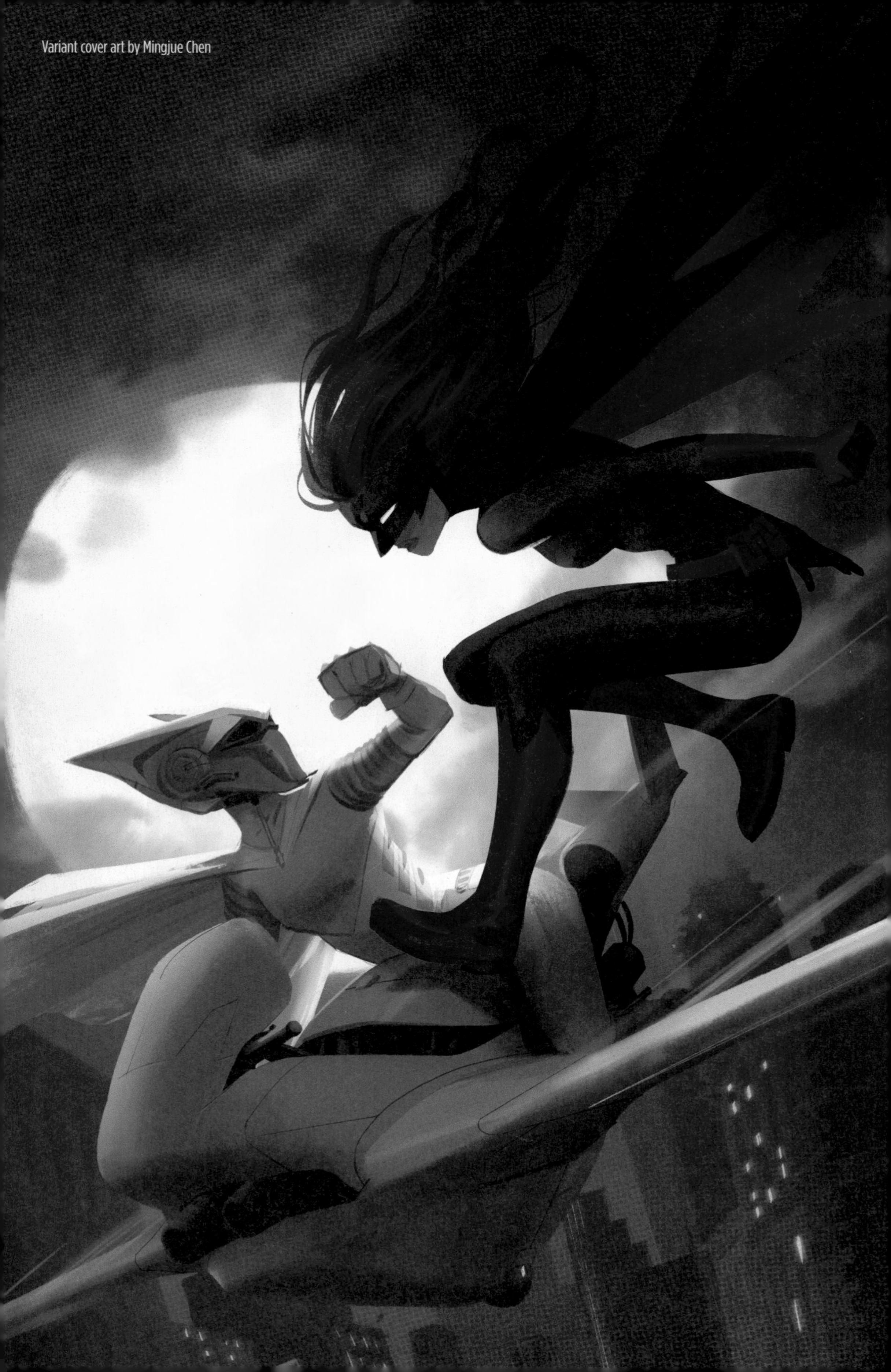

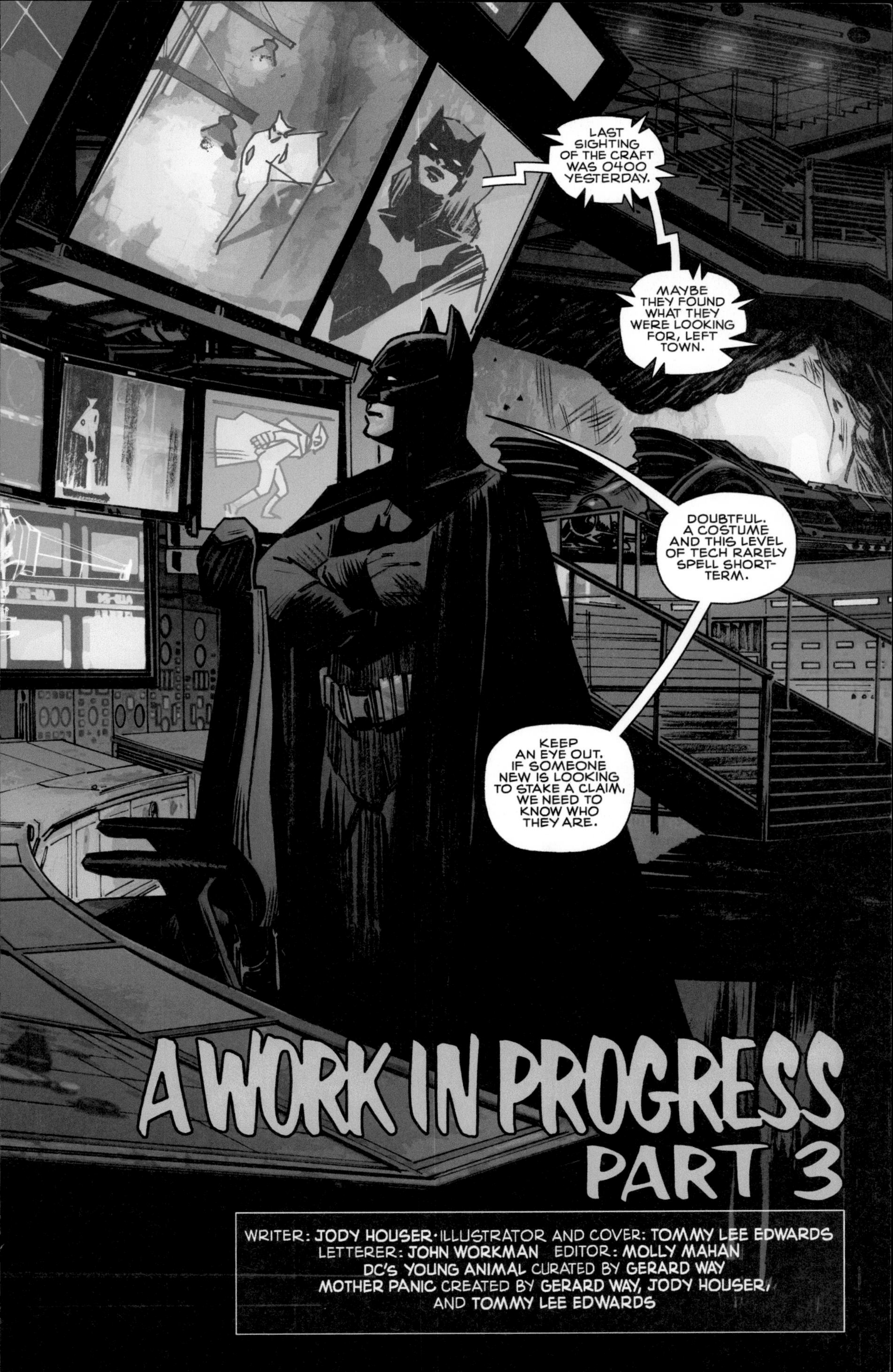
LAST SIGHTING OF THE CRAFT WAS 0400 YESTERDAY.
MAYBE THEY FOUND WHAT THEY WERE LOOKING FOR, LEFT TOWN.
DOUBTFUL. A COSTUME AND THIS LEVEL OF TECH RARELY SPELL SHORT-TERM.
KEEP AN EYE OUT. IF SOMEONE NEW IS LOOKING TO STAKE A CLAIM, WE NEED TO KNOW WHO THEY ARE.
A WORK IN PROGRESS
PART 3
WRITER: JODY HOUSER · ILLUSTRATOR AND COVER: TOMMY LEE EDWARDS
LETTERER: JOHN WORKMAN EDITOR: MOLLY MAHAN
DC'S YOUNG ANIMAL CURATED BY GERARD WAY
MOTHER PANIC CREATED BY GERARD WAY, JODY HOUSER, AND TOMMY LEE EDWARDS

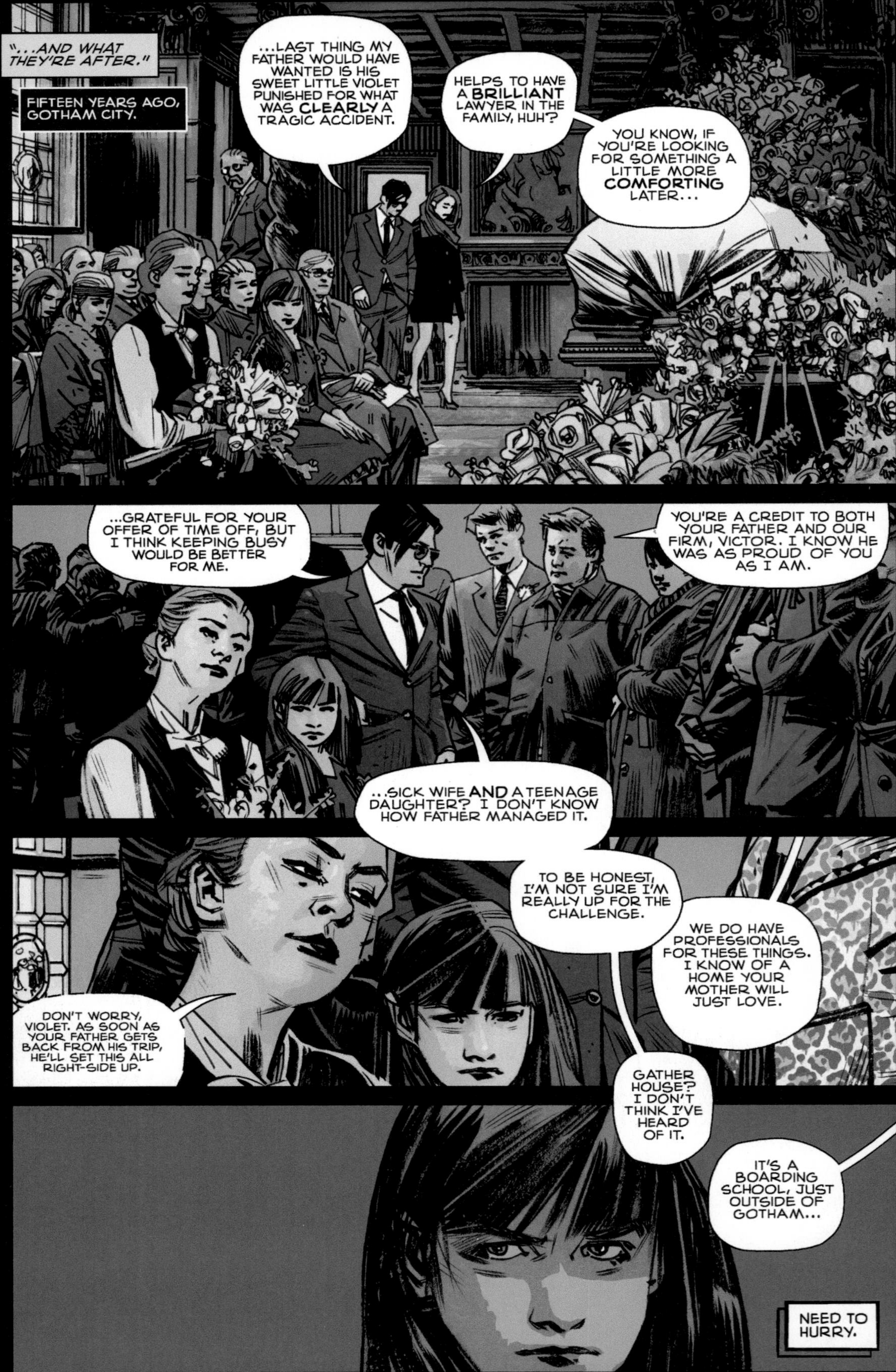
"...AND WHAT THEY'RE AFTER."
FIFTEEN YEARS AGO, GOTHAM CITY.
...LAST THING MY FATHER WOULD HAVE WANTED IS HIS SWEET LITTLE VIOLET PUNISHED FOR WHAT WAS CLEARLY A TRAGIC ACCIDENT.
HELPS TO HAVE A BRILLIANT LAWYER IN THE FAMILY, HUH?
YOU KNOW, IF YOU'RE LOOKING FOR SOMETHING A LITTLE MORE COMFORTING LATER...
...GRATEFUL FOR YOUR OFFER OF TIME OFF, BUT I THINK KEEPING BUSY WOULD BE BETTER FOR ME.
YOU'RE A CREDIT TO BOTH YOUR FATHER AND OUR FIRM, VICTOR. I KNOW HE WAS AS PROUD OF YOU AS I AM.
...SICK WIFE AND A TEENAGE DAUGHTER? I DON'T KNOW HOW FATHER MANAGED IT.
TO BE HONEST, I'M NOT SURE I'M REALLY UP FOR THE CHALLENGE.
WE DO HAVE PROFESSIONALS FOR THESE THINGS. I KNOW OF A HOME YOUR MOTHER WILL JUST LOVE.
DON'T WORRY, VIOLET. AS SOON AS YOUR FATHER GETS BACK FROM HIS TRIP, HE'LL SET THIS ALL RIGHT-SIDE UP.
GATHER HOUSE? I DON'T THINK I'VE HEARD OF IT.
IT'S A BOARDING SCHOOL, JUST OUTSIDE OF GOTHAM...
NEED TO HURRY.

SHOULD HAVE KILLED HEMSLEY. WANTED TO.
SO WHY COULDN'T I DO IT?
ALL I DID WAS LET HIM KNOW I'M COMING.
TAKING AWAY HIS TOYS WILL HAVE TO DO FOR NOW.

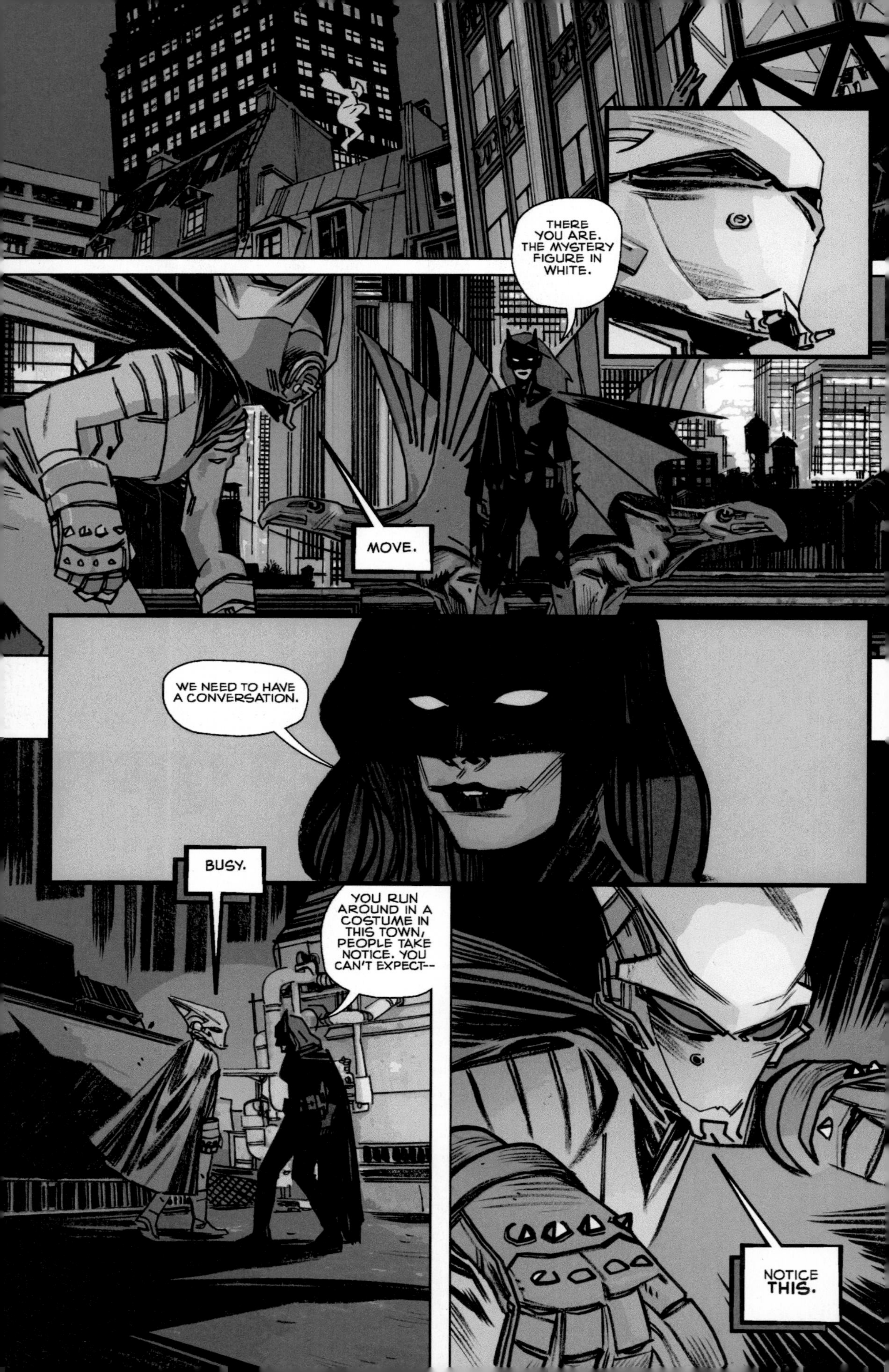
THERE YOU ARE. THE MYSTERY FIGURE IN WHITE.
MOVE.
WE NEED TO HAVE A CONVERSATION.
BUSY.
YOU RUN AROUND IN A COSTUME IN THIS TOWN, PEOPLE TAKE NOTICE. YOU CAN'T EXPECT--
NOTICE THIS.

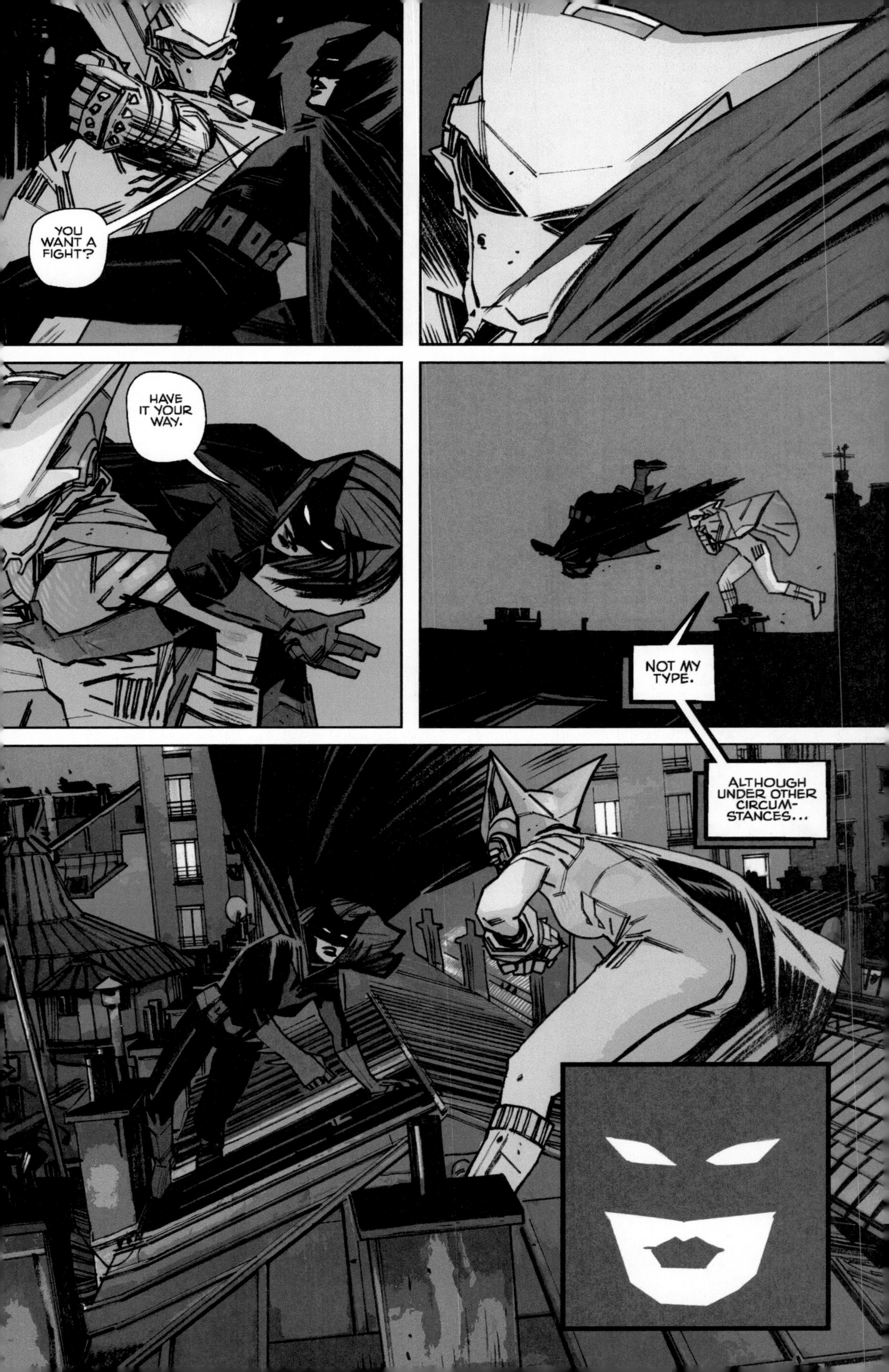
YOU WANT A FIGHT?
HAVE IT YOUR WAY.
NOT MY TYPE.
ALTHOUGH UNDER OTHER CIRCUM-STANCES...

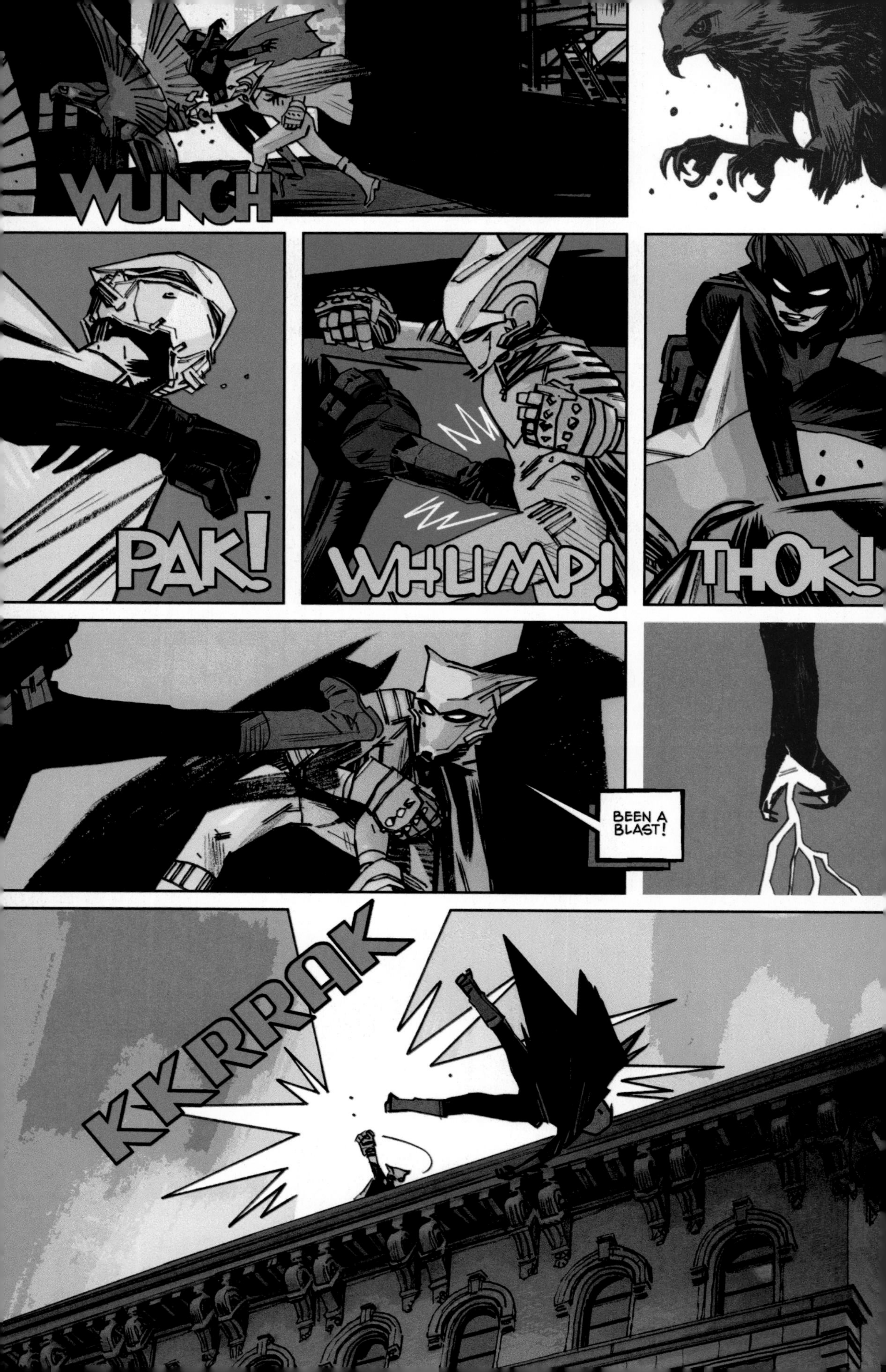
WUNCH
PAK!
WHUMP!
THOK!
BEEN A BLAST!
KKRRAK

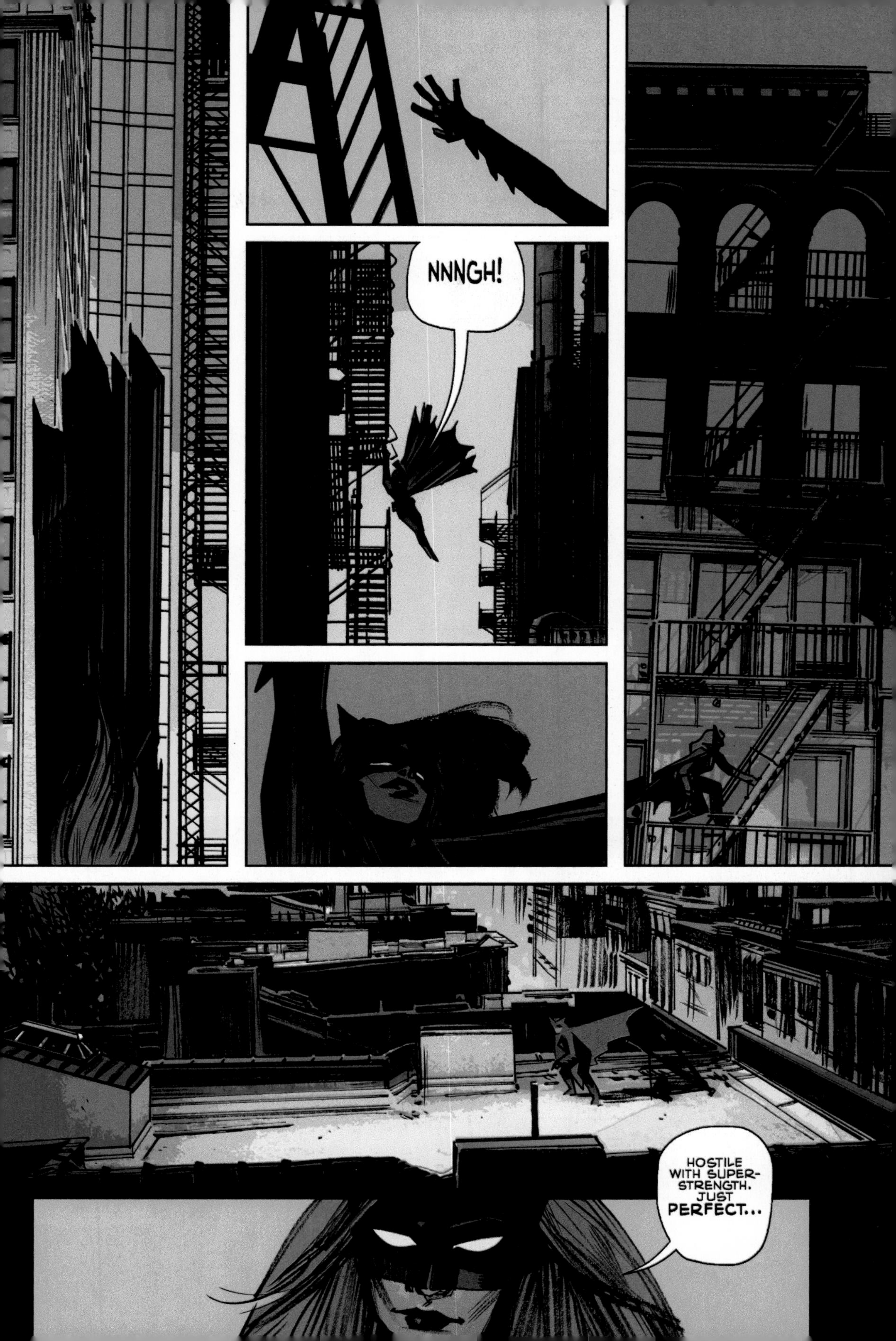
NNNGH!
HOSTILE WITH SUPER-STRENGTH. JUST PERFECT...

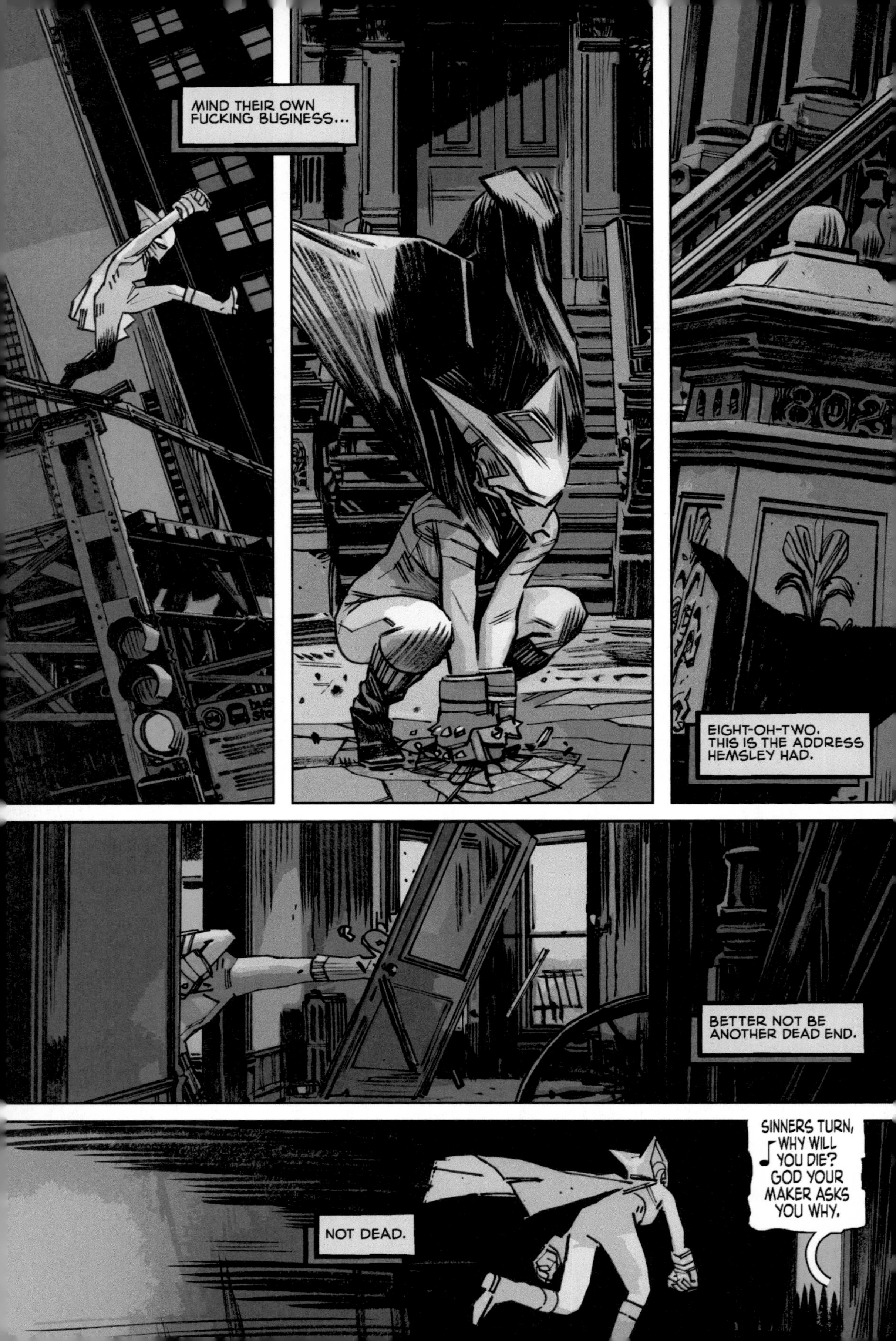
MIND THEIR OWN FUCKING BUSINESS...
EIGHT-OH-TWO. THIS IS THE ADDRESS HEMSLEY HAD.
BETTER NOT BE ANOTHER DEAD END.
NOT DEAD.
SINNERS TURN, ♪ WHY WILL YOU DIE? GOD YOUR MAKER ASKS YOU WHY.

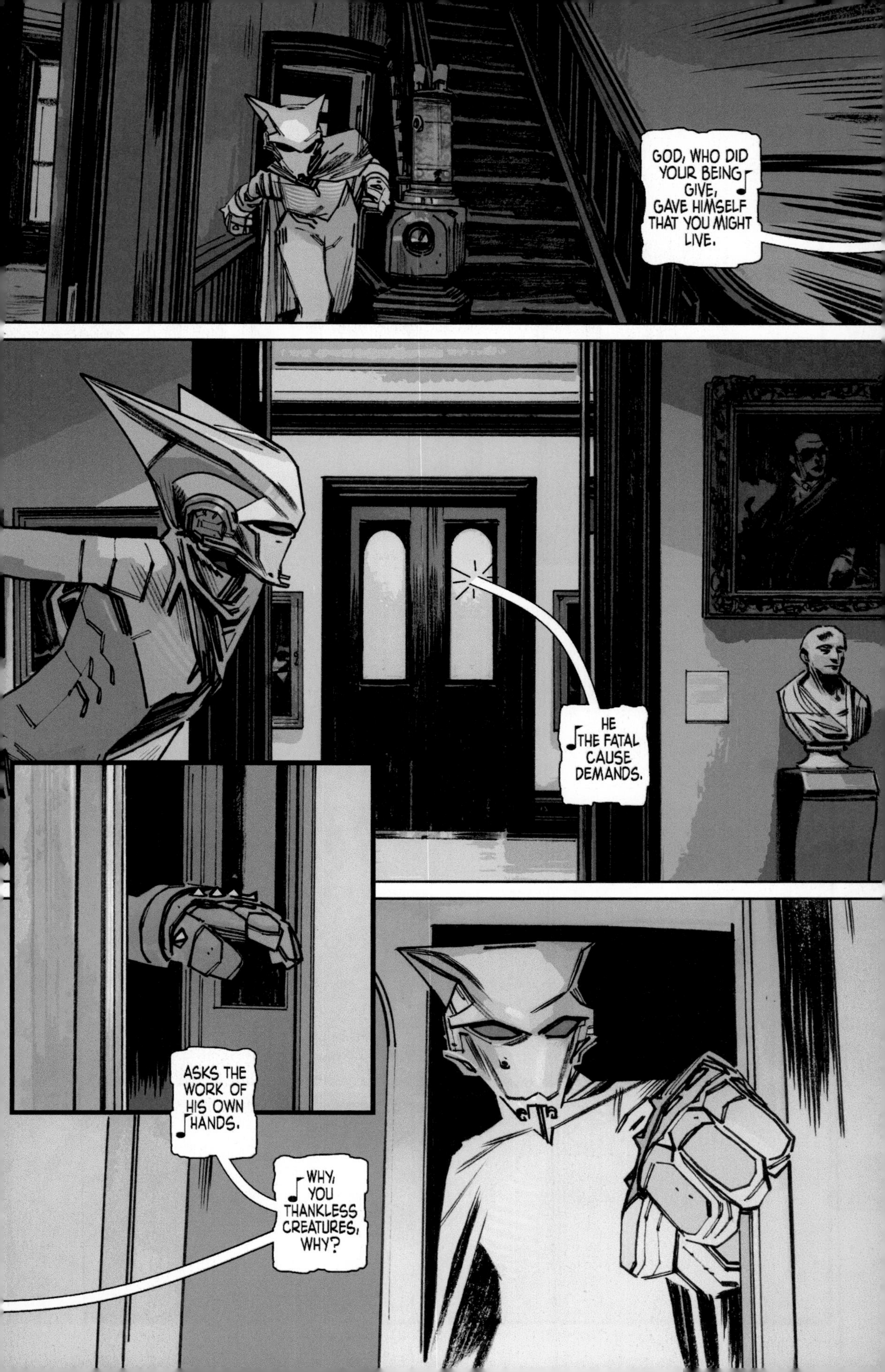

GOD, WHO DID YOUR BEING GIVE, GAVE HIMSELF THAT YOU MIGHT LIVE.
HE THE FATAL CAUSE DEMANDS.
ASKS THE WORK OF HIS OWN HANDS.
WHY, YOU THANKLESS CREATURES, WHY?

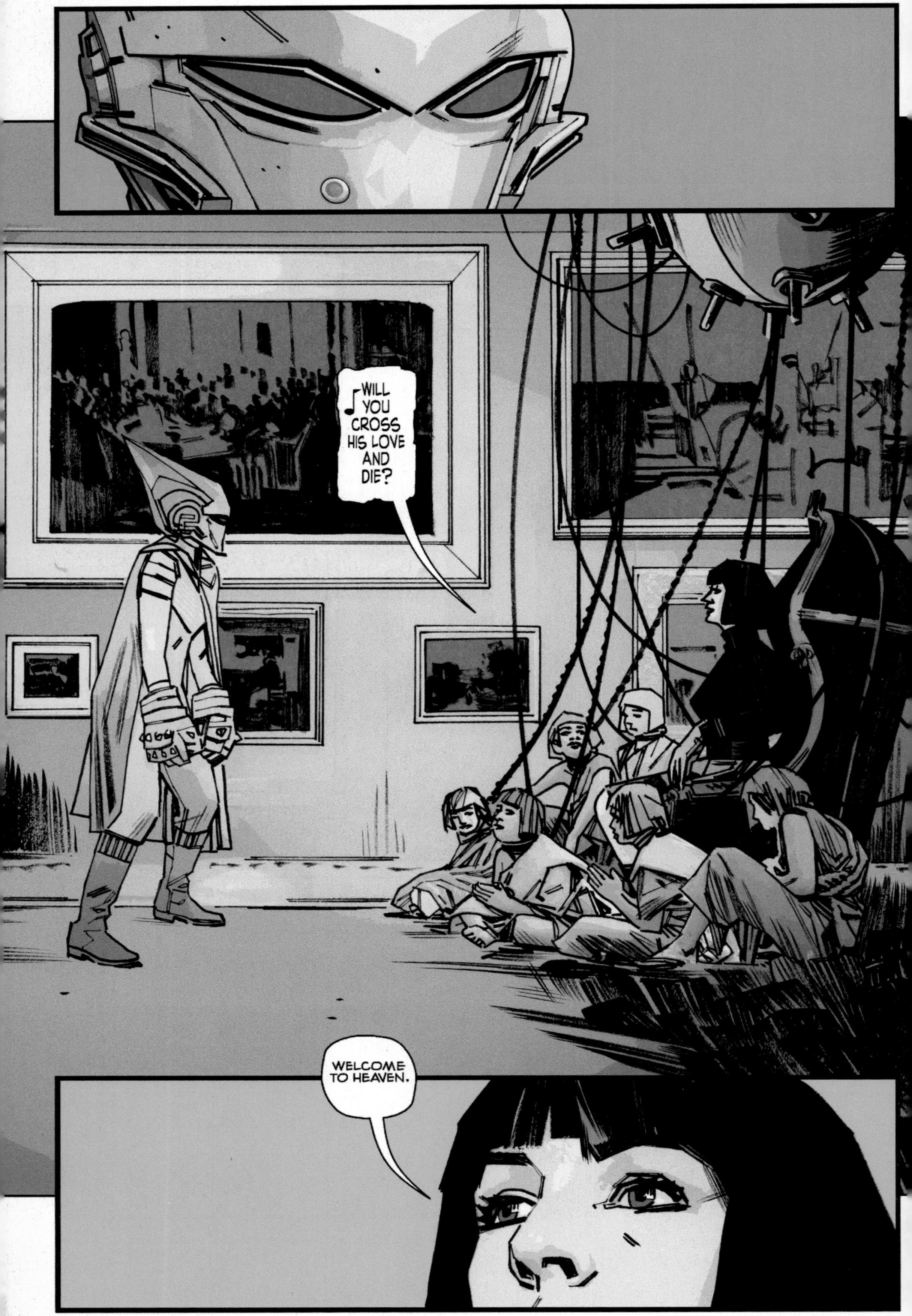
♩WILL YOU CROSS HIS LOVE AND DIE?
WELCOME TO HEAVEN.

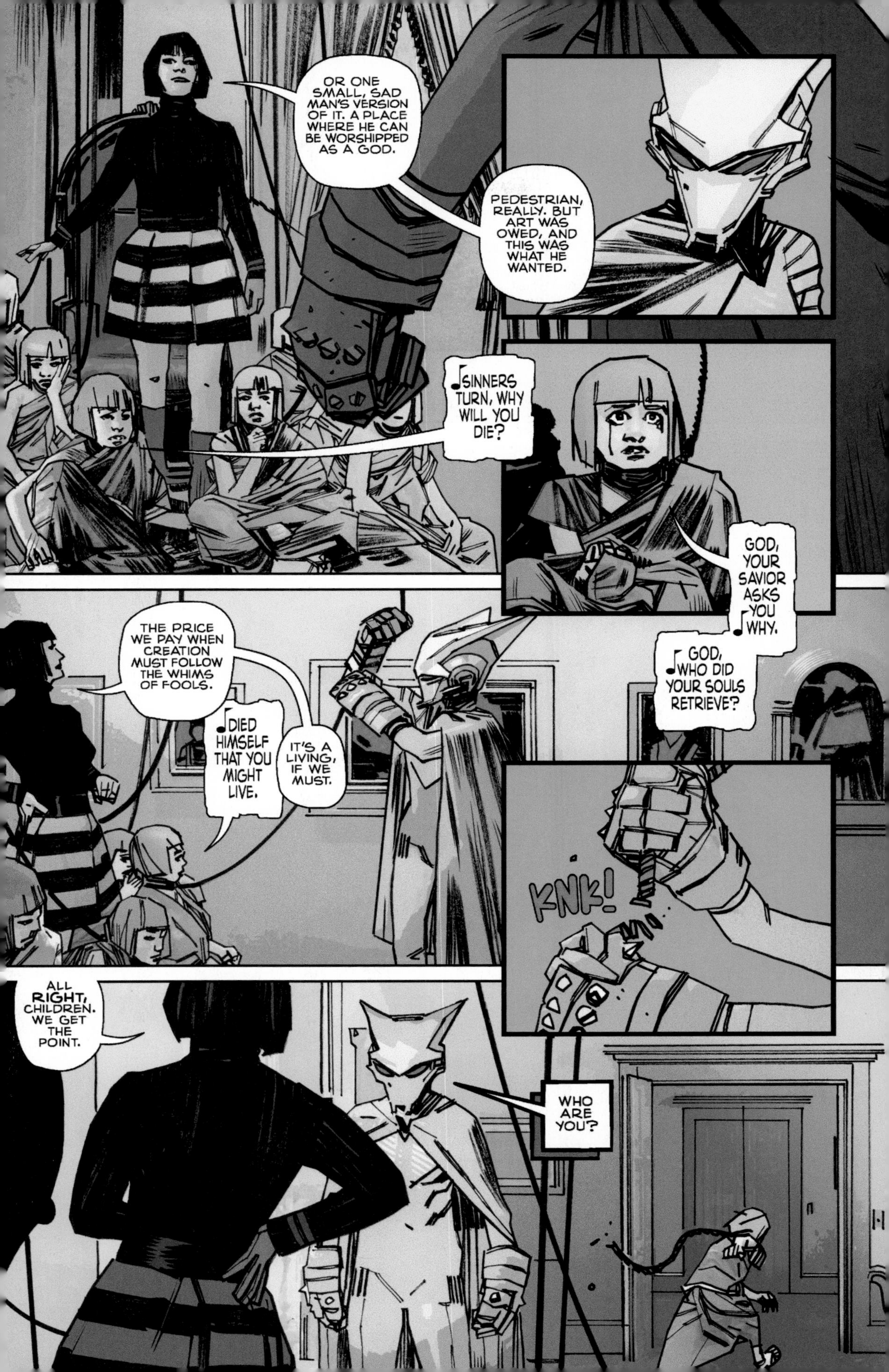
OR ONE SMALL, SAD MAN'S VERSION OF IT. A PLACE WHERE HE CAN BE WORSHIPPED AS A GOD.
PEDESTRIAN, REALLY. BUT ART WAS OWED, AND THIS WAS WHAT HE WANTED.
♪SINNERS TURN, WHY WILL YOU DIE?
GOD, YOUR SAVIOR ASKS YOU ♪WHY.
♪GOD, WHO DID YOUR SOULS RETRIEVE?
THE PRICE WE PAY WHEN CREATION MUST FOLLOW THE WHIMS OF FOOLS.
♪DIED HIMSELF THAT YOU MIGHT LIVE.
IT'S A LIVING, IF WE MUST.
KNK!
ALL RIGHT, CHILDREN. WE GET THE POINT.
WHO ARE YOU?

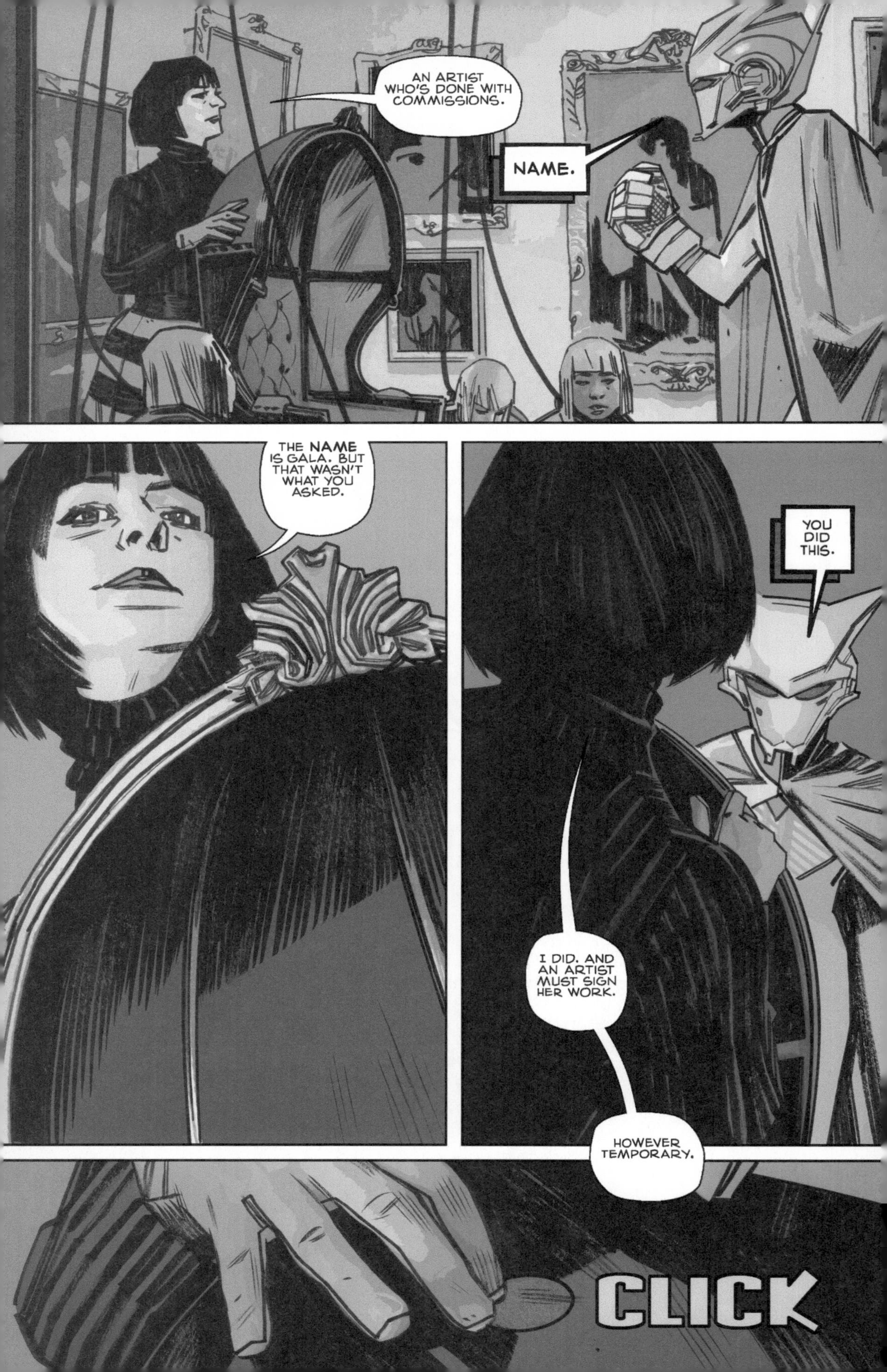
AN ARTIST WHO'S DONE WITH COMMISSIONS.
NAME.
THE NAME IS GALA. BUT THAT WASN'T WHAT YOU ASKED.
YOU DID THIS.
I DID. AND AN ARTIST MUST SIGN HER WORK.
HOWEVER TEMPORARY.
CLICK

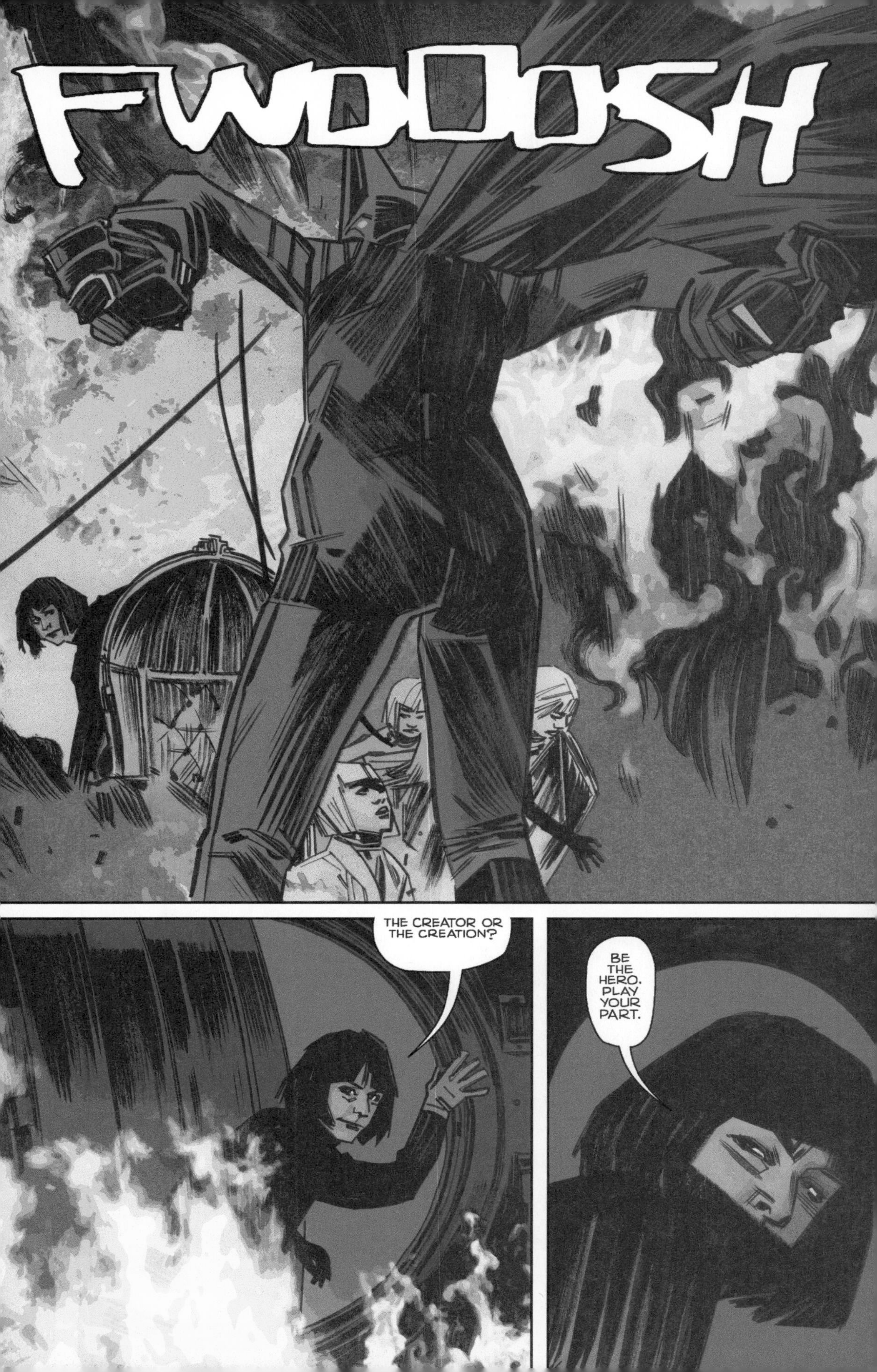
FWOOOSH
THE CREATOR OR THE CREATION?
BE THE HERO. PLAY YOUR PART.

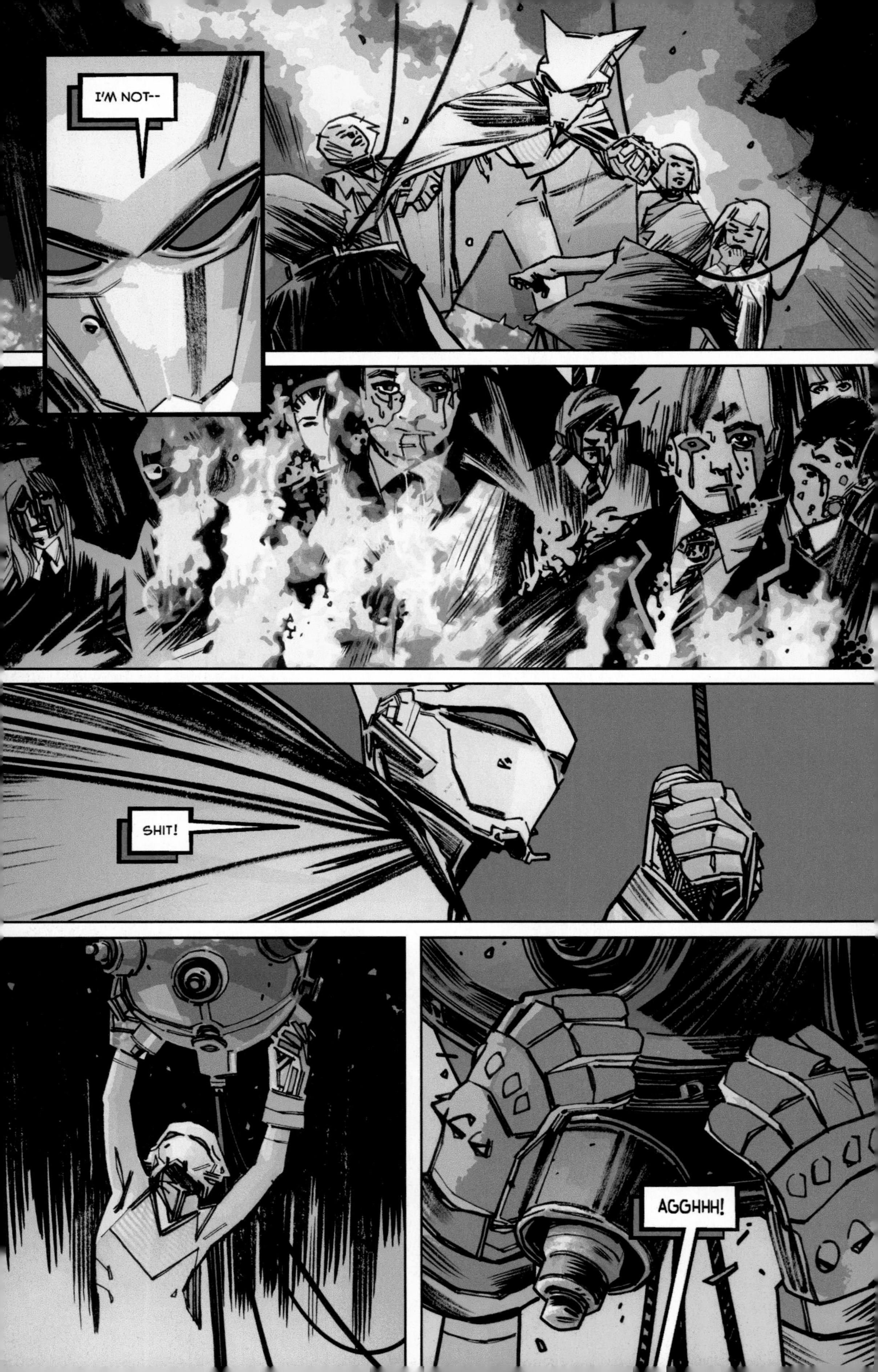
I'M NOT--
SHIT!
AGGHHH!

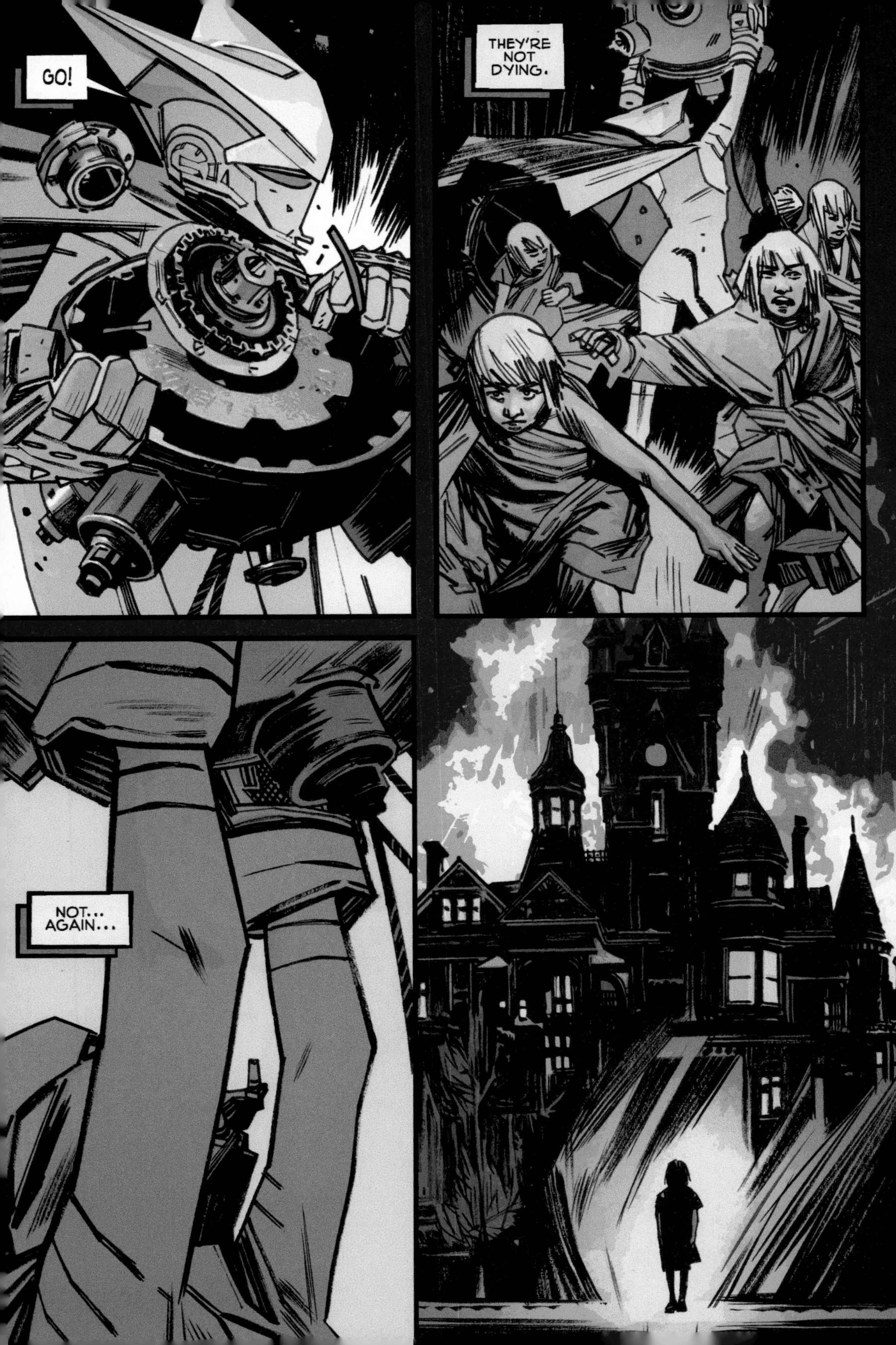
GO!
THEY'RE NOT DYING.
NOT... AGAIN...

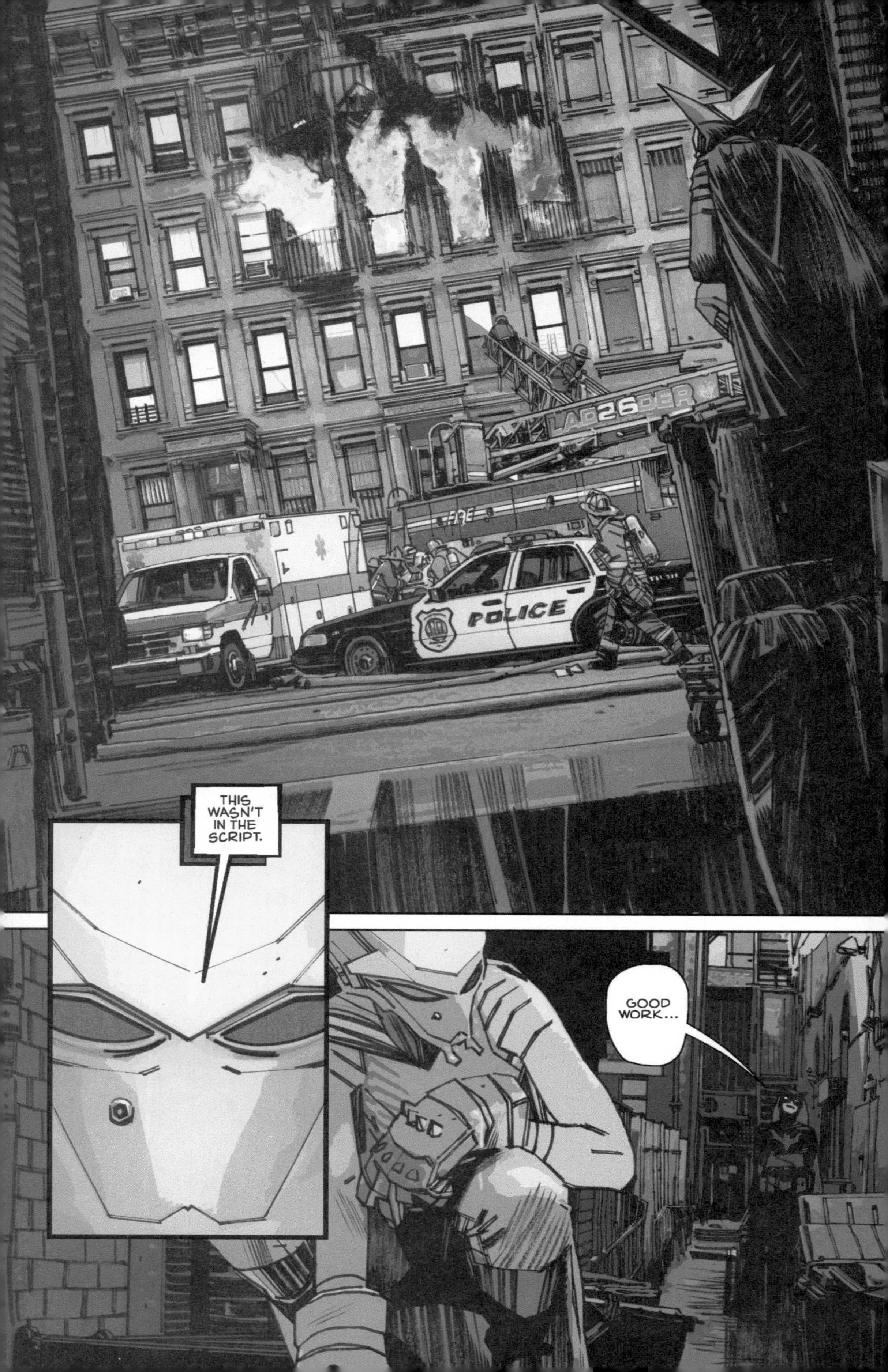
LAD26DER
FIRE
POLICE
THIS WASN'T IN THE SCRIPT.
GOOD WORK...

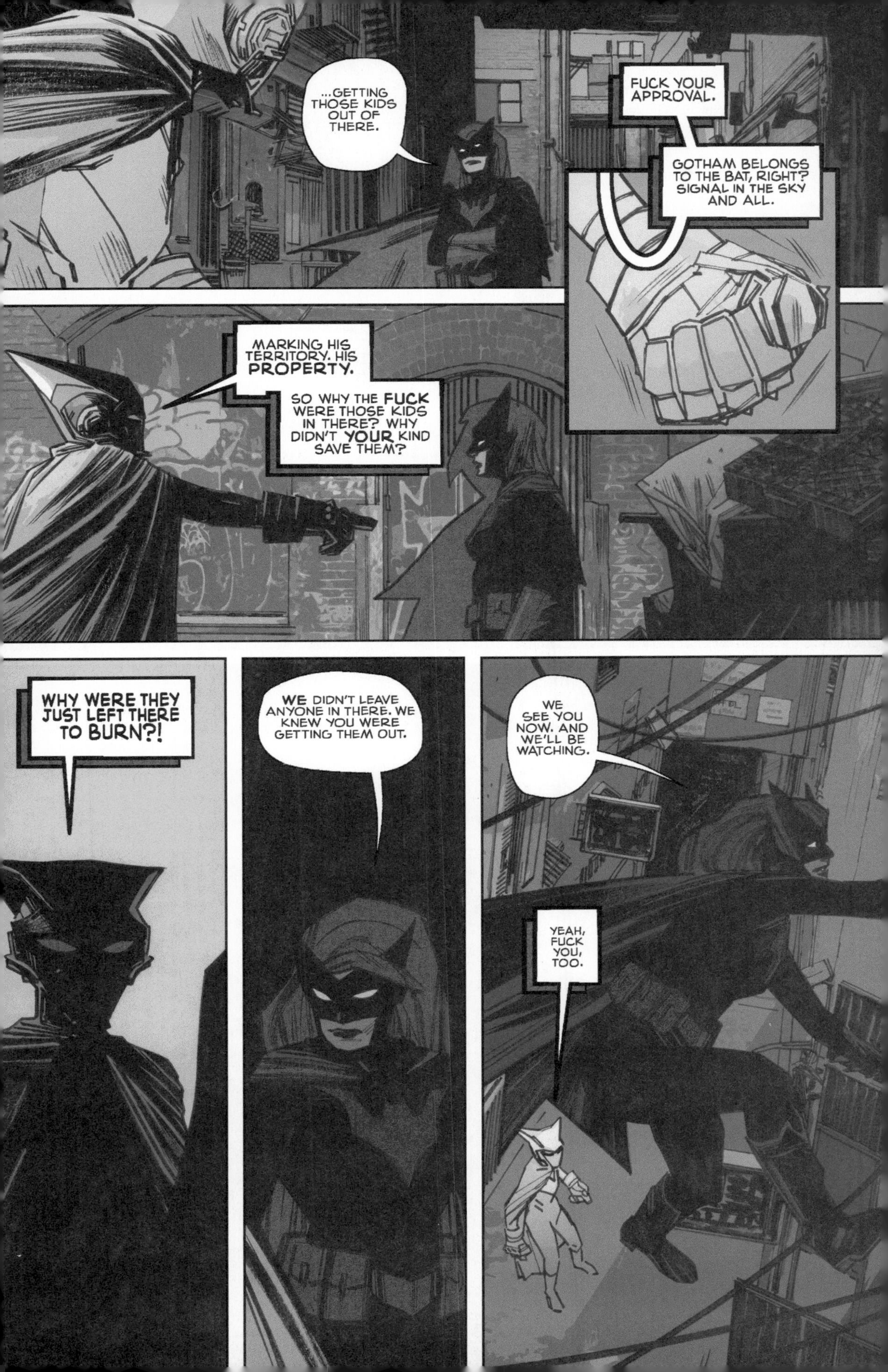

...GETTING THOSE KIDS OUT OF THERE.
FUCK YOUR APPROVAL.
GOTHAM BELONGS TO THE BAT, RIGHT? SIGNAL IN THE SKY AND ALL.
MARKING HIS TERRITORY. HIS PROPERTY.
SO WHY THE FUCK WERE THOSE KIDS IN THERE? WHY DIDN'T YOUR KIND SAVE THEM?
WHY WERE THEY JUST LEFT THERE TO BURN?!
WE DIDN'T LEAVE ANYONE IN THERE. WE KNEW YOU WERE GETTING THEM OUT.
WE SEE YOU NOW. AND WE'LL BE WATCHING.
YEAH, FUCK YOU, TOO.

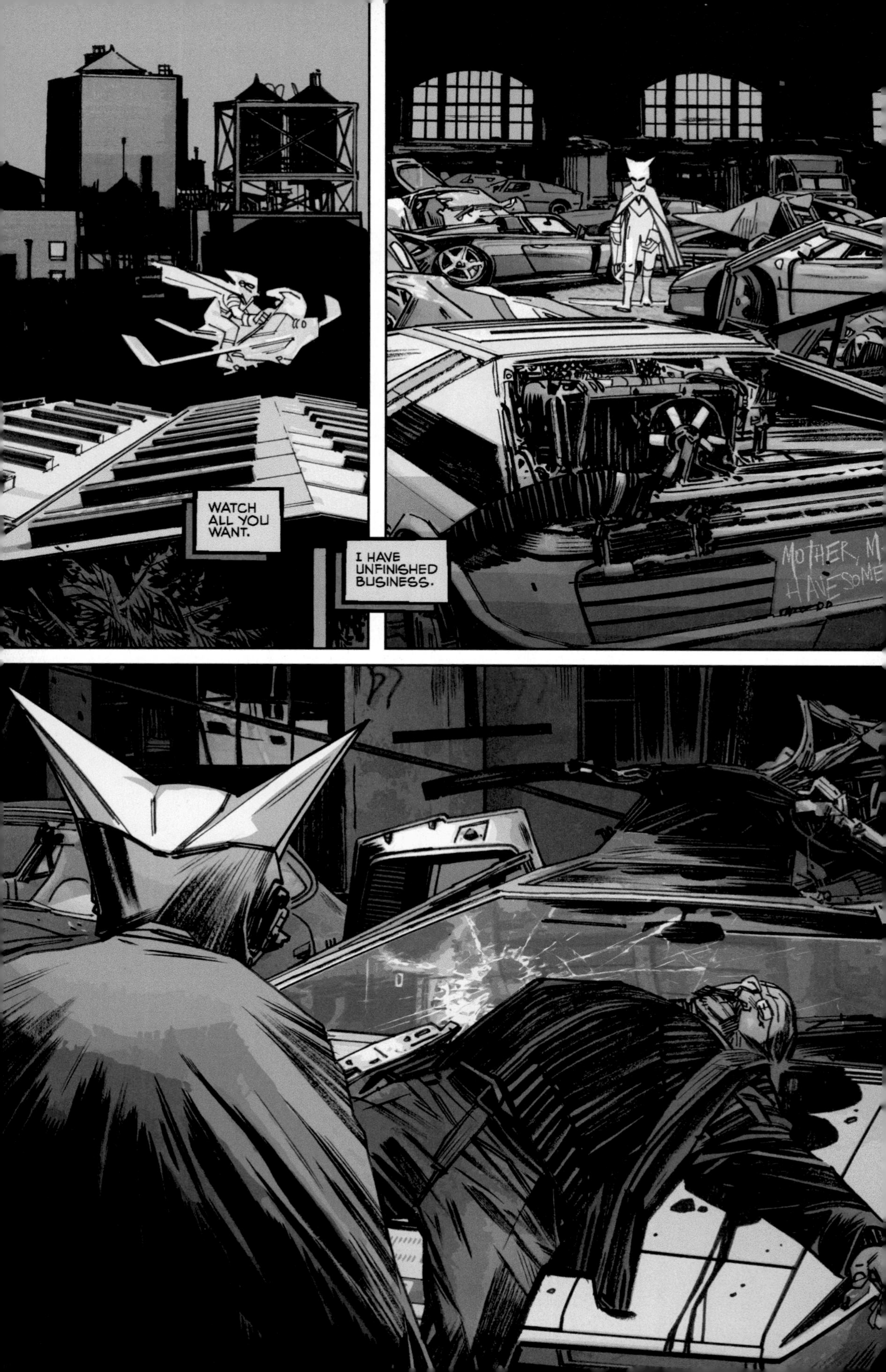
WATCH ALL YOU WANT.
I HAVE UNFINISHED BUSINESS.

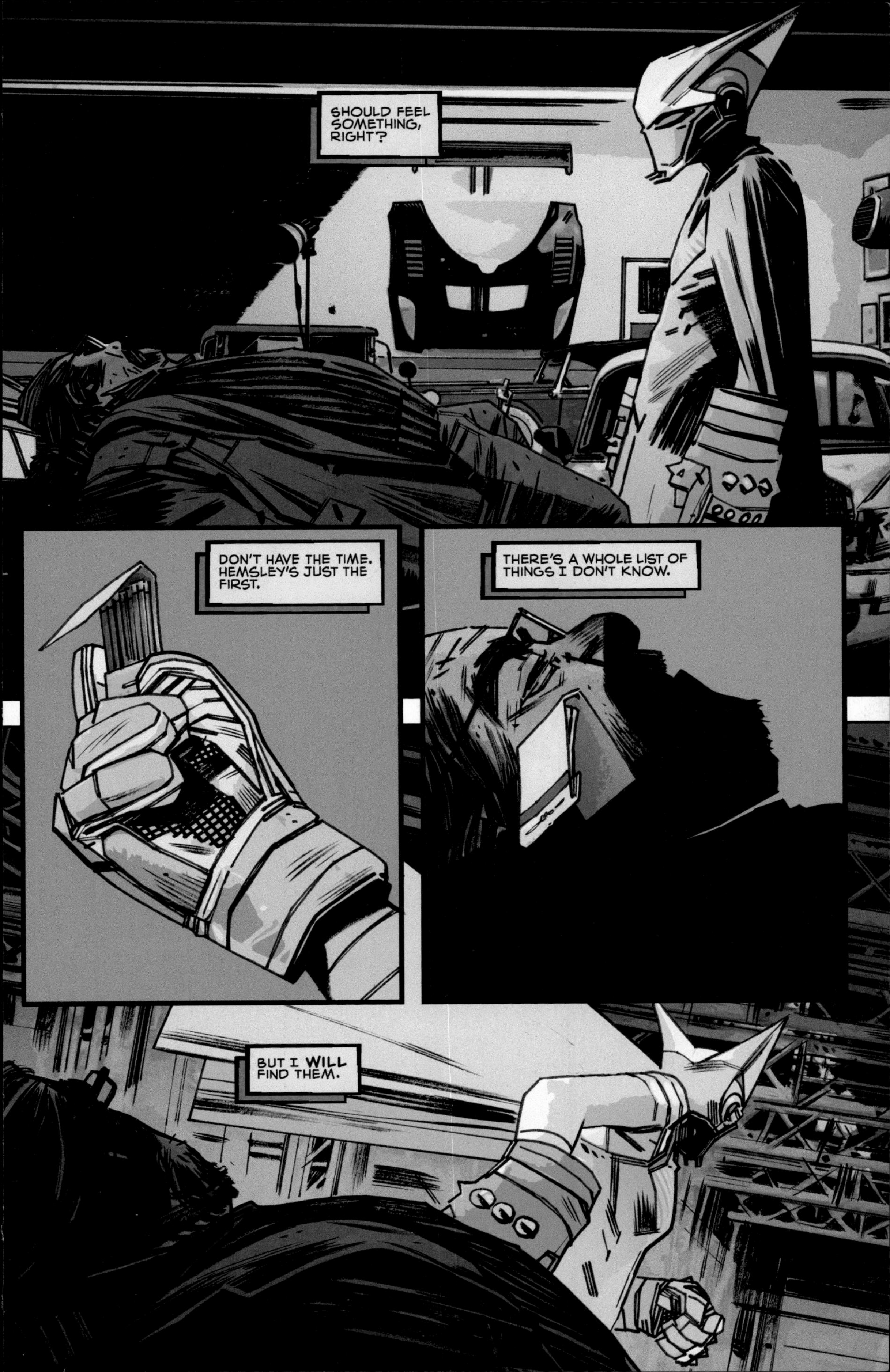
SHOULD FEEL SOMETHING, RIGHT?
DON'T HAVE THE TIME. HEMSLEY'S JUST THE FIRST.
THERE'S A WHOLE LIST OF THINGS I DON'T KNOW.
BUT I **WILL** FIND THEM.

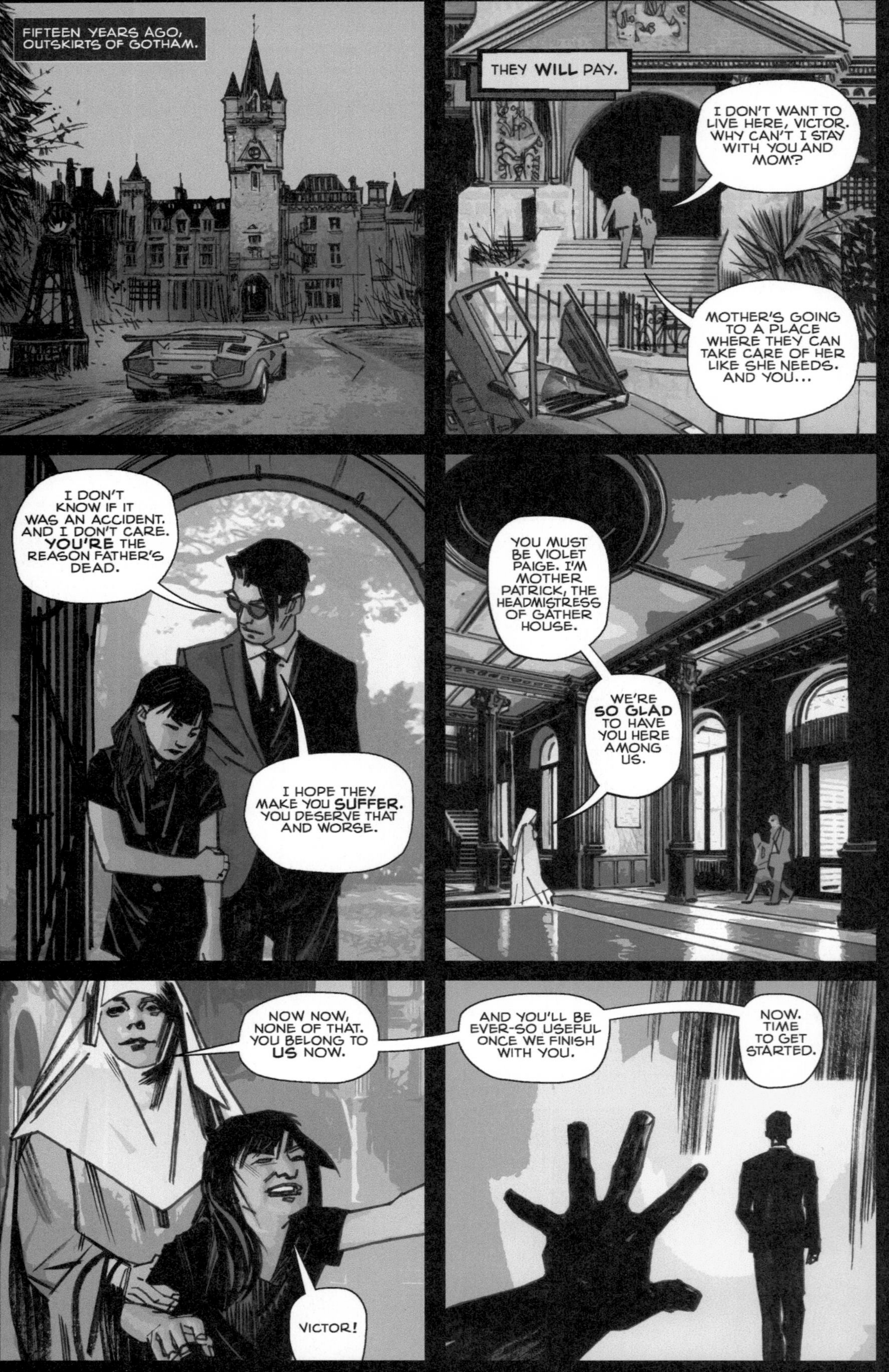
FIFTEEN YEARS AGO, OUTSKIRTS OF GOTHAM.
THEY WILL PAY.
I DON'T WANT TO LIVE HERE, VICTOR. WHY CAN'T I STAY WITH YOU AND MOM?
MOTHER'S GOING TO A PLACE WHERE THEY CAN TAKE CARE OF HER LIKE SHE NEEDS. AND YOU...
I DON'T KNOW IF IT WAS AN ACCIDENT. AND I DON'T CARE. YOU'RE THE REASON FATHER'S DEAD.
I HOPE THEY MAKE YOU SUFFER. YOU DESERVE THAT AND WORSE.
YOU MUST BE VIOLET PAIGE. I'M MOTHER PATRICK, THE HEADMISTRESS OF GATHER HOUSE.
WE'RE SO GLAD TO HAVE YOU HERE AMONG US.
NOW NOW, NONE OF THAT. YOU BELONG TO US NOW.
VICTOR!
AND YOU'LL BE EVER-SO USEFUL ONCE WE FINISH WITH YOU.
NOW. TIME TO GET STARTED.

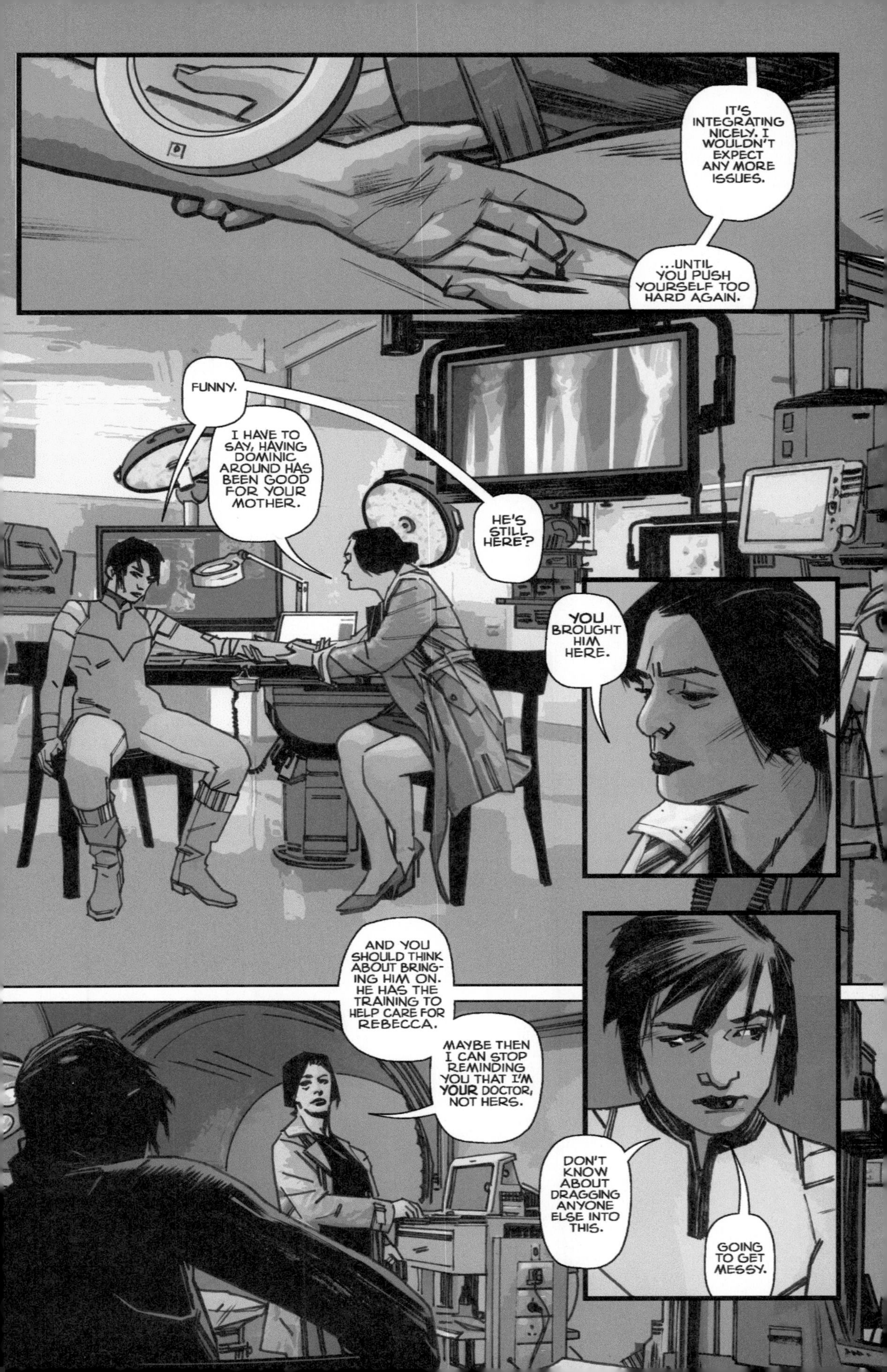

IT'S INTEGRATING NICELY. I WOULDN'T EXPECT ANY MORE ISSUES.
...UNTIL YOU PUSH YOURSELF TOO HARD AGAIN.
FUNNY.
I HAVE TO SAY, HAVING DOMINIC AROUND HAS BEEN GOOD FOR YOUR MOTHER.
HE'S STILL HERE?
YOU BROUGHT HIM HERE.
AND YOU SHOULD THINK ABOUT BRING-ING HIM ON. HE HAS THE TRAINING TO HELP CARE FOR REBECCA.
MAYBE THEN I CAN STOP REMINDING YOU THAT I'M YOUR DOCTOR, NOT HERS.
DON'T KNOW ABOUT DRAGGING ANYONE ELSE INTO THIS.
GOING TO GET MESSY.

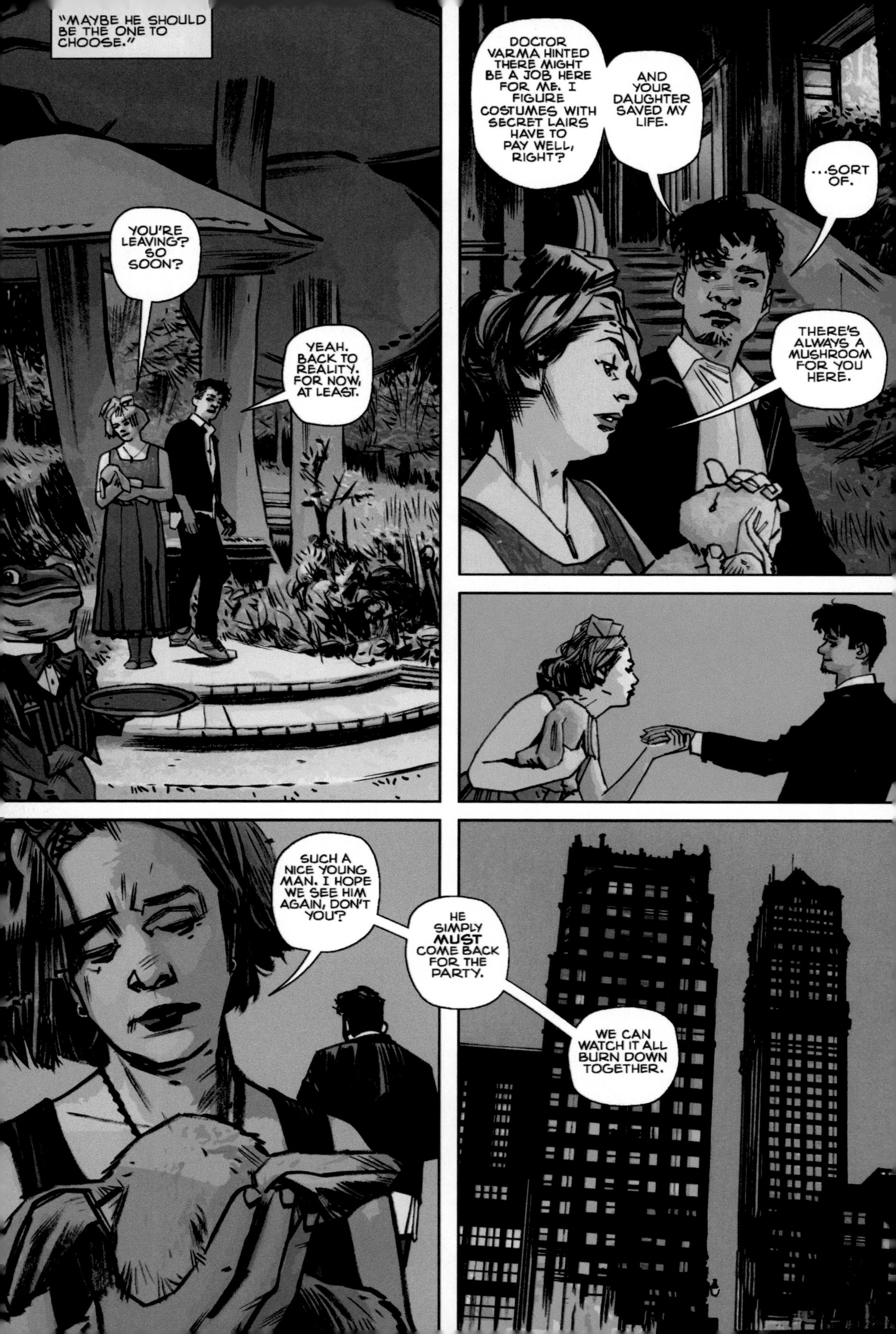
"MAYBE HE SHOULD BE THE ONE TO CHOOSE."
YOU'RE LEAVING? SO SOON?
YEAH. BACK TO REALITY. FOR NOW, AT LEAST.
DOCTOR VARMA HINTED THERE MIGHT BE A JOB HERE FOR ME. I FIGURE COSTUMES WITH SECRET LAIRS HAVE TO PAY WELL, RIGHT?
AND YOUR DAUGHTER SAVED MY LIFE.
...SORT OF.
THERE'S ALWAYS A MUSHROOM FOR YOU HERE.
SUCH A NICE YOUNG MAN. I HOPE WE SEE HIM AGAIN, DON'T YOU?
HE SIMPLY MUST COME BACK FOR THE PARTY.
WE CAN WATCH IT ALL BURN DOWN TOGETHER.

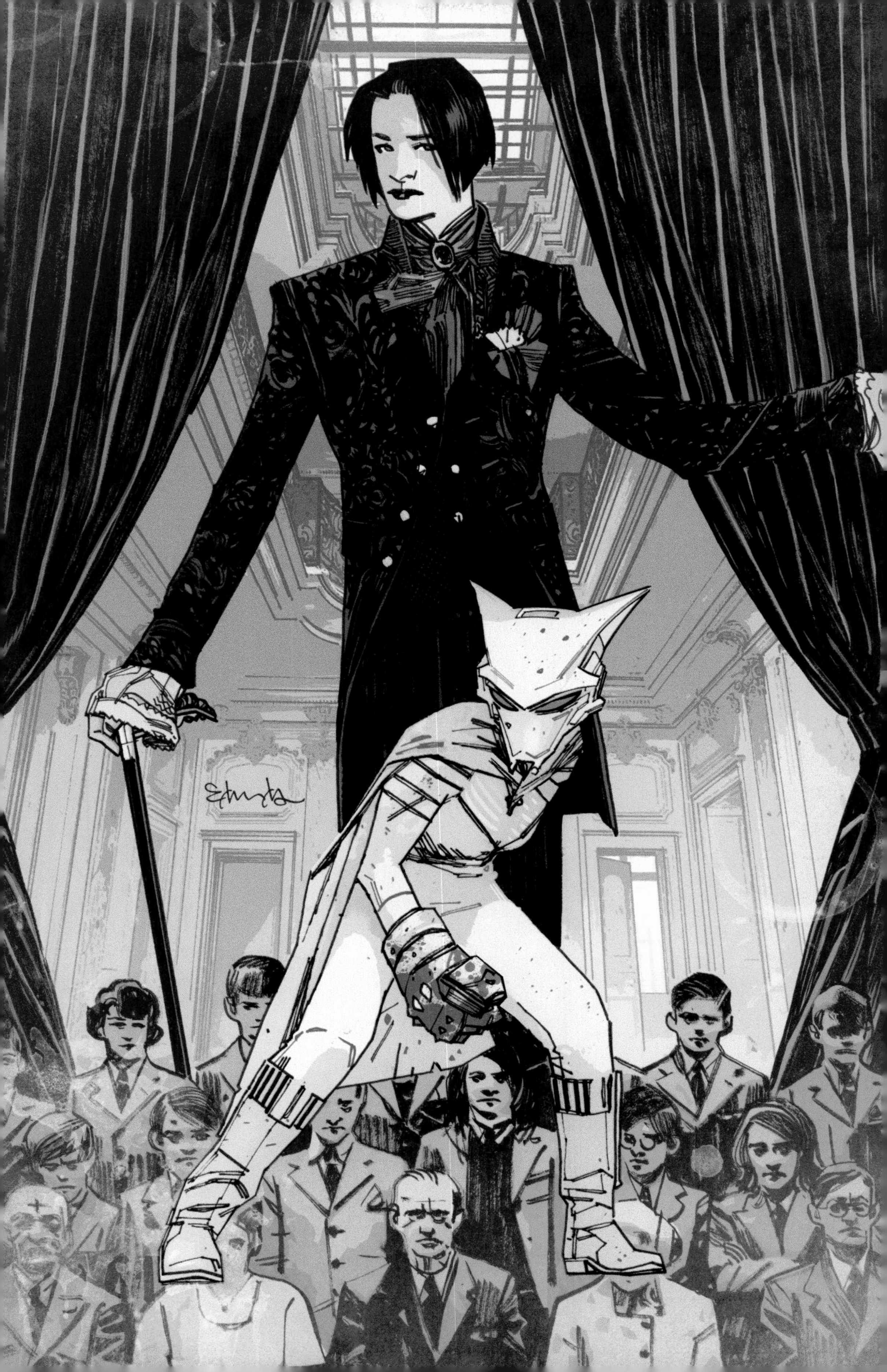

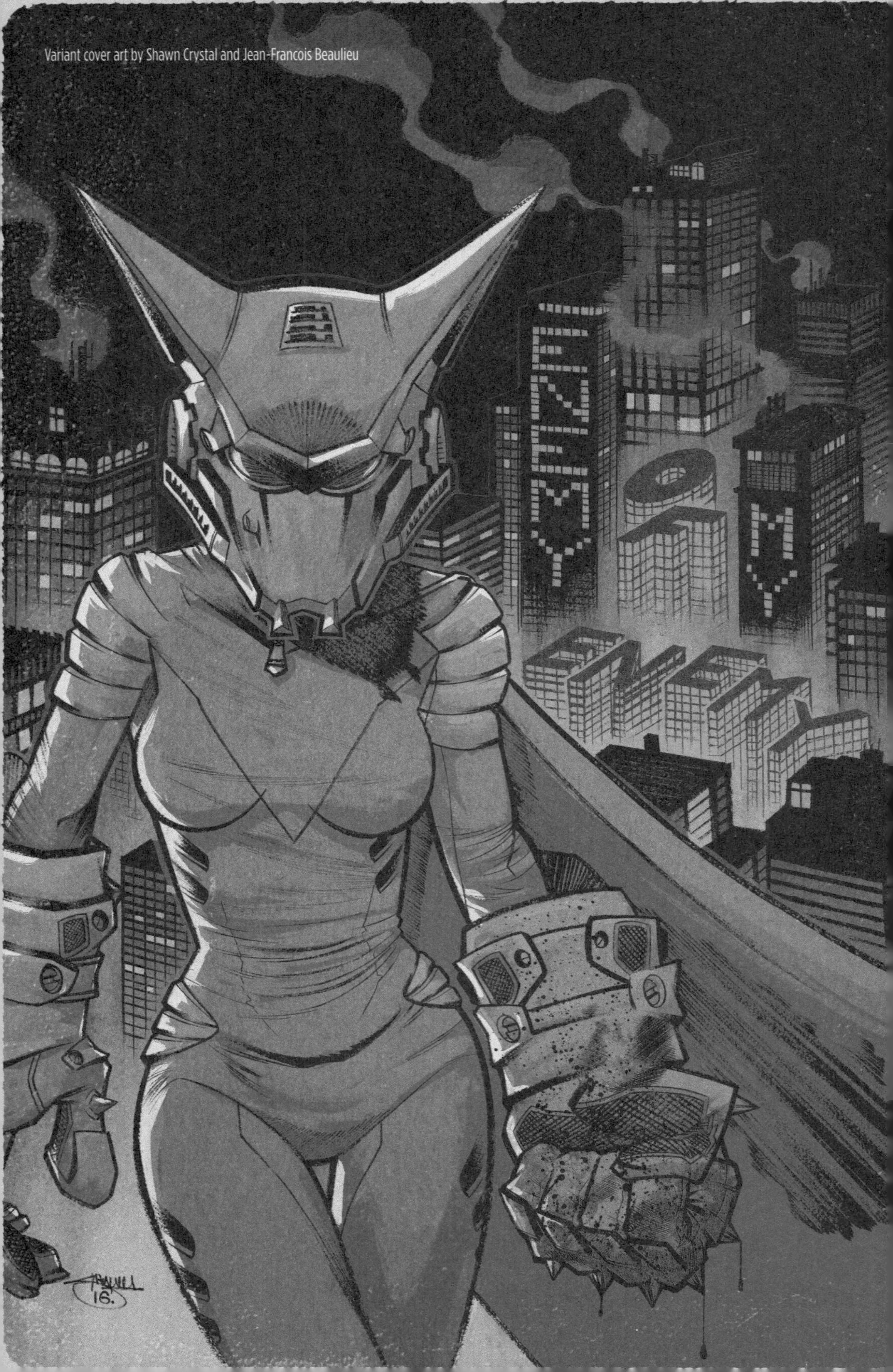
ENEMY
OF
MY
ENEMY

Variant cover art by Shawn Crystal and Jean-Francois Beaulieu

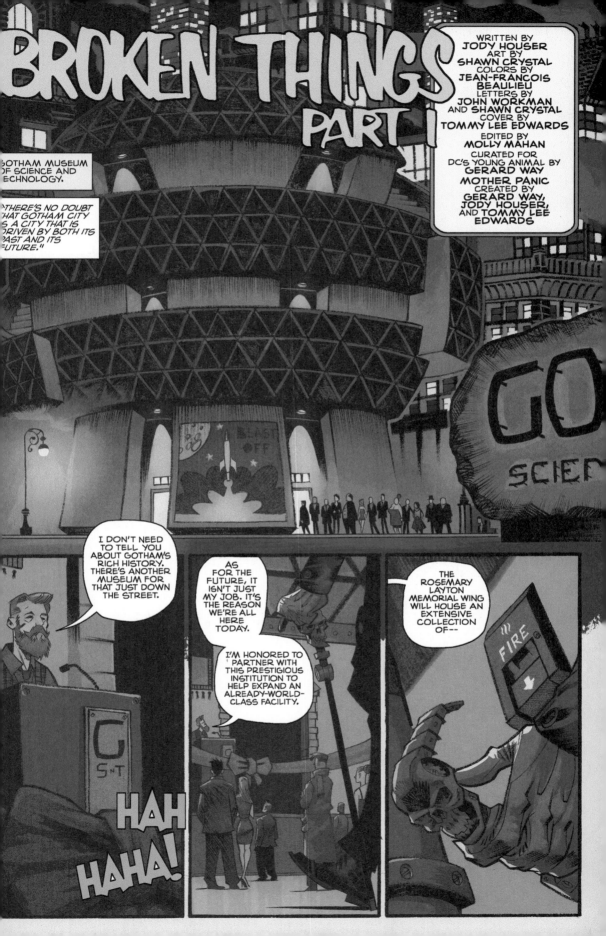

# BROKEN THINGS
## PART 1

WRITTEN BY
JODY HOUSER
ART BY
SHAWN CRYSTAL
COLORS BY
JEAN-FRANÇOIS
BEAULIEU
LETTERS BY
JOHN WORKMAN
AND SHAWN CRYSTAL
COVER BY
TOMMY LEE EDWARDS
EDITED BY
MOLLY MAHAN
CURATED FOR
DC'S YOUNG ANIMAL BY
GERARD WAY
MOTHER PANIC
CREATED BY
GERARD WAY,
JODY HOUSER,
AND TOMMY LEE
EDWARDS

GOTHAM MUSEUM OF SCIENCE AND TECHNOLOGY.

"THERE'S NO DOUBT THAT GOTHAM CITY IS A CITY THAT IS DRIVEN BY BOTH ITS PAST AND ITS FUTURE."

I DON'T NEED TO TELL YOU ABOUT GOTHAM'S RICH HISTORY. THERE'S ANOTHER MUSEUM FOR THAT JUST DOWN THE STREET.

AS FOR THE FUTURE, IT ISN'T JUST MY JOB. IT'S THE REASON WE'RE ALL HERE TODAY.

I'M HONORED TO PARTNER WITH THIS PRESTIGIOUS INSTITUTION TO HELP EXPAND AN ALREADY-WORLD-CLASS FACILITY.

THE ROSEMARY LAYTON MEMORIAL WING WILL HOUSE AN EXTENSIVE COLLECTION OF--

HAH HAHA!

FIRE

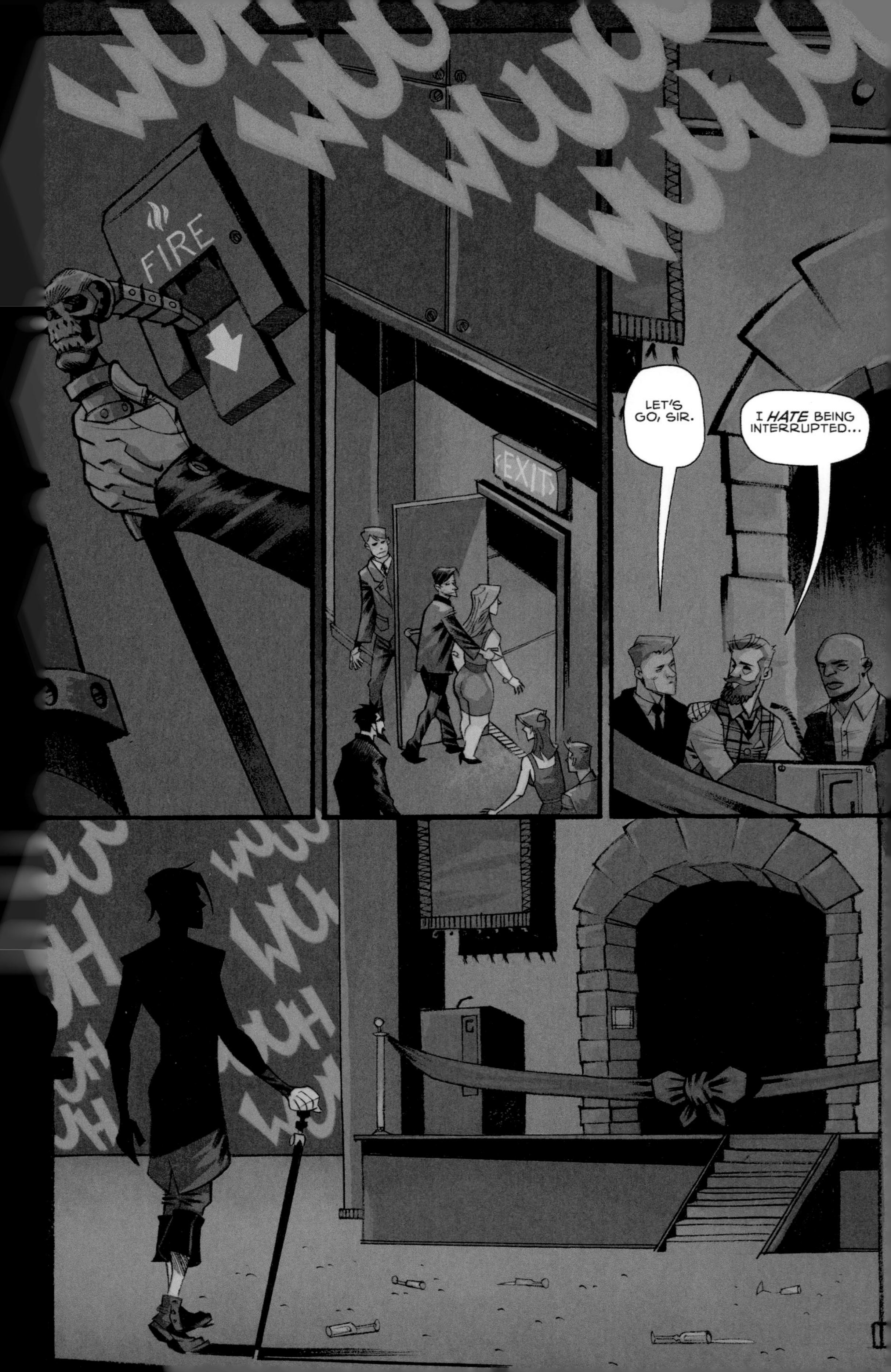
WUH WUH WUH
FIRE
EXIT
LET'S GO, SIR.
I *HATE* BEING INTERRUPTED...

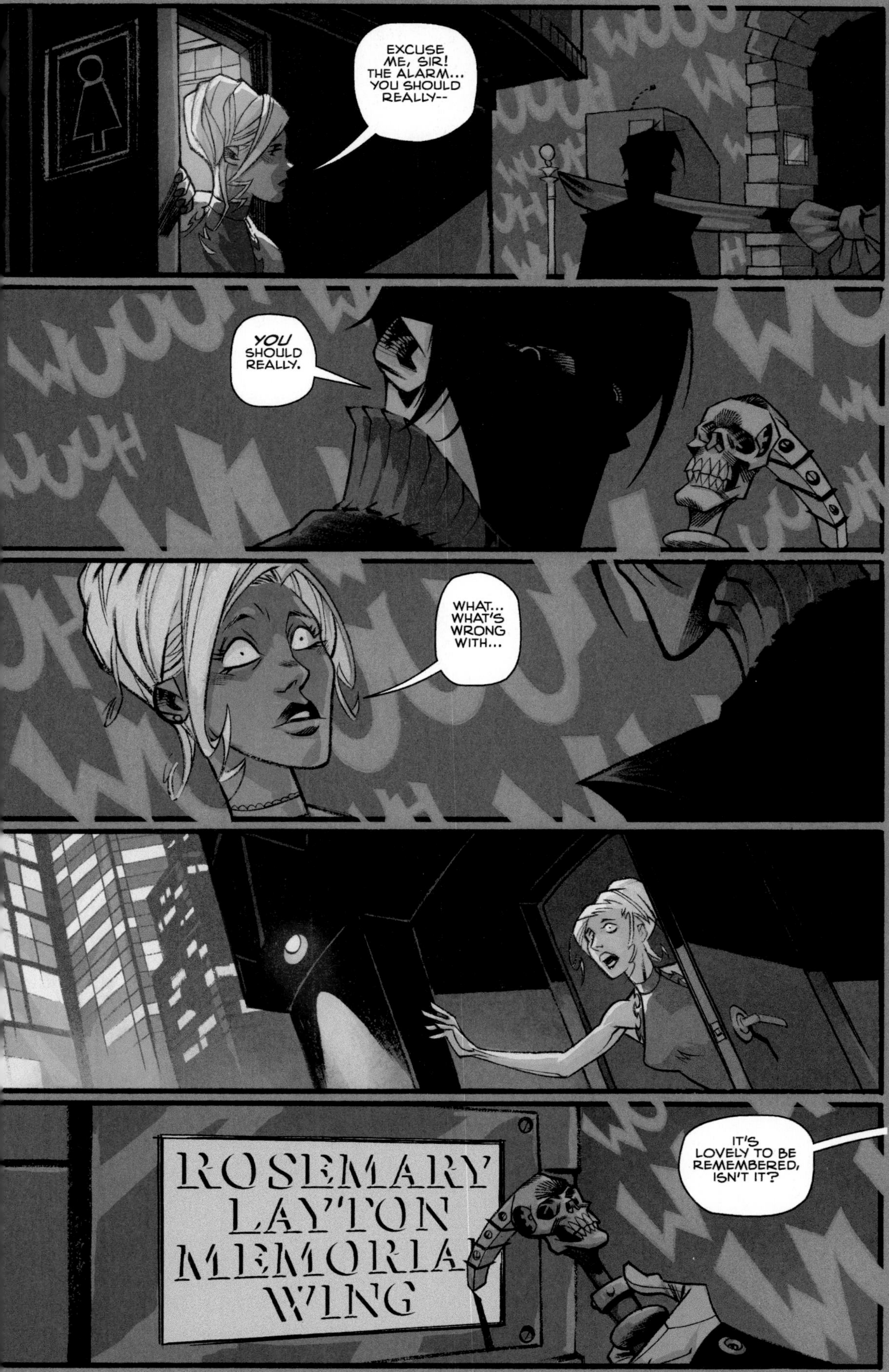
EXCUSE ME, SIR! THE ALARM... YOU SHOULD REALLY--
YOU SHOULD REALLY.
WHAT... WHAT'S WRONG WITH...
ROSEMARY LAYTON MEMORIAL WING
IT'S LOVELY TO BE REMEMBERED, ISN'T IT?

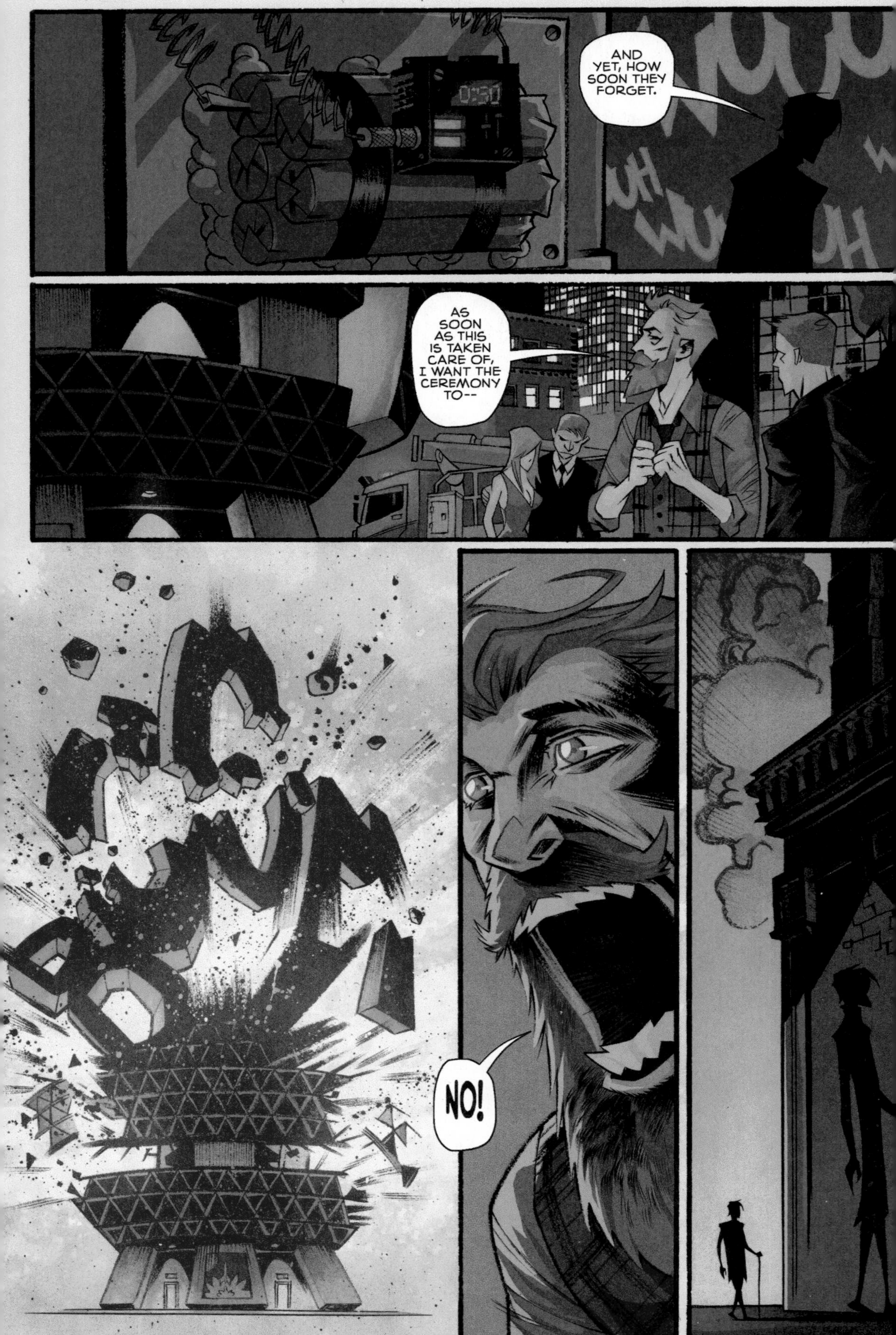
AND YET, HOW SOON THEY FORGET.
AS SOON AS THIS IS TAKEN CARE OF, I WANT THE CEREMONY TO--
NO!

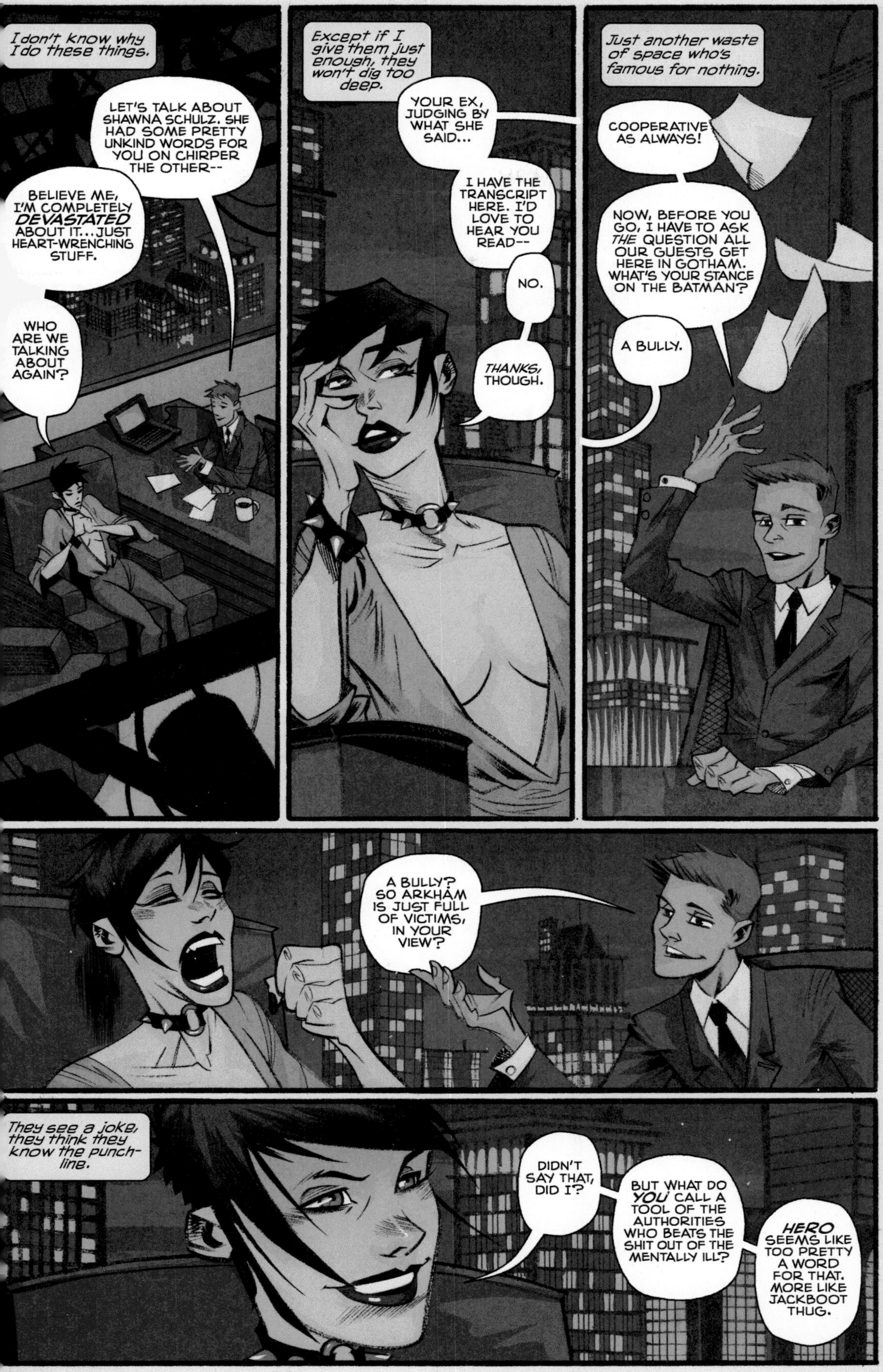
I don't know why I do these things.
LET'S TALK ABOUT SHAWNA SCHULZ. SHE HAD SOME PRETTY UNKIND WORDS FOR YOU ON CHIRPER THE OTHER--
BELIEVE ME, I'M COMPLETELY DEVASTATED ABOUT IT... JUST HEART-WRENCHING STUFF.
WHO ARE WE TALKING ABOUT AGAIN?
Except if I give them just enough, they won't dig too deep.
YOUR EX, JUDGING BY WHAT SHE SAID...
I HAVE THE TRANSCRIPT HERE. I'D LOVE TO HEAR YOU READ--
NO.
THANKS, THOUGH.
Just another waste of space who's famous for nothing.
COOPERATIVE AS ALWAYS!
NOW, BEFORE YOU GO, I HAVE TO ASK THE QUESTION ALL OUR GUESTS GET HERE IN GOTHAM. WHAT'S YOUR STANCE ON THE BATMAN?
A BULLY.
A BULLY? SO ARKHAM IS JUST FULL OF VICTIMS, IN YOUR VIEW?
They see a joke, they think they know the punch-line.
DIDN'T SAY THAT, DID I?
BUT WHAT DO YOU CALL A TOOL OF THE AUTHORITIES WHO BEATS THE SHIT OUT OF THE MENTALLY ILL?
HERO SEEMS LIKE TOO PRETTY A WORD FOR THAT. MORE LIKE JACKBOOT THUG.

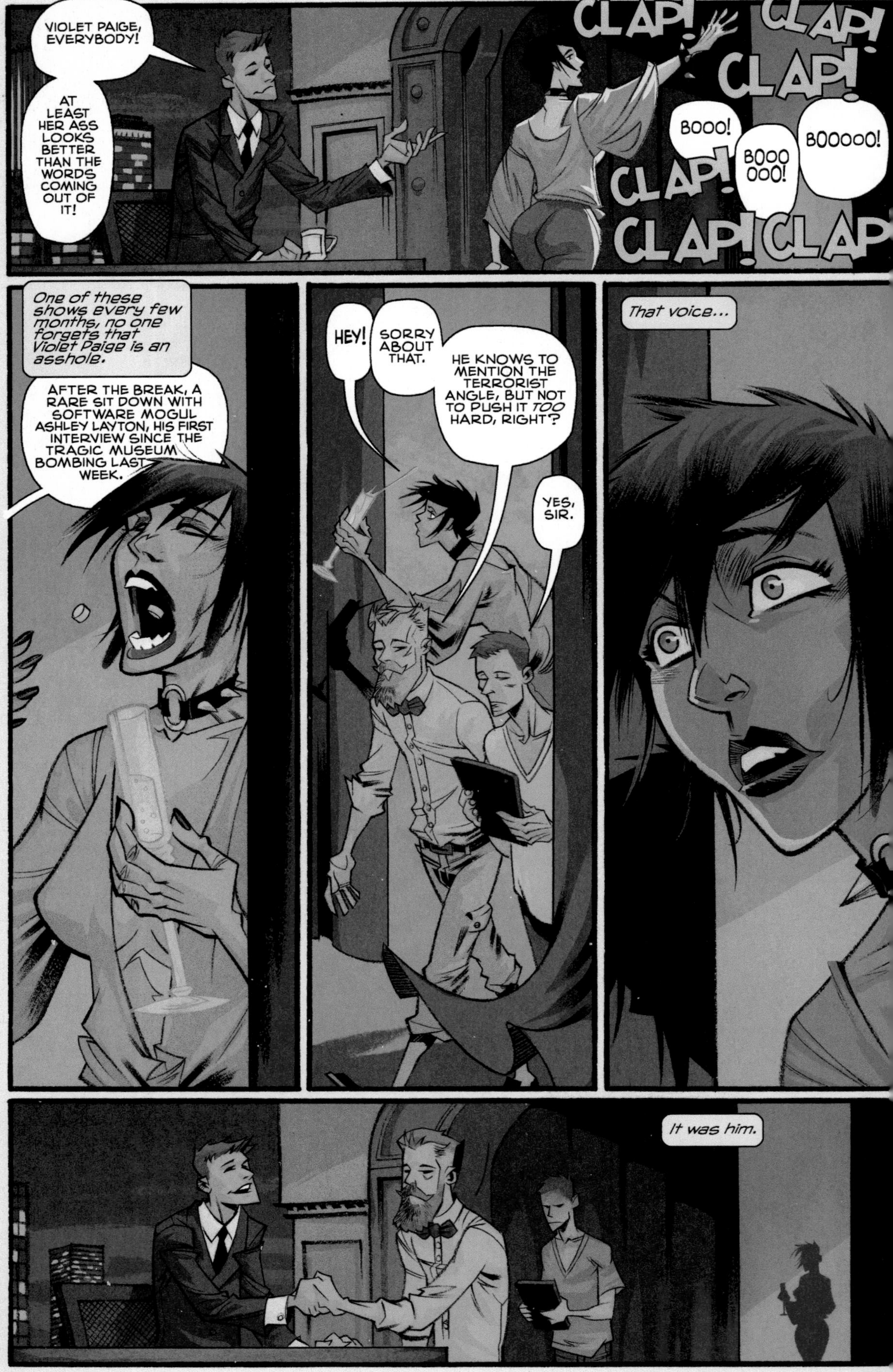

VIOLET PAIGE, EVERYBODY!
AT LEAST HER ASS LOOKS BETTER THAN THE WORDS COMING OUT OF IT!
CLAP! CLAP! CLAP!
BOOO!
BOOO OOO!
BOOOOO!
CLAP! CLAP! CLAP
One of these shows every few months, no one forgets that Violet Paige is an asshole.
AFTER THE BREAK, A RARE SIT DOWN WITH SOFTWARE MOGUL ASHLEY LAYTON, HIS FIRST INTERVIEW SINCE THE TRAGIC MUSEUM BOMBING LAST WEEK.
HEY!
SORRY ABOUT THAT.
HE KNOWS TO MENTION THE TERRORIST ANGLE, BUT NOT TO PUSH IT *TOO* HARD, RIGHT?
YES, SIR.
That voice...
It was him.

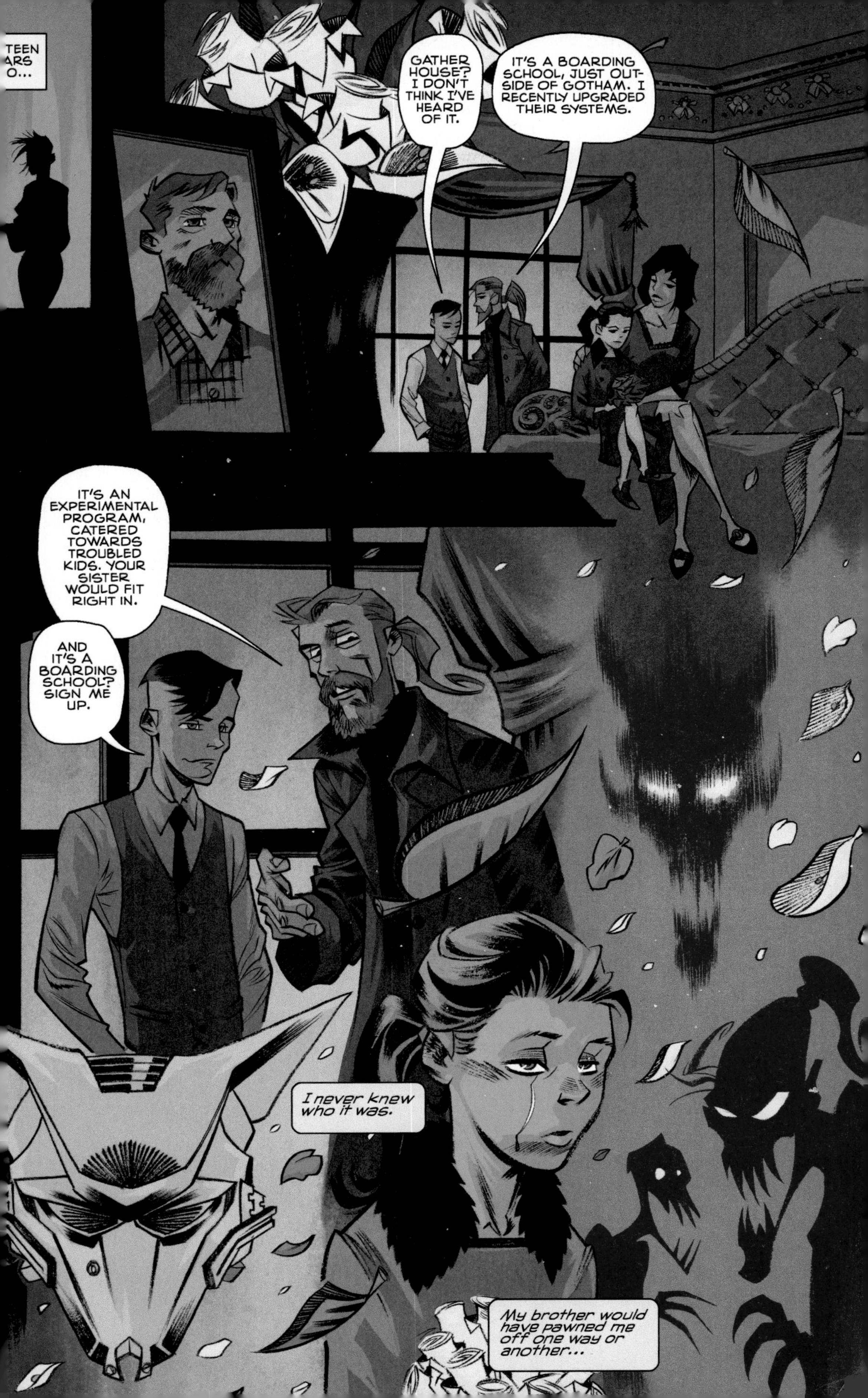

TEEN
ARS
O...
GATHER HOUSE? I DON'T THINK I'VE HEARD OF IT.
IT'S A BOARDING SCHOOL, JUST OUTSIDE OF GOTHAM. I RECENTLY UPGRADED THEIR SYSTEMS.
IT'S AN EXPERIMENTAL PROGRAM, CATERED TOWARDS TROUBLED KIDS. YOUR SISTER WOULD FIT RIGHT IN.
AND IT'S A BOARDING SCHOOL? SIGN ME UP.
I never knew who it was.
My brother would have pawned me off one way or another...

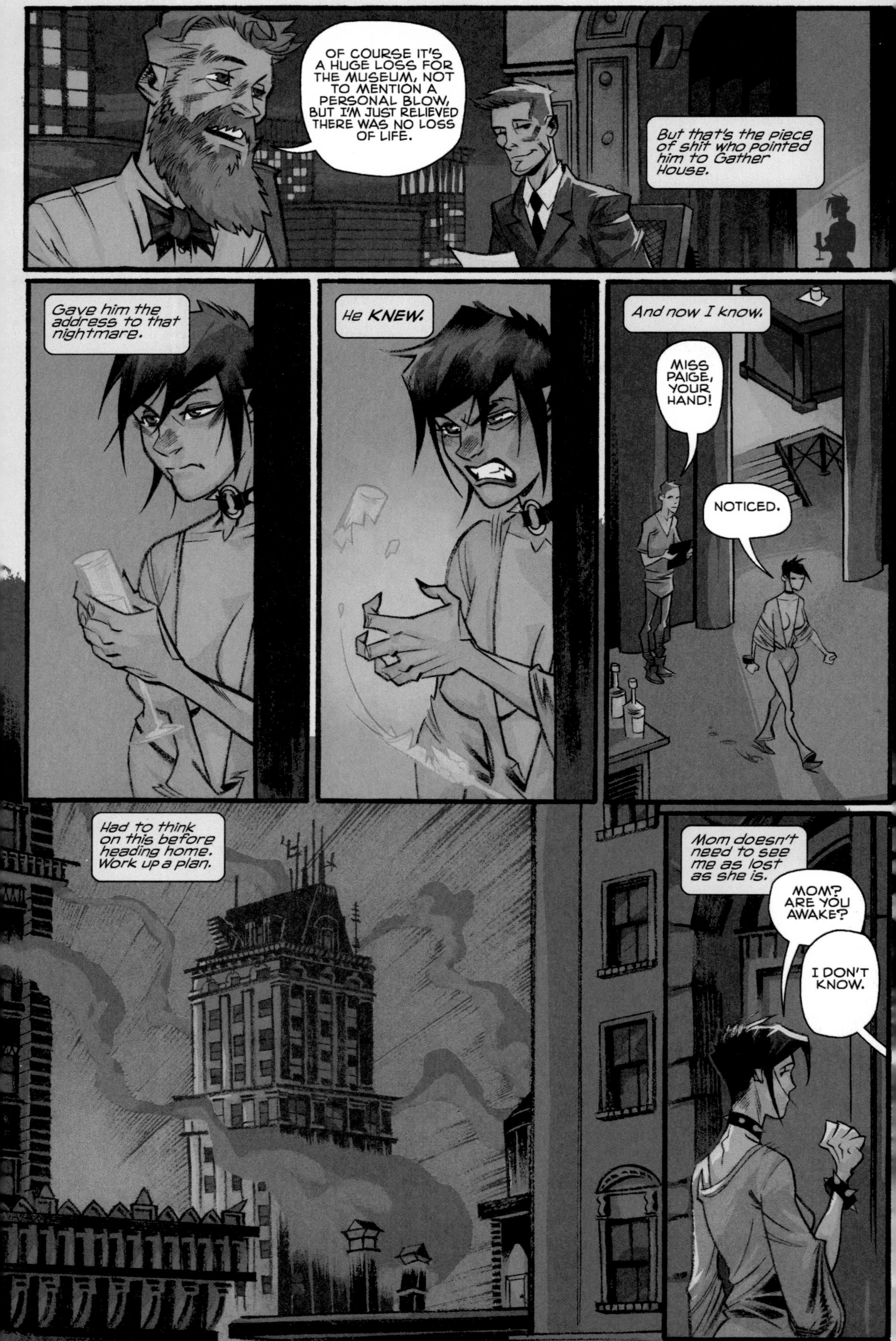
OF COURSE IT'S A HUGE LOSS FOR THE MUSEUM, NOT TO MENTION A PERSONAL BLOW, BUT I'M JUST RELIEVED THERE WAS NO LOSS OF LIFE.
But that's the piece of shit who pointed him to Gather House.
Gave him the address to that nightmare.
He KNEW.
And now I know.
MISS PAIGE, YOUR HAND!
NOTICED.
Had to think on this before heading home. Work up a plan.
Mom doesn't need to see me as lost as she is.
MOM? ARE YOU AWAKE?
I DON'T KNOW.

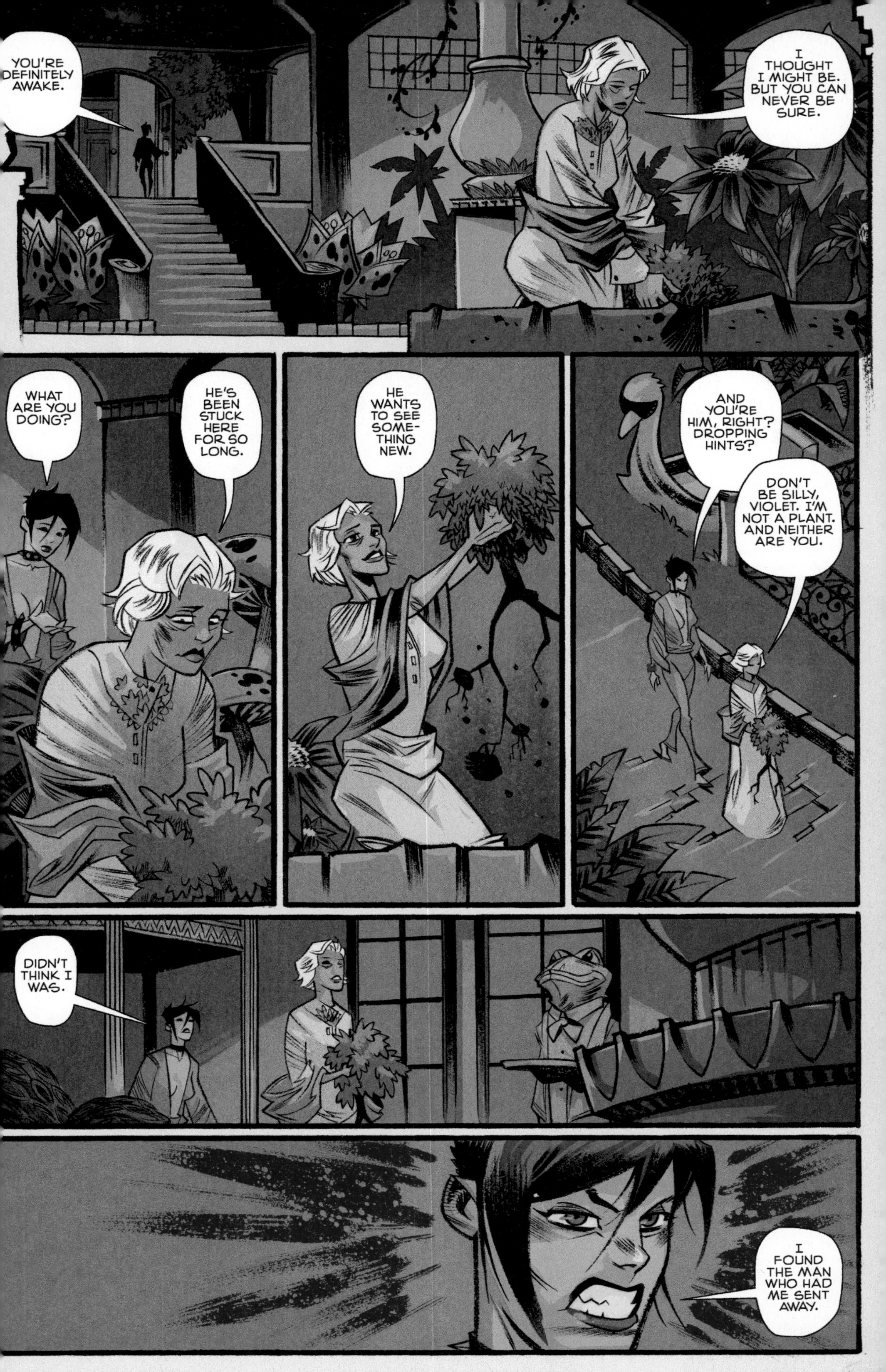

YOU'RE DEFINITELY AWAKE.
I THOUGHT I MIGHT BE. BUT YOU CAN NEVER BE SURE.
WHAT ARE YOU DOING?
HE'S BEEN STUCK HERE FOR SO LONG.
HE WANTS TO SEE SOME-THING NEW.
AND YOU'RE HIM, RIGHT? DROPPING HINTS?
DON'T BE SILLY, VIOLET. I'M NOT A PLANT. AND NEITHER ARE YOU.
DIDN'T THINK I WAS.
I FOUND THE MAN WHO HAD ME SENT AWAY.

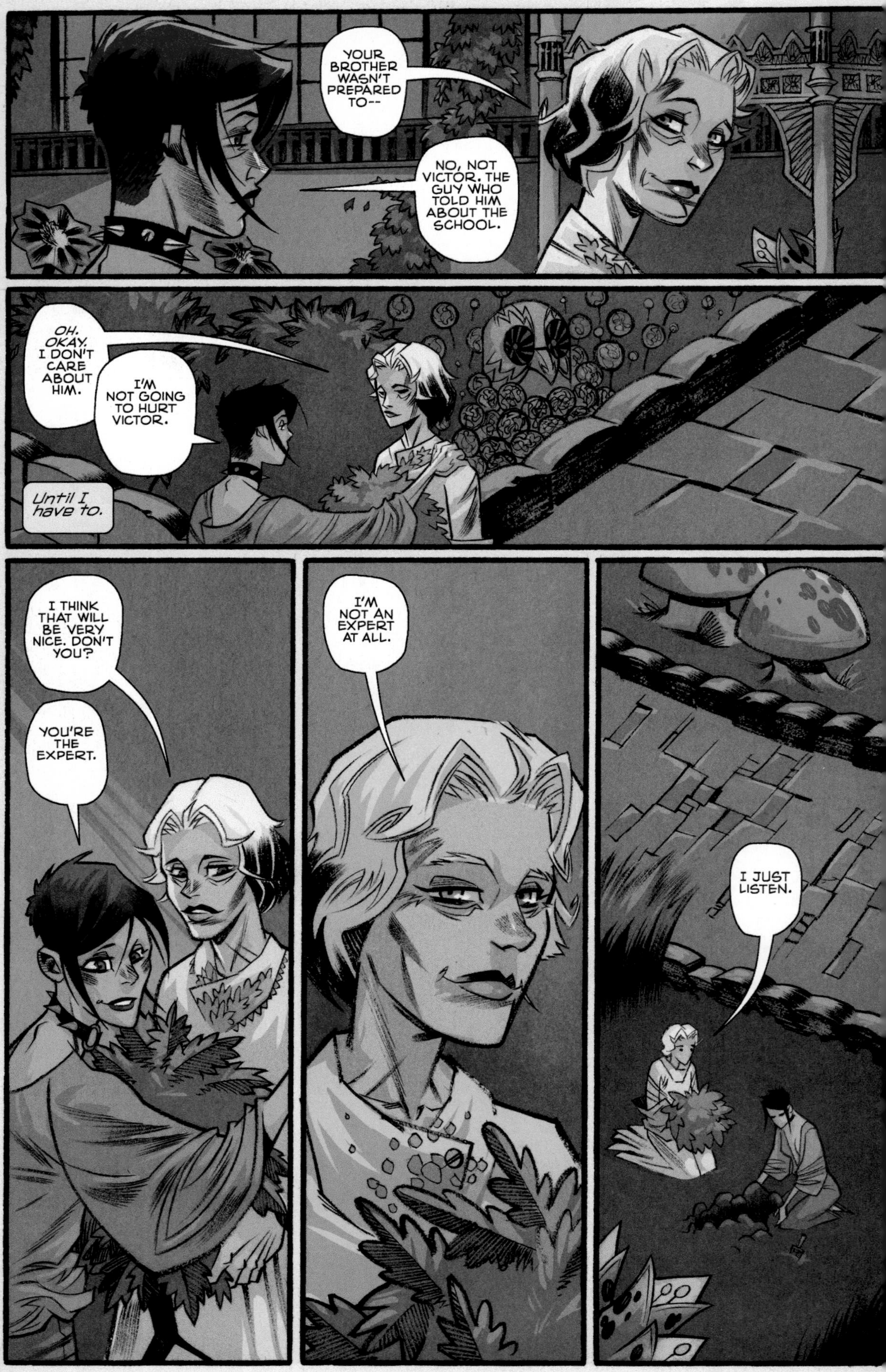
YOUR BROTHER WASN'T PREPARED TO--
NO, NOT VICTOR. THE GUY WHO TOLD HIM ABOUT THE SCHOOL.
OH. OKAY. I DON'T CARE ABOUT HIM.
I'M NOT GOING TO HURT VICTOR.
Until I have to.
I THINK THAT WILL BE VERY NICE. DON'T YOU?
YOU'RE THE EXPERT.
I'M NOT AN EXPERT AT ALL.
I JUST LISTEN.

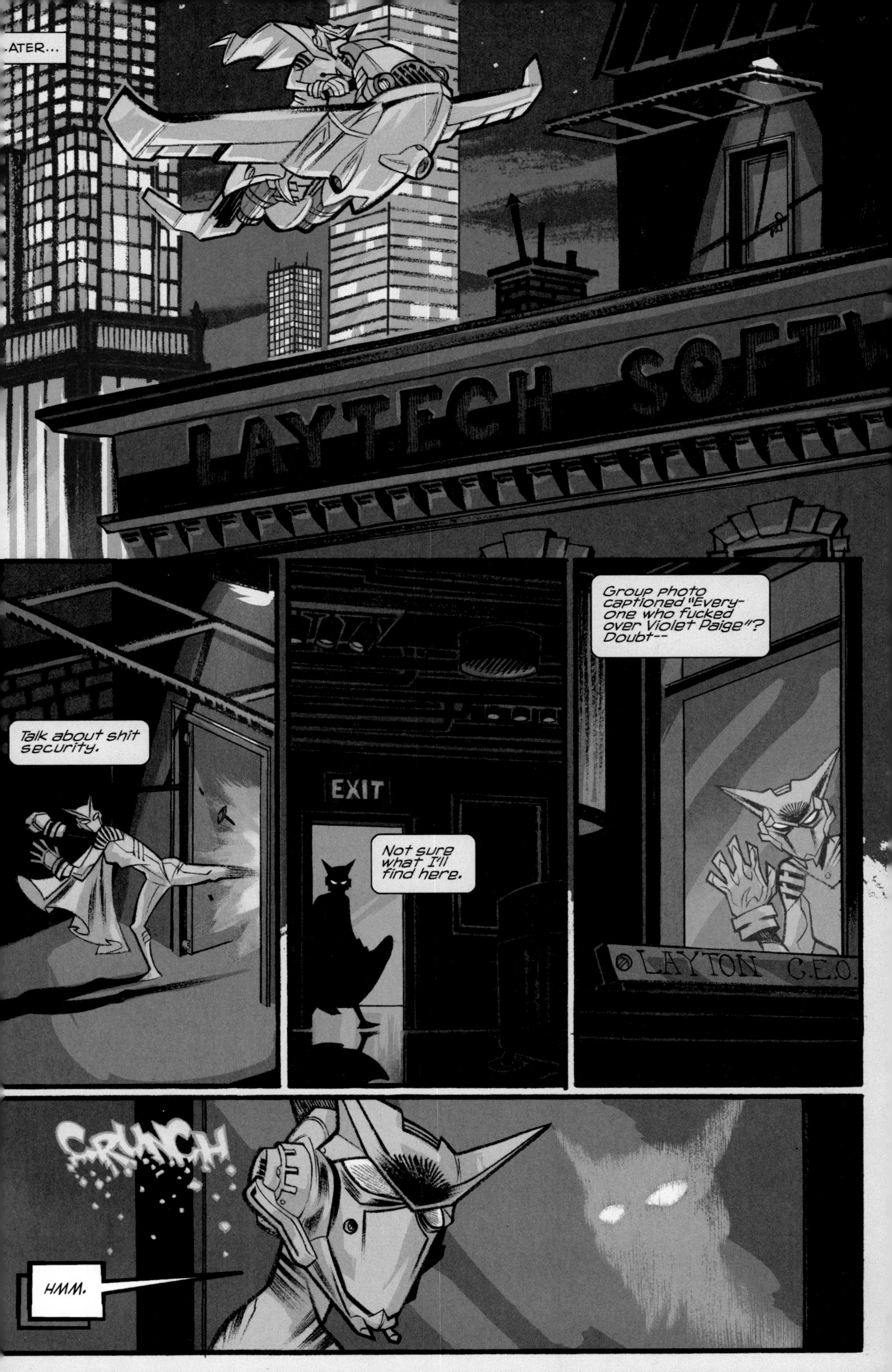

ATER...
LAYTECH SOFT
Talk about shit security.
EXIT
Not sure what I'll find here.
Group photo captioned "Every-one who fucked over Violet Paige"? Doubt--
LAYTON C.E.O.
CRUNCH
HMM.

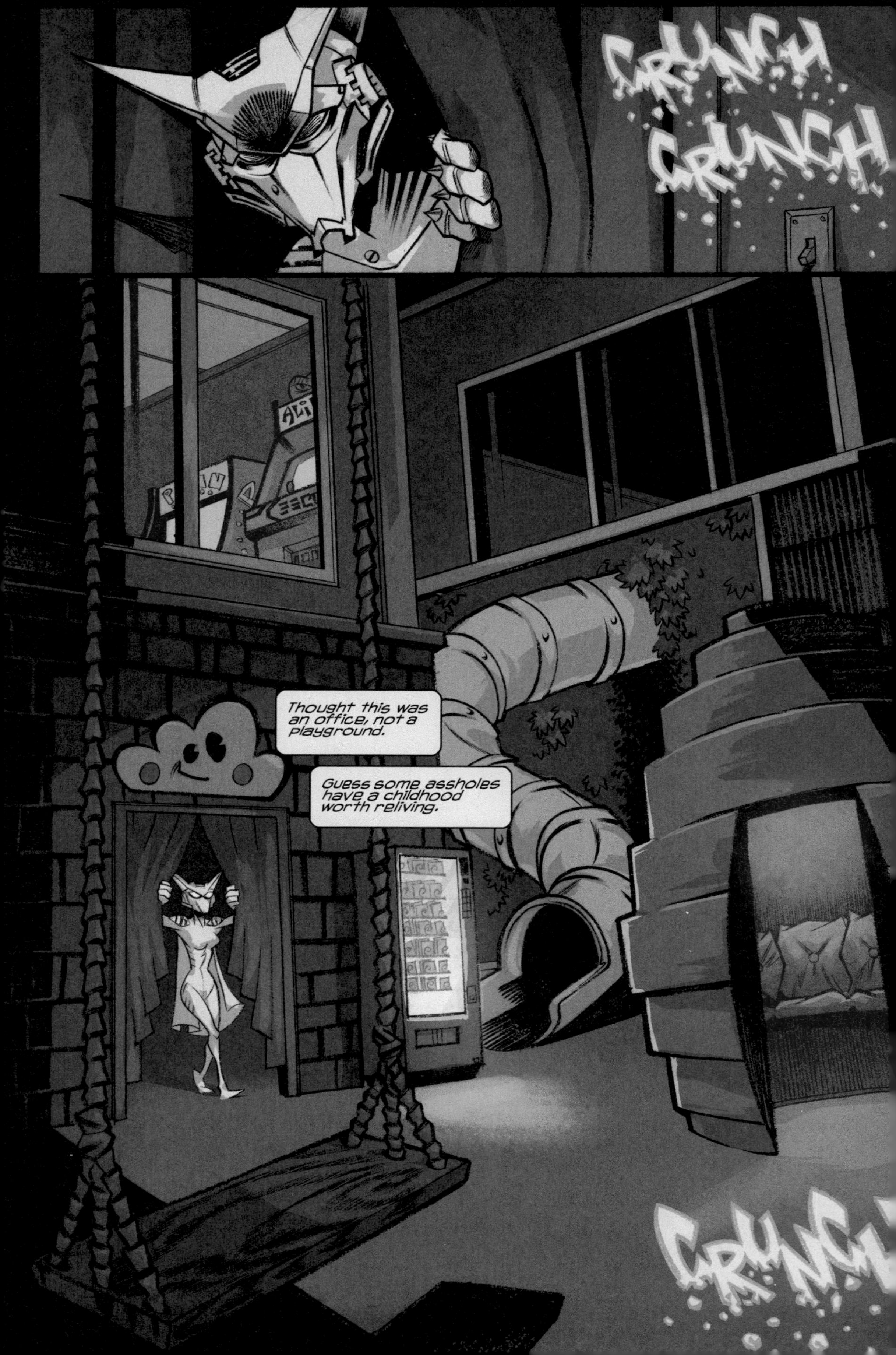

CRUNCH
CRUNCH
Thought this was an office, not a playground.
Guess some assholes have a childhood worth reliving.
CRUNCH

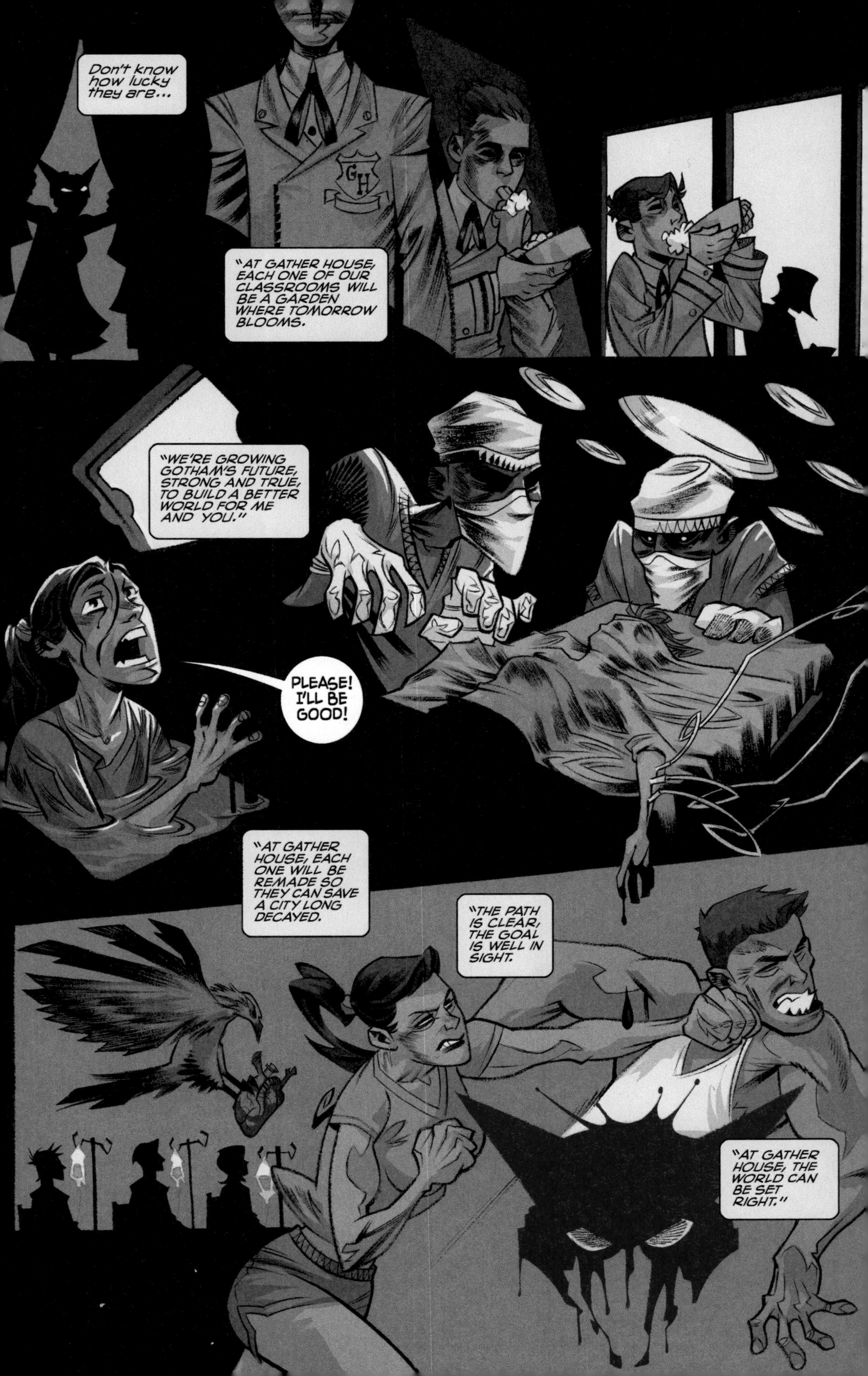
Don't know how lucky they are...
"AT GATHER HOUSE, EACH ONE OF OUR CLASSROOMS WILL BE A GARDEN WHERE TOMORROW BLOOMS.
"WE'RE GROWING GOTHAM'S FUTURE, STRONG AND TRUE, TO BUILD A BETTER WORLD FOR ME AND YOU."
PLEASE! I'LL BE GOOD!
"AT GATHER HOUSE, EACH ONE WILL BE REMADE SO THEY CAN SAVE A CITY LONG DECAYED.
"THE PATH IS CLEAR, THE GOAL IS WELL IN SIGHT.
"AT GATHER HOUSE, THE WORLD CAN BE SET RIGHT."

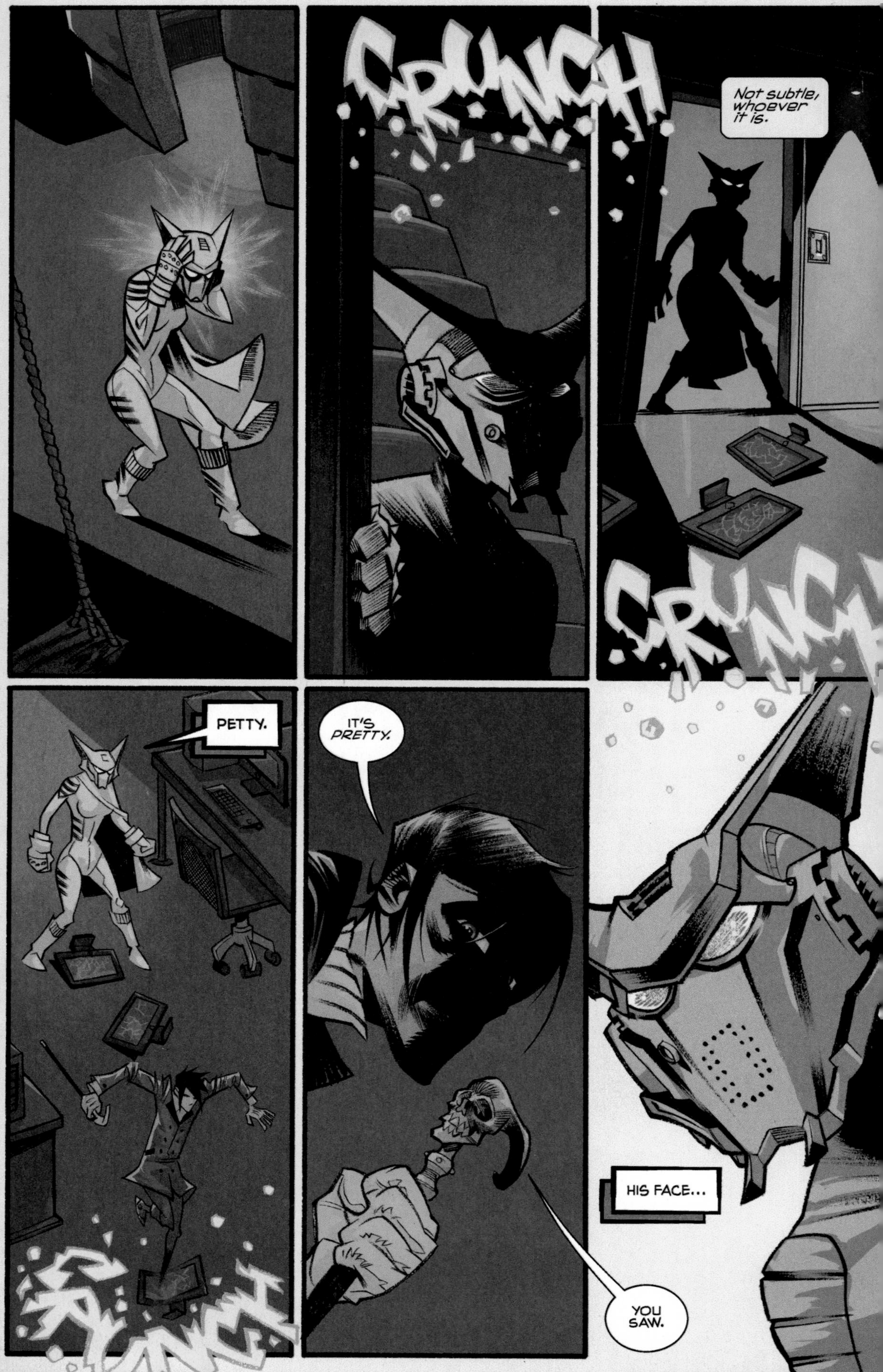
CRUNCH
Not subtle, whoever it is.
CRUNCH
PETTY.
IT'S PRETTY.
HIS FACE...
YOU SAW.
CRUNCH

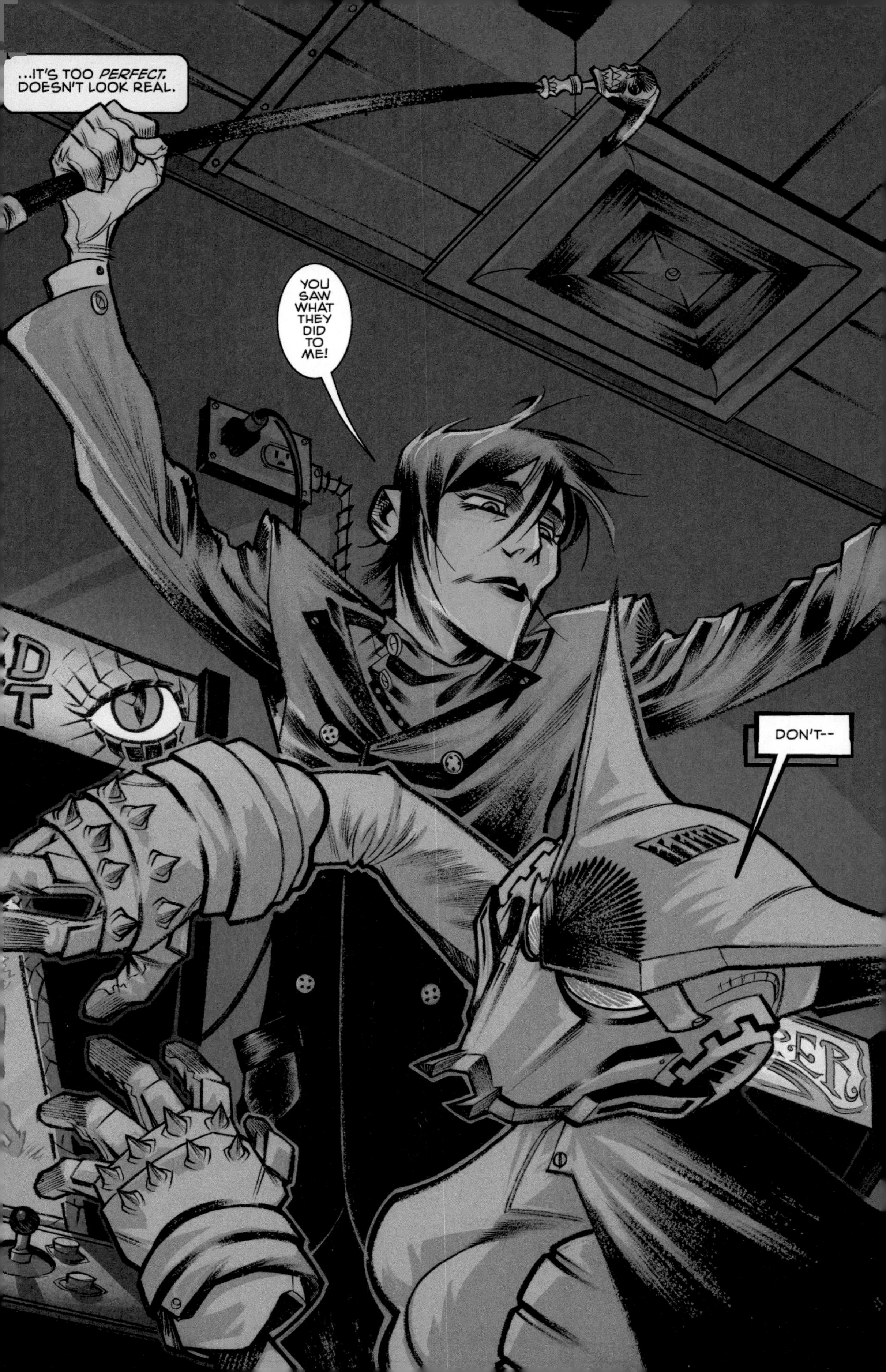
...IT'S TOO *PERFECT.* DOESN'T LOOK REAL.
YOU SAW WHAT THEY DID TO ME!
DON'T--

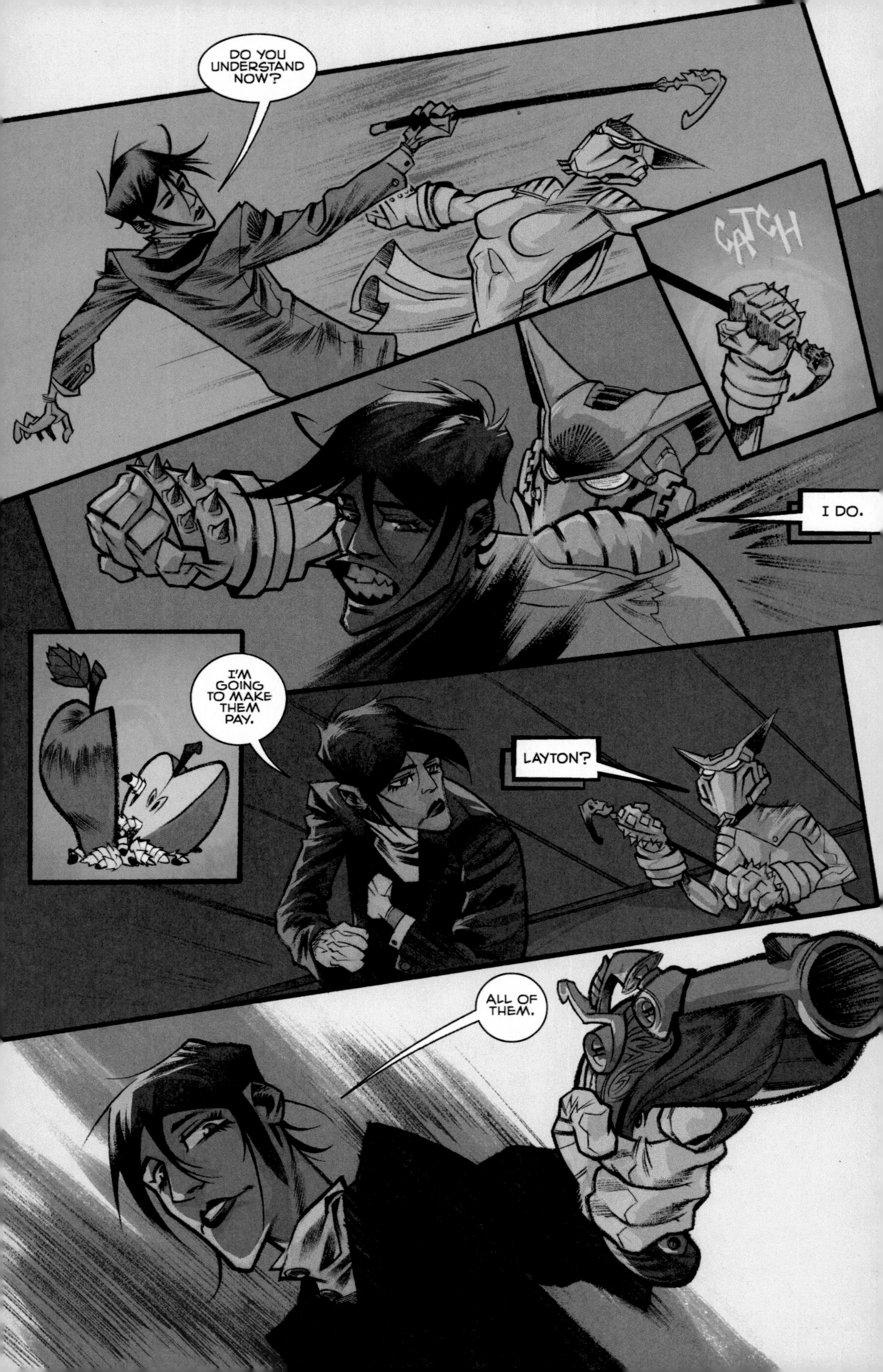
DO YOU UNDERSTAND NOW?
CATCH
I DO.
I'M GOING TO MAKE THEM PAY.
LAYTON?
ALL OF THEM.

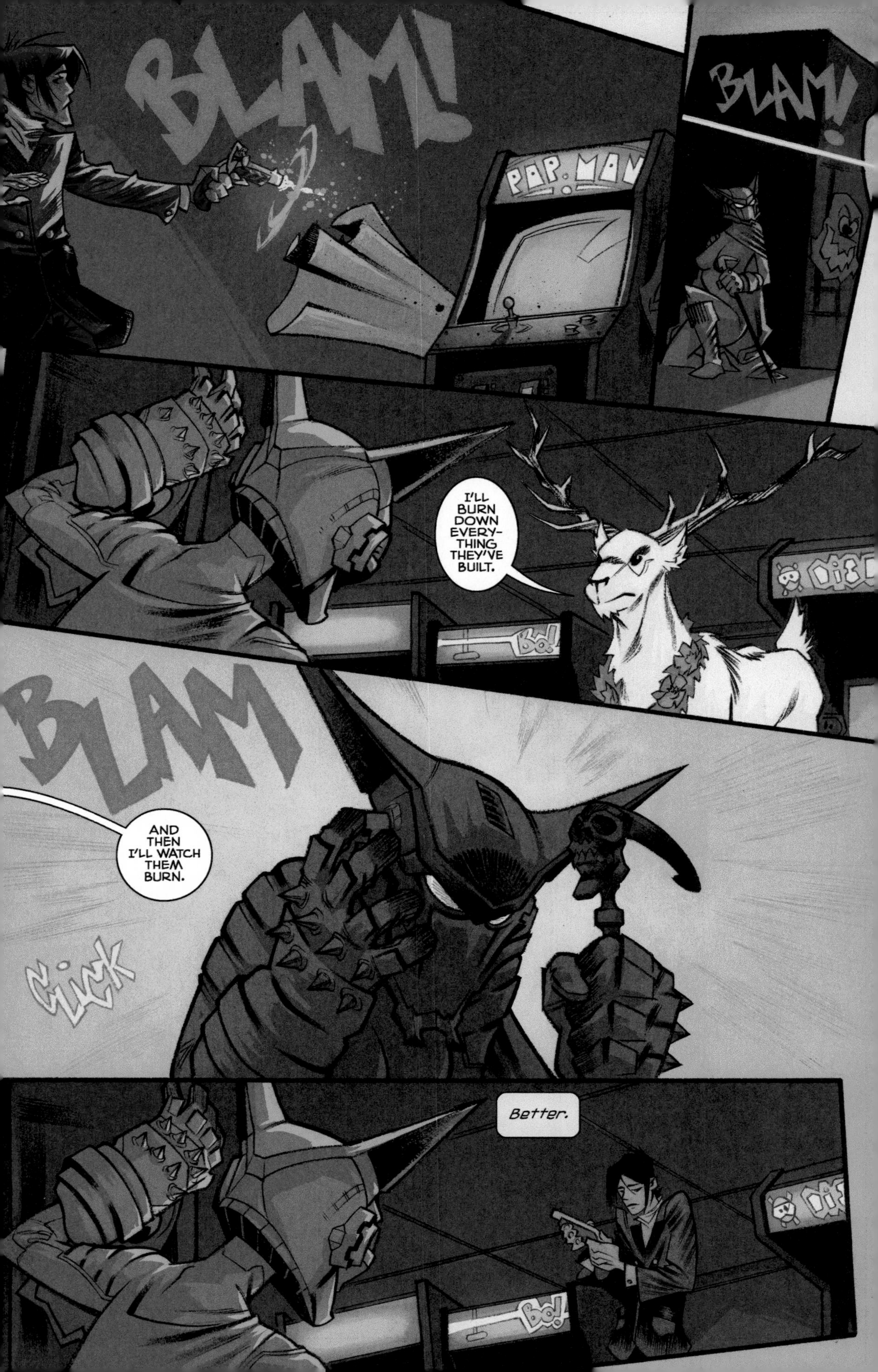
BLAM!
POP.MAN
BLAM!
I'LL BURN DOWN EVERY-THING THEY'VE BUILT.
BLAM
AND THEN I'LL WATCH THEM BURN.
CLICK
Better.

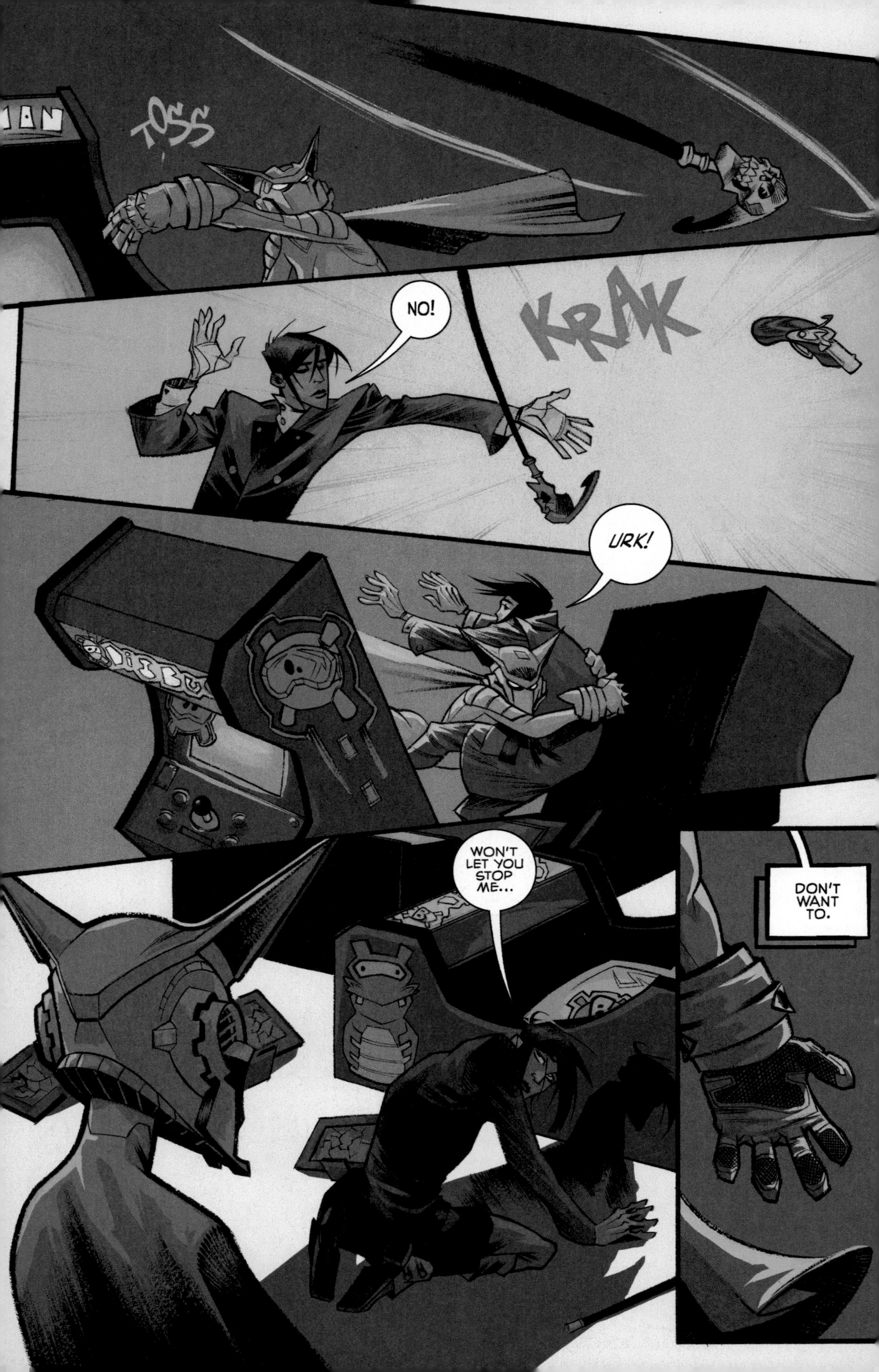
TOSS
NO!
KRAK
URK!
WON'T LET YOU STOP ME...
DON'T WANT TO.

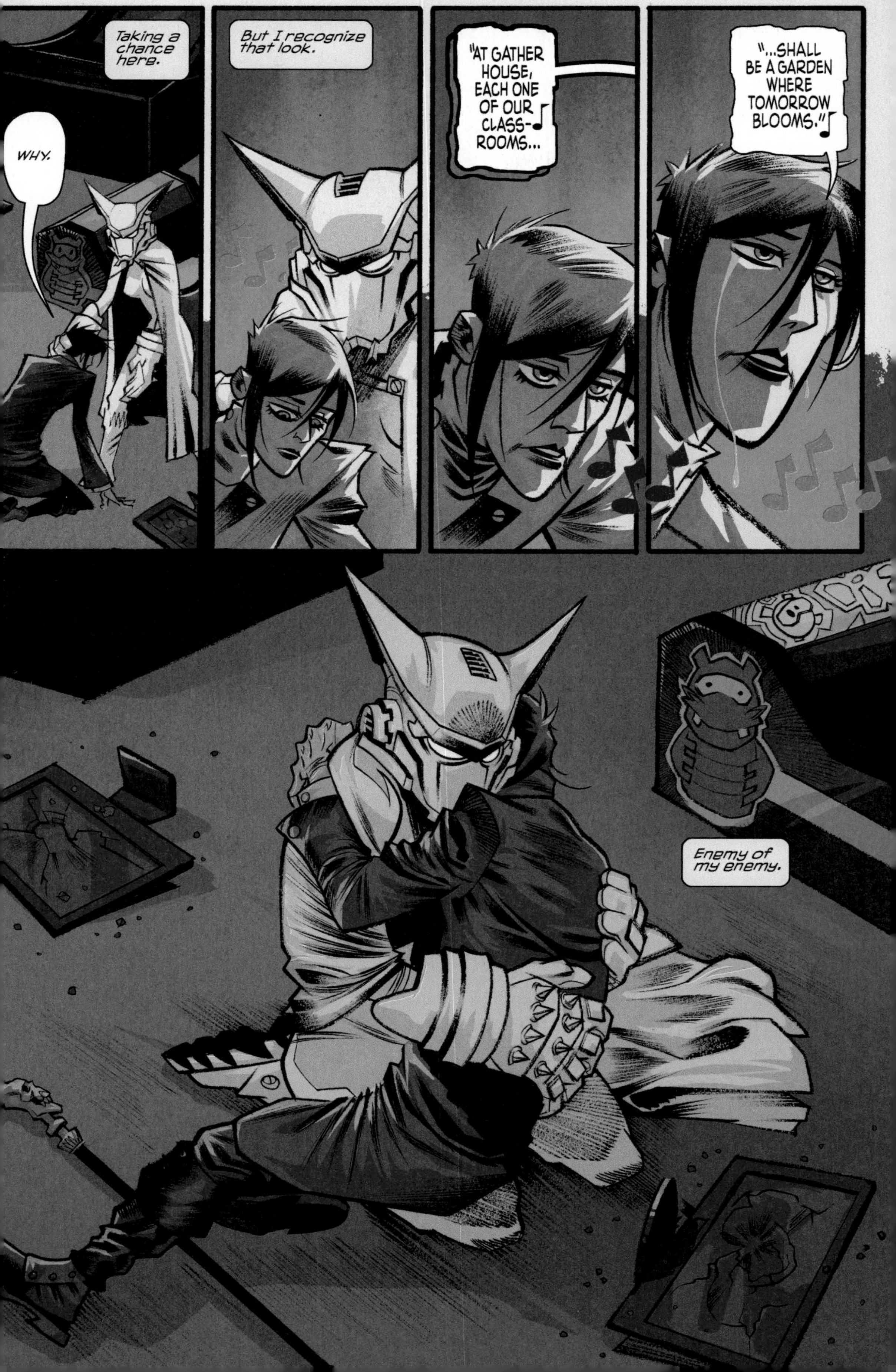
Taking a chance here.
WHY.
But I recognize that look.
"AT GATHER HOUSE, EACH ONE OF OUR CLASS-ROOMS...
"...SHALL BE A GARDEN WHERE TOMORROW BLOOMS."
Enemy of my enemy.

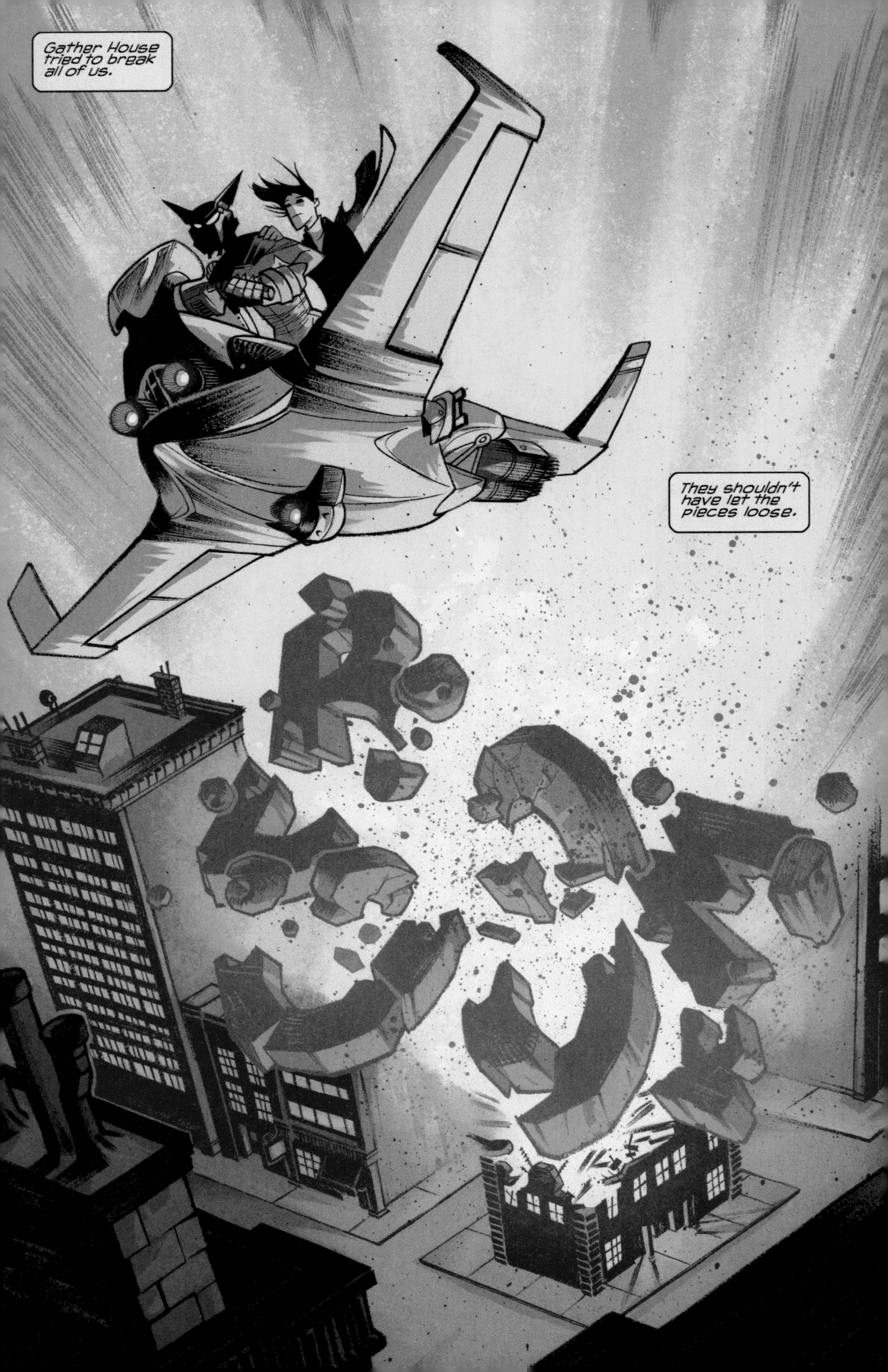
Gather House tried to break all of us.
They shouldn't have let the pieces loose.

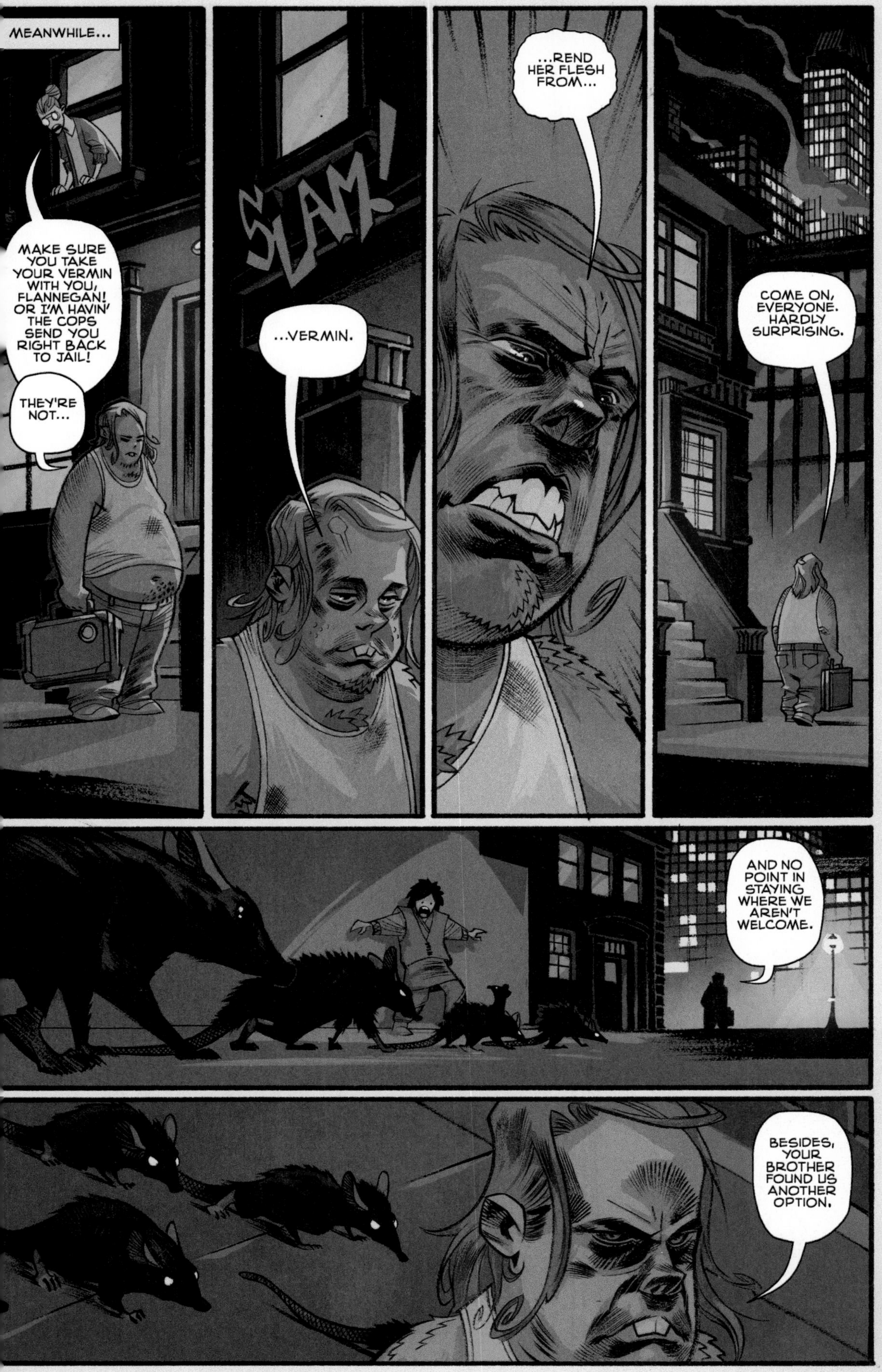
MEANWHILE...
MAKE SURE YOU TAKE YOUR VERMIN WITH YOU, FLANNEGAN! OR I'M HAVIN' THE COPS SEND YOU RIGHT BACK TO JAIL!
THEY'RE NOT...
SLAM!
...VERMIN.
...REND HER FLESH FROM...
COME ON, EVERYONE. HARDLY SURPRISING.
AND NO POINT IN STAYING WHERE WE AREN'T WELCOME.
BESIDES, YOUR BROTHER FOUND US ANOTHER OPTION.

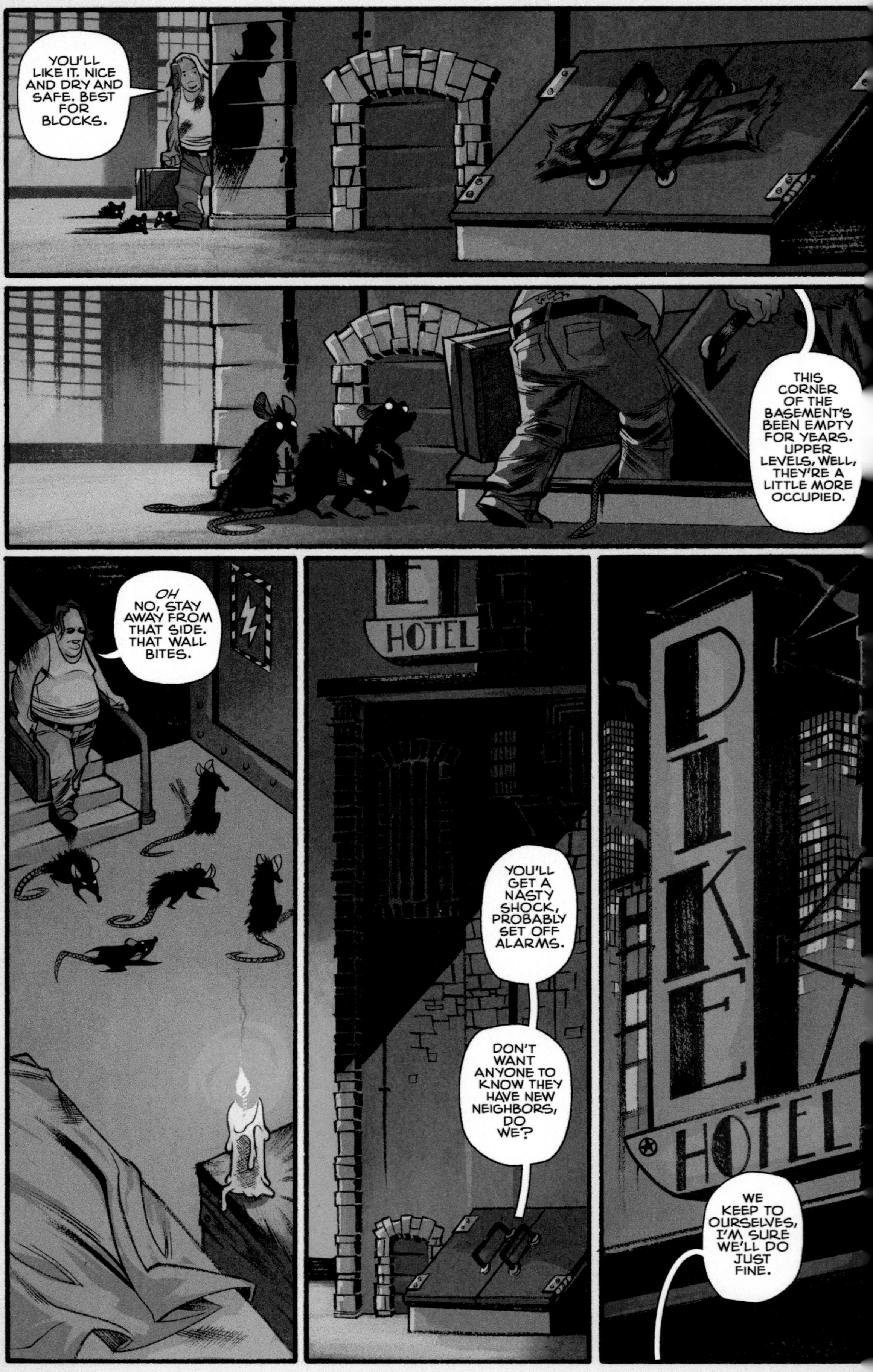
YOU'LL LIKE IT. NICE AND DRY AND SAFE. BEST FOR BLOCKS.
THIS CORNER OF THE BASEMENT'S BEEN EMPTY FOR YEARS. UPPER LEVELS, WELL, THEY'RE A LITTLE MORE OCCUPIED.
OH NO, STAY AWAY FROM THAT SIDE. THAT WALL BITES.
HOTEL
YOU'LL GET A NASTY SHOCK, PROBABLY SET OFF ALARMS.
DON'T WANT ANYONE TO KNOW THEY HAVE NEW NEIGHBORS, DO WE?
PIKE
HOTEL
WE KEEP TO OURSELVES, I'M SURE WE'LL DO JUST FINE.

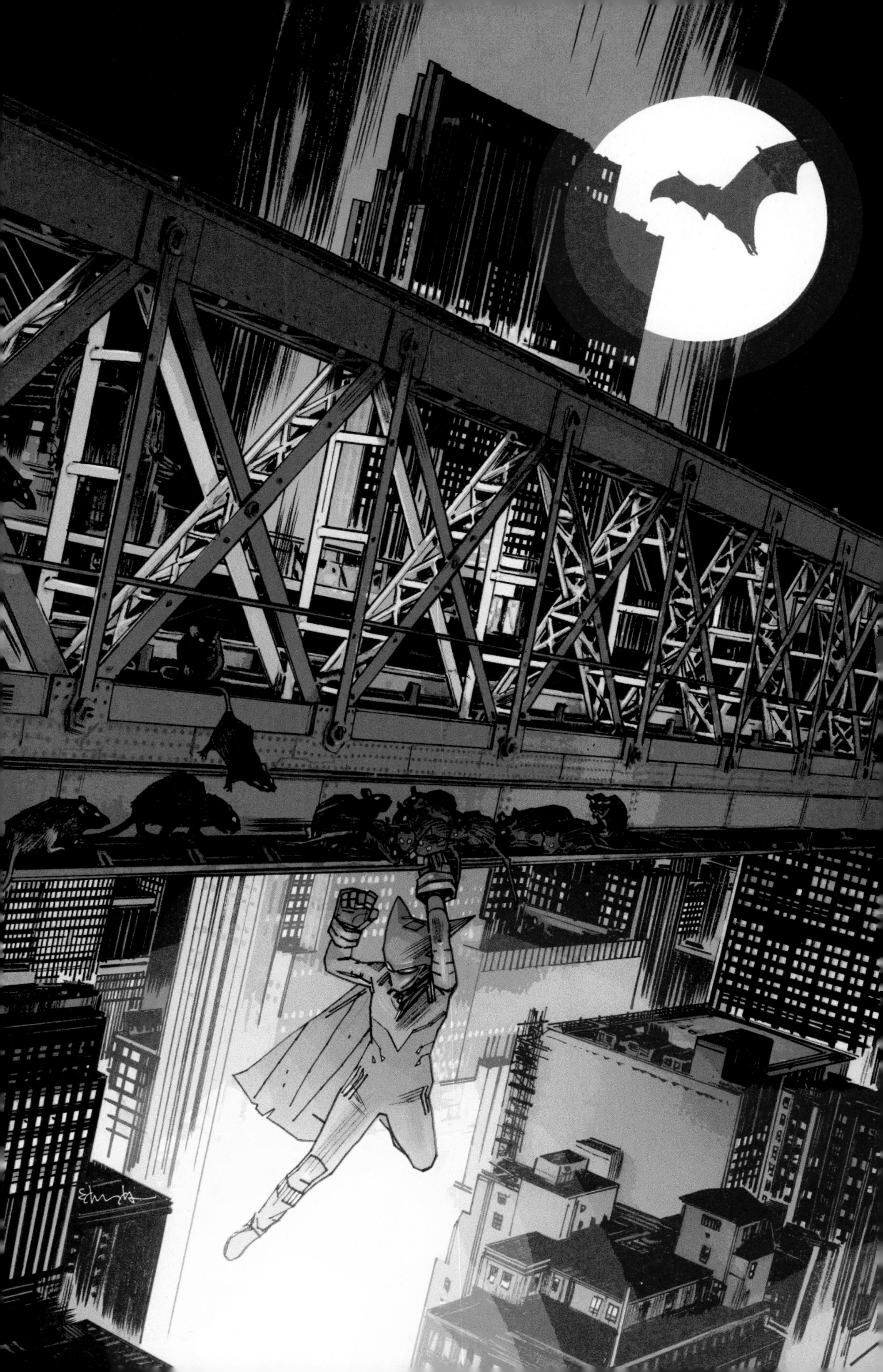

Variant cover art by Michael Cho

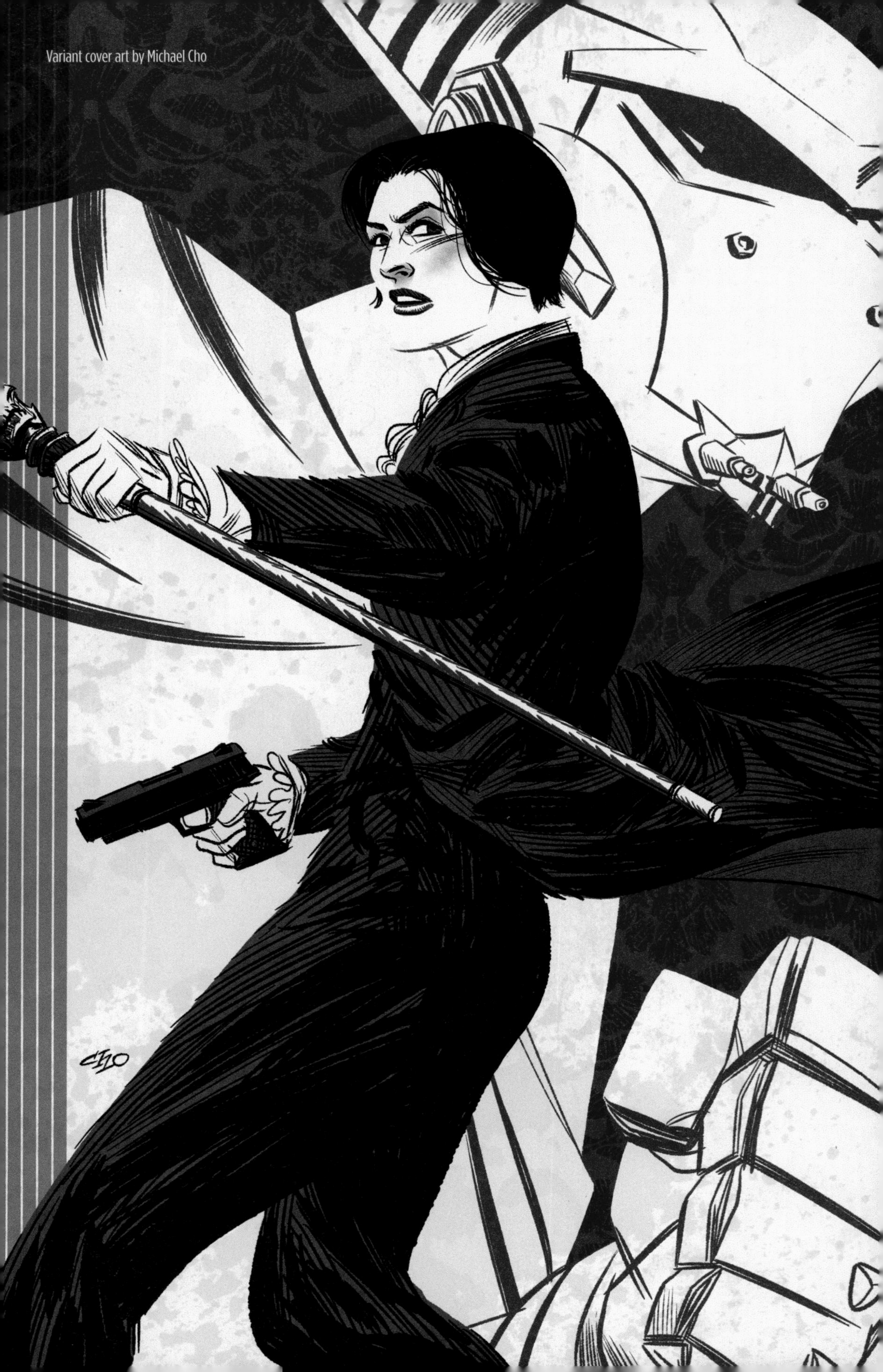
CHO

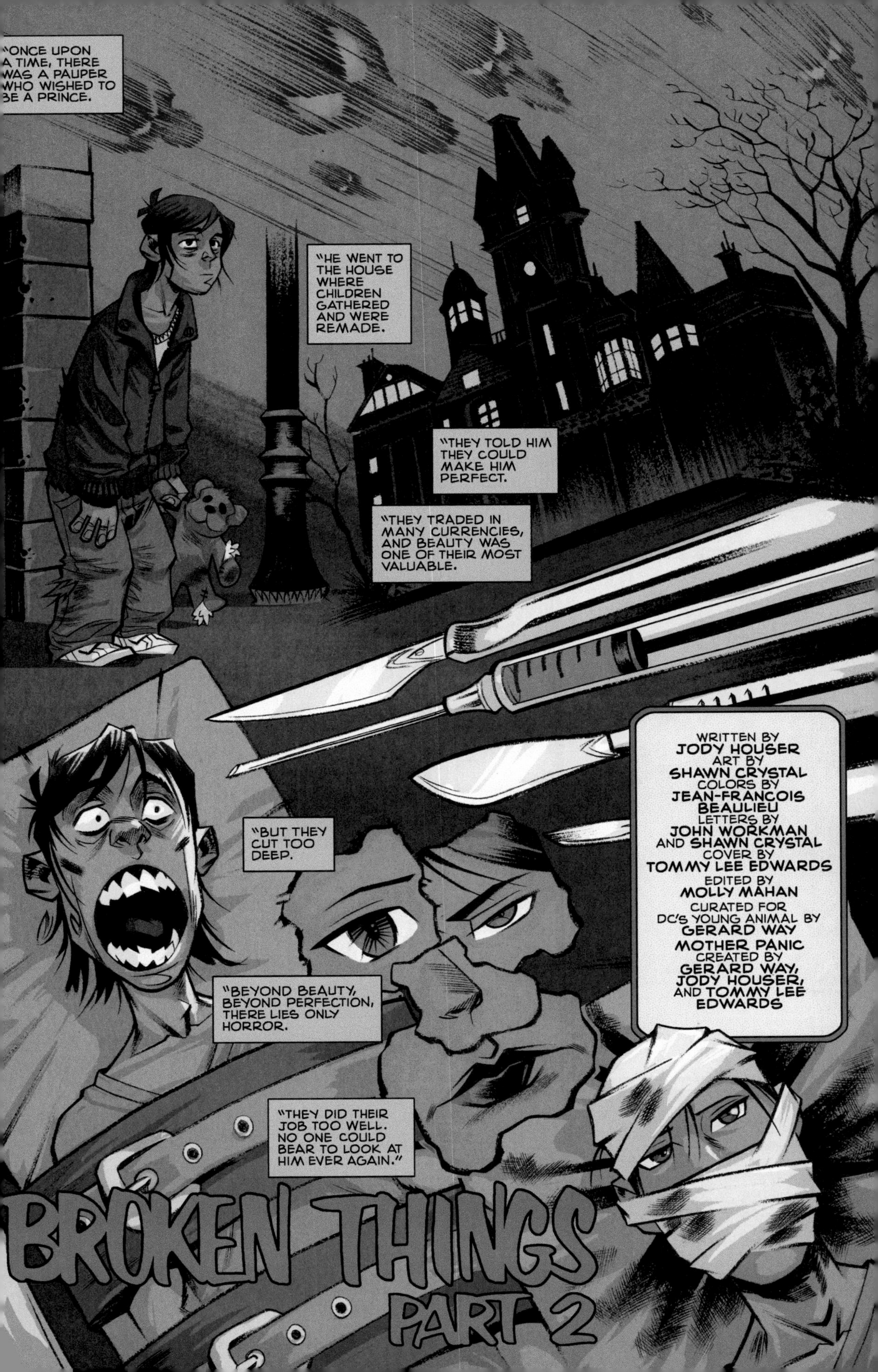
"ONCE UPON A TIME, THERE WAS A PAUPER WHO WISHED TO BE A PRINCE.
"HE WENT TO THE HOUSE WHERE CHILDREN GATHERED AND WERE REMADE.
"THEY TOLD HIM THEY COULD MAKE HIM PERFECT.
"THEY TRADED IN MANY CURRENCIES, AND BEAUTY WAS ONE OF THEIR MOST VALUABLE.
"BUT THEY CUT TOO DEEP.
"BEYOND BEAUTY, BEYOND PERFECTION, THERE LIES ONLY HORROR.
"THEY DID THEIR JOB TOO WELL. NO ONE COULD BEAR TO LOOK AT HIM EVER AGAIN."
WRITTEN BY JODY HOUSER ART BY SHAWN CRYSTAL COLORS BY JEAN-FRANCOIS BEAULIEU LETTERS BY JOHN WORKMAN AND SHAWN CRYSTAL COVER BY TOMMY LEE EDWARDS EDITED BY MOLLY MAHAN CURATED FOR DC'S YOUNG ANIMAL BY GERARD WAY MOTHER PANIC CREATED BY GERARD WAY, JODY HOUSER, AND TOMMY LEE EDWARDS
BROKEN THINGS
PART 2

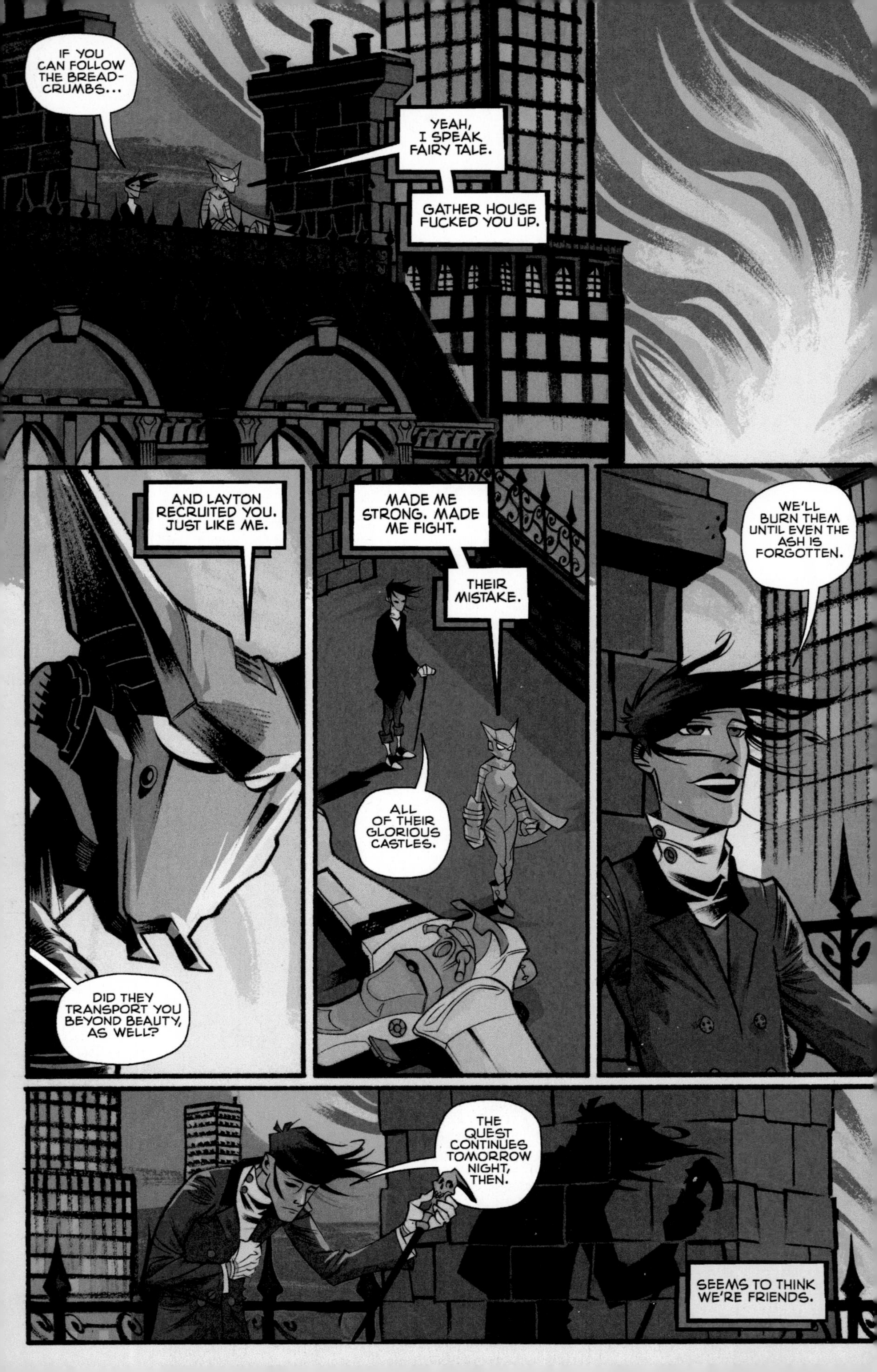
IF YOU CAN FOLLOW THE BREAD-CRUMBS...
YEAH, I SPEAK FAIRY TALE.
GATHER HOUSE FUCKED YOU UP.
AND LAYTON RECRUITED YOU. JUST LIKE ME.
DID THEY TRANSPORT YOU BEYOND BEAUTY, AS WELL?
MADE ME STRONG. MADE ME FIGHT.
THEIR MISTAKE.
ALL OF THEIR GLORIOUS CASTLES.
WE'LL BURN THEM UNTIL EVEN THE ASH IS FORGOTTEN.
THE QUEST CONTINUES TOMORROW NIGHT, THEN.
SEEMS TO THINK WE'RE FRIENDS.

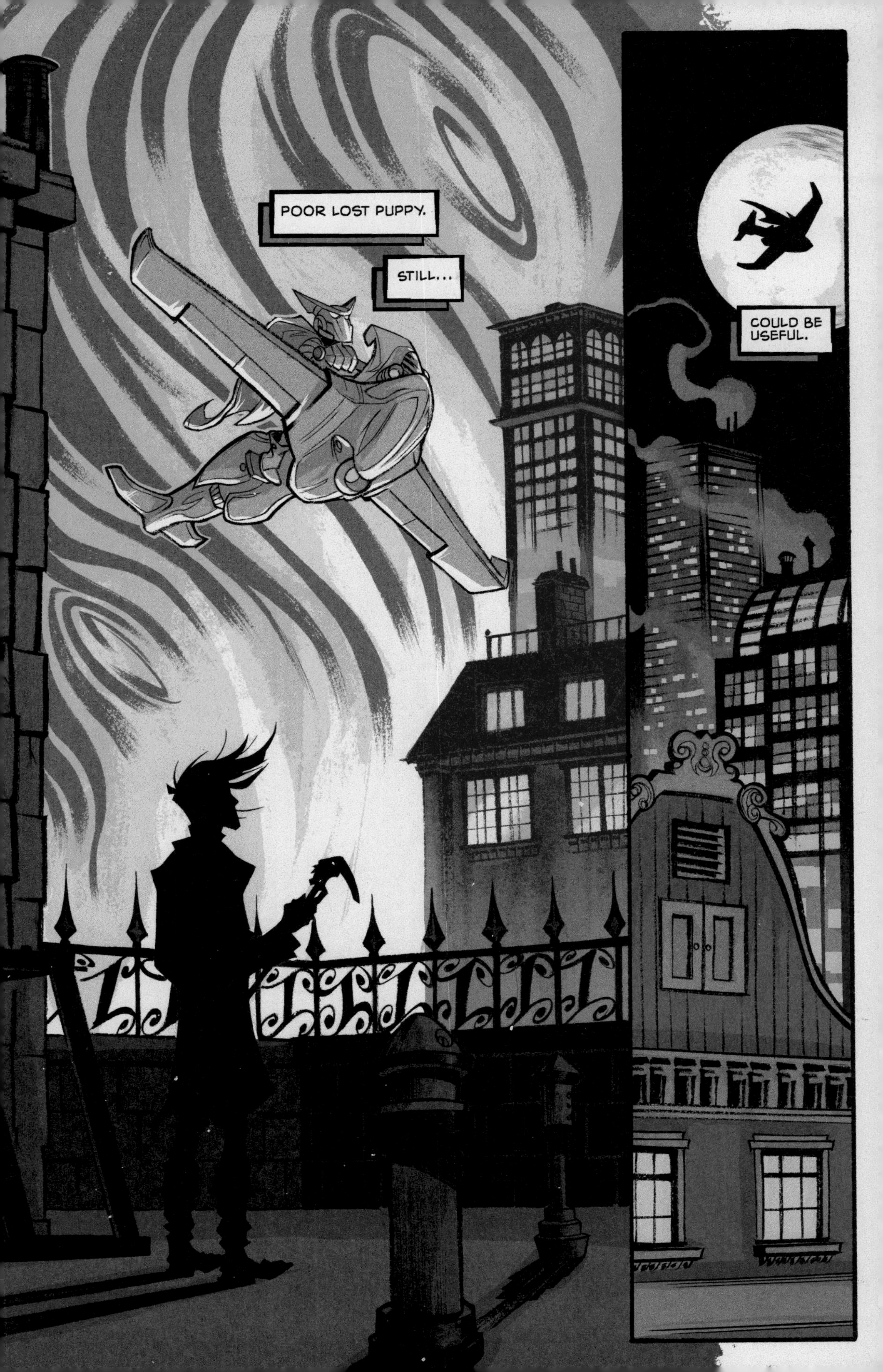
POOR LOST PUPPY.
STILL...
COULD BE USEFUL.

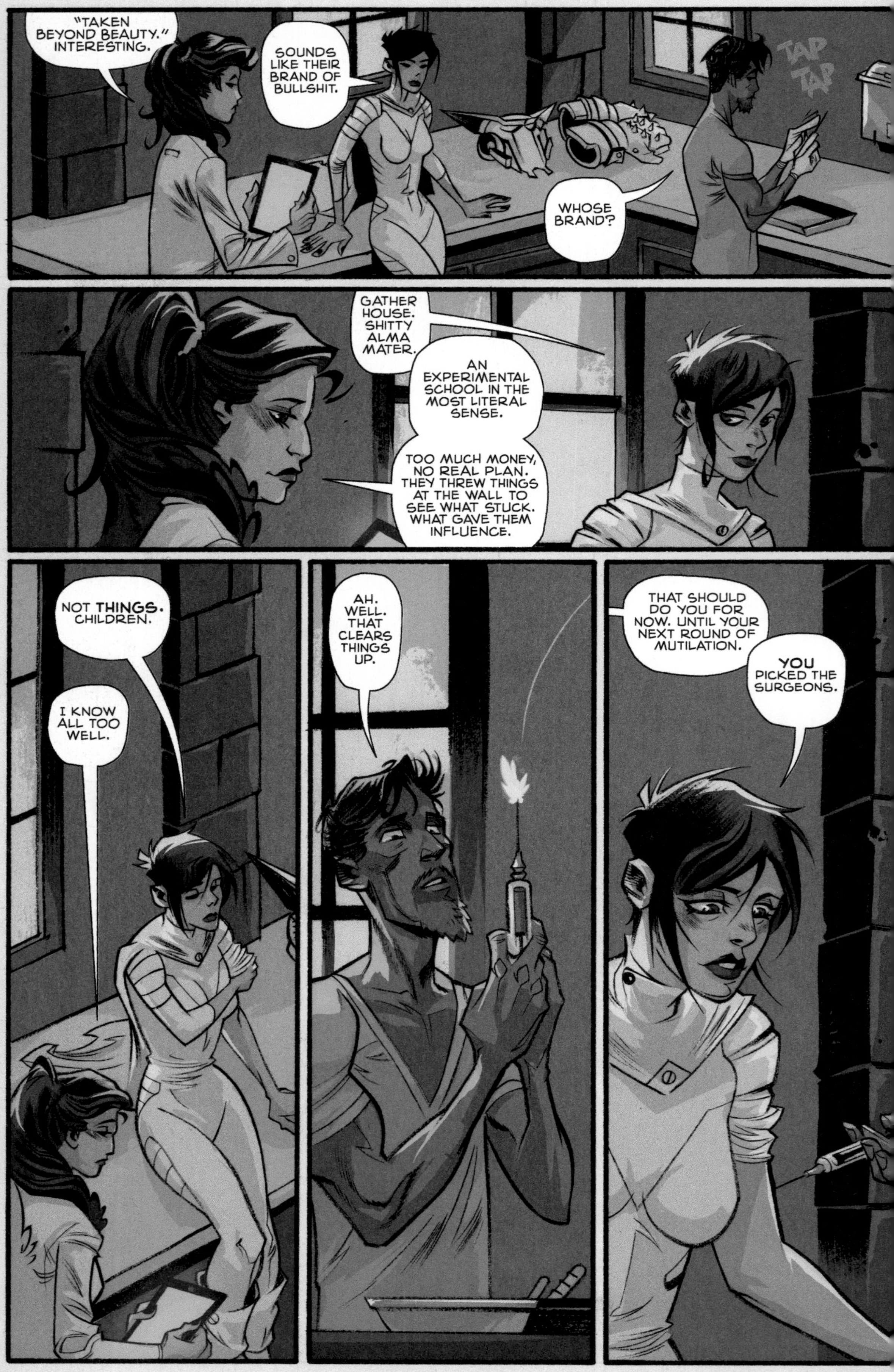
"TAKEN BEYOND BEAUTY." INTERESTING.
SOUNDS LIKE THEIR BRAND OF BULLSHIT.
TAP TAP
WHOSE BRAND?
GATHER HOUSE. SHITTY ALMA MATER.
AN EXPERIMENTAL SCHOOL IN THE MOST LITERAL SENSE.
TOO MUCH MONEY, NO REAL PLAN. THEY THREW THINGS AT THE WALL TO SEE WHAT STUCK. WHAT GAVE THEM INFLUENCE.
NOT **THINGS.** CHILDREN.
I KNOW ALL TOO WELL.
AH. WELL. THAT CLEARS THINGS UP.
THAT SHOULD DO YOU FOR NOW. UNTIL YOUR NEXT ROUND OF MUTILATION.
**YOU** PICKED THE SURGEONS.

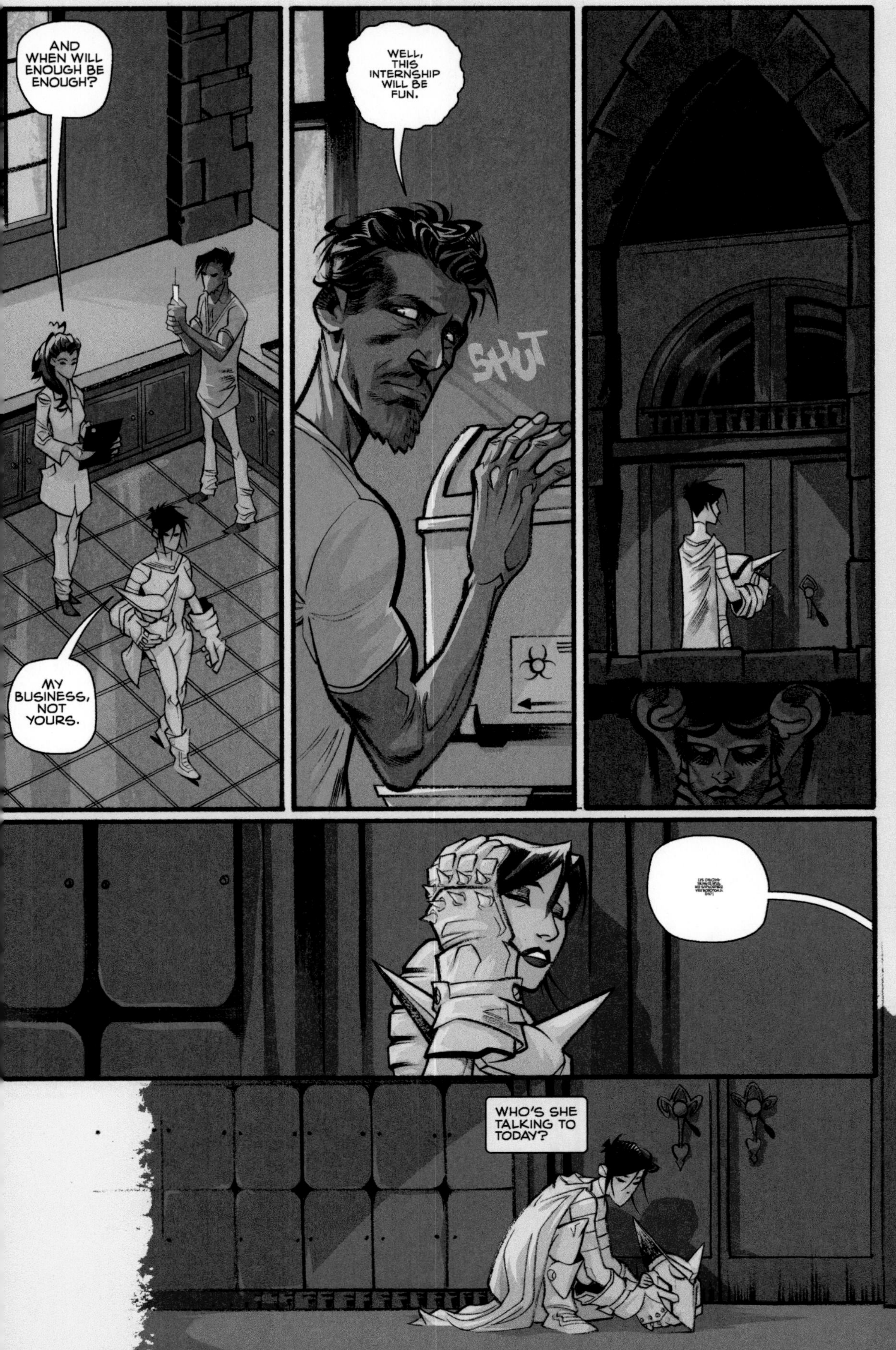
AND WHEN WILL ENOUGH BE ENOUGH?
MY BUSINESS, NOT YOURS.
WELL, THIS INTERNSHIP WILL BE FUN.
SHUT
WHO'S SHE TALKING TO TODAY?

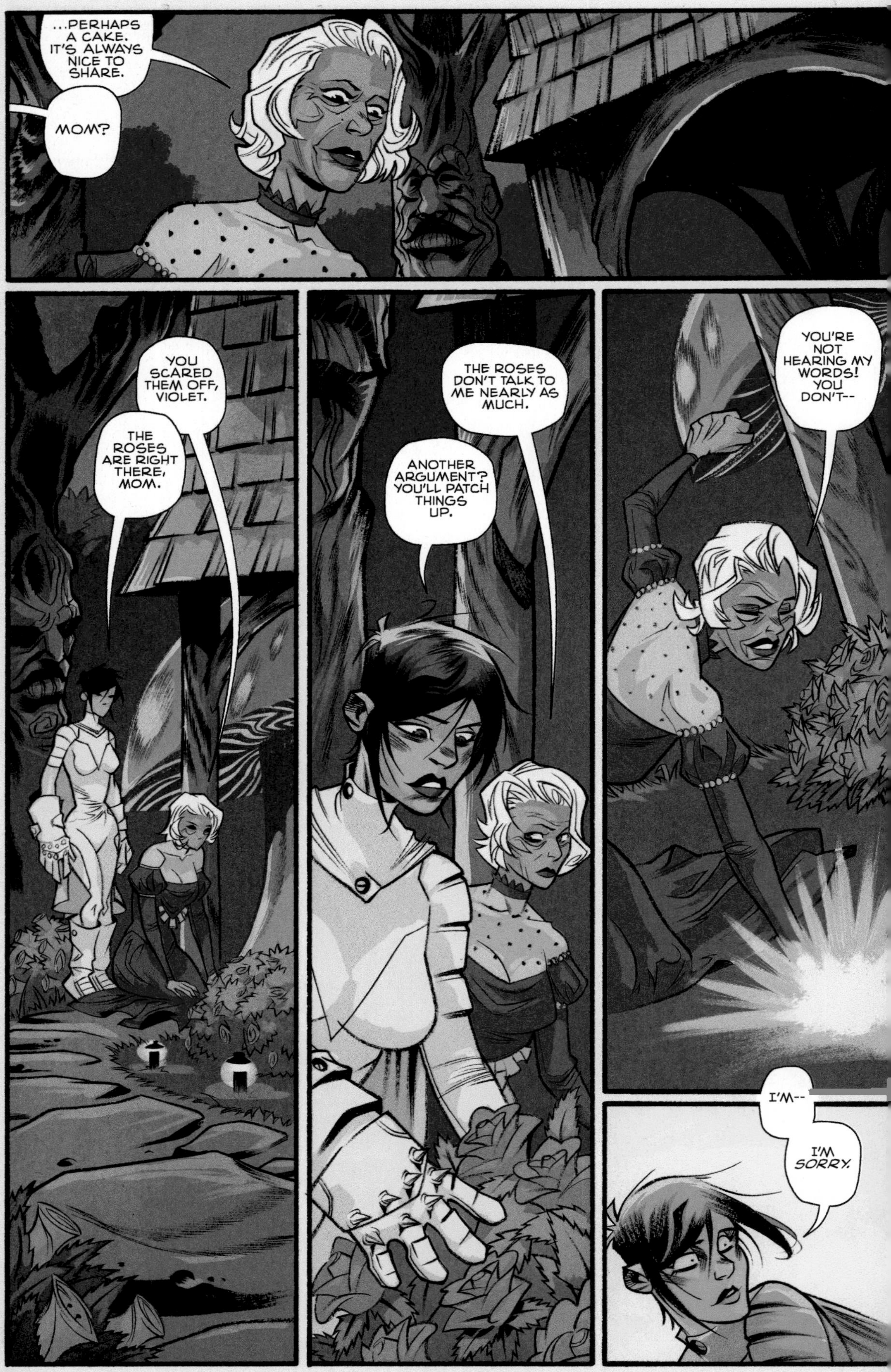
...PERHAPS A CAKE. IT'S ALWAYS NICE TO SHARE.
MOM?
YOU SCARED THEM OFF, VIOLET.
THE ROSES ARE RIGHT THERE, MOM.
THE ROSES DON'T TALK TO ME NEARLY AS MUCH.
ANOTHER ARGUMENT? YOU'LL PATCH THINGS UP.
YOU'RE NOT HEARING MY WORDS! YOU DON'T--
I'M--
I'M SORRY.

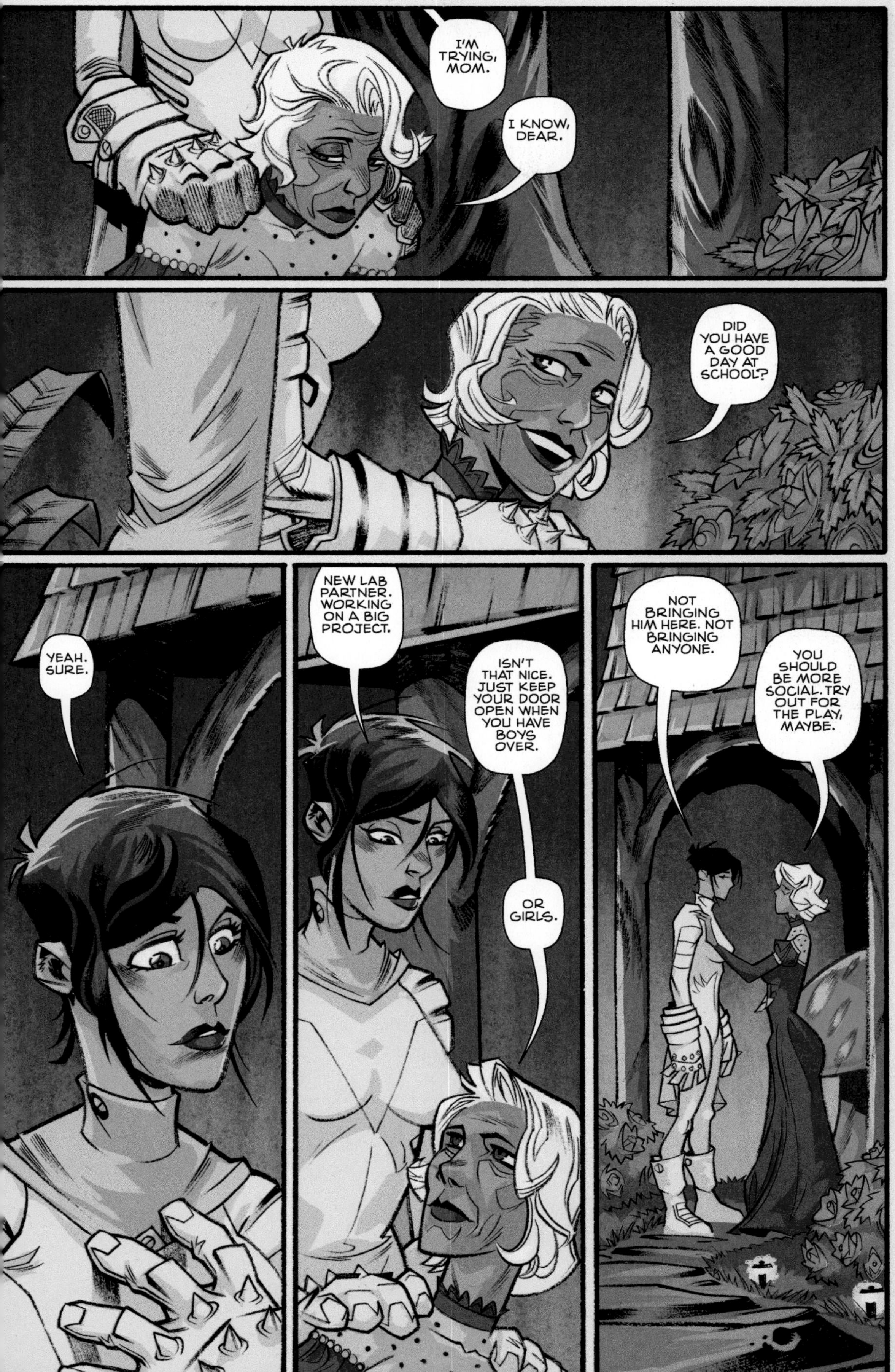
I'M TRYING, MOM.
I KNOW, DEAR.
DID YOU HAVE A GOOD DAY AT SCHOOL?
YEAH. SURE.
NEW LAB PARTNER. WORKING ON A BIG PROJECT.
ISN'T THAT NICE. JUST KEEP YOUR DOOR OPEN WHEN YOU HAVE BOYS OVER.
OR GIRLS.
NOT BRINGING HIM HERE. NOT BRINGING ANYONE.
YOU SHOULD BE MORE SOCIAL. TRY OUT FOR THE PLAY, MAYBE.

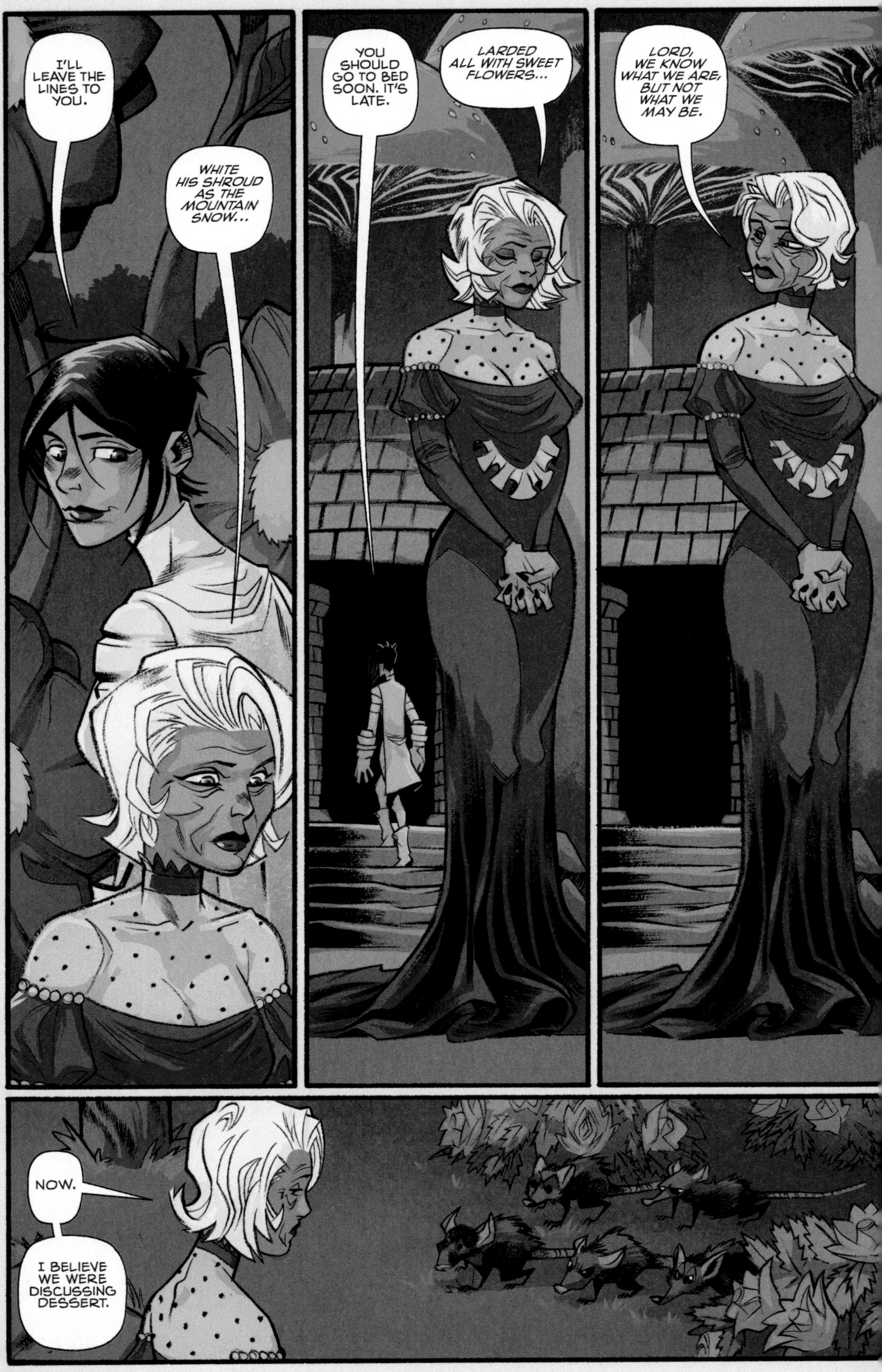
I'LL LEAVE THE LINES TO YOU.
WHITE HIS SHROUD AS THE MOUNTAIN SNOW...
YOU SHOULD GO TO BED SOON. IT'S LATE.
LARDED ALL WITH SWEET FLOWERS...
LORD, WE KNOW WHAT WE ARE, BUT NOT WHAT WE MAY BE.
NOW.
I BELIEVE WE WERE DISCUSSING DESSERT.

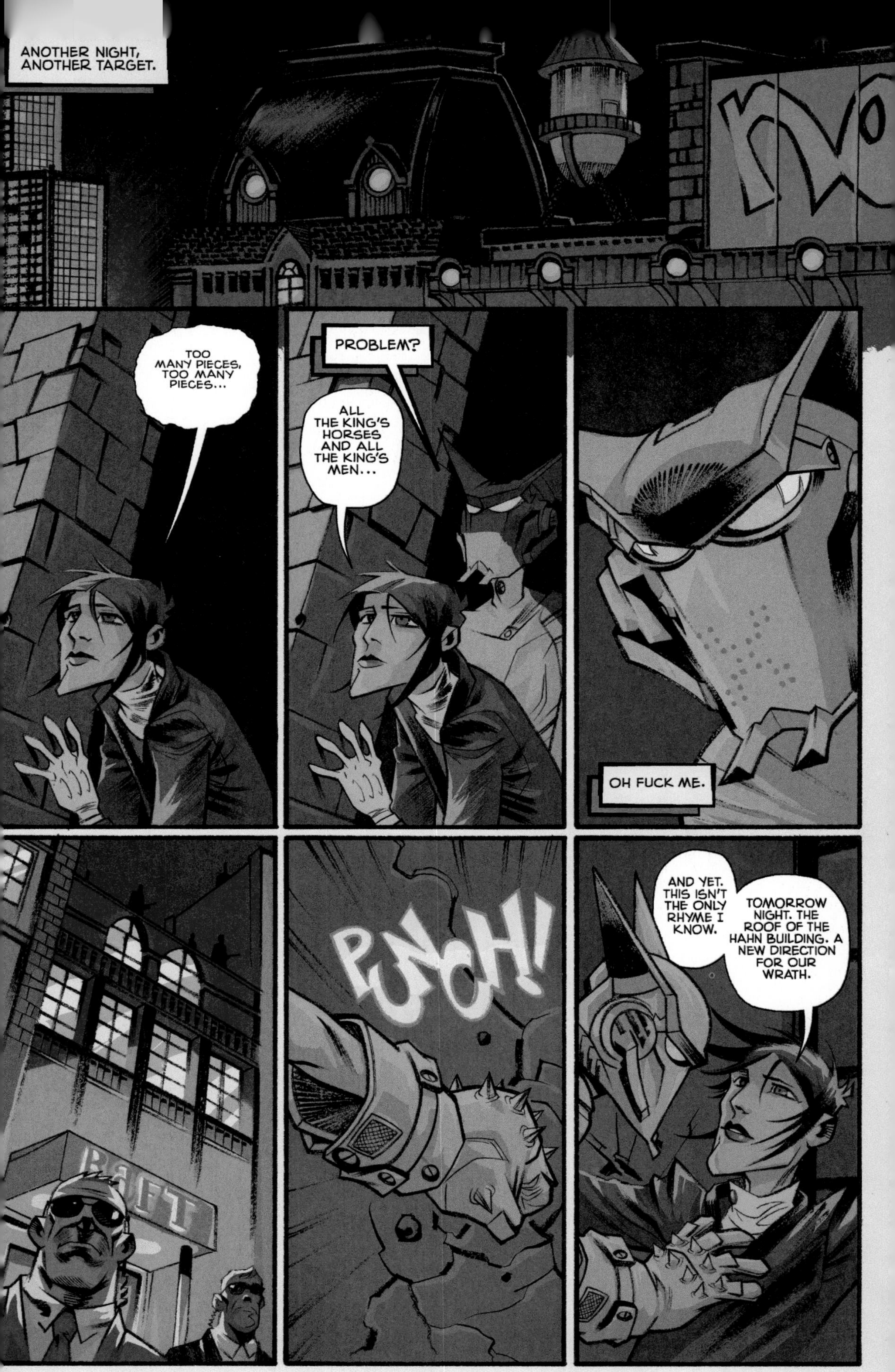
ANOTHER NIGHT, ANOTHER TARGET.
TOO MANY PIECES, TOO MANY PIECES...
PROBLEM?
ALL THE KING'S HORSES AND ALL THE KING'S MEN...
OH FUCK ME.
PUNCH!
AND YET. THIS ISN'T THE ONLY RHYME I KNOW.
TOMORROW NIGHT. THE ROOF OF THE HAHN BUILDING. A NEW DIRECTION FOR OUR WRATH.

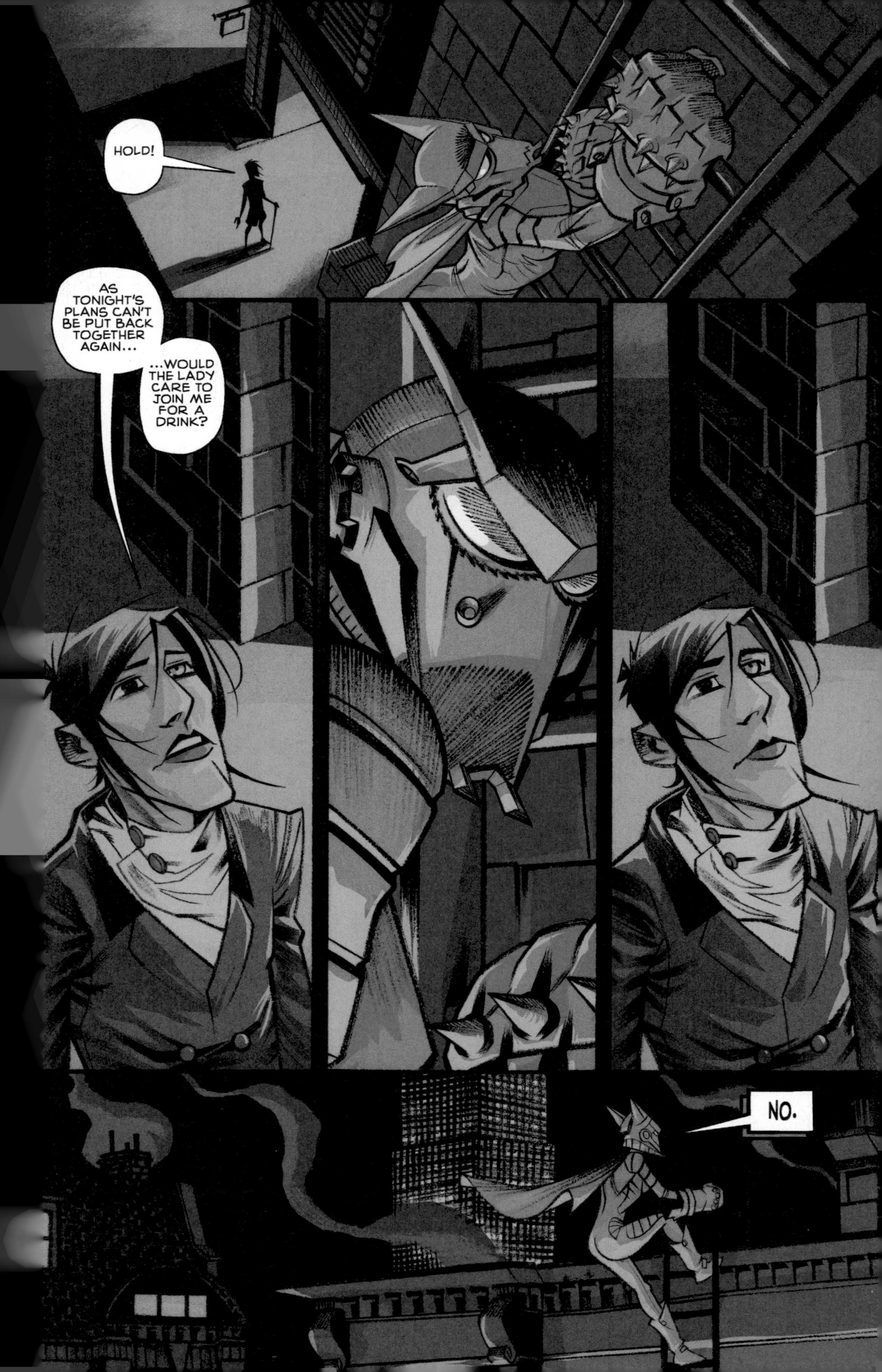
HOLD!
AS TONIGHT'S PLANS CAN'T BE PUT BACK TOGETHER AGAIN...
...WOULD THE LADY CARE TO JOIN ME FOR A DRINK?
NO.

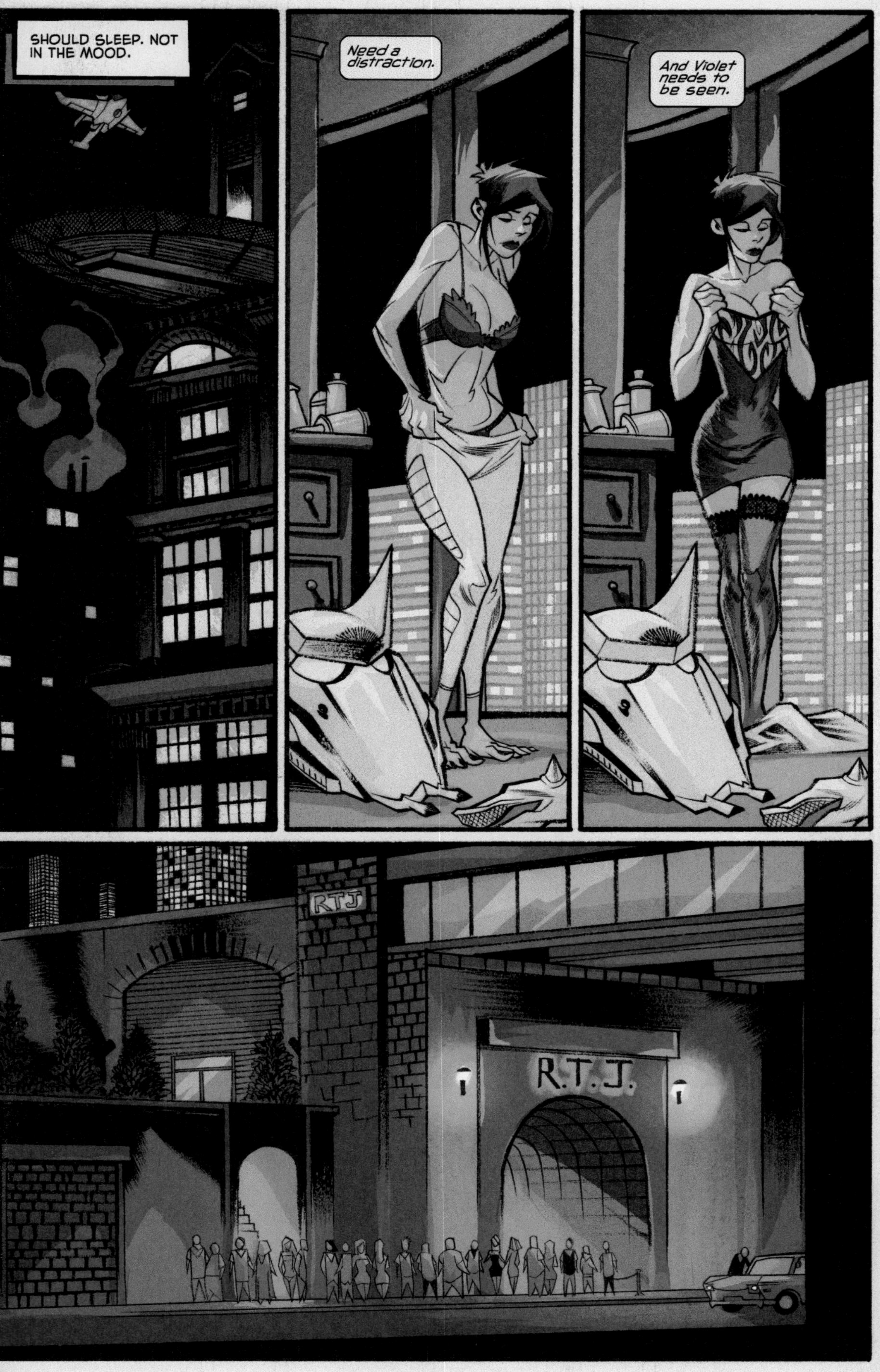
SHOULD SLEEP. NOT IN THE MOOD.
Need a distraction.
And Violet needs to be seen.
RTJ
R.T.J.

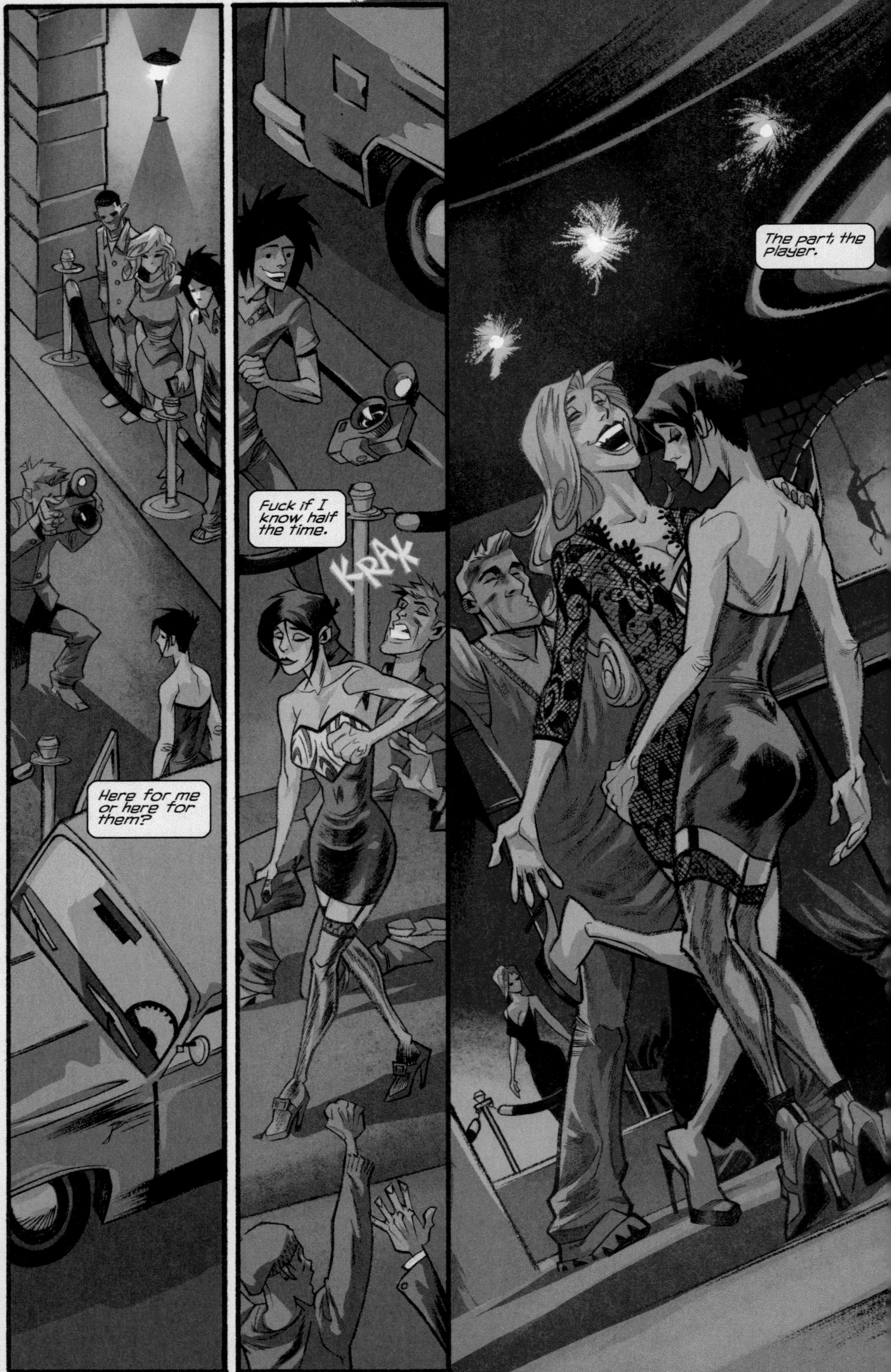
Here for me or here for them?
Fuck if I know half the time.
KRAK
The part; the player.

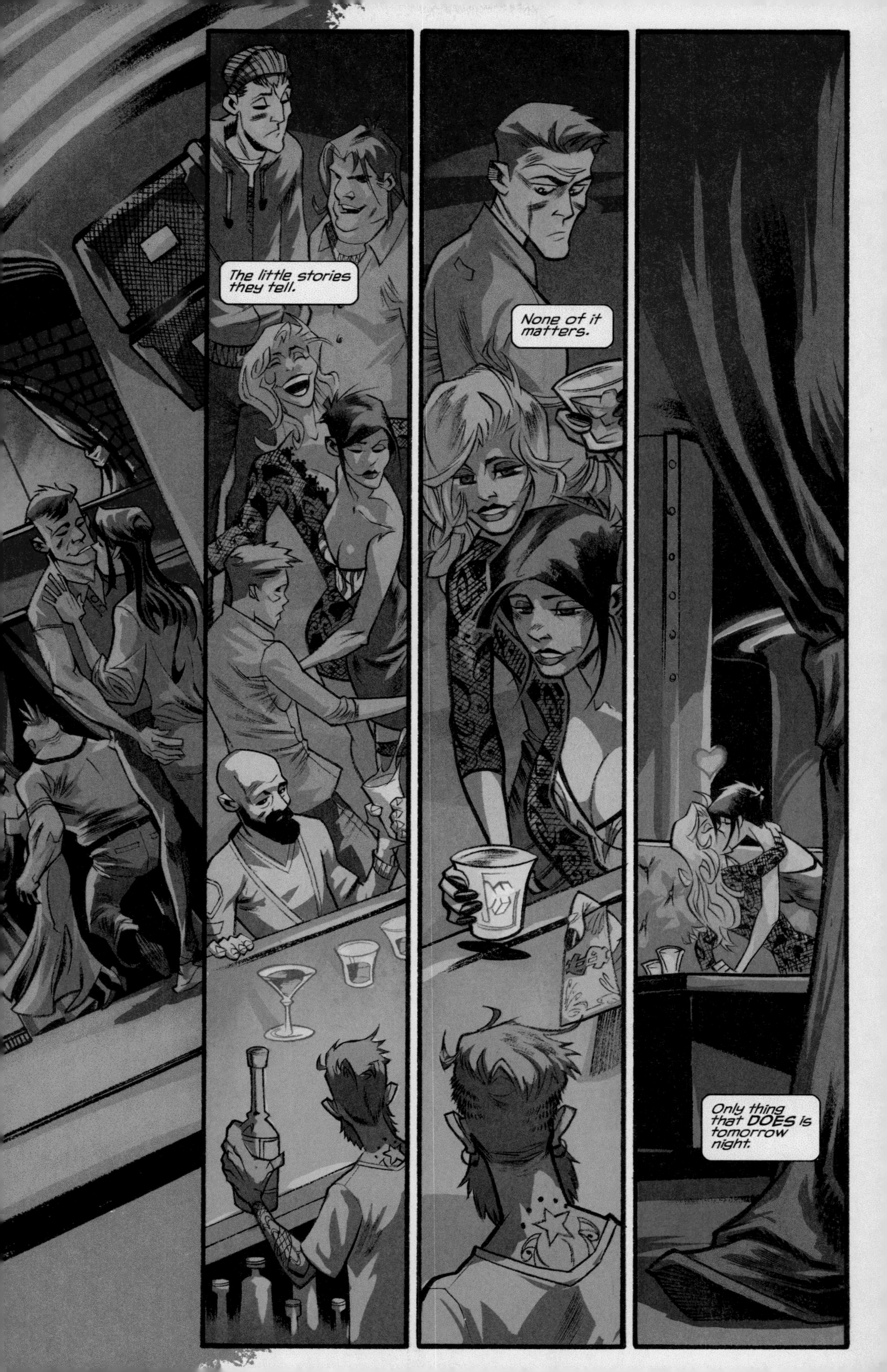
The little stories they tell.
None of it matters.
Only thing that DOES is tomorrow night.

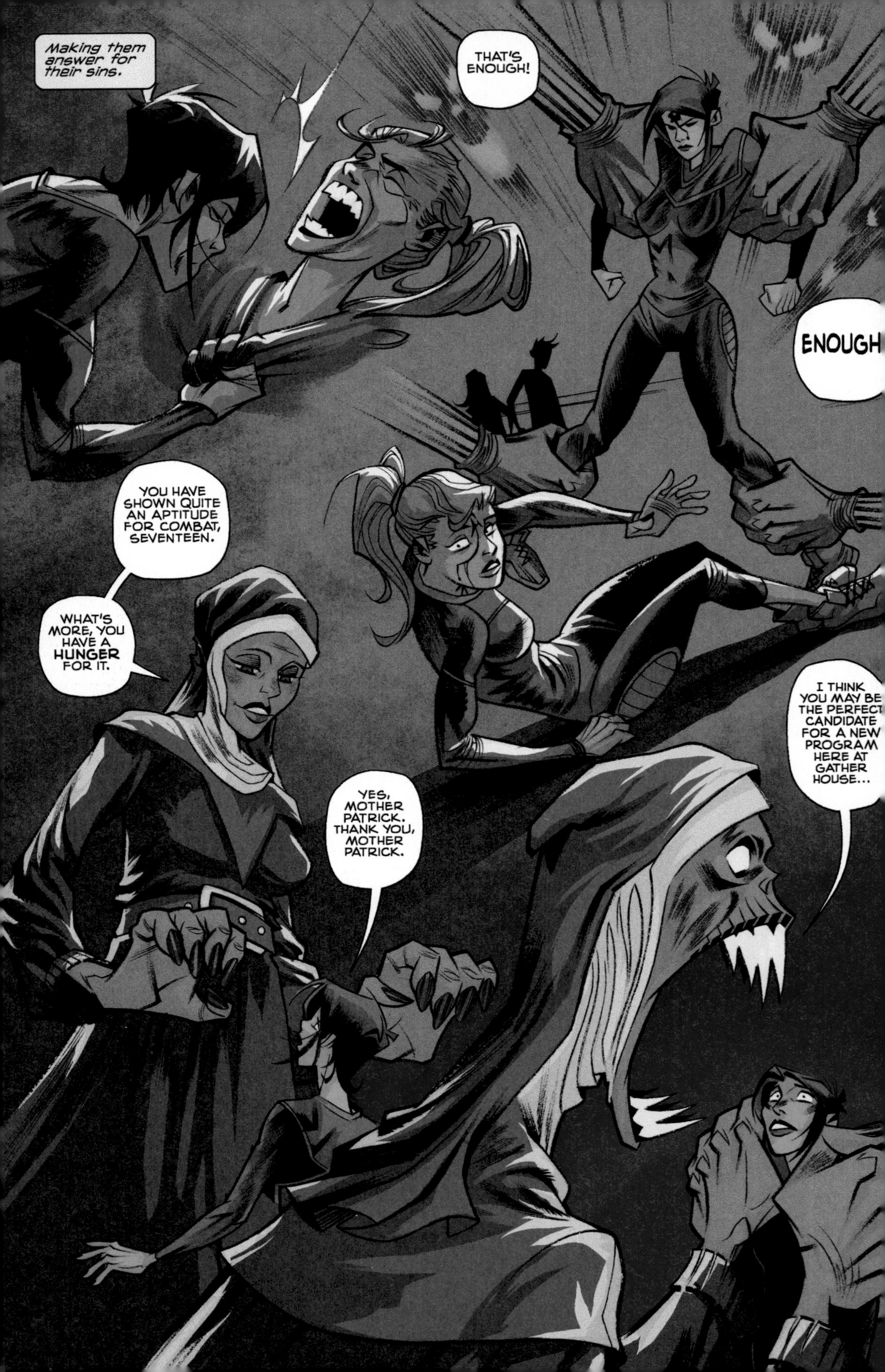
Making them answer for their sins.
THAT'S ENOUGH!
ENOUGH
YOU HAVE SHOWN QUITE AN APTITUDE FOR COMBAT, SEVENTEEN.
WHAT'S MORE, YOU HAVE A **HUNGER** FOR IT.
YES, MOTHER PATRICK. THANK YOU, MOTHER PATRICK.
I THINK YOU MAY BE THE PERFECT CANDIDATE FOR A NEW PROGRAM HERE AT GATHER HOUSE...

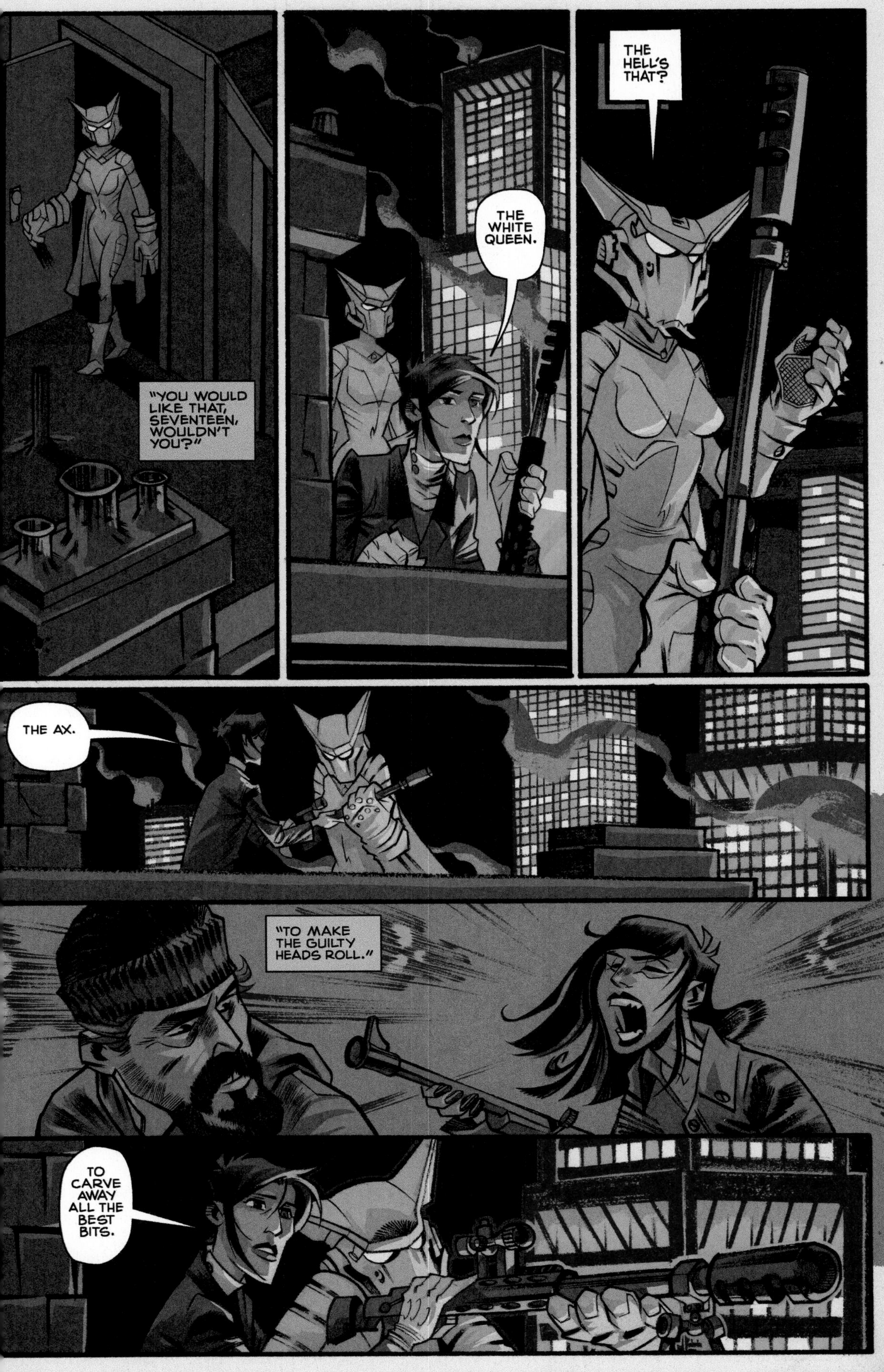
"YOU WOULD LIKE THAT, SEVENTEEN, WOULDN'T YOU?"
THE WHITE QUEEN.
THE HELL'S THAT?
THE AX.
"TO MAKE THE GUILTY HEADS ROLL."
TO CARVE AWAY ALL THE BEST BITS.

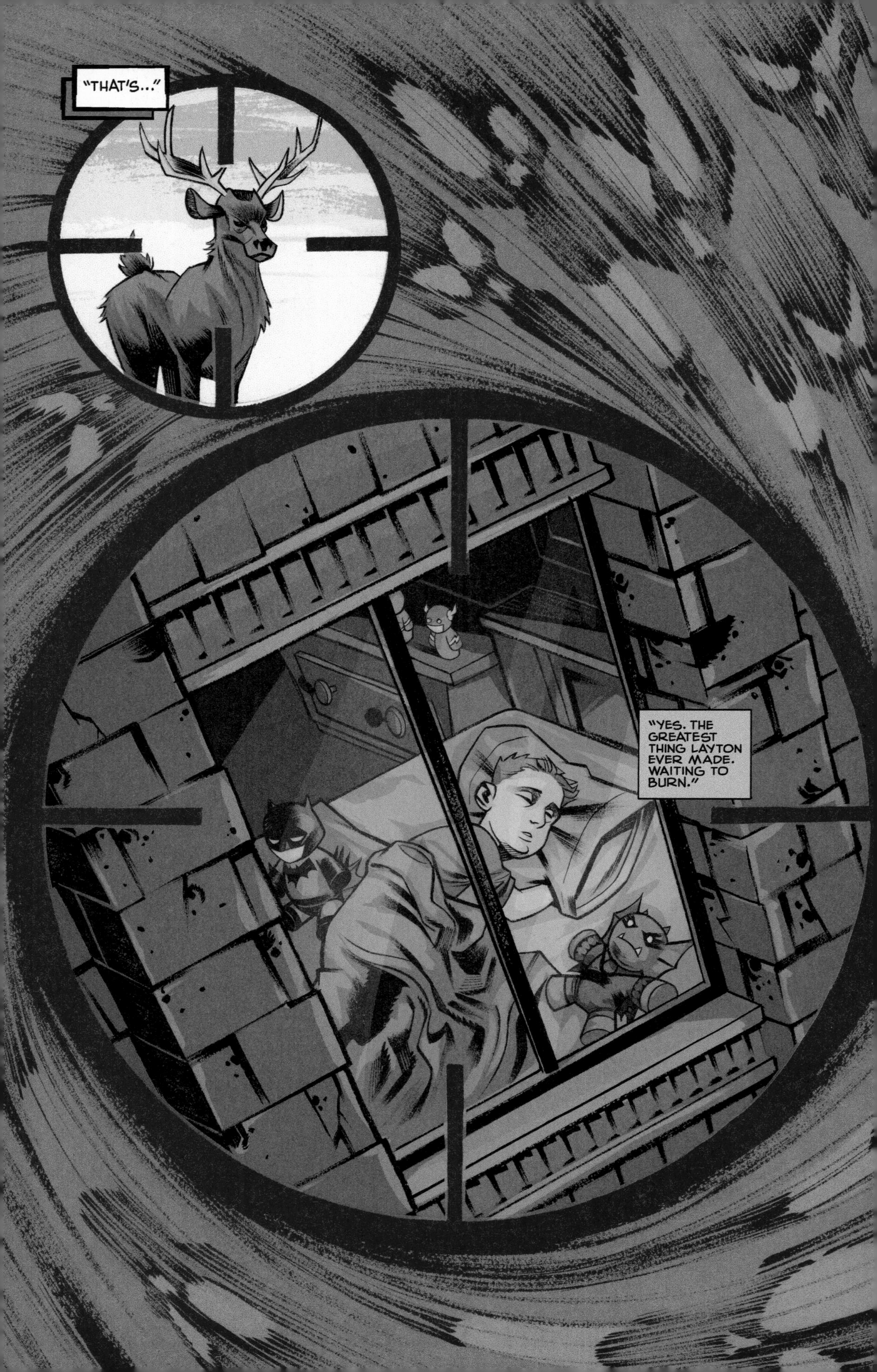
"THAT'S..."
"YES. THE GREATEST THING LAYTON EVER MADE. WAITING TO BURN."

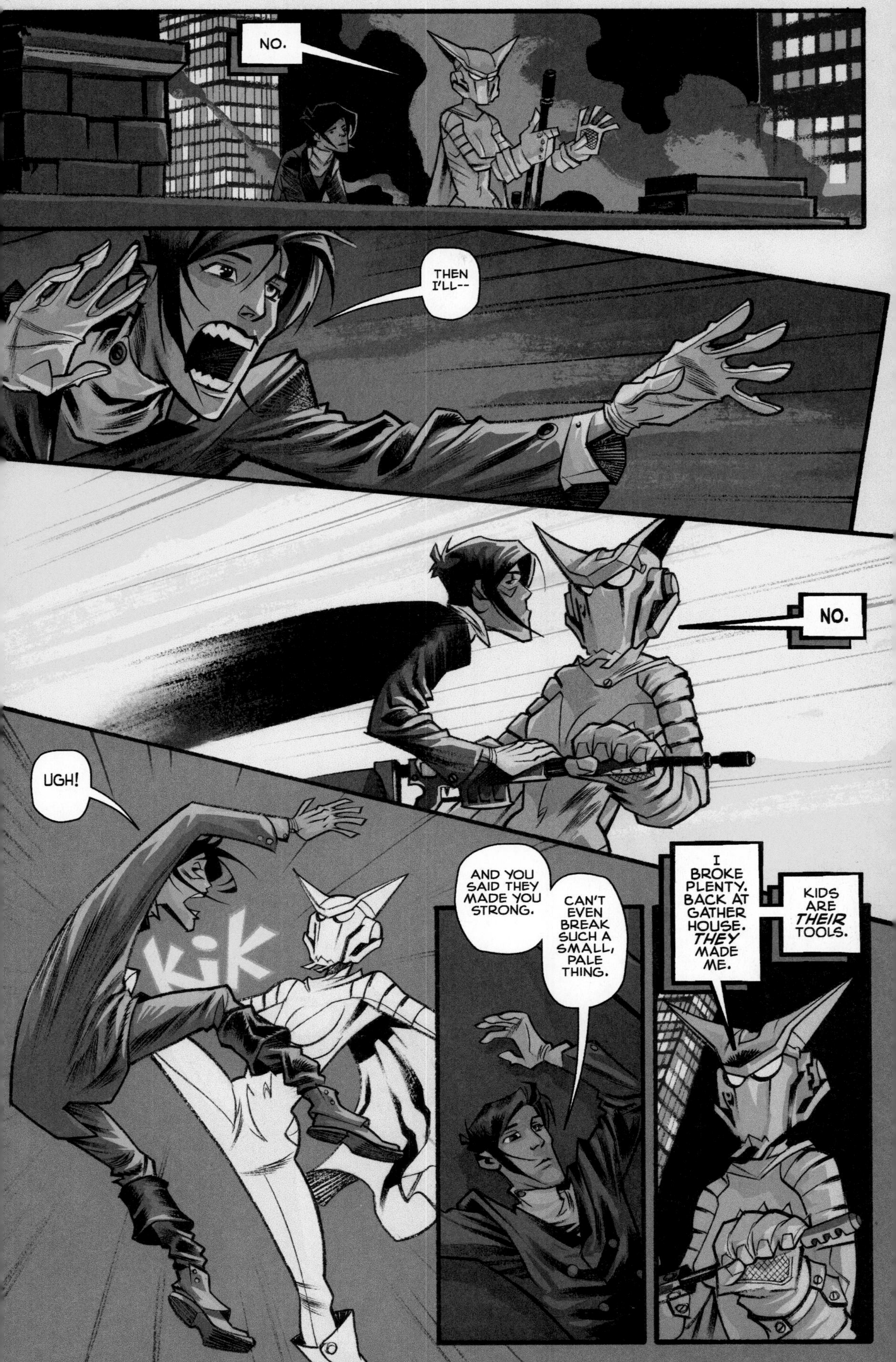
NO.
THEN I'LL--
NO.
UGH!
KIK
AND YOU SAID THEY MADE YOU STRONG.
CAN'T EVEN BREAK SUCH A SMALL, PALE THING.
I BROKE PLENTY. BACK AT GATHER HOUSE. *THEY* MADE ME.
KIDS ARE *THEIR* TOOLS.

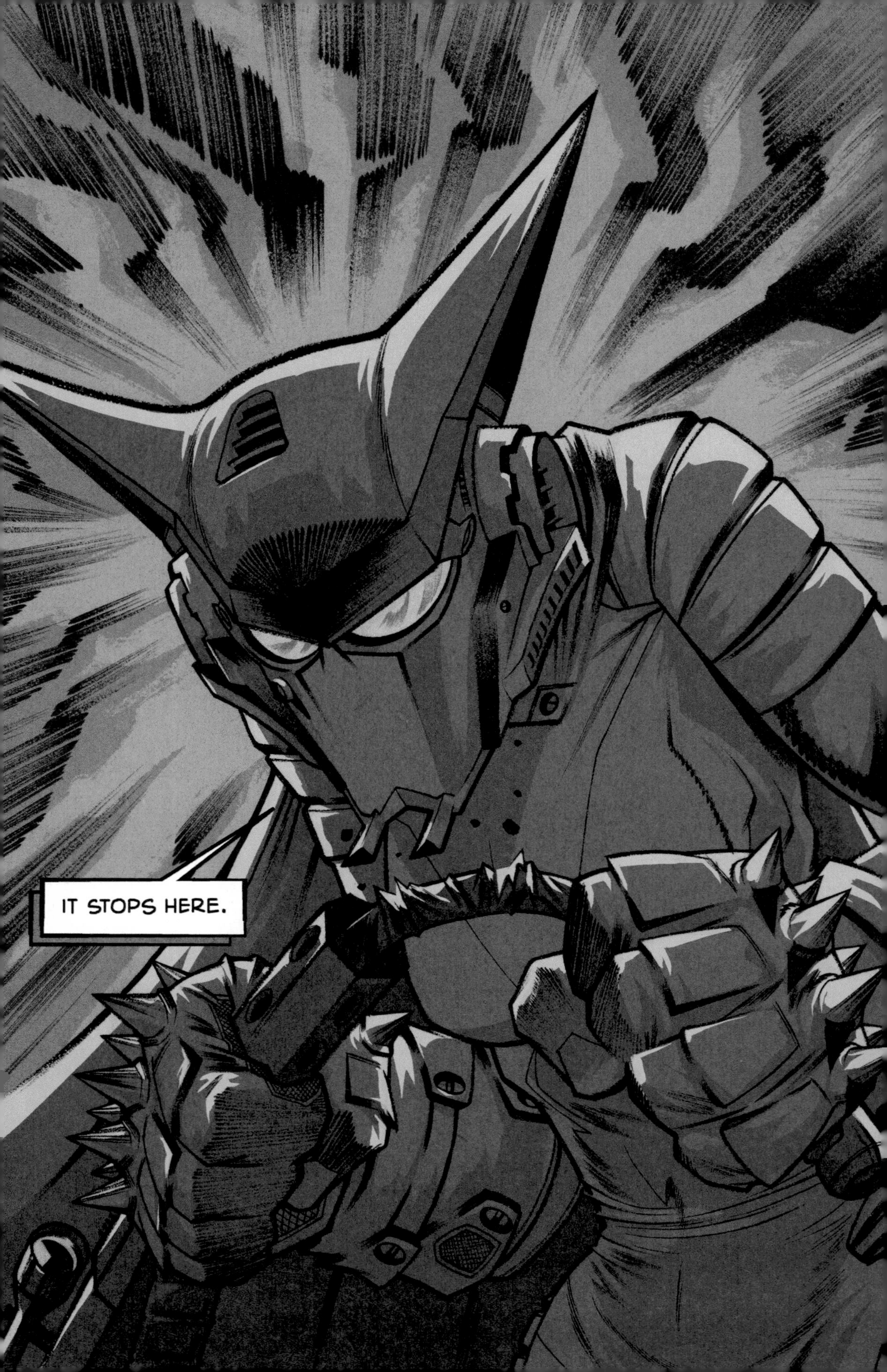
IT STOPS HERE.

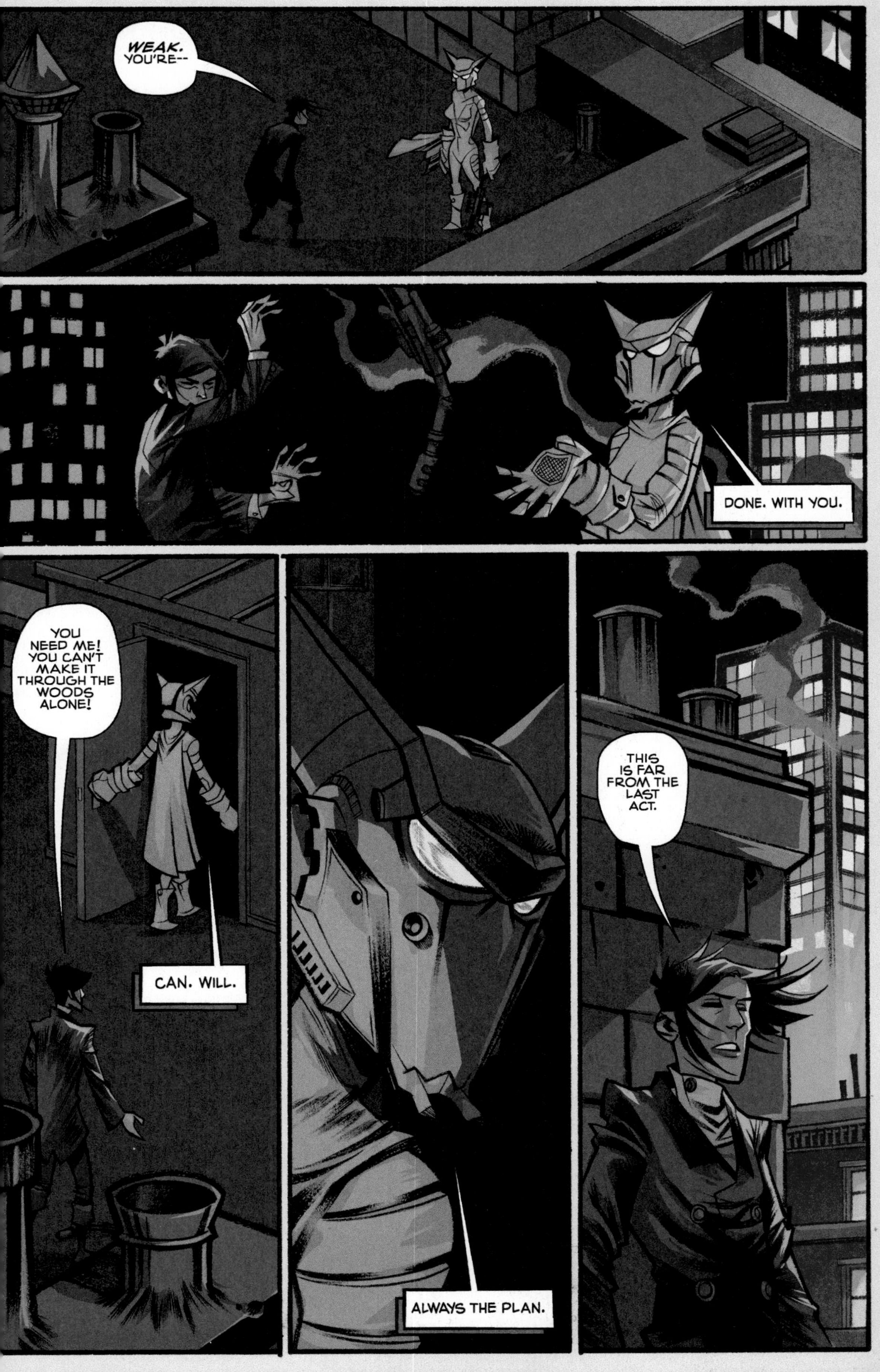
WEAK. YOU'RE--
DONE. WITH YOU.
YOU NEED ME! YOU CAN'T MAKE IT THROUGH THE WOODS ALONE!
CAN. WILL.
ALWAYS THE PLAN.
THIS IS FAR FROM THE LAST ACT.

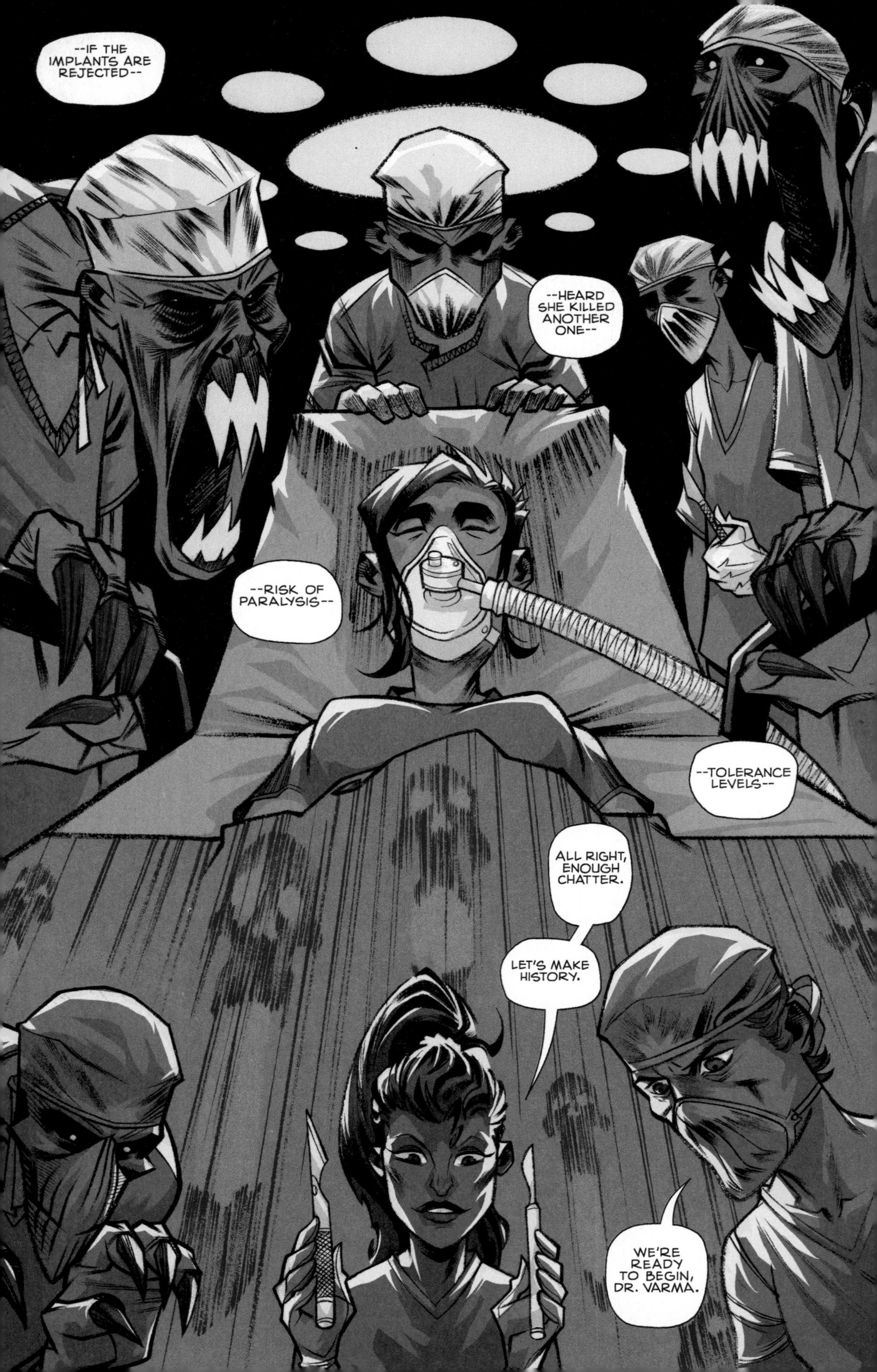
--IF THE IMPLANTS ARE REJECTED--
--HEARD SHE KILLED ANOTHER ONE--
--RISK OF PARALYSIS--
--TOLERANCE LEVELS--
ALL RIGHT, ENOUGH CHATTER.
LET'S MAKE HISTORY.
WE'RE READY TO BEGIN, DR. VARMA.

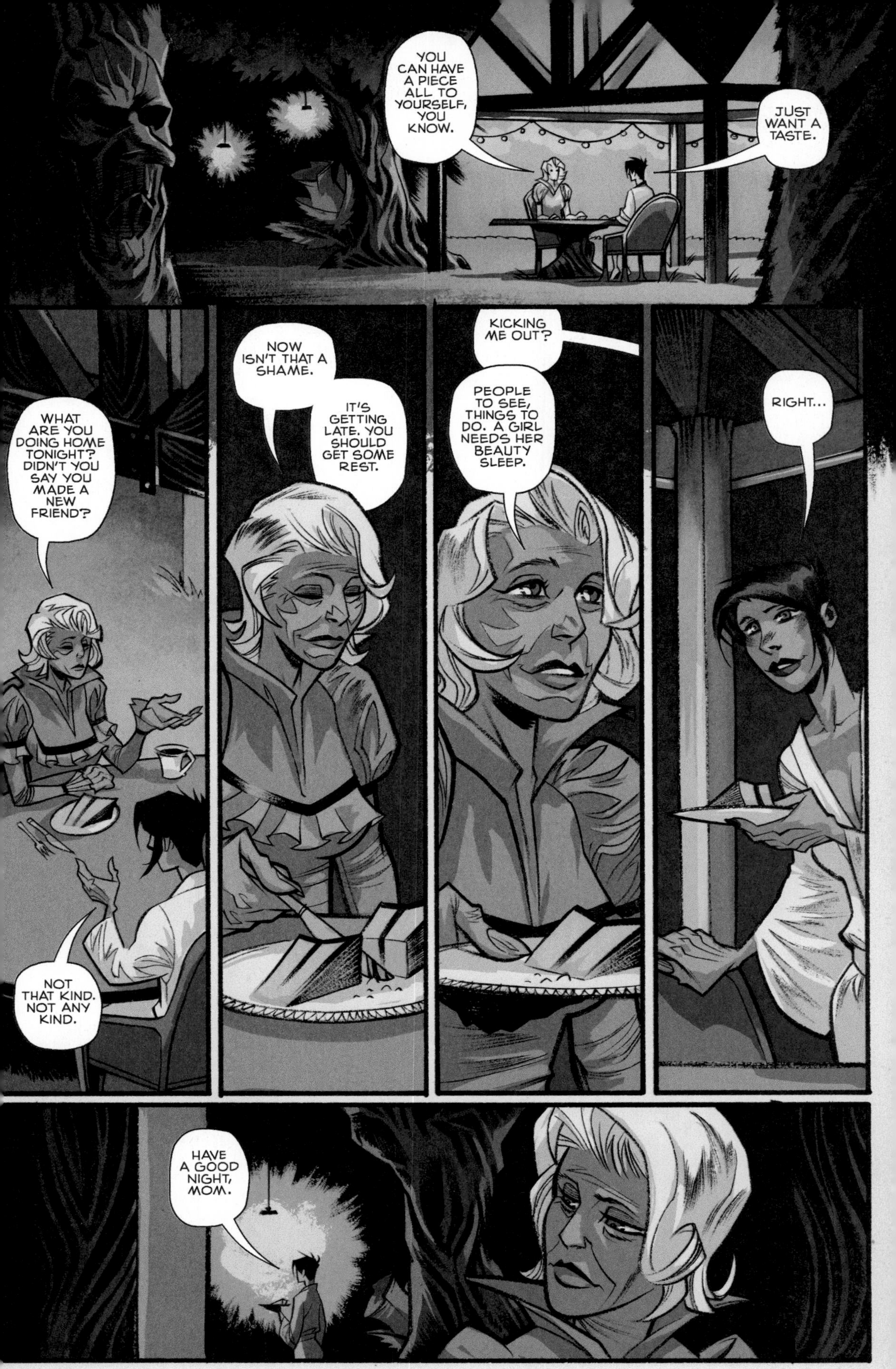
YOU CAN HAVE A PIECE ALL TO YOURSELF, YOU KNOW.
JUST WANT A TASTE.
WHAT ARE YOU DOING HOME TONIGHT? DIDN'T YOU SAY YOU MADE A NEW FRIEND?
NOT THAT KIND. NOT ANY KIND.
NOW ISN'T THAT A SHAME.
IT'S GETTING LATE. YOU SHOULD GET SOME REST.
KICKING ME OUT?
PEOPLE TO SEE, THINGS TO DO. A GIRL NEEDS HER BEAUTY SLEEP.
RIGHT...
HAVE A GOOD NIGHT, MOM.

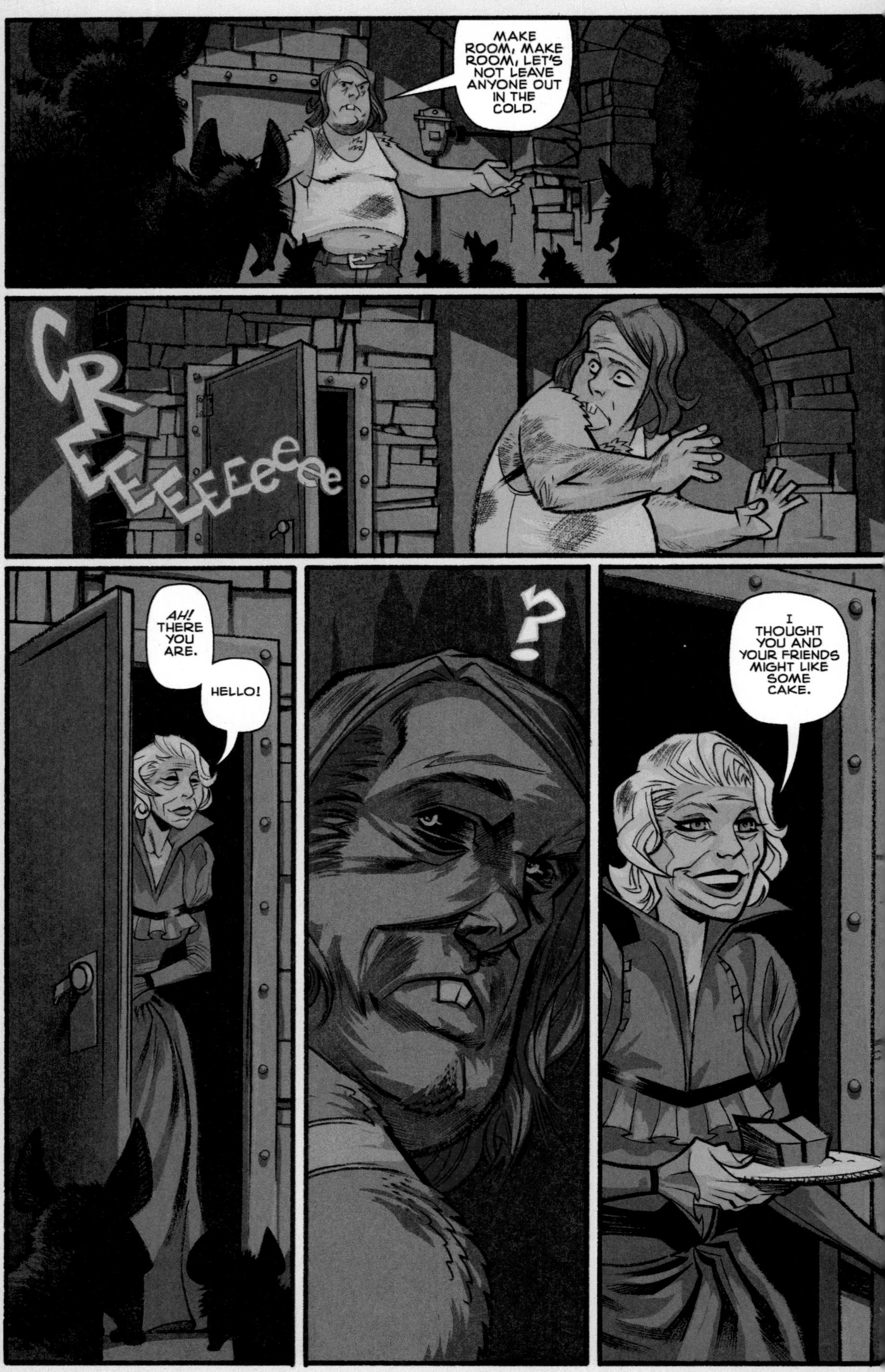
MAKE ROOM, MAKE ROOM, LET'S NOT LEAVE ANYONE OUT IN THE COLD.
CREEEEEeeeee
AH! THERE YOU ARE.
HELLO!
?
I THOUGHT YOU AND YOUR FRIENDS MIGHT LIKE SOME CAKE.

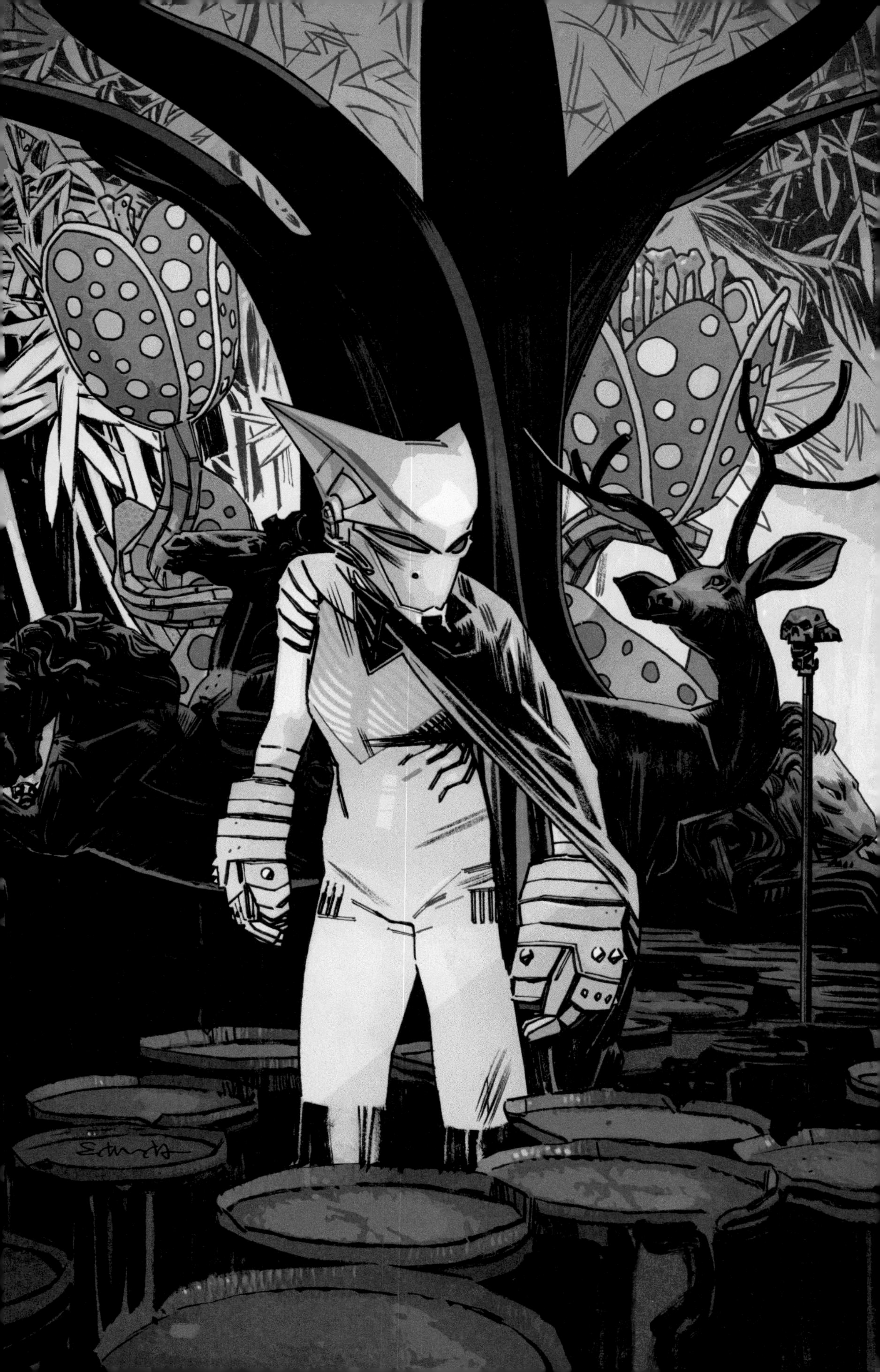

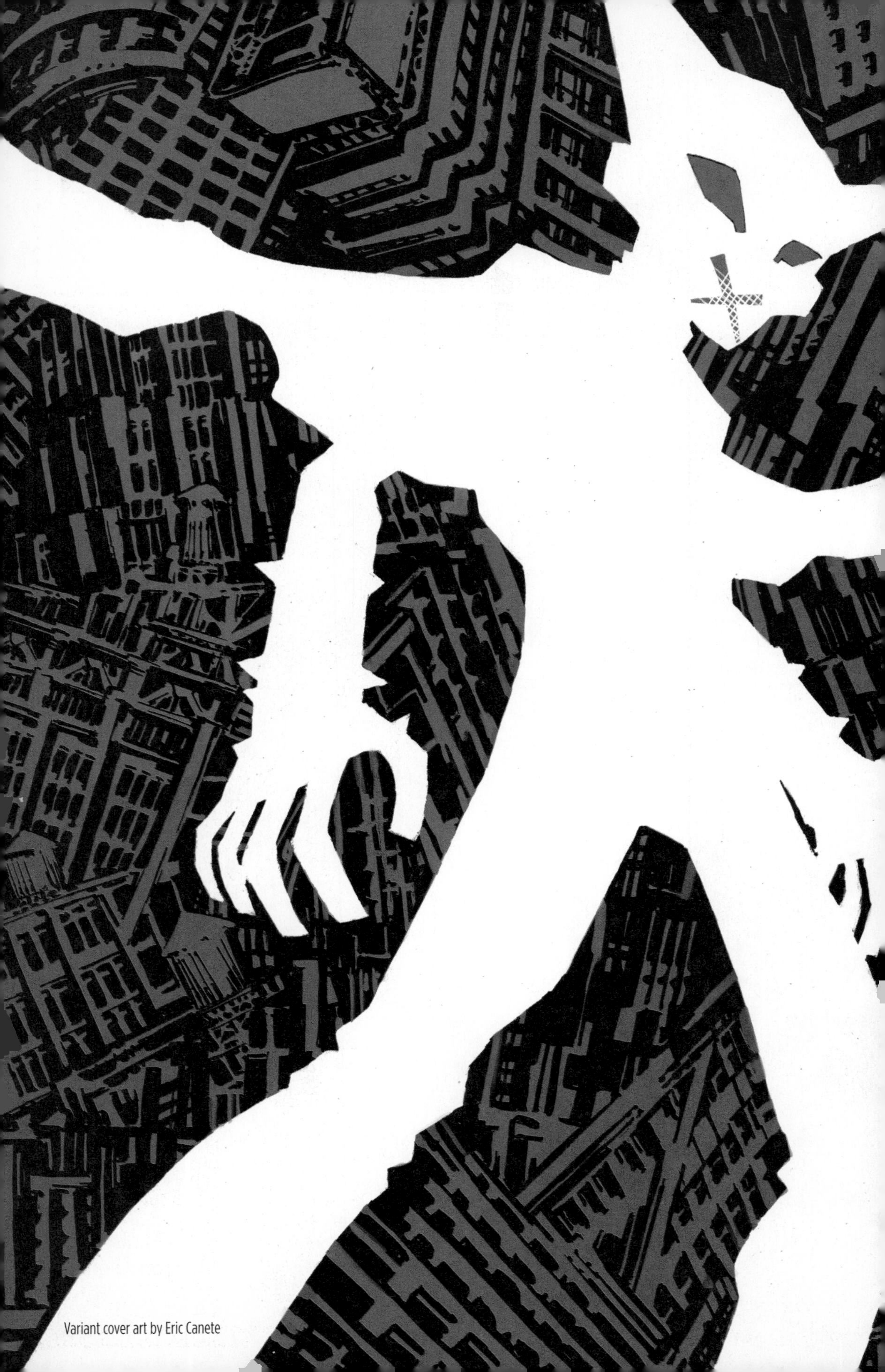

Variant cover art by Eric Canete

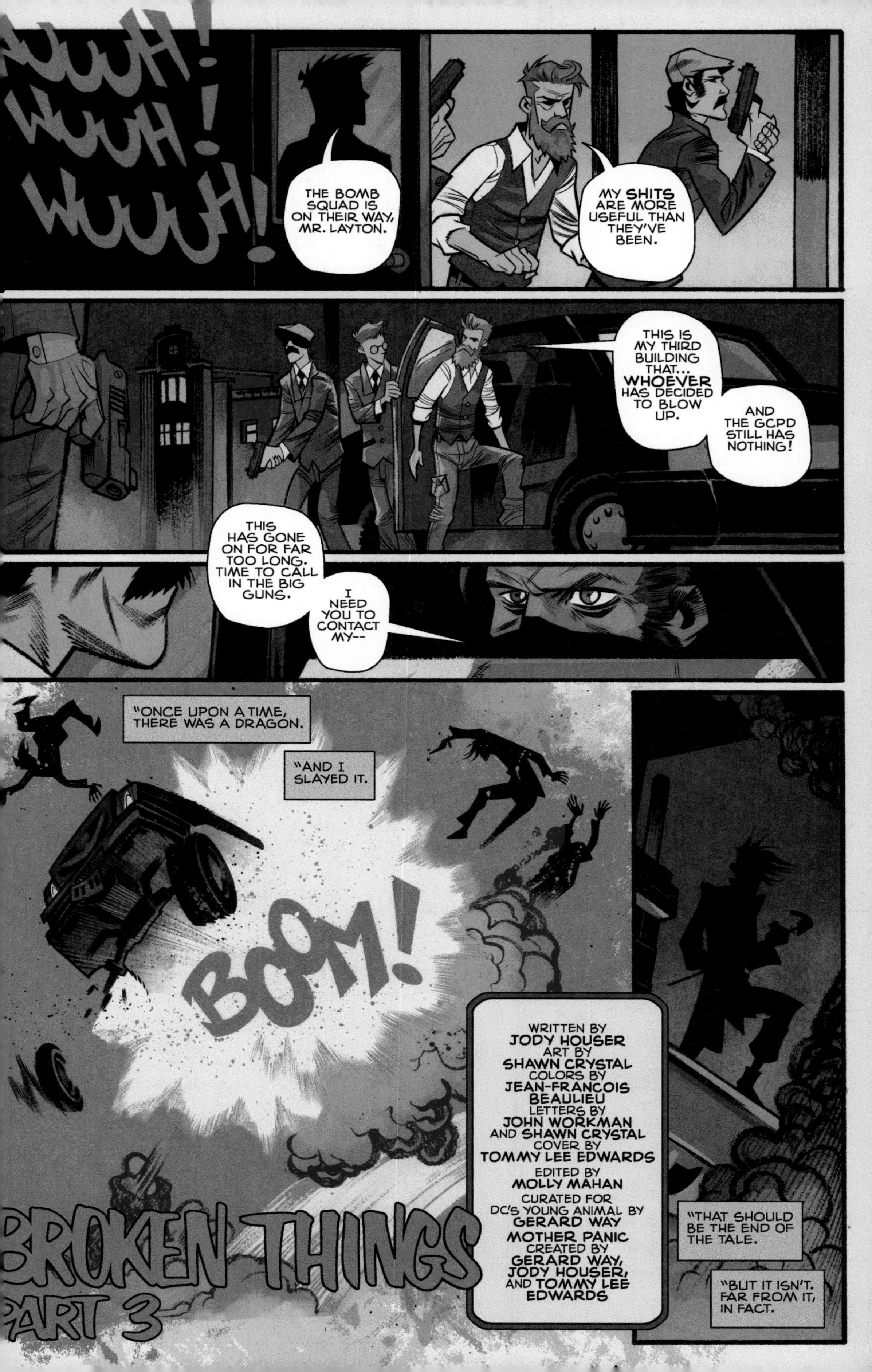
WUUUH! WUUH! WUUUH!
THE BOMB SQUAD IS ON THEIR WAY, MR. LAYTON.
MY SHITS ARE MORE USEFUL THAN THEY'VE BEEN.
THIS IS MY THIRD BUILDING THAT... WHOEVER HAS DECIDED TO BLOW UP.
AND THE GCPD STILL HAS NOTHING!
THIS HAS GONE ON FOR FAR TOO LONG. TIME TO CALL IN THE BIG GUNS.
I NEED YOU TO CONTACT MY--
"ONCE UPON A TIME, THERE WAS A DRAGON.
"AND I SLAYED IT.
BOOM!
WRITTEN BY JODY HOUSER ART BY SHAWN CRYSTAL COLORS BY JEAN-FRANCOIS BEAULIEU LETTERS BY JOHN WORKMAN AND SHAWN CRYSTAL COVER BY TOMMY LEE EDWARDS EDITED BY MOLLY MAHAN CURATED FOR DC'S YOUNG ANIMAL BY GERARD WAY MOTHER PANIC CREATED BY GERARD WAY, JODY HOUSER, AND TOMMY LEE EDWARDS
BROKEN THINGS PART 3
"THAT SHOULD BE THE END OF THE TALE.
"BUT IT ISN'T. FAR FROM IT, IN FACT.

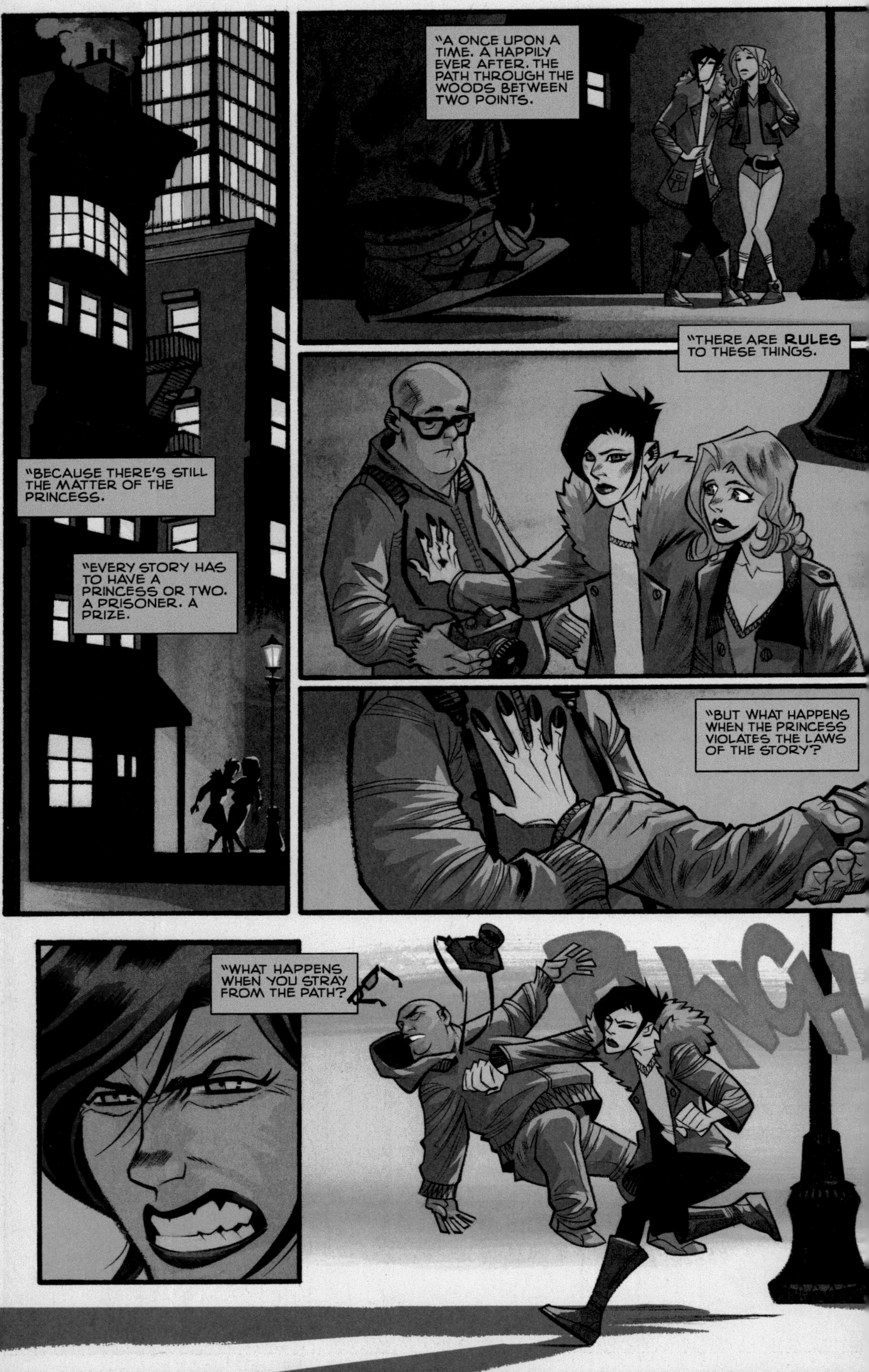
"A ONCE UPON A TIME. A HAPPILY EVER AFTER. THE PATH THROUGH THE WOODS BETWEEN TWO POINTS.
"BECAUSE THERE'S STILL THE MATTER OF THE PRINCESS.
"EVERY STORY HAS TO HAVE A PRINCESS OR TWO. A PRISONER. A PRIZE.
"THERE ARE RULES TO THESE THINGS.
"BUT WHAT HAPPENS WHEN THE PRINCESS VIOLATES THE LAWS OF THE STORY?
"WHAT HAPPENS WHEN YOU STRAY FROM THE PATH?

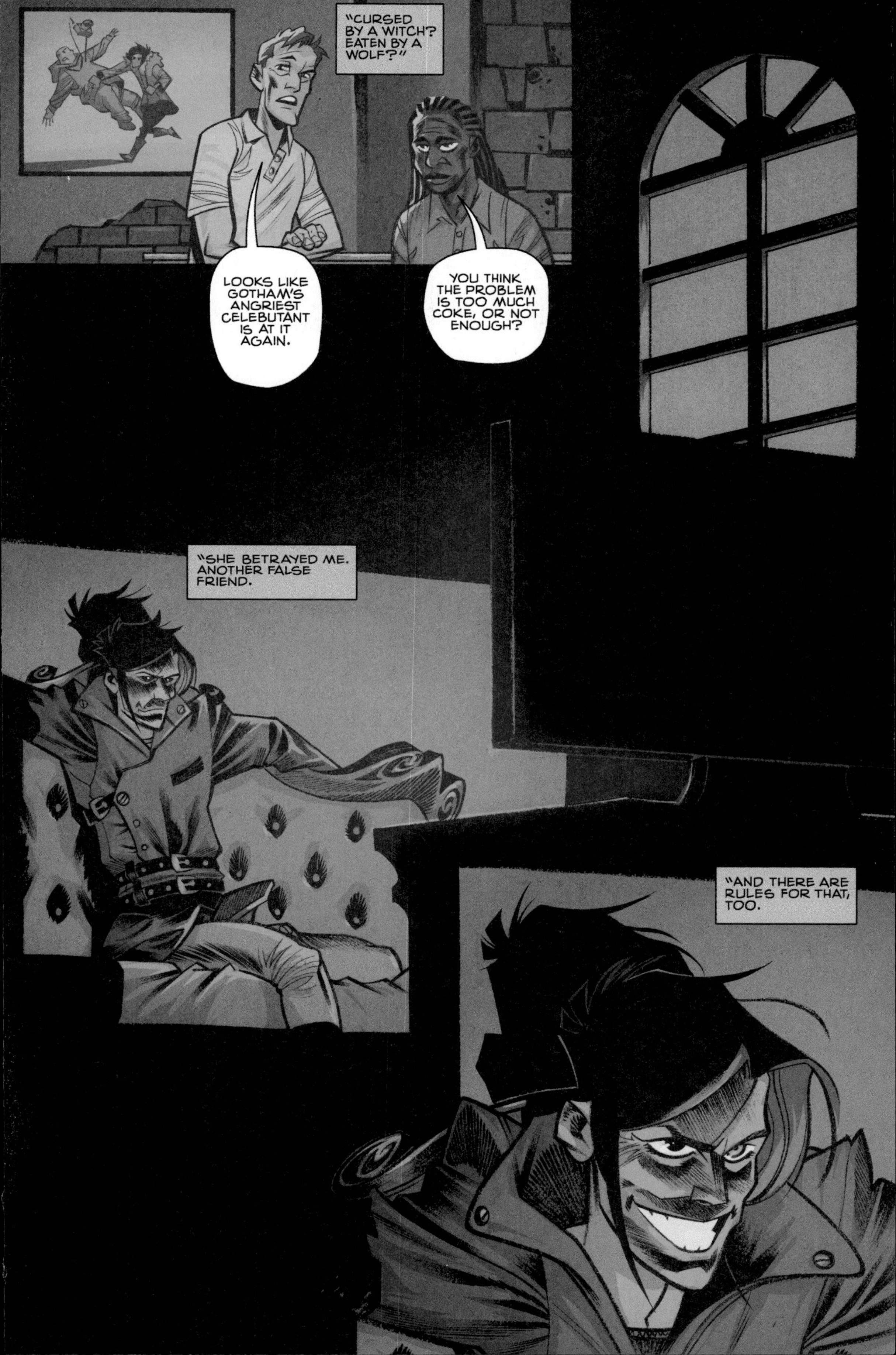
"CURSED BY A WITCH? EATEN BY A WOLF?"
LOOKS LIKE GOTHAM'S ANGRIEST CELEBUTANT IS AT IT AGAIN.
YOU THINK THE PROBLEM IS TOO MUCH COKE, OR NOT ENOUGH?
"SHE BETRAYED ME. ANOTHER FALSE FRIEND.
"AND THERE ARE RULES FOR THAT, TOO.

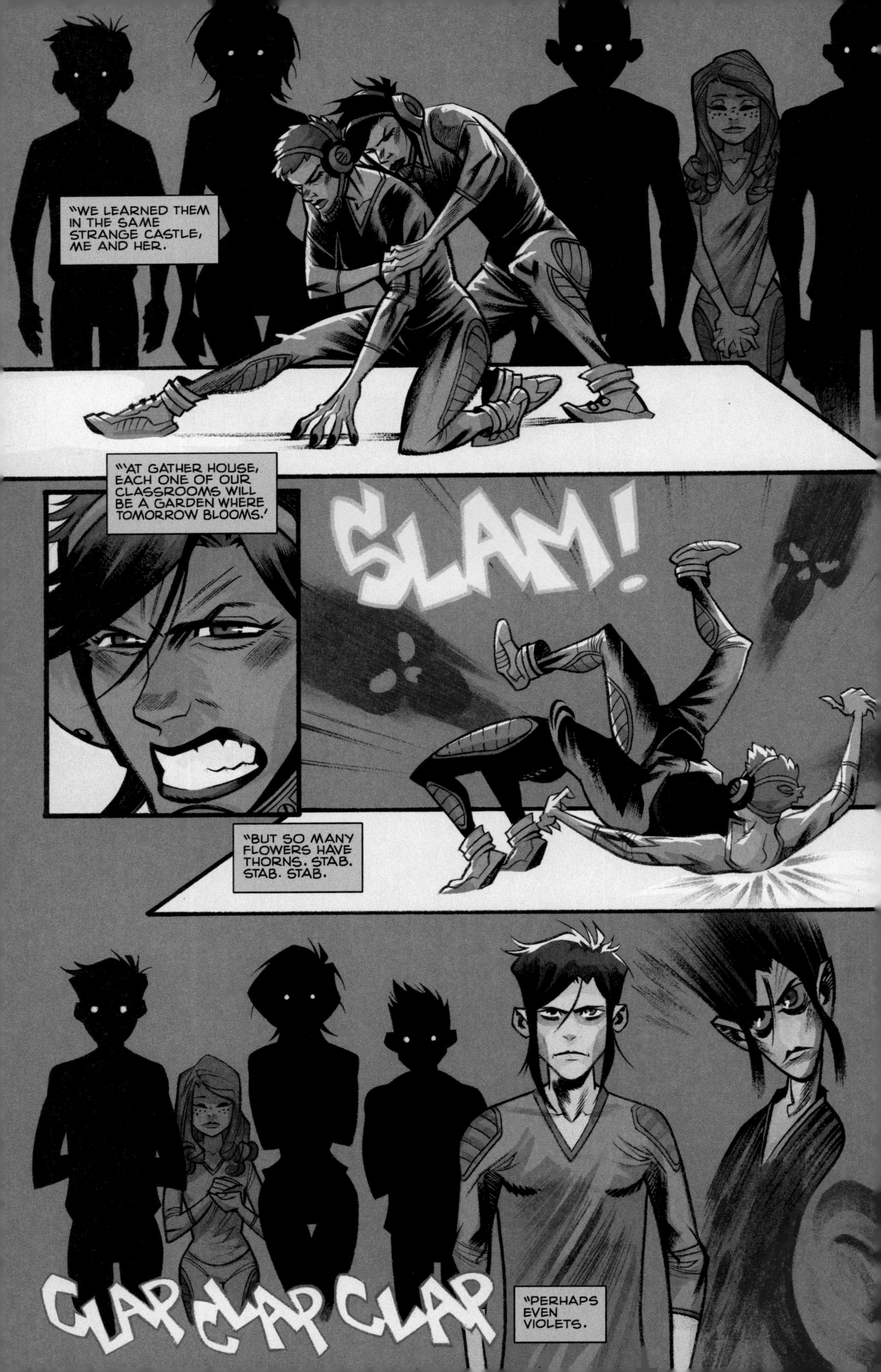
"WE LEARNED THEM IN THE SAME STRANGE CASTLE, ME AND HER.
"AT GATHER HOUSE, EACH ONE OF OUR CLASSROOMS WILL BE A GARDEN WHERE TOMORROW BLOOMS.'
SLAM!
"BUT SO MANY FLOWERS HAVE THORNS. STAB. STAB. STAB.
CLAP CLAP CLAP
"PERHAPS EVEN VIOLETS.

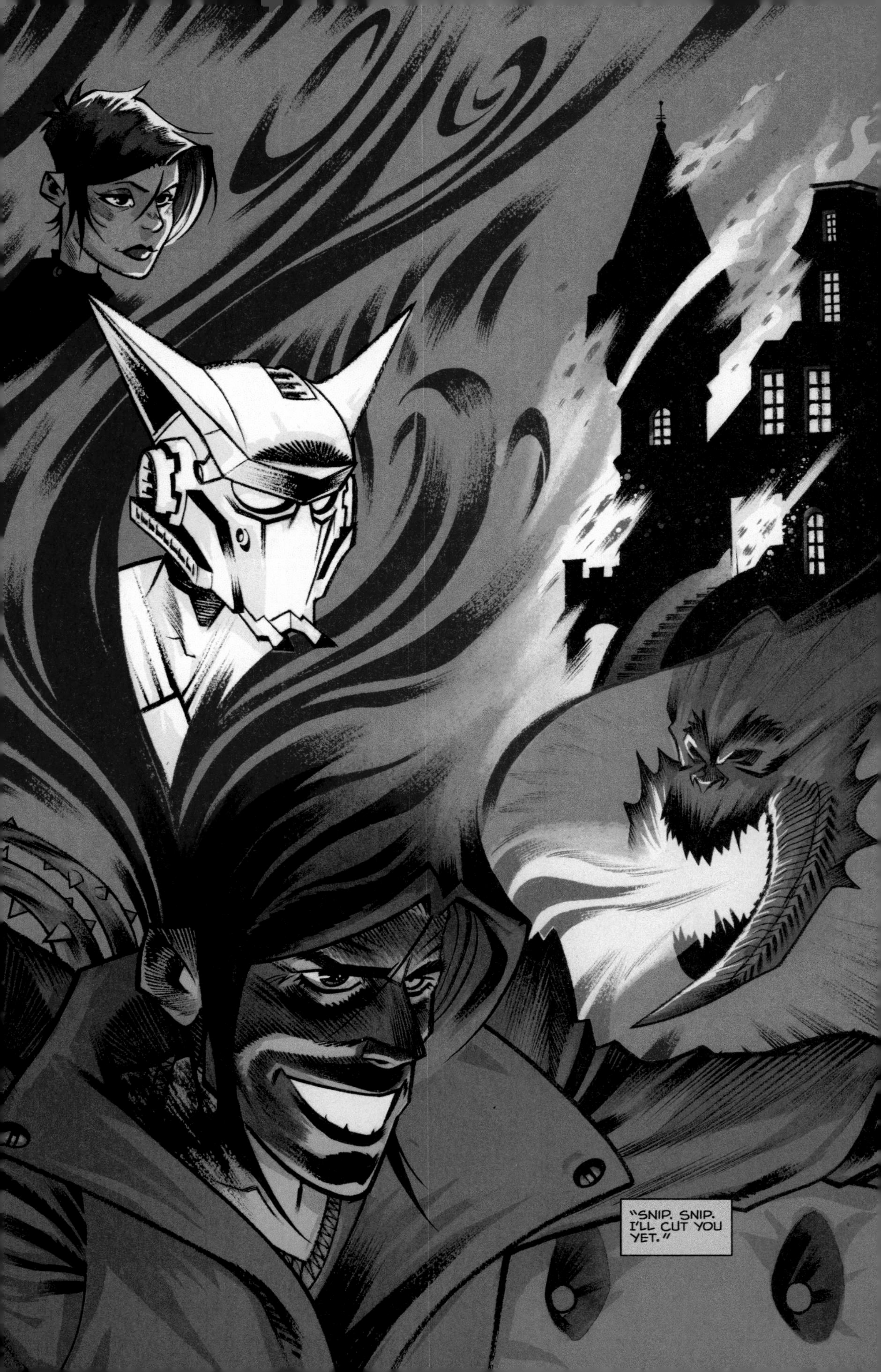
"SNIP. SNIP. I'LL CUT YOU YET."

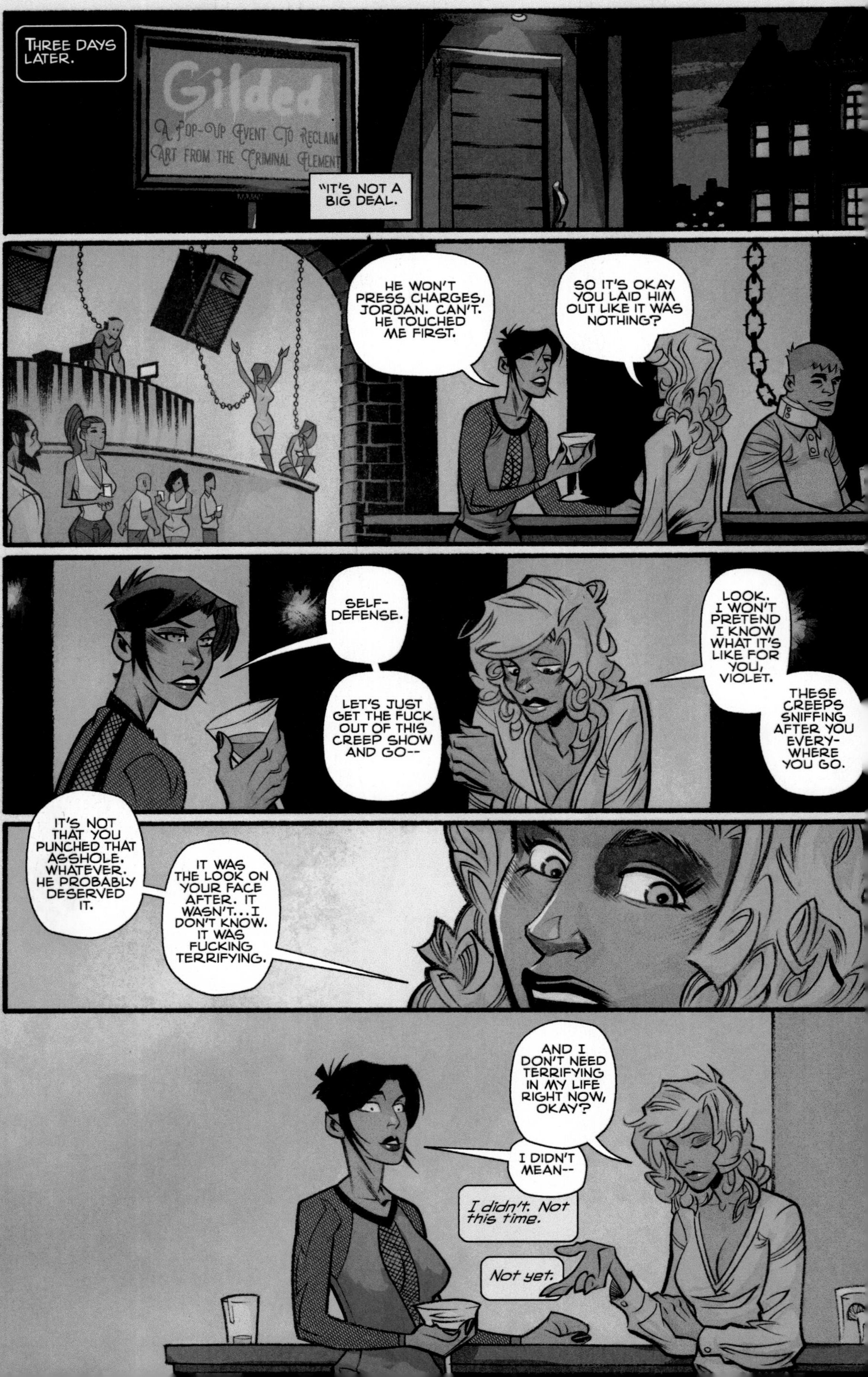
THREE DAYS LATER.
Gilded
A POP-UP EVENT TO RECLAIM ART FROM THE CRIMINAL ELEMENT
"IT'S NOT A BIG DEAL.
HE WON'T PRESS CHARGES, JORDAN. CAN'T. HE TOUCHED ME FIRST.
SO IT'S OKAY YOU LAID HIM OUT LIKE IT WAS NOTHING?
SELF-DEFENSE.
LET'S JUST GET THE FUCK OUT OF THIS CREEP SHOW AND GO--
LOOK. I WON'T PRETEND I KNOW WHAT IT'S LIKE FOR YOU, VIOLET.
THESE CREEPS SNIFFING AFTER YOU EVERY-WHERE YOU GO.
IT'S NOT THAT YOU PUNCHED THAT ASSHOLE. WHATEVER. HE PROBABLY DESERVED IT.
IT WAS THE LOOK ON YOUR FACE AFTER. IT WASN'T...I DON'T KNOW. IT WAS FUCKING TERRIFYING.
AND I DON'T NEED TERRIFYING IN MY LIFE RIGHT NOW, OKAY?
I DIDN'T MEAN--
*I didn't. Not this time.*
*Not yet.*

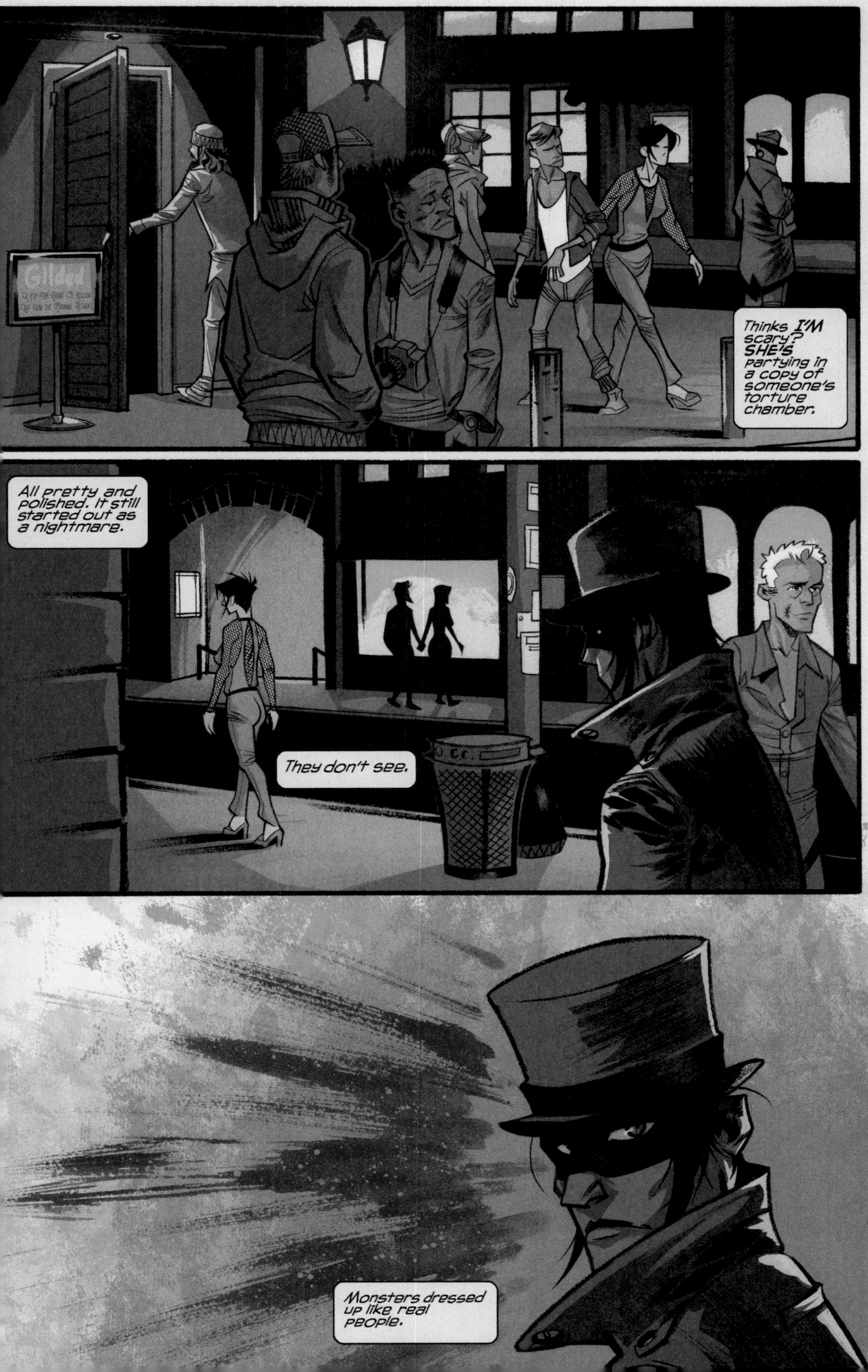
Gilded
Thinks I'M scary? SHE'S partying in a copy of someone's torture chamber.
All pretty and polished. It still started out as a nightmare.
They don't see.
Monsters dressed up like real people.

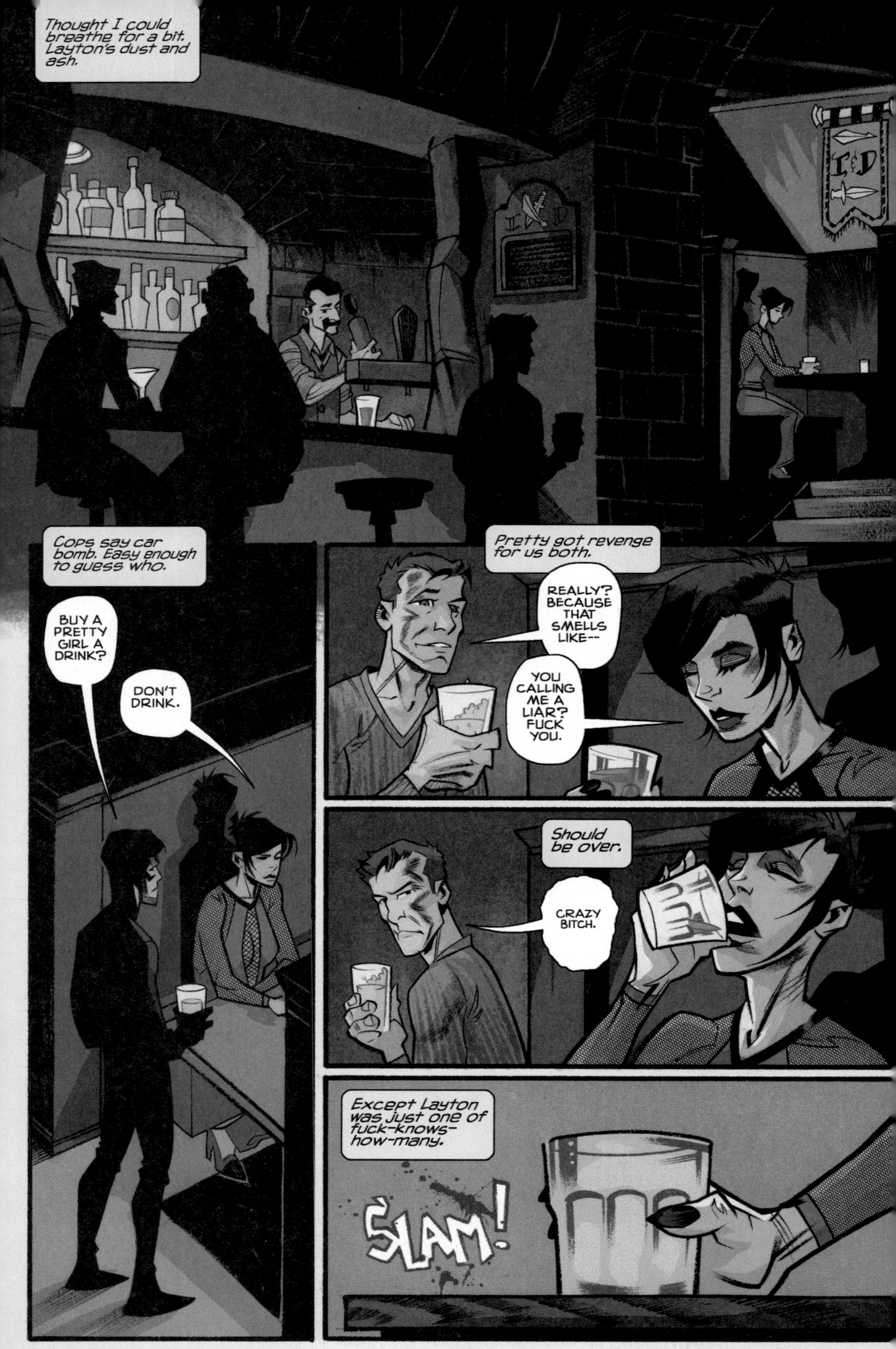
Thought I could breathe for a bit. Layton's dust and ash.
Cops say car bomb. Easy enough to guess who.
BUY A PRETTY GIRL A DRINK?
DON'T DRINK.
Pretty got revenge for us both.
REALLY? BECAUSE THAT SMELLS LIKE--
YOU CALLING ME A LIAR? FUCK YOU.
Should be over.
CRAZY BITCH.
Except Layton was just one of fuck-knows-how-many.
SLAM!

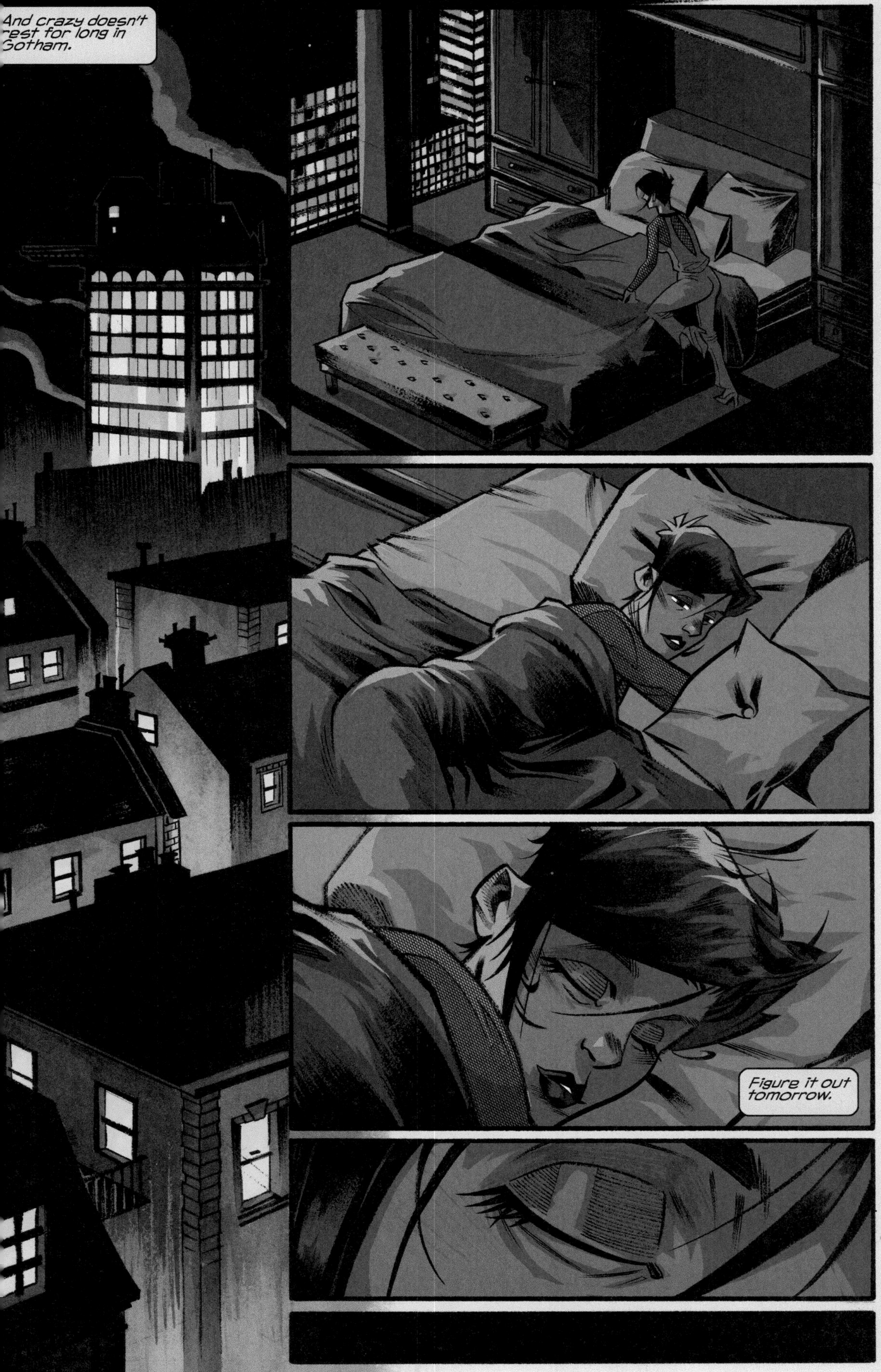
And crazy doesn't rest for long in Gotham.
Figure it out tomorrow.

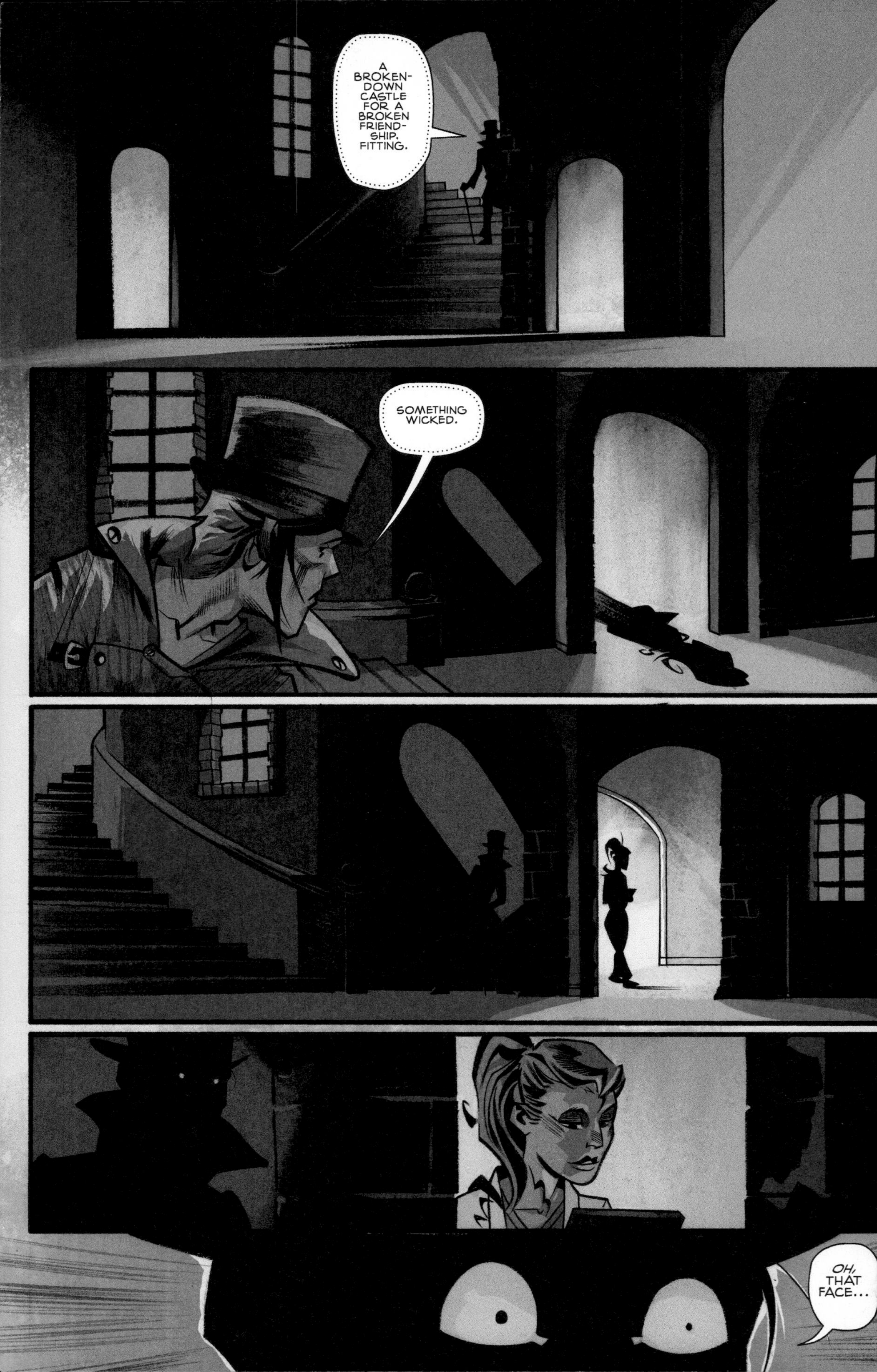
A BROKEN-DOWN CASTLE FOR A BROKEN FRIENDSHIP. FITTING.
SOMETHING WICKED.
OH, THAT FACE...

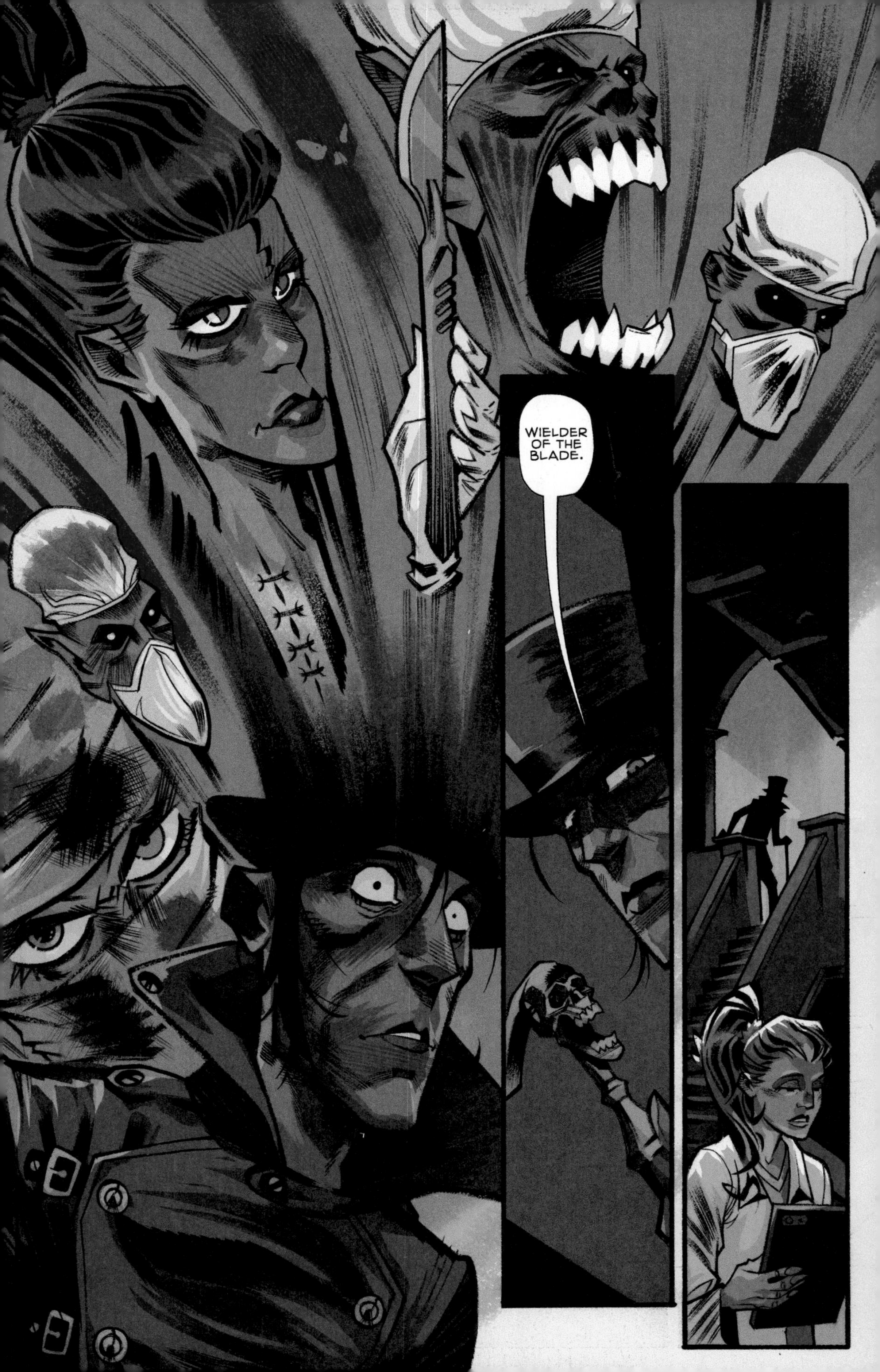
WIELDER OF THE BLADE.

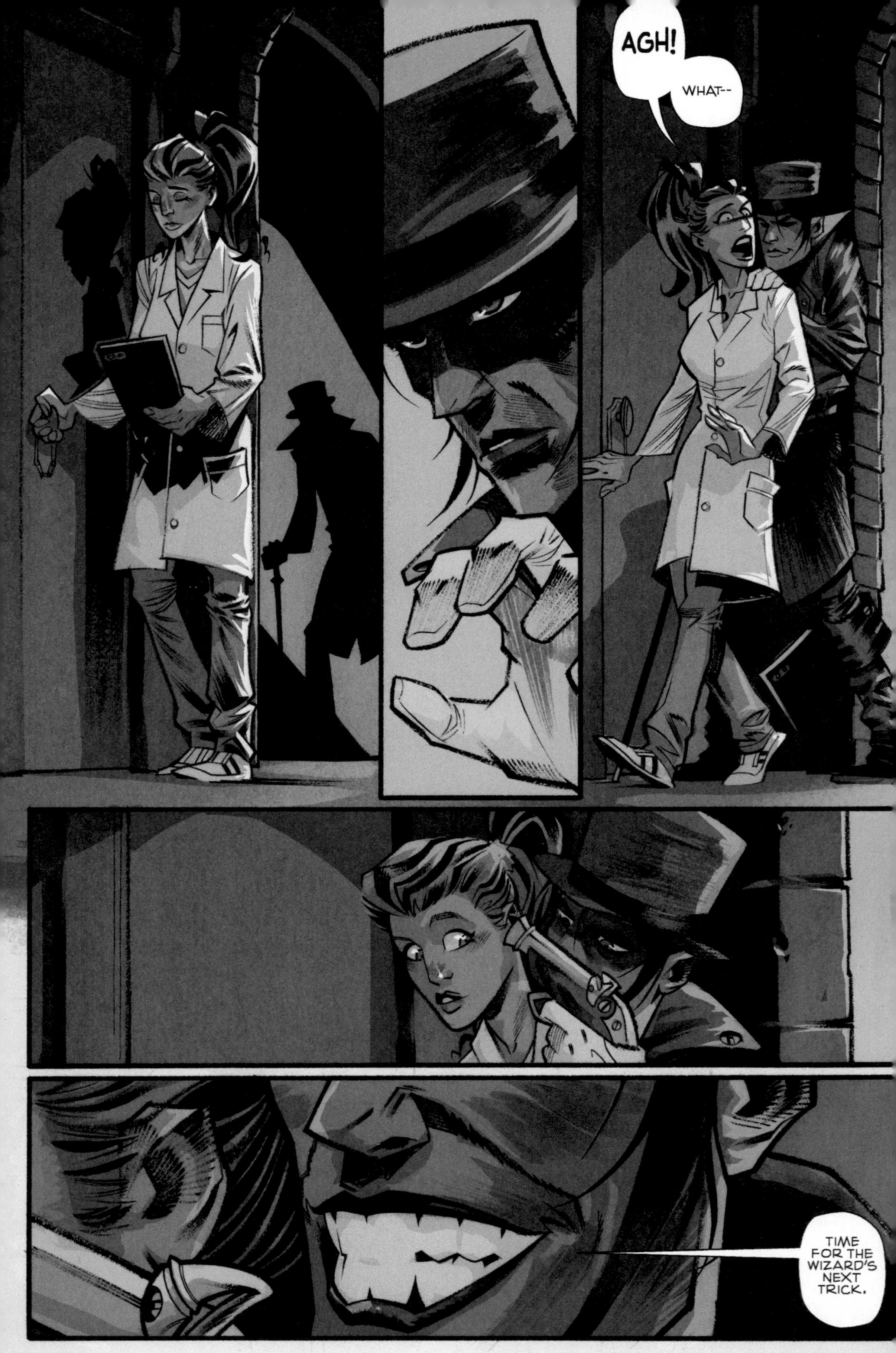
AGH!
WHAT--
TIME FOR THE WIZARD'S NEXT TRICK.

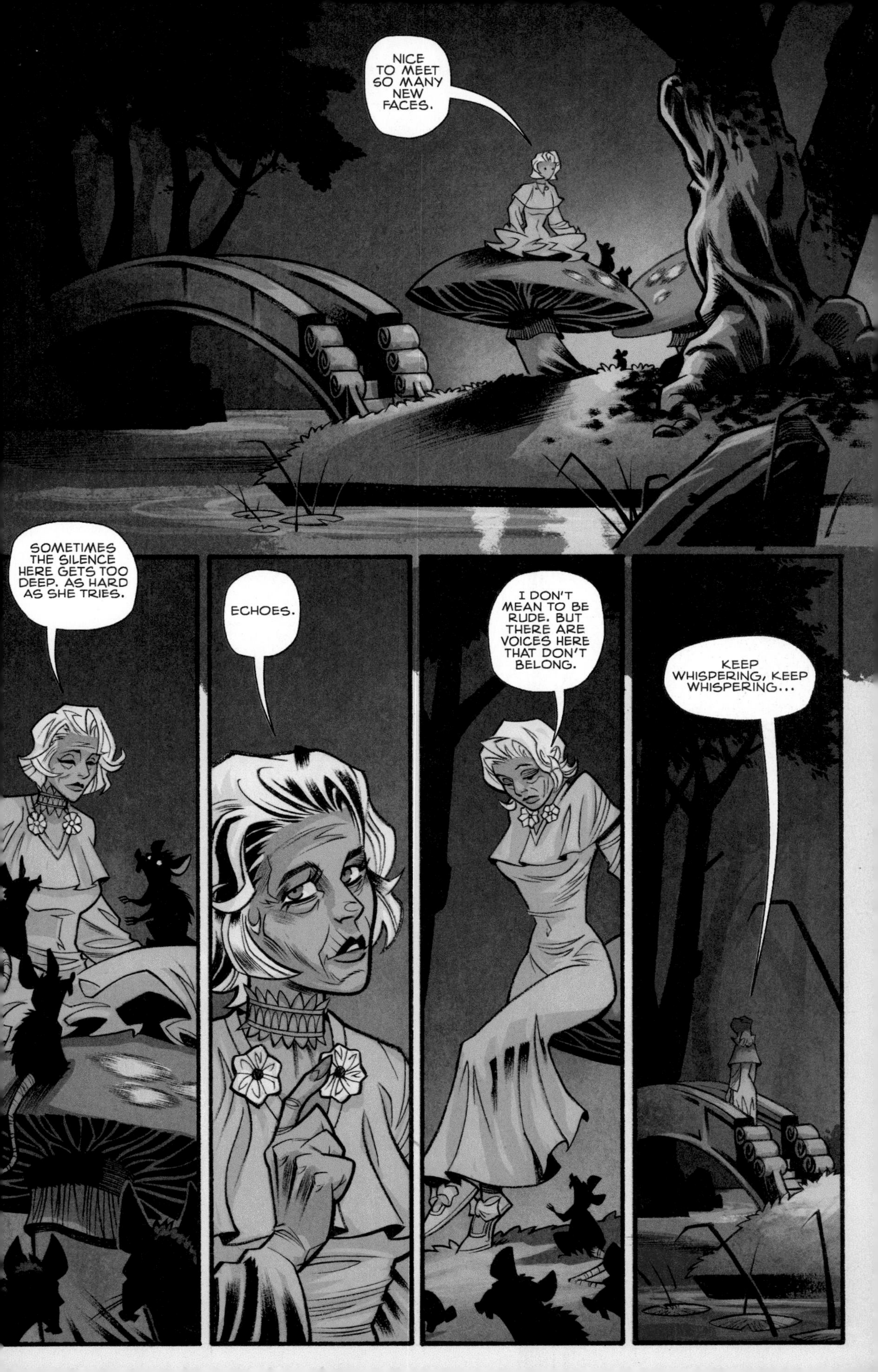
NICE TO MEET SO MANY NEW FACES.
SOMETIMES THE SILENCE HERE GETS TOO DEEP. AS HARD AS SHE TRIES.
ECHOES.
I DON'T MEAN TO BE RUDE. BUT THERE ARE VOICES HERE THAT DON'T BELONG.
KEEP WHISPERING, KEEP WHISPERING...

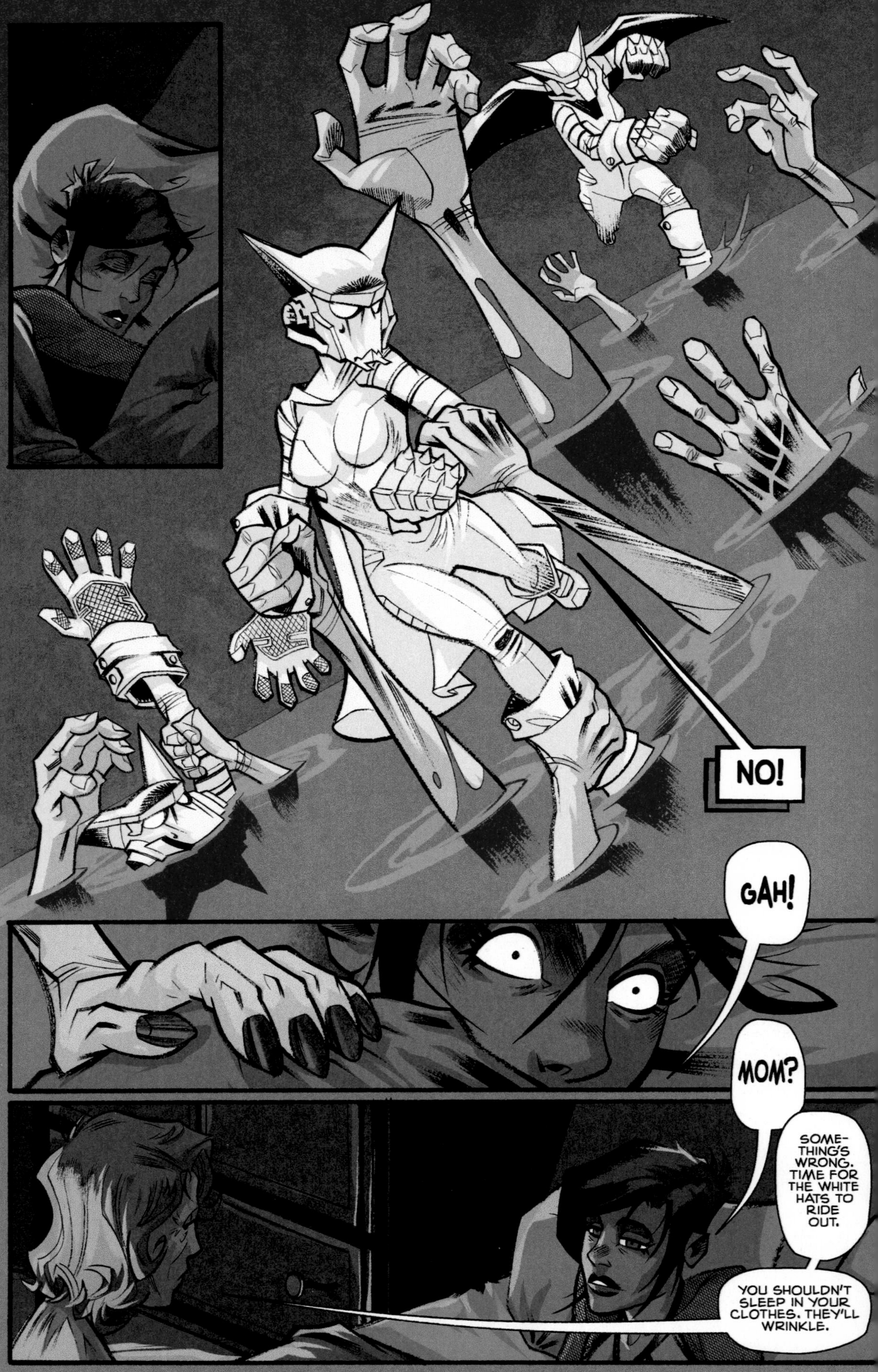
NO!
GAH!
MOM?
SOME-THING'S WRONG. TIME FOR THE WHITE HATS TO RIDE OUT.
YOU SHOULDN'T SLEEP IN YOUR CLOTHES. THEY'LL WRINKLE.

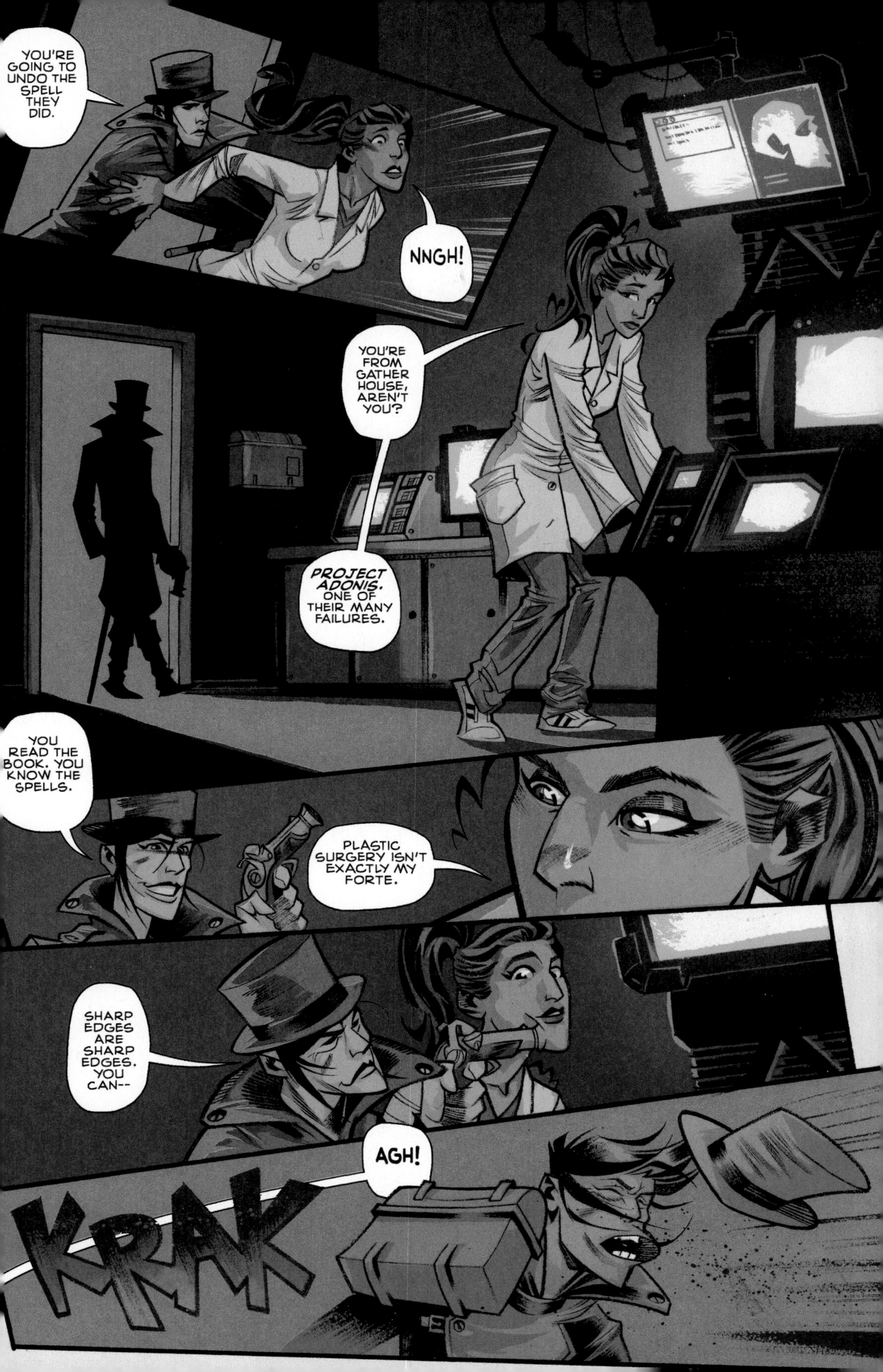
YOU'RE GOING TO UNDO THE SPELL THEY DID.
NNGH!
YOU'RE FROM GATHER HOUSE, AREN'T YOU?
*PROJECT ADONIS.* ONE OF THEIR MANY FAILURES.
YOU READ THE BOOK. YOU KNOW THE SPELLS.
PLASTIC SURGERY ISN'T EXACTLY MY FORTE.
SHARP EDGES ARE SHARP EDGES. YOU CAN--
AGH!
KRAK

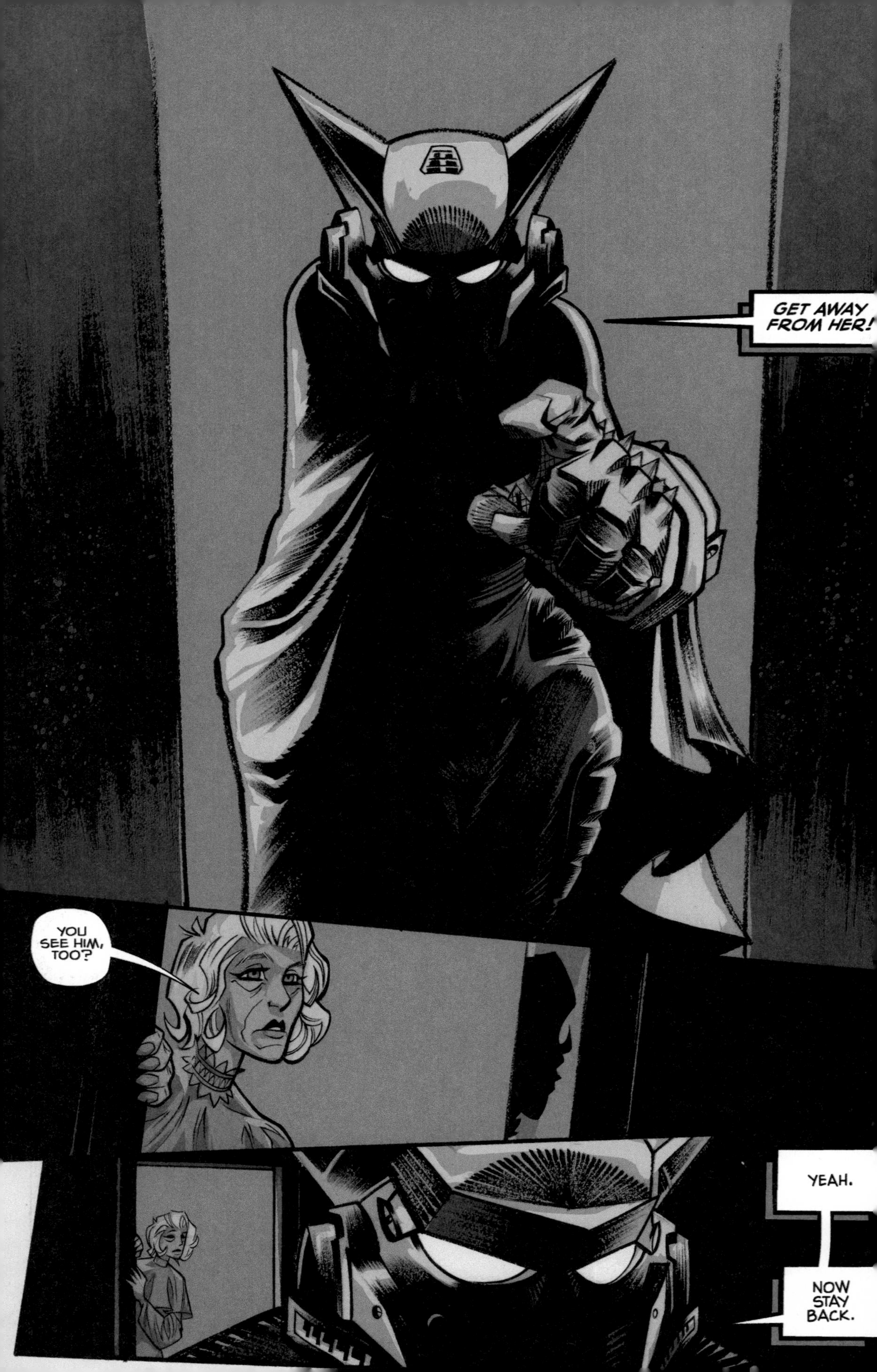
GET AWAY FROM HER!
YOU SEE HIM, TOO?
YEAH.
NOW STAY BACK.

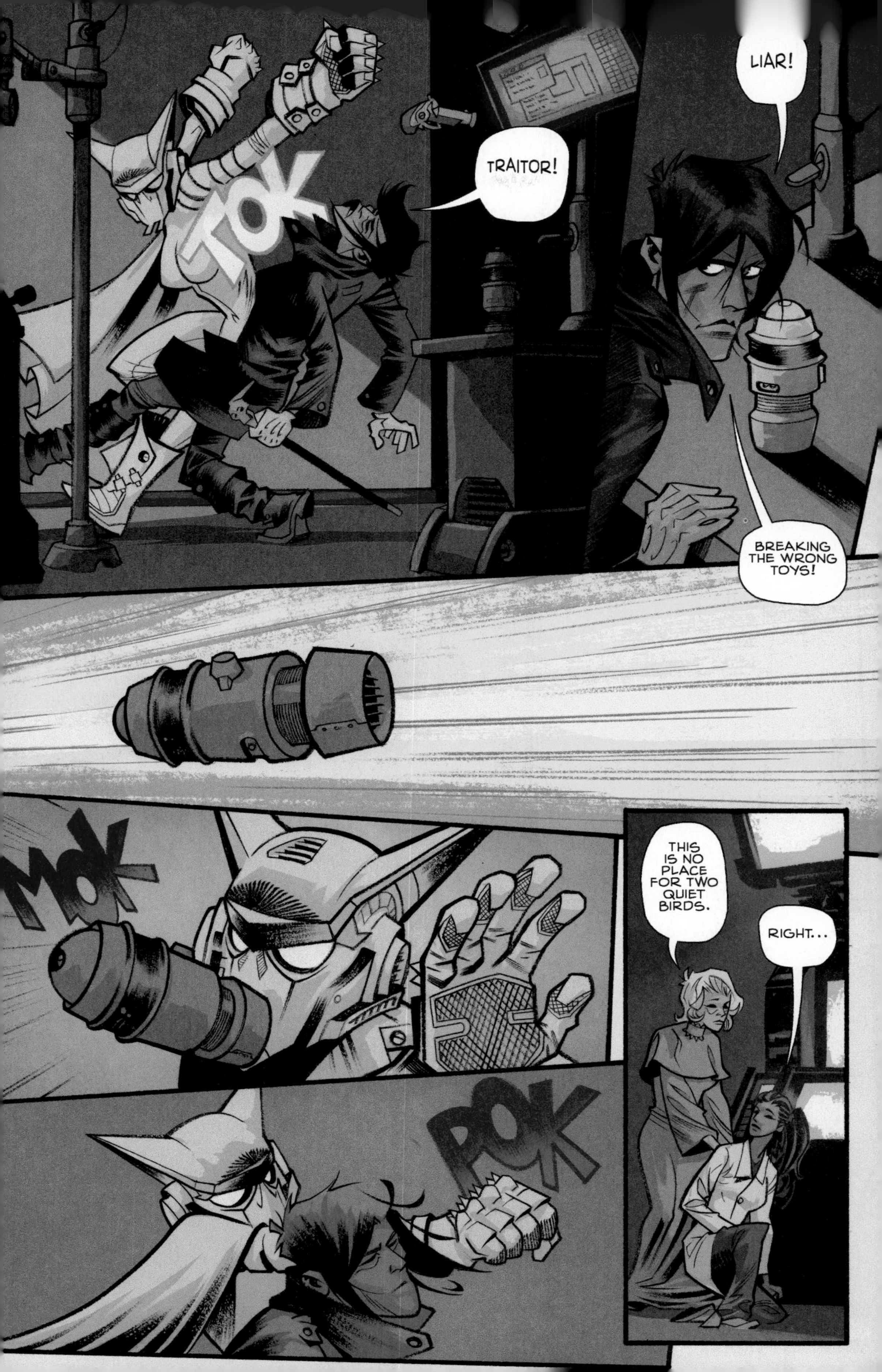
TOK
TRAITOR!
LIAR!
BREAKING THE WRONG TOYS!
MOK
THIS IS NO PLACE FOR TWO QUIET BIRDS.
RIGHT...
POK

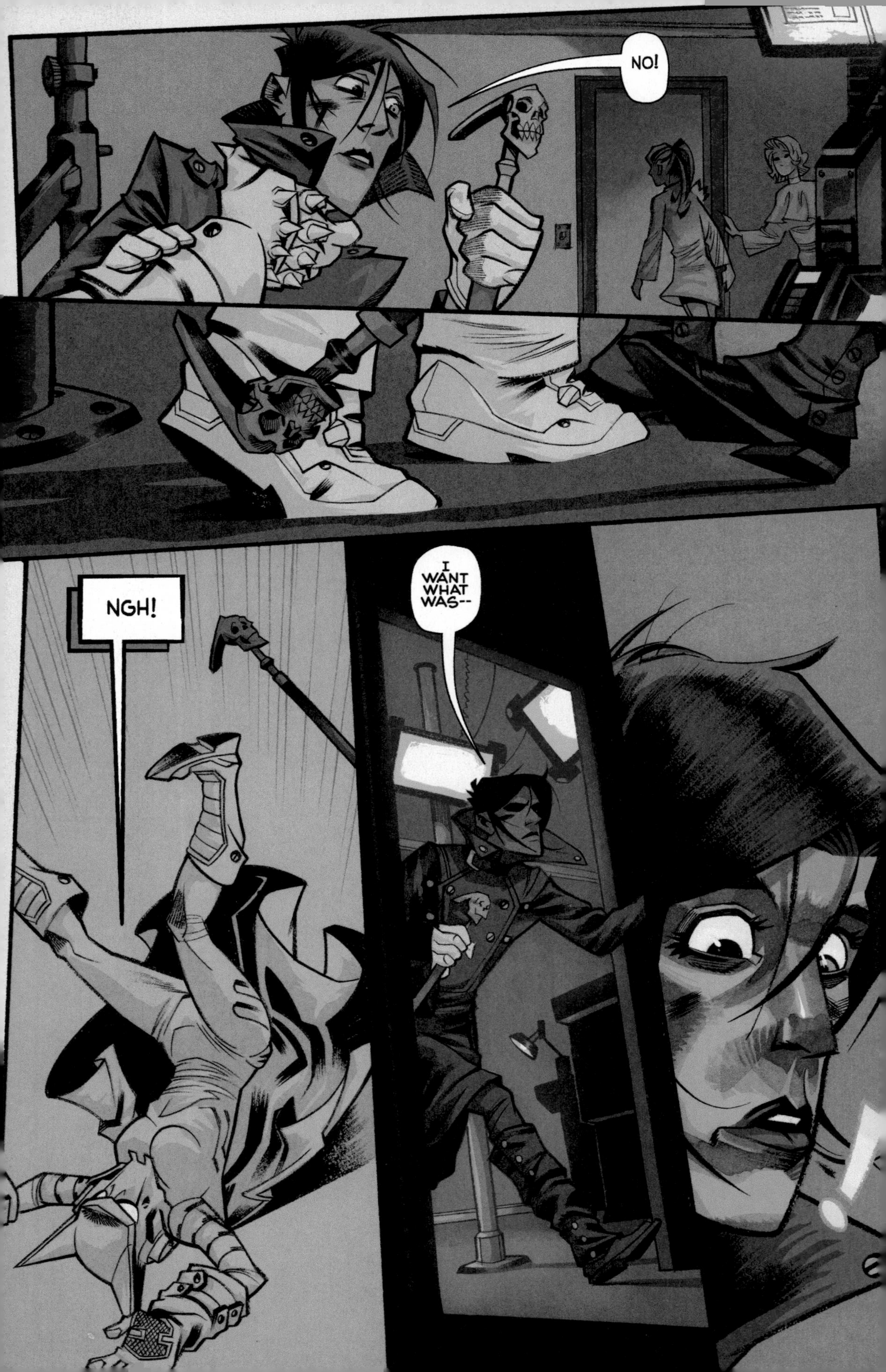
NO!
NGH!
I WANT WHAT WAS--

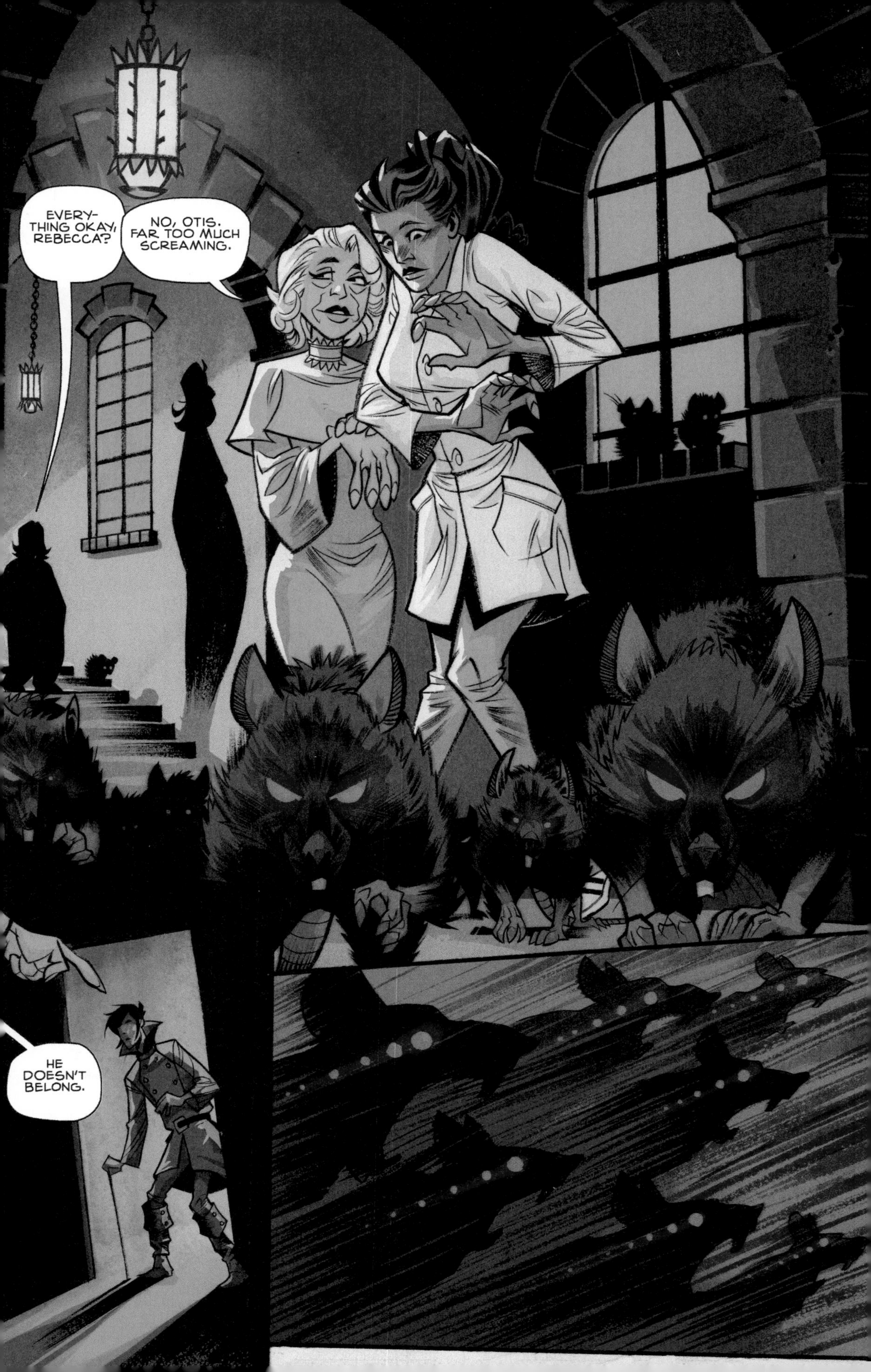
EVERYTHING OKAY, REBECCA?
NO, OTIS. FAR TOO MUCH SCREAMING.
HE DOESN'T BELONG.

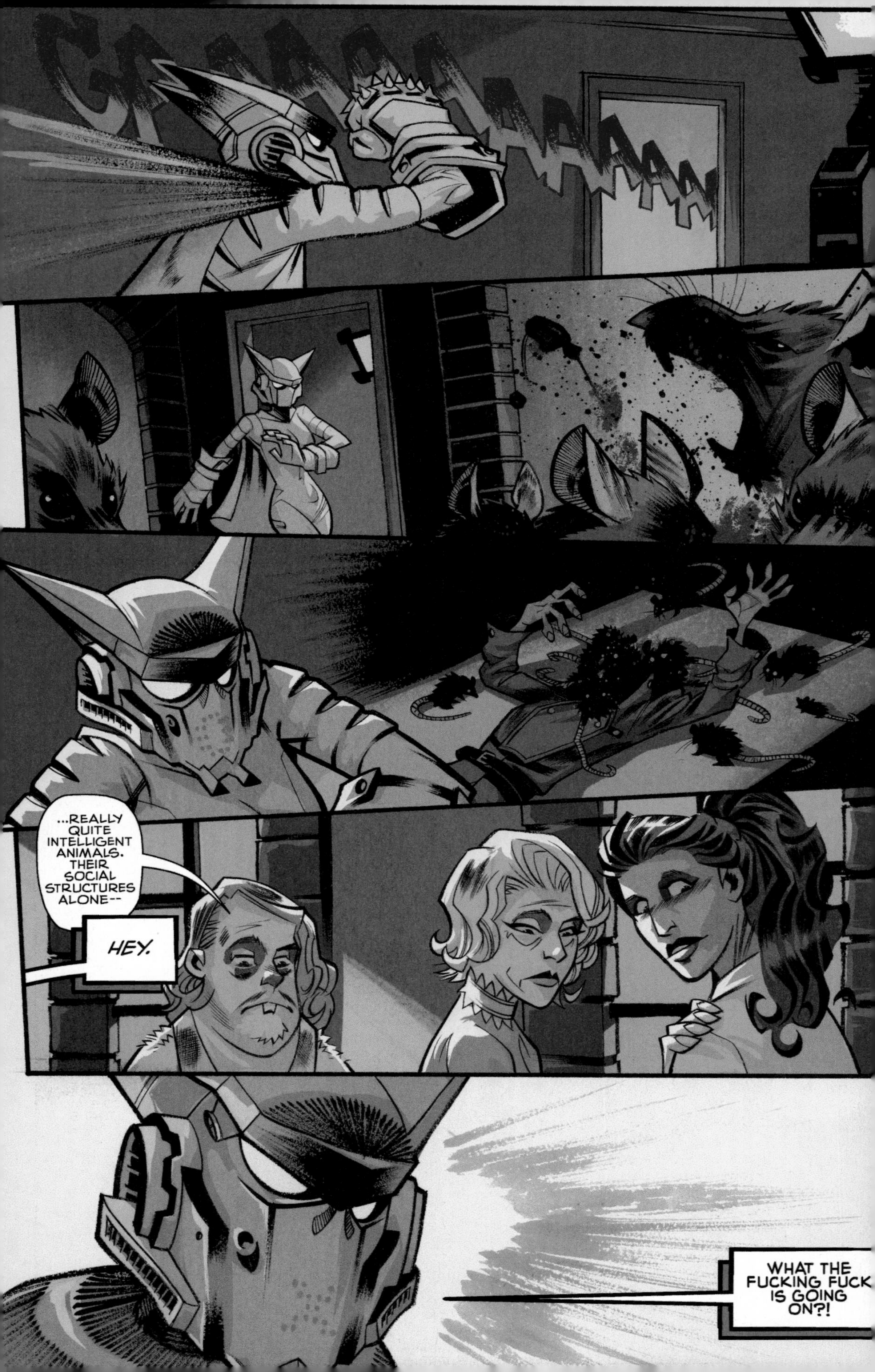
...REALLY QUITE INTELLIGENT ANIMALS. THEIR SOCIAL STRUCTURES ALONE--
HEY.
WHAT THE FUCKING FUCK IS GOING ON?!

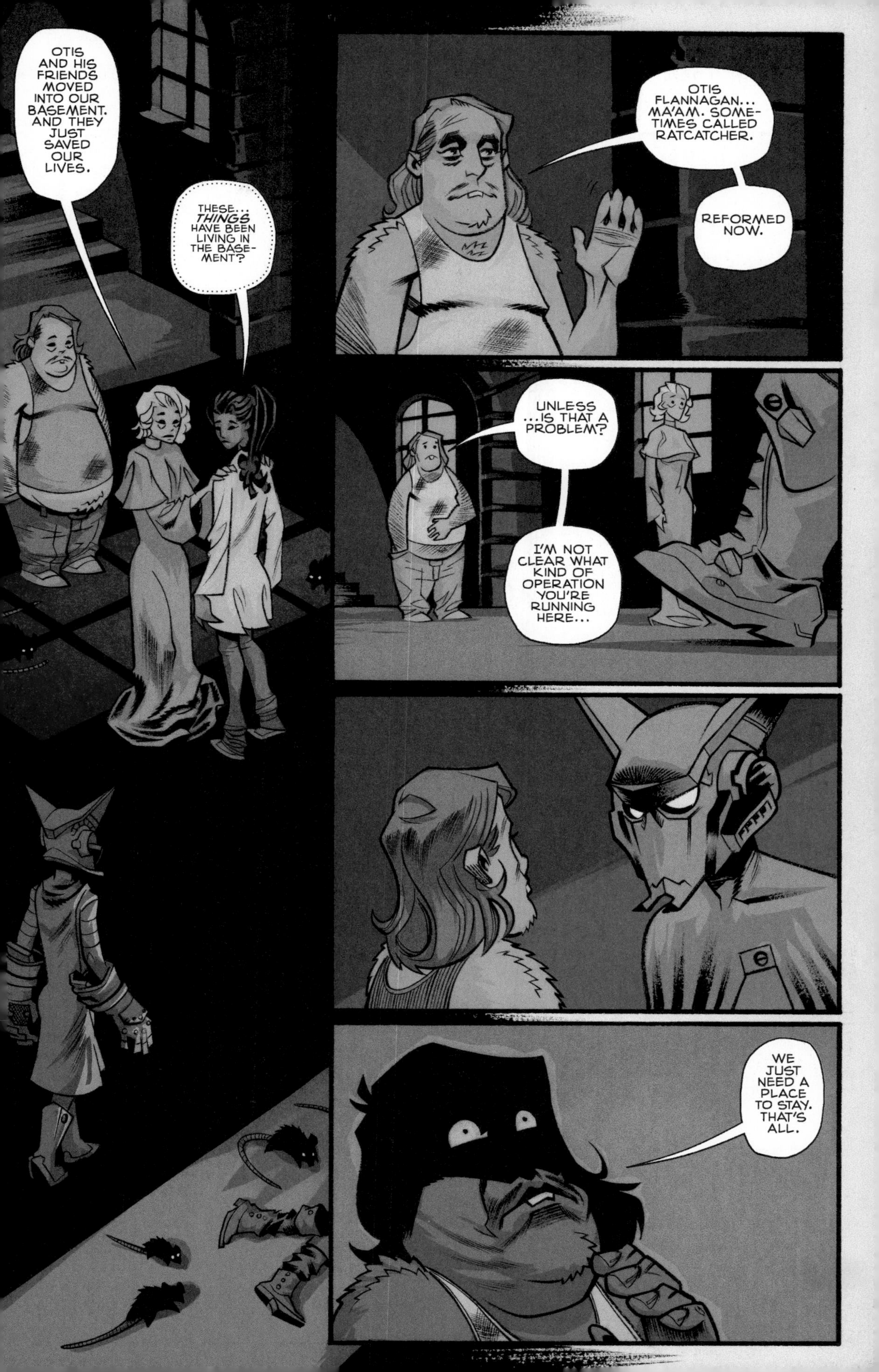
OTIS AND HIS FRIENDS MOVED INTO OUR BASEMENT. AND THEY JUST SAVED OUR LIVES.
THESE... THINGS HAVE BEEN LIVING IN THE BASE-MENT?
OTIS FLANNAGAN... MA'AM. SOME-TIMES CALLED RATCATCHER.
REFORMED NOW.
UNLESS ...IS THAT A PROBLEM?
I'M NOT CLEAR WHAT KIND OF OPERATION YOU'RE RUNNING HERE...
WE JUST NEED A PLACE TO STAY. THAT'S ALL.

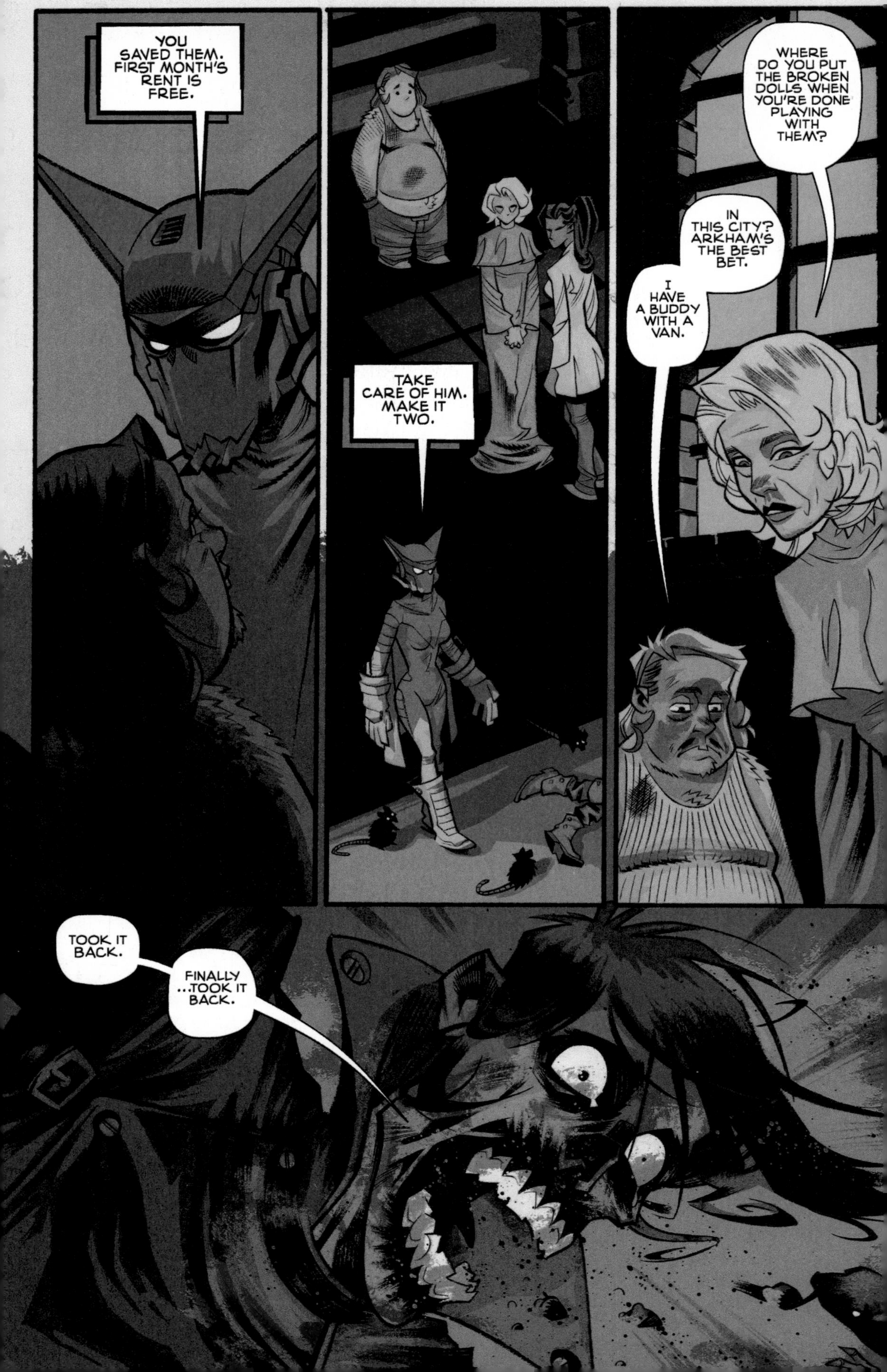
YOU SAVED THEM. FIRST MONTH'S RENT IS FREE.
TAKE CARE OF HIM. MAKE IT TWO.
WHERE DO YOU PUT THE BROKEN DOLLS WHEN YOU'RE DONE PLAYING WITH THEM?
IN THIS CITY? ARKHAM'S THE BEST BET.
I HAVE A BUDDY WITH A VAN.
TOOK IT BACK.
FINALLY ...TOOK IT BACK.

What you're holdi
It is, technically, t
under the Young
are working on th
would be great to
been up to since
City Comicon.

This throws back
of the past, becau
Young Animal as
liberty of updating
our collective per
contained inspira

# AFTERWORD By **Gerard Way**

The concept of Mother Panic started as a couple of scribbles in a notebook while waiting in a dentist's office. The character went on to be co-created and fully realized by Jody Houser, Tommy Lee Edwards, and myself, but the initial spark was the result of thinking about Bruce Wayne's playboy persona and what that kind of assumed identity would look like in our current climate, and whether or not it would actually still work as a cover for a superhero.

I thought about Bruce drinking apple juice instead of champagne and about all of the other falsehoods he has to create in order to protect his alter ego, and I wondered what it would be like if the lines were more blurred in terms of what is real and what is deception. What would a current-day celebrity act like and have to deal with while being a vigilante at the same time?

The allure of fame is a dangerous thing. It makes people irrational, detached, and desperate to cling to it when it starts to slip away. Not to lecture you on what you already know, but we are a culture obsessed with celebrities—ever more interested in large personalities

and wealth instead of ability and achievement, fascinated by scandal over substance, living in a scripted non-reality reality broadcast into all of our homes. Tension, friction, combat—this modern kind of celebrity represents more of an ideal lifestyle than an idea itself. Lifestyle worship has always been around, of course, but it seems to be more at the forefront these days—excess is access—and with it comes the media's portrayal of what your body and your life are supposed to look like.

I feel like Violet Paige was created as an answer to all of that. Just as her vigilante persona is an answer to Batman, her overall existence is an answer to Gotham itself. In fact, even though MOTHER PANIC started as a potential creator-owned independent project, it was bringing the character into Gotham that gave us a lot more room to explore all of the nastiness that comes with celebrity status in general and that dark, cold city in particular. There's history there, an old guard that Bruce Wayne and Batman represent, but now there's a new guard stepping up—Gather House, Violet, and the emergence of Mother Panic.

Being in an internationally acknowledged band, I have found myself in some strange places, and the further up the ladder we got, the weirder—and darker—it became. That was something I wanted us to bring to MOTHER PANIC—the darkness, the addiction, the oddity of it all. When you are in a life like that, you have to keep a grip on any normalcy that you came in with, and when you meet like-minded people you have to hold on to them. But you're always in danger of turning a dark corner and losing yourself completely—something else I wanted us to explore. I feel like Violet is locked in that struggle, with the added complication of a developing addiction to pain medication—a problem that is growing in our own world day by day. It's also through Violet's surgical augmentation that we are able to address the growing pressure to possess what is perceived to be an acceptable body. In our world, people become addicted to plastic surgery to make themselves more beautiful, but what if you became addicted to surgery that makes you a more efficient weapon?

Working on this book, even from the sidelines, has been an enlightening experience—one that has allowed me to personally explore the themes of fame and addiction through whatever insights I could provide. But it is Jody Houser, Tommy Lee Edwards, Shawn Crystal, Jean-Francois Beaulieu, and John Workman who have truly formed these stories. Tommy and I initially started talking about and developing the character, discussing everything about her, down to what Violet would wear in her high-profile civilian life—the kind of "I paid $4,000 to look like I spent $20" type of style that you commonly see in Los Angeles. Tommy also spent a great deal of time working out Mother Panic's outfit and building her glider and other pieces of hardware using 3D modeling to make sure they could work in the real world. In terms of her appearance, we wanted a vigilante costume that looked as if it could have been designed by Karl Lagerfeld—high-fashion violence, a witch in white. With the addition of Jody Houser, the book began to solidify further—she added whole new layers to both Violet and Mother Panic. Jody gives a wonderful directness to the way Violet speaks and acts, and she has created a superb supporting cast to accompany her. I am a fan of them both. We all got to witness the magic of John Workman's lettering—a lot of time and care went into making the art and the text work together, and to this day it is some of my favorite lettering. Tommy also brought Shawn Crystal into the fold to take over after issue #3, and his expressive style—together with Jean-Francois' colors—acted as a nice contrast to the first three issues, taking the book in a different but no less impactful direction. Finally, Molly Mahan guides the book in an editorial sense, and she has a very deep understanding of the characters, which is always one of her greatest strengths, along with getting the best work out of her charges. It has been a rewarding collaboration, and I am continuing to learn from absolutely everyone on the team.

I hope that you enjoyed the first volume of MOTHER PANIC, and I hope that you are looking forward to more stories with these characters, because we have a lot of them to tell. It's only going to get darker and uglier from here.

Love, Cristal, and broken glass,

**G**

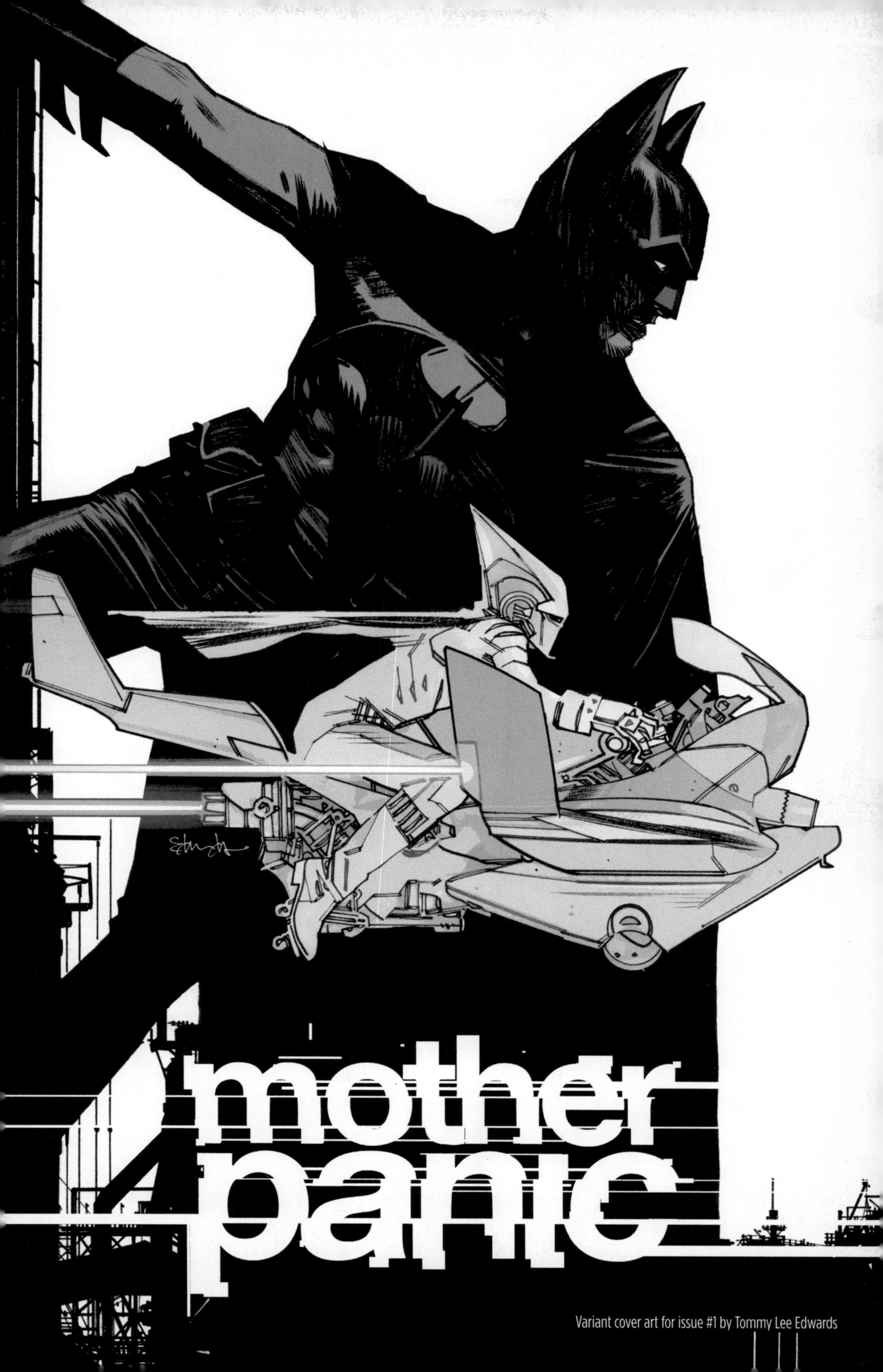
mother
panic

Variant cover art for issue #1 by Tommy Lee Edwards

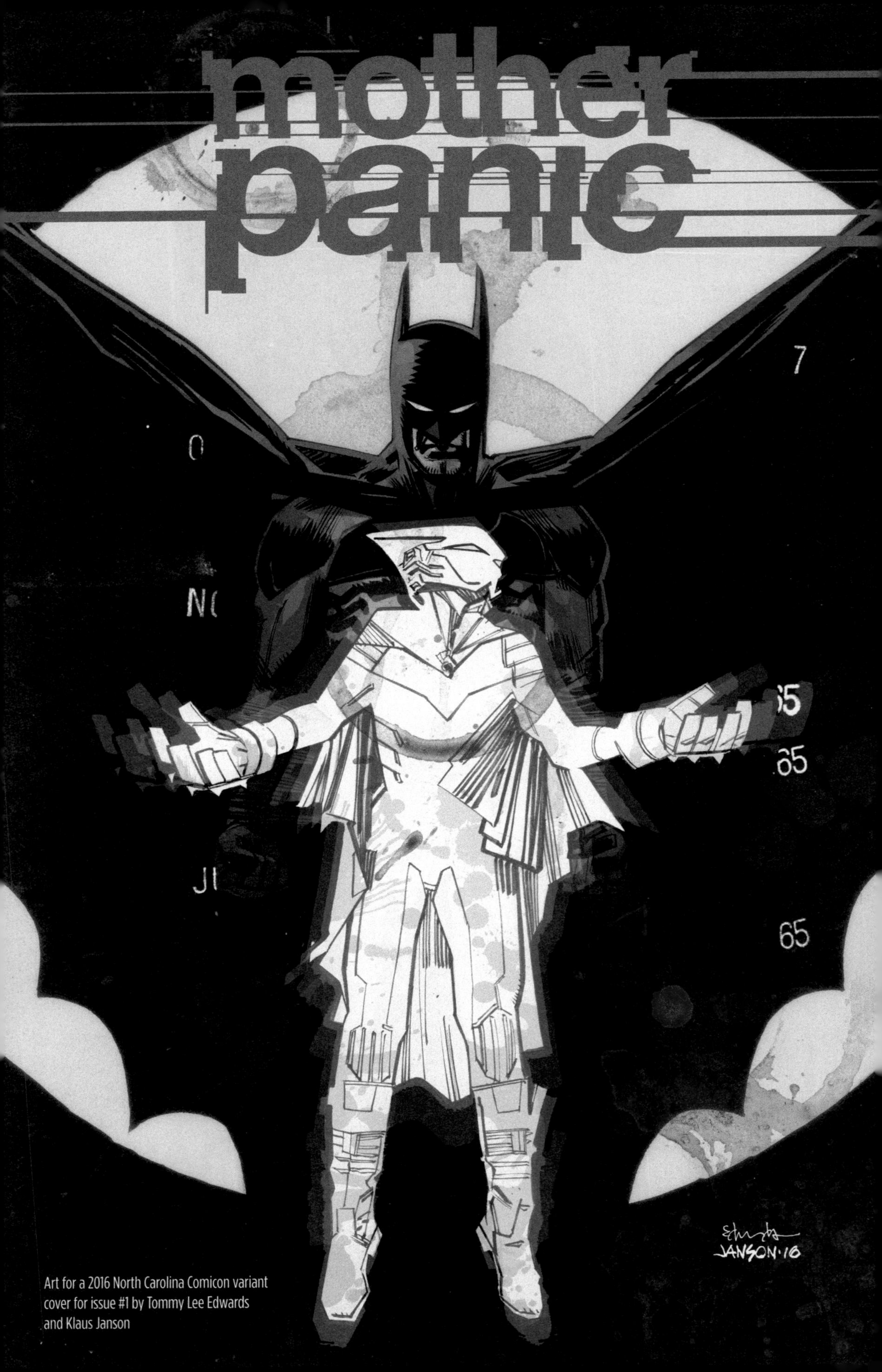
mother
panic
7
0
NC
65
65
JU
65
JANSON·16

Art for a 2016 North Carolina Comicon variant cover for issue #1 by Tommy Lee Edwards and Klaus Janson

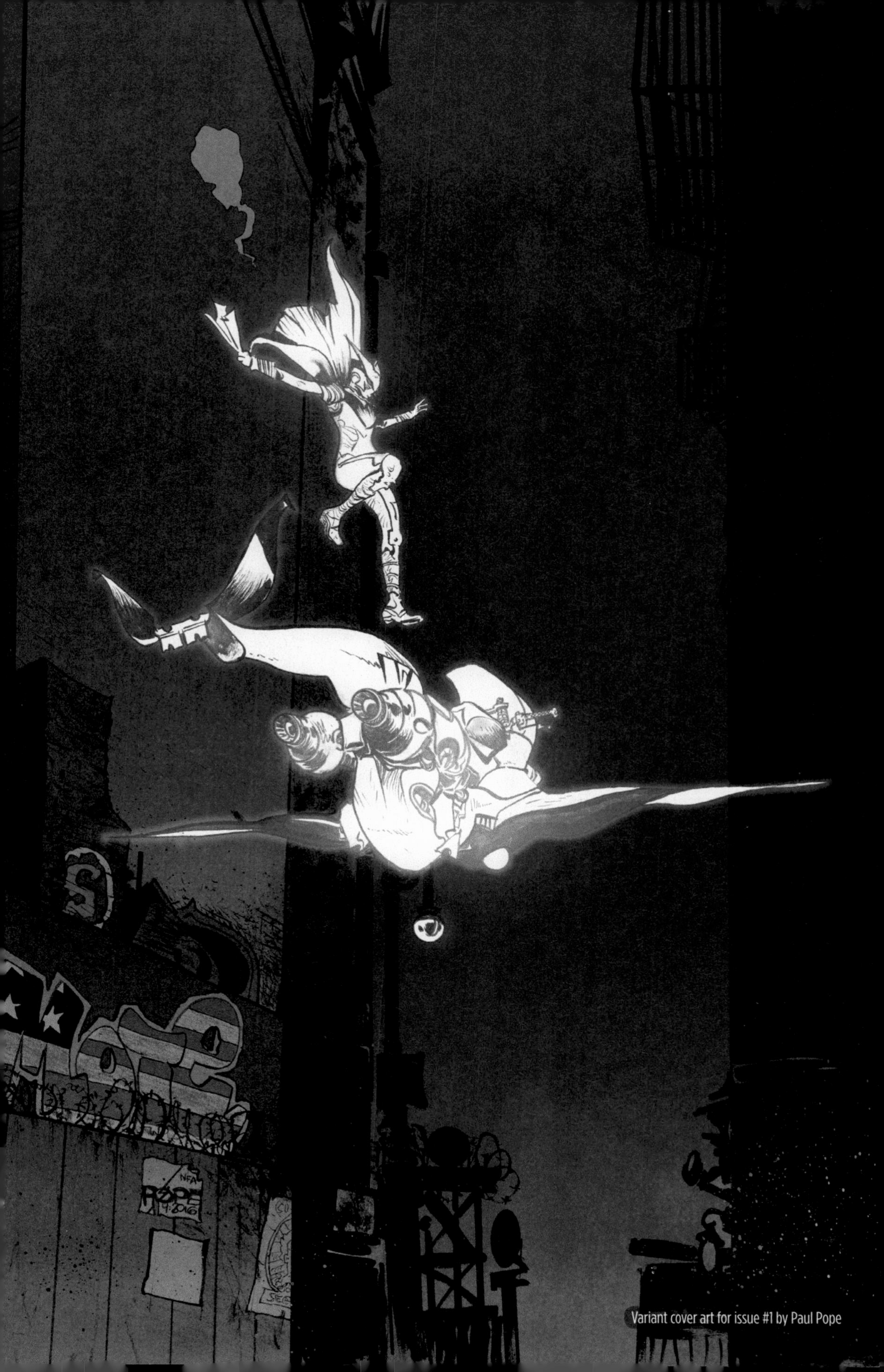

Variant cover art for issue #1 by Paul Pope

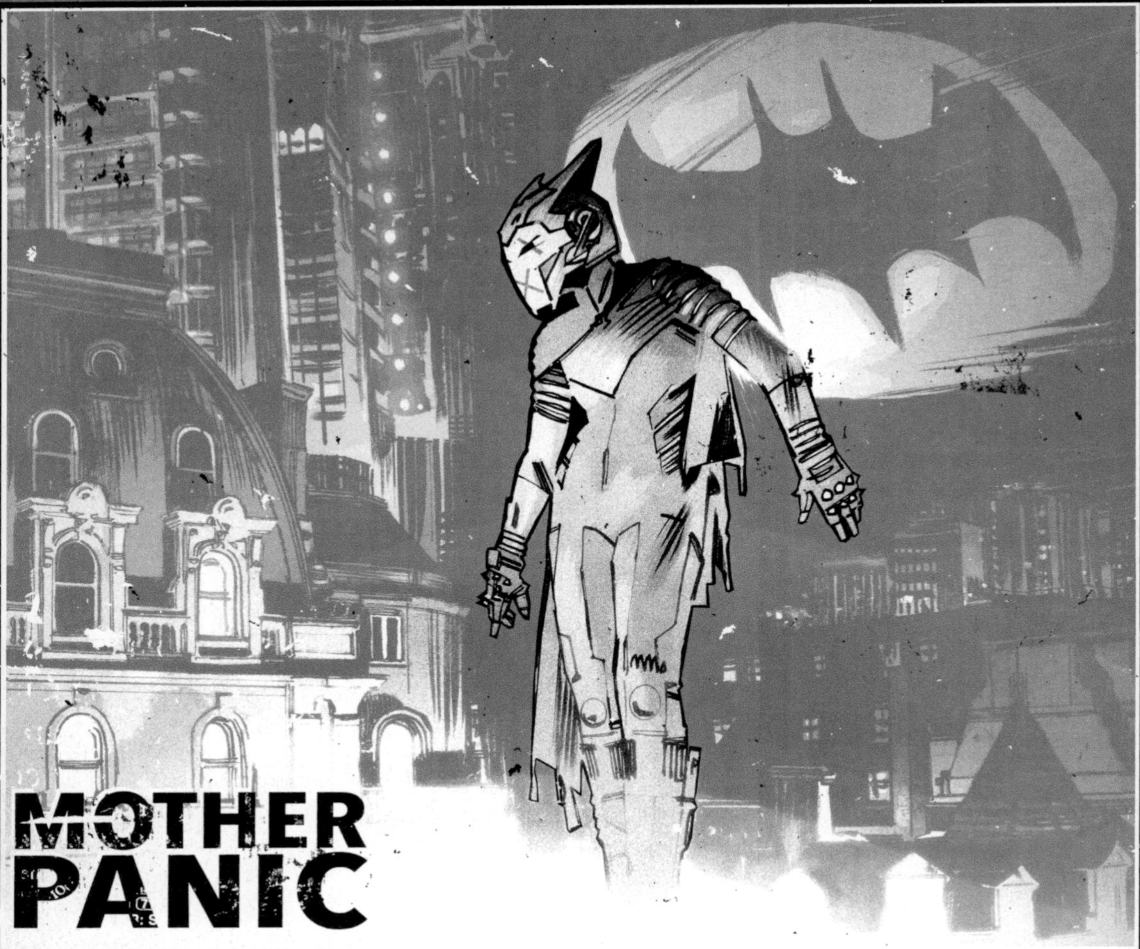

# MOTHER PANIC

## PERSONAL DATA

**Name:** Mother Panic
**Alter Ego:** Violet Paige
**Occupation:** Celebutant
**Known Relatives:** Rebecca (mother), Martin (father, deceased), Victor (brother)
**Group Affiliations:** None
**Base of Operations:** Gotham City
**Height:** 6'0"
**Weight:** 180 lbs.
**Hair:** Black
**Eyes:** Green

## HISTORY

Born and raised in Gotham City, Violet Paige was daddy's little girl. Her mother, Rebecca, was diagnosed with early-onset Alzheimer's when Violet was still young, not always remembering who she was. As Violet's brother, Victor, was quite a bit older than her, already making his mark on the legal world before she reached her teens, they were never close. Her father, Martin, spoiled her and took her on many of his outdoor excursions.

Everything changed when Violet was thirteen. On a hunting trip with his daughter and a business associate, Martin was shot and killed in what appeared to be a hunting accident. Without her husband to care for her, Rebecca Paige was institutionalized, while Victor had no place in his life for a traumatized young girl. On the advisement of one of his colleagues, Victor sent her to a new experimental private boarding school called Gather House, right outside of Gotham.

No one heard from Violet for ten years. Then she reappeared in Gotham high society. Her wild antics on the party scene soon made her a favorite target of the paparazzi, along with the lingering mystery surrounding her father's death. While rumors circulate that she's involved with several different men and women, no serious relationships have been witnessed and surprisingly little is known about her personal life outside of public social gatherings. There have been few sightings of Mother Panic and little is known about her or her motives. There has been no sign as of yet that she is allied with any of the other costumed heroes of Gotham.

## POWERS & WEAPONS

Mother Panic has extensive hand-to-hand combat skills enhanced by superhuman strength, the source of which is currently unknown. The technological capabilities of her costume and glider are unknown, but the design of both appears to be highly advanced.

## Rebecca Paige

### PERSONAL DATA

**Who's Who:** Rebecca Paige
**Marital Status:** Widowed
**Height:** 5'9"
**Weight:** 150 lbs
**Hair Color:** Gray
**Eye Color:** Green

### HISTORY

Rebecca Paige, née Barrow, was born and raised in a solidly middle-class family in the suburbs outside of Gotham. Working at her father's landscaping company in her late teens, she met the son of one of his clients, Martin Paige. After several years of courtship and with the very grudging approval of both sets of parents, the two were wed.

Although not born to the elite, Rebecca took to the life of a socialite, her kind and gregarious nature making her well-liked. Their son, Victor, was born early in their marriage and was their only child for fifteen years, until Violet was born.

Violet was still fairly young when Rebecca began to experience strange cognitive issues. After an unnerving episode while visiting Martin at his office, an episode Martin never spoke about, Rebecca was taken to the hospital. The best neuro-specialist the Paiges' money could buy diagnosed her with an early-onset degenerative brain disorder.

As Rebecca's health and memory continued to decline, she was cared for at home by Martin and Violet. When Martin was killed in a mysterious hunting accident, Rebecca was sent to a nursing home by Victor, just as Violet was sent to the school known as Gather House.

Rebecca lingered in the home, alone, until Violet reappeared as an adult. Now she lives in a suite-turned-enchanted forest in the Pike Hotel, Violet's secret home and Mother Panic's headquarters. She mostly keeps to her own devices. How much she knows and understands of her daughter's mission remains a mystery.

### PERSONAL DATA

**Who's Who:** Dr. Suditi Varma
**Marital Status:** Single
**Height:** 5'7"
**Weight:** 145 lbs
**Hair Color:** Black
**Eye Color:** Brown

### HISTORY

One of the foremost biomechanical implant surgeons in the world, Dr. Suditi Varma was born and raised in London, the daughter of a pediatrician and an office manager. She excelled at school, particularly in the sciences, from a very young age. She knew early on that she wanted to be a doctor like her mother, although she wanted to do something different than working with children.

## Dr. Suditi Varma

After receiving her M.D. at the University of Cambridge and completing her surgical residency, Dr. Varma was hired by a private practice that specialized in state-of-the-art prosthetics. Through her work there, she developed a fascination with making the human body better, helping it to reach its fullest potential. She moved from research group to research group, sometimes working with teams that pushed the ethical limits of how much one could engineer the human body, particularly for military purposes.

Eventually, she was found and hired by Violet Paige. She has served as Violet's "private physician" ever since. She currently lives at the Pike Hotel and does her best to temper Violet's most self-destructive tendencies in an effort to keep her greatest work in one piece.

# MOTHER OF INVENTION

## CHARACTER DESIGNS AND PROMOTIONAL ART BY TOMMY LEE EDWARDS

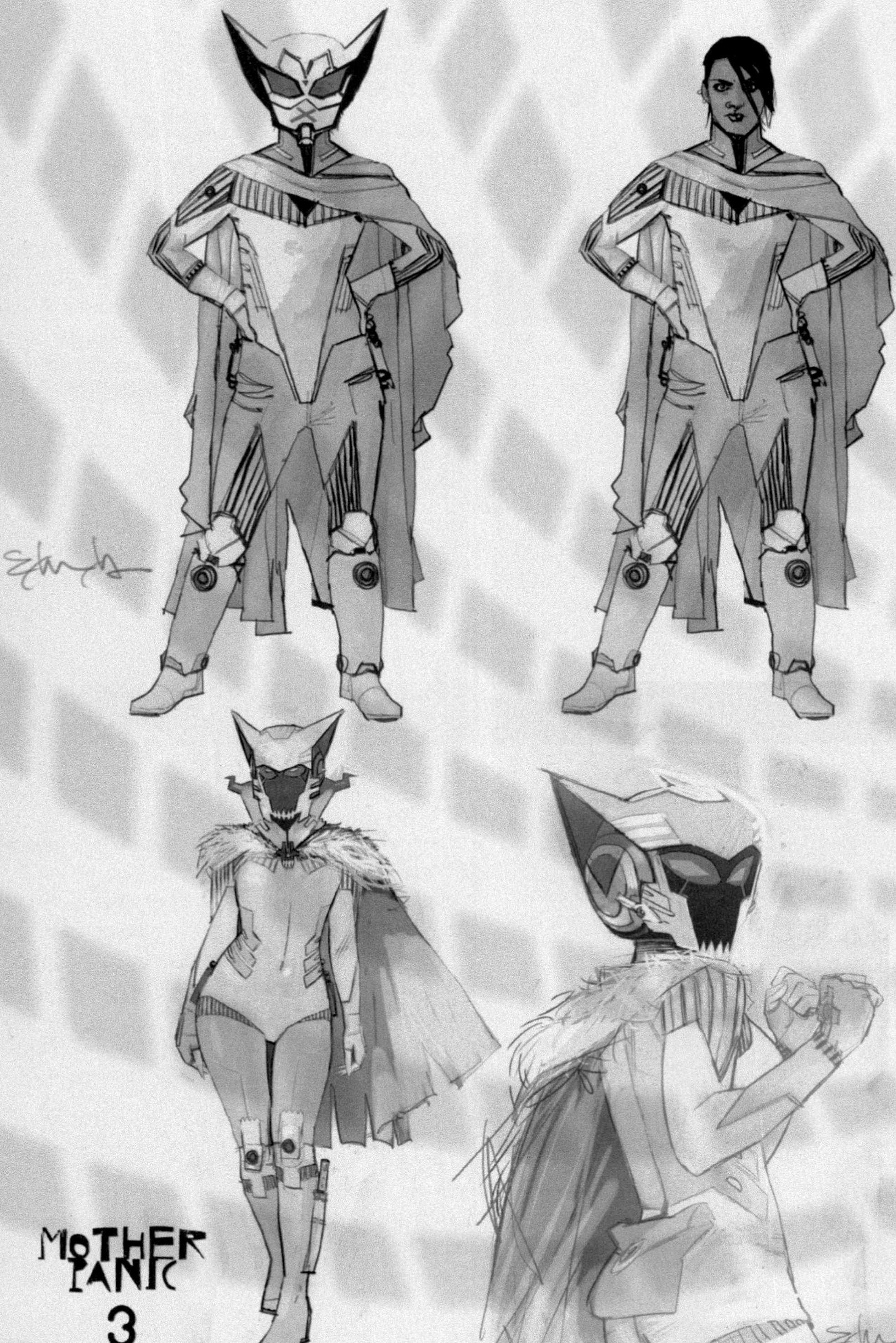
MOTHER
PANIC
3

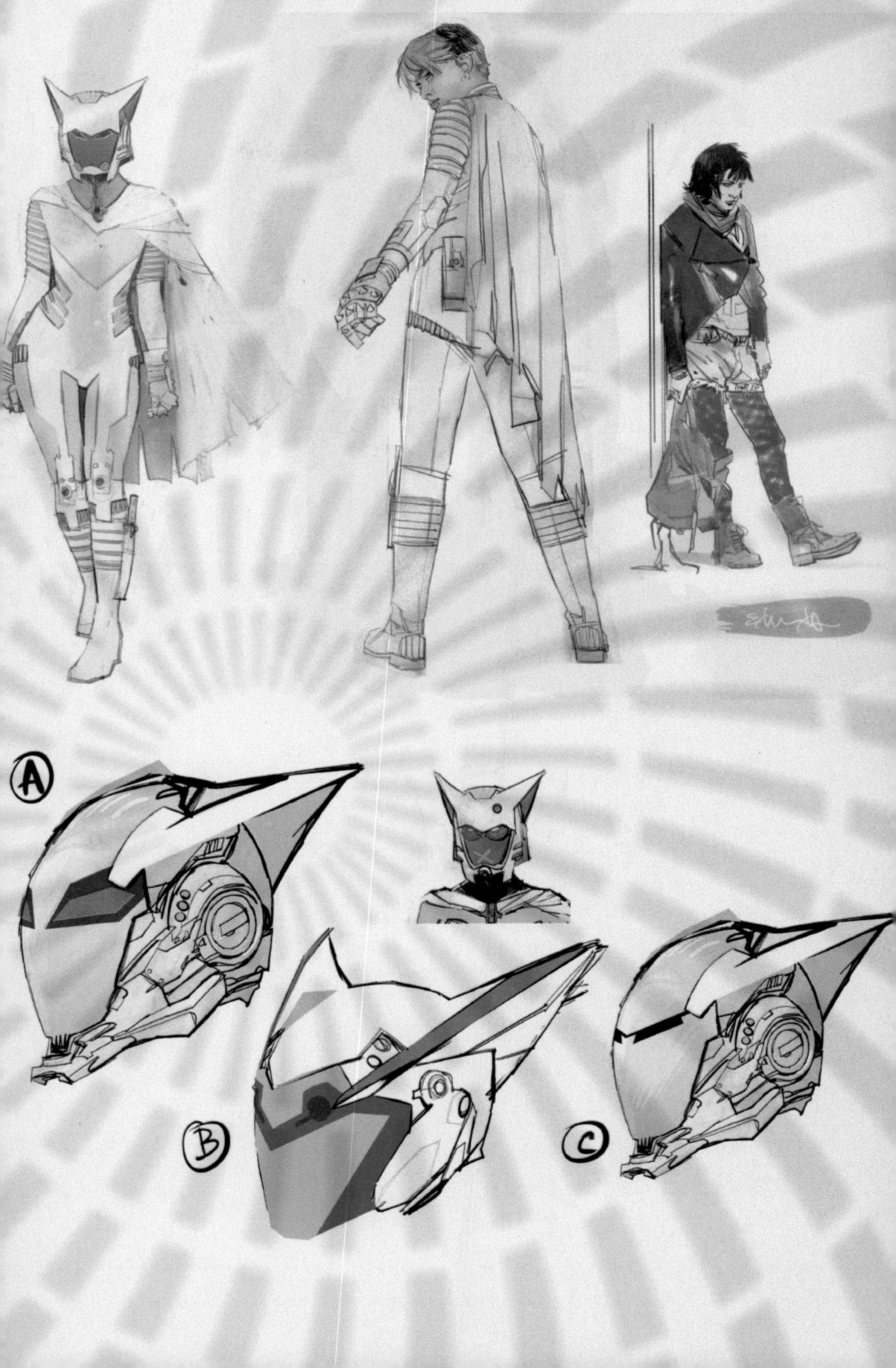
A
B
C

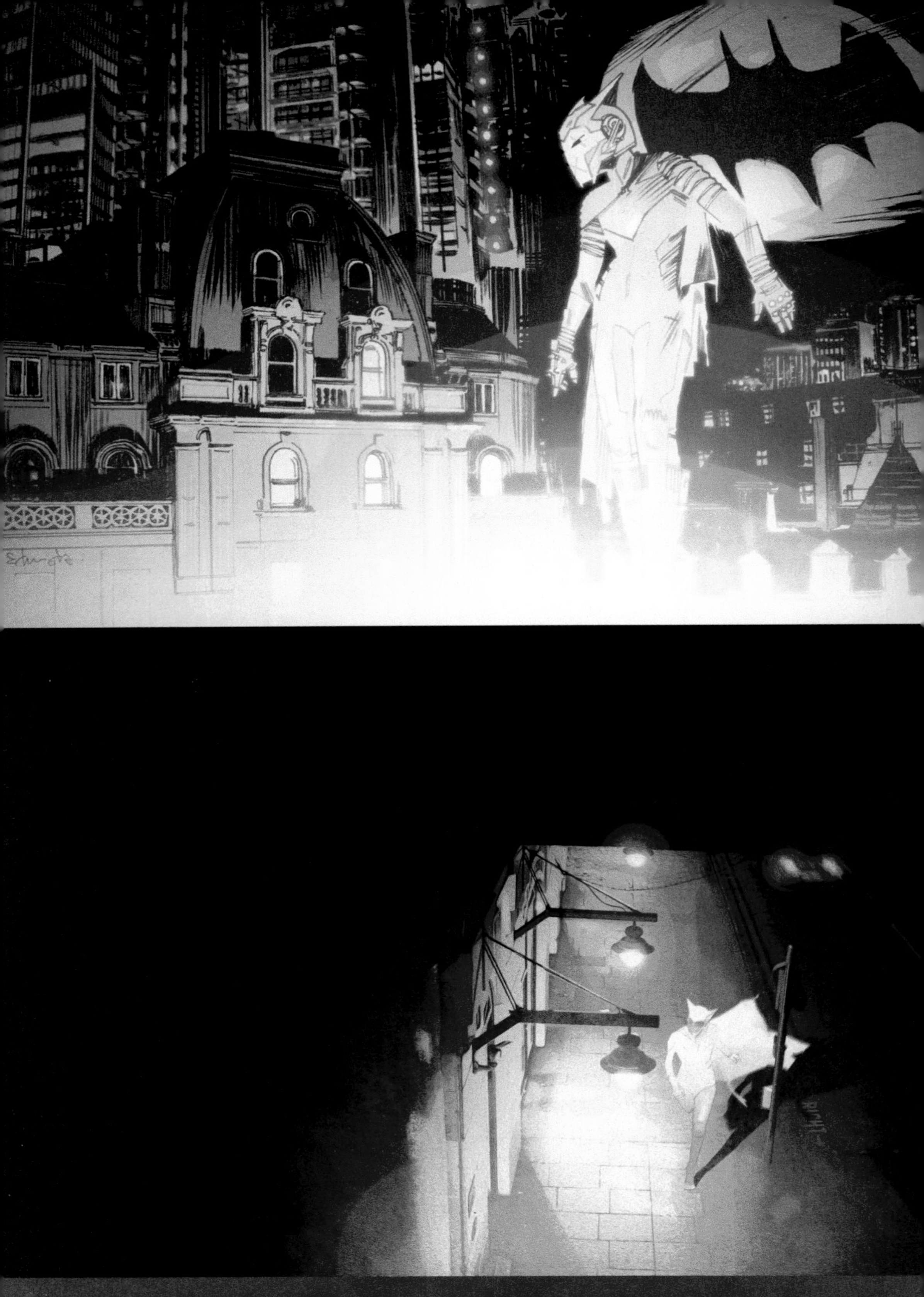

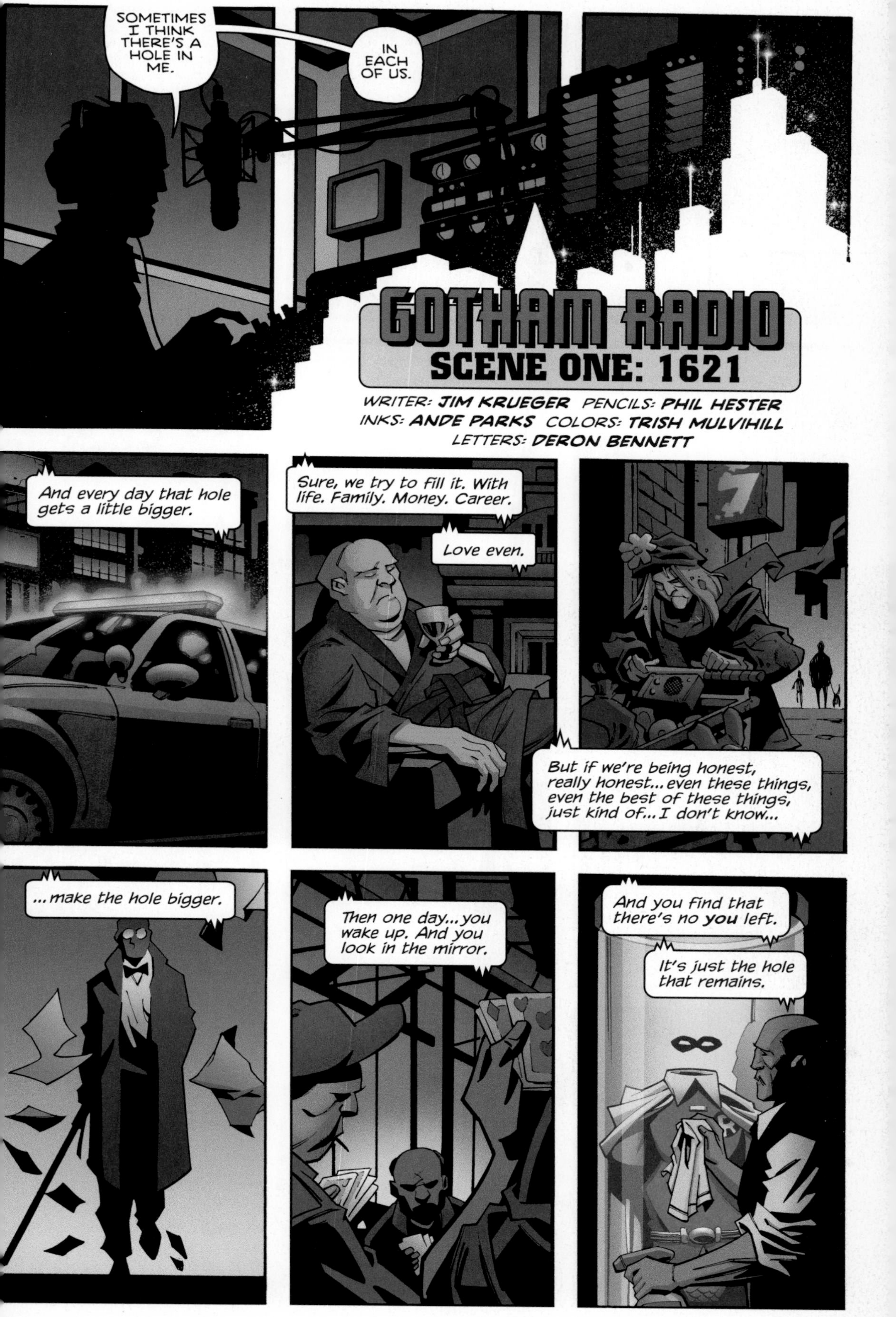

SOMETIMES I THINK THERE'S A HOLE IN ME.
IN EACH OF US.
GOTHAM RADIO
SCENE ONE: 1621
WRITER: JIM KRUEGER PENCILS: PHIL HESTER
INKS: ANDE PARKS COLORS: TRISH MULVIHILL
LETTERS: DERON BENNETT
And every day that hole gets a little bigger.
Sure, we try to fill it. With life. Family. Money. Career.
Love even.
But if we're being honest, really honest... even these things, even the best of these things, just kind of... I don't know...
...make the hole bigger.
Then one day... you wake up. And you look in the mirror.
And you find that there's no you left.
It's just the hole that remains.

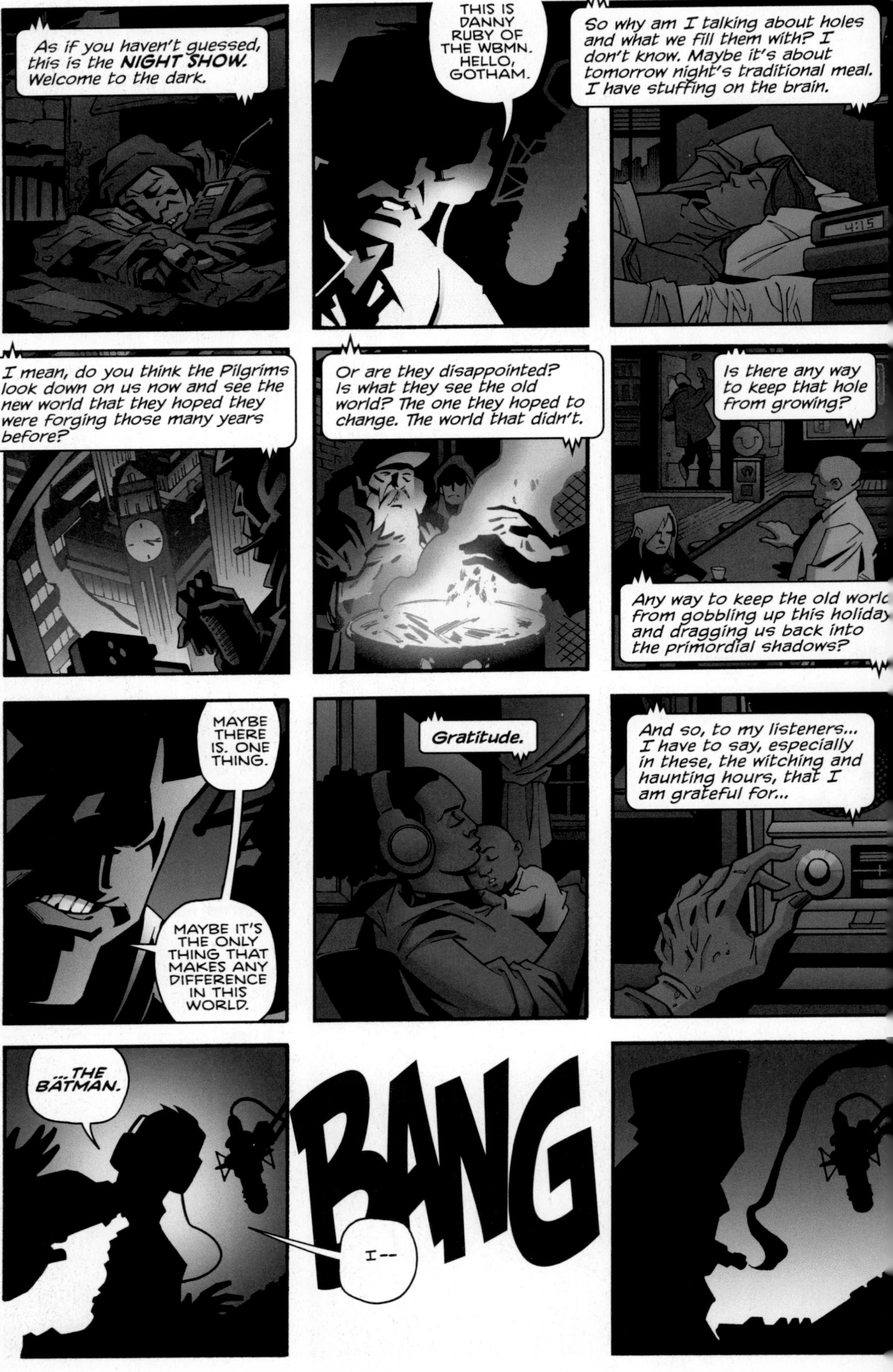

As if you haven't guessed, this is the NIGHT SHOW. Welcome to the dark.
THIS IS DANNY RUBY OF THE WBMN. HELLO, GOTHAM.
So why am I talking about holes and what we fill them with? I don't know. Maybe it's about tomorrow night's traditional meal. I have stuffing on the brain.
4:15
I mean, do you think the Pilgrims look down on us now and see the new world that they hoped they were forging those many years before?
Or are they disappointed? Is what they see the old world? The one they hoped to change. The world that didn't.
Is there any way to keep that hole from growing?
Any way to keep the old world from gobbling up this holiday and dragging us back into the primordial shadows?
MAYBE THERE IS. ONE THING.
MAYBE IT'S THE ONLY THING THAT MAKES ANY DIFFERENCE IN THIS WORLD.
Gratitude.
And so, to my listeners... I have to say, especially in these, the witching and haunting hours, that I am grateful for...
...THE BATMAN.
BANG
I--

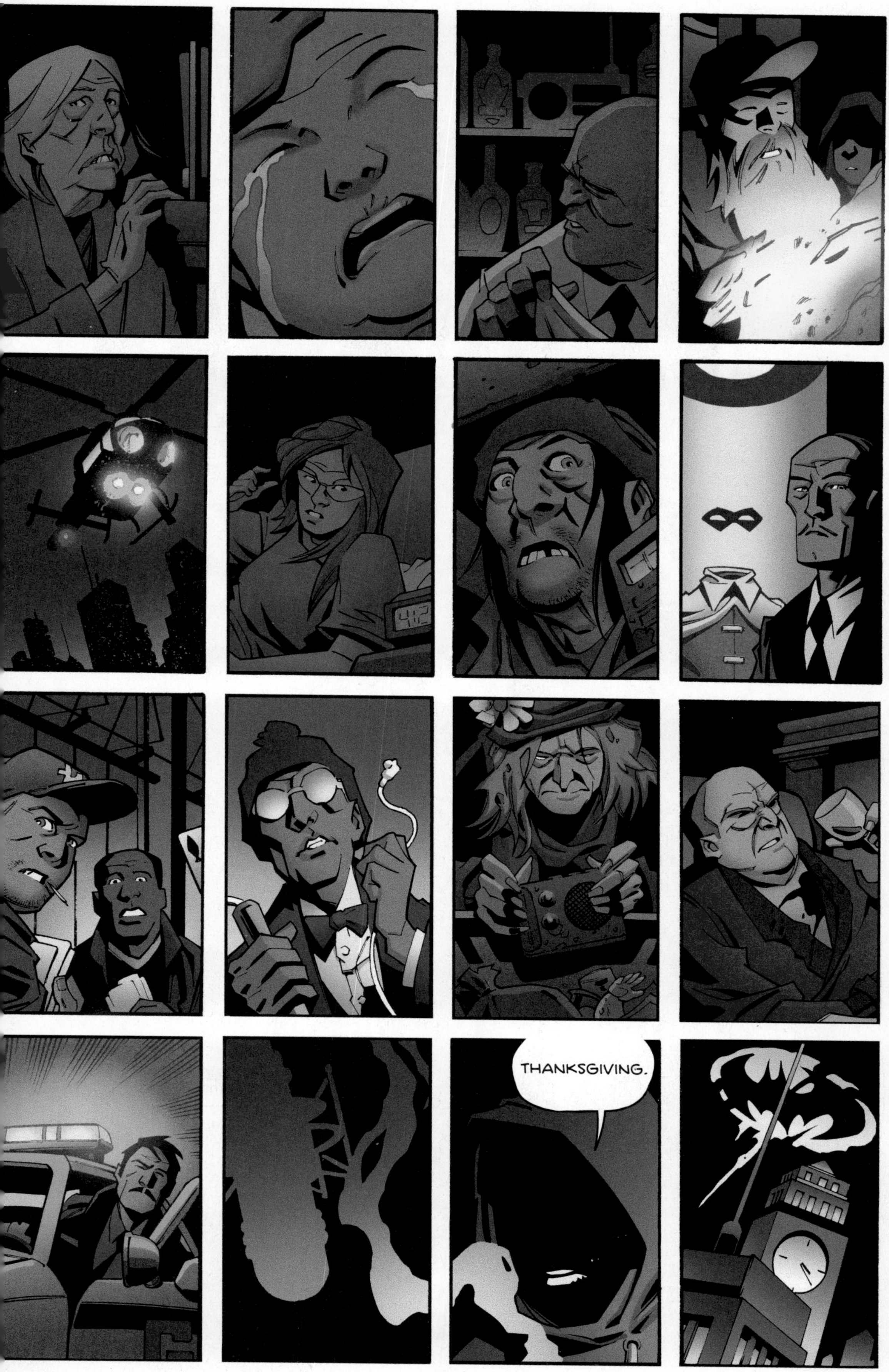
THANKSGIVING.

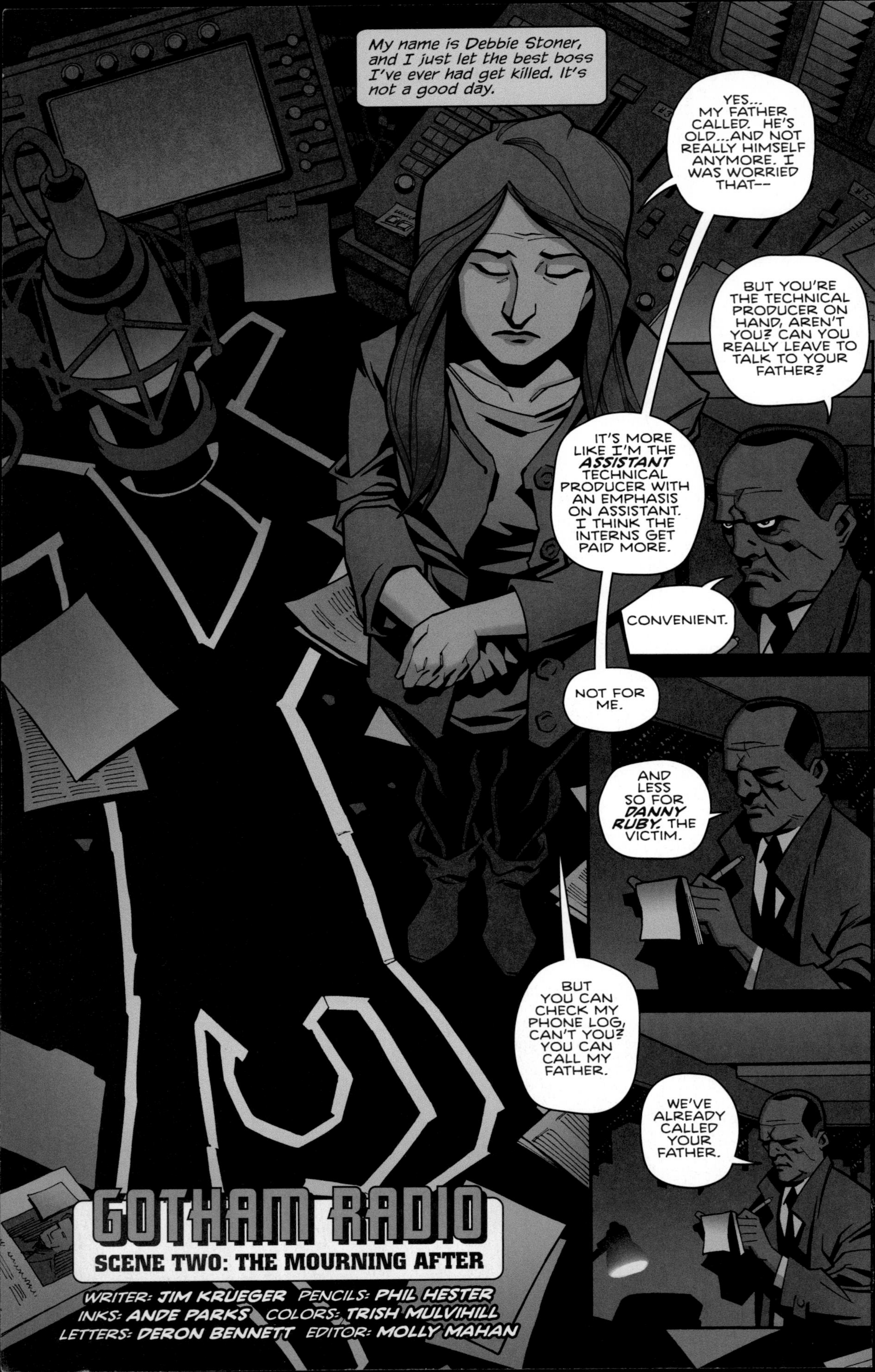
My name is Debbie Stoner, and I just let the best boss I've ever had get killed. It's not a good day.
YES... MY FATHER CALLED. HE'S OLD...AND NOT REALLY HIMSELF ANYMORE. I WAS WORRIED THAT--
BUT YOU'RE THE TECHNICAL PRODUCER ON HAND, AREN'T YOU? CAN YOU REALLY LEAVE TO TALK TO YOUR FATHER?
IT'S MORE LIKE I'M THE ASSISTANT TECHNICAL PRODUCER WITH AN EMPHASIS ON ASSISTANT. I THINK THE INTERNS GET PAID MORE.
CONVENIENT.
NOT FOR ME.
AND LESS SO FOR DANNY RUBY. THE VICTIM.
BUT YOU CAN CHECK MY PHONE LOG, CAN'T YOU? YOU CAN CALL MY FATHER.
WE'VE ALREADY CALLED YOUR FATHER.
GOTHAM RADIO
SCENE TWO: THE MOURNING AFTER
WRITER: JIM KRUEGER PENCILS: PHIL HESTER
INKS: ANDE PARKS COLORS: TRISH MULVIHILL
LETTERS: DERON BENNETT EDITOR: MOLLY MAHAN

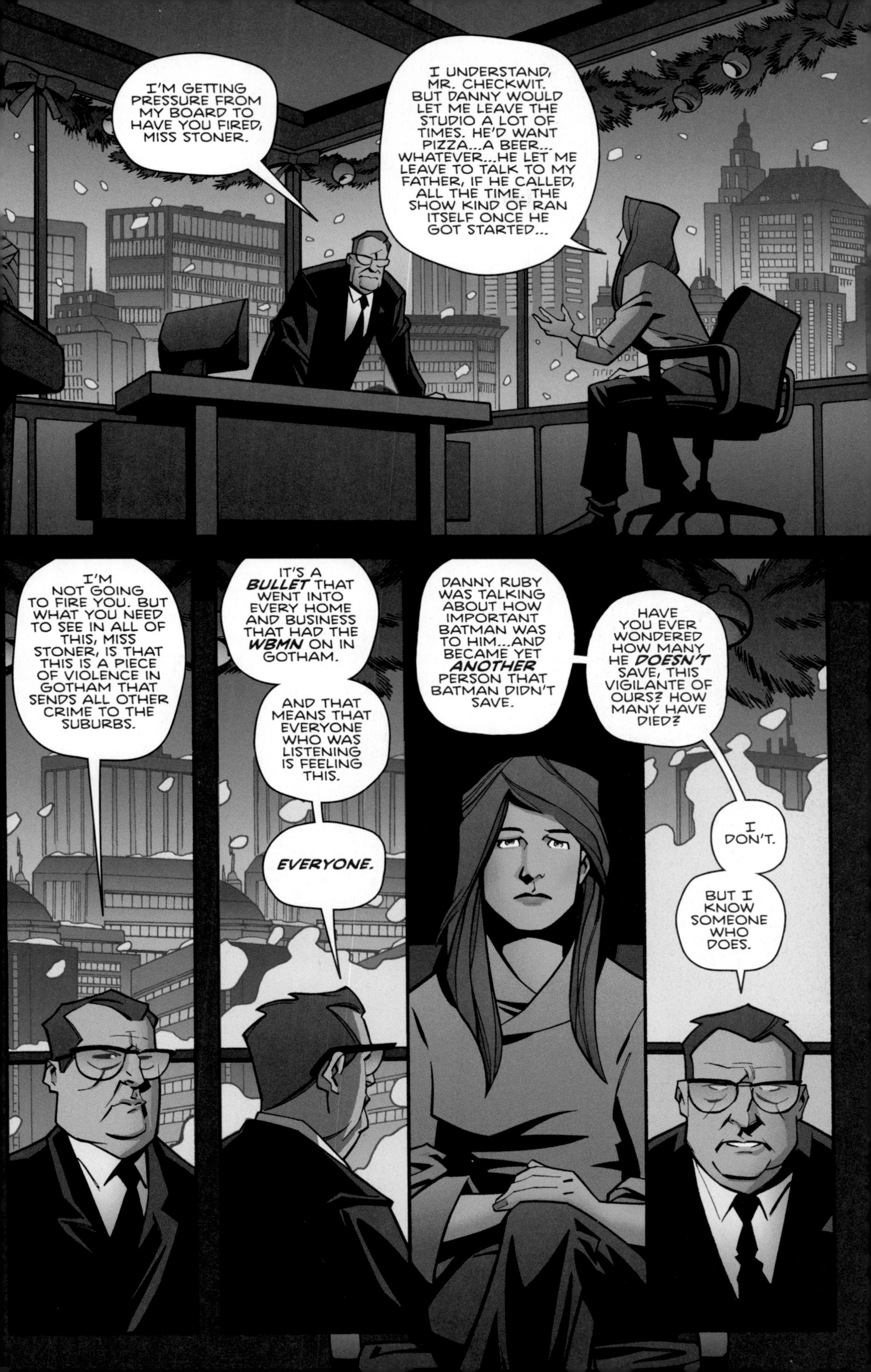
I'M GETTING PRESSURE FROM MY BOARD TO HAVE YOU FIRED, MISS STONER.
I UNDERSTAND, MR. CHECKWIT. BUT DANNY WOULD LET ME LEAVE THE STUDIO A LOT OF TIMES. HE'D WANT PIZZA... A BEER... WHATEVER... HE LET ME LEAVE TO TALK TO MY FATHER, IF HE CALLED, ALL THE TIME. THE SHOW KIND OF RAN ITSELF ONCE HE GOT STARTED...
I'M NOT GOING TO FIRE YOU. BUT WHAT YOU NEED TO SEE IN ALL OF THIS, MISS STONER, IS THAT THIS IS A PIECE OF VIOLENCE IN GOTHAM THAT SENDS ALL OTHER CRIME TO THE SUBURBS.
IT'S A **BULLET** THAT WENT INTO EVERY HOME AND BUSINESS THAT HAD THE **WBMN** ON IN GOTHAM.
AND THAT MEANS THAT EVERYONE WHO WAS LISTENING IS FEELING THIS.
**EVERYONE.**
DANNY RUBY WAS TALKING ABOUT HOW IMPORTANT BATMAN WAS TO HIM... AND BECAME YET **ANOTHER** PERSON THAT BATMAN DIDN'T SAVE.
HAVE YOU EVER WONDERED HOW MANY HE **DOESN'T** SAVE, THIS VIGILANTE OF OURS? HOW MANY HAVE DIED?
I DON'T.
BUT I KNOW SOMEONE WHO DOES.

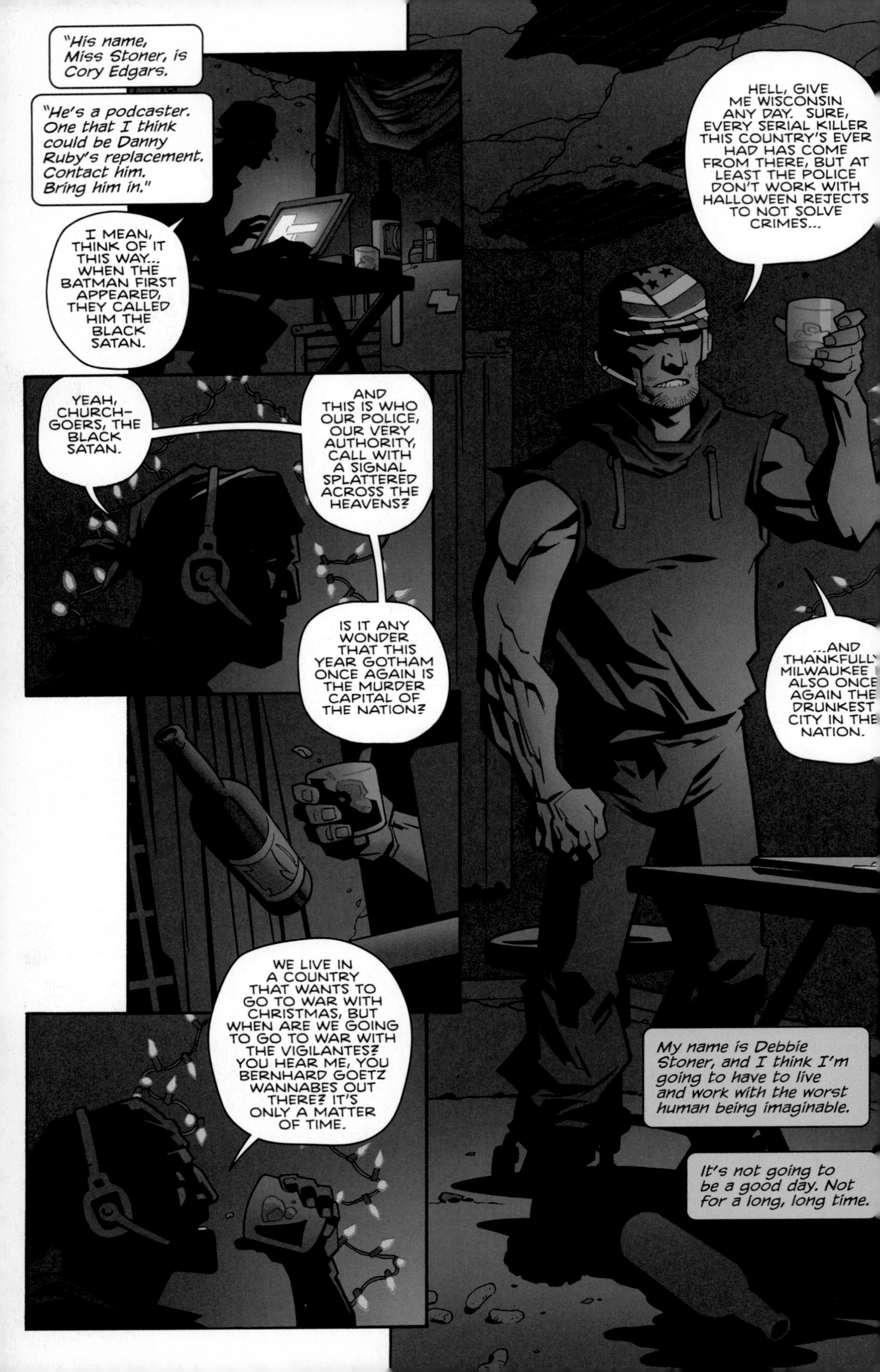
"His name, Miss Stoner, is Cory Edgars.
"He's a podcaster. One that I think could be Danny Ruby's replacement. Contact him. Bring him in."
I MEAN, THINK OF IT THIS WAY... WHEN THE BATMAN FIRST APPEARED, THEY CALLED HIM THE BLACK SATAN.
HELL, GIVE ME WISCONSIN ANY DAY. SURE, EVERY SERIAL KILLER THIS COUNTRY'S EVER HAD HAS COME FROM THERE, BUT AT LEAST THE POLICE DON'T WORK WITH HALLOWEEN REJECTS TO NOT SOLVE CRIMES...
YEAH, CHURCH-GOERS, THE BLACK SATAN.
AND THIS IS WHO OUR POLICE, OUR VERY AUTHORITY, CALL WITH A SIGNAL SPLATTERED ACROSS THE HEAVENS?
IS IT ANY WONDER THAT THIS YEAR GOTHAM ONCE AGAIN IS THE MURDER CAPITAL OF THE NATION?
...AND THANKFULLY MILWAUKEE IS ALSO ONCE AGAIN THE DRUNKEST CITY IN THE NATION.
WE LIVE IN A COUNTRY THAT WANTS TO GO TO WAR WITH CHRISTMAS, BUT WHEN ARE WE GOING TO GO TO WAR WITH THE VIGILANTES? YOU HEAR ME, YOU BERNHARD GOETZ WANNABES OUT THERE? IT'S ONLY A MATTER OF TIME.
My name is Debbie Stoner, and I think I'm going to have to live and work with the worst human being imaginable.
It's not going to be a good day. Not for a long, long time.

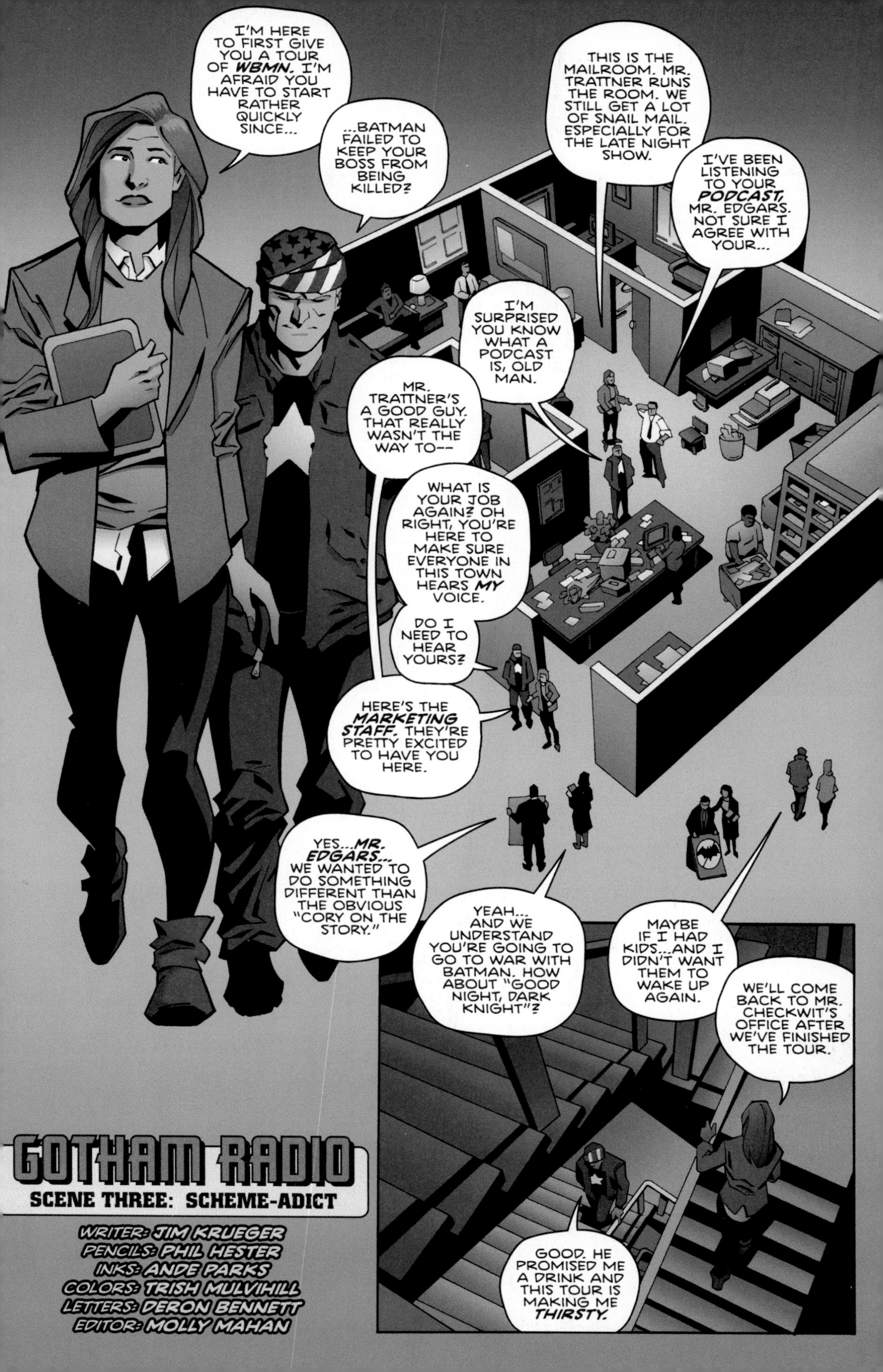

I'M HERE TO FIRST GIVE YOU A TOUR OF WBMN. I'M AFRAID YOU HAVE TO START RATHER QUICKLY SINCE...
...BATMAN FAILED TO KEEP YOUR BOSS FROM BEING KILLED?
THIS IS THE MAILROOM. MR. TRATTNER RUNS THE ROOM. WE STILL GET A LOT OF SNAIL MAIL. ESPECIALLY FOR THE LATE NIGHT SHOW.
I'VE BEEN LISTENING TO YOUR PODCAST, MR. EDGARS. NOT SURE I AGREE WITH YOUR...
I'M SURPRISED YOU KNOW WHAT A PODCAST IS, OLD MAN.
MR. TRATTNER'S A GOOD GUY. THAT REALLY WASN'T THE WAY TO--
WHAT IS YOUR JOB AGAIN? OH RIGHT, YOU'RE HERE TO MAKE SURE EVERYONE IN THIS TOWN HEARS MY VOICE.
DO I NEED TO HEAR YOURS?
HERE'S THE MARKETING STAFF. THEY'RE PRETTY EXCITED TO HAVE YOU HERE.
YES...MR. EDGARS... WE WANTED TO DO SOMETHING DIFFERENT THAN THE OBVIOUS "CORY ON THE STORY."
YEAH... AND WE UNDERSTAND YOU'RE GOING TO GO TO WAR WITH BATMAN. HOW ABOUT "GOOD NIGHT, DARK KNIGHT"?
MAYBE IF I HAD KIDS...AND I DIDN'T WANT THEM TO WAKE UP AGAIN.
WE'LL COME BACK TO MR. CHECKWIT'S OFFICE AFTER WE'VE FINISHED THE TOUR.
GOOD. HE PROMISED ME A DRINK AND THIS TOUR IS MAKING ME THIRSTY.
GOTHAM RADIO
SCENE THREE: SCHEME-ADICT
WRITER: JIM KRUEGER
PENCILS: PHIL HESTER
INKS: ANDE PARKS
COLORS: TRISH MULVIHILL
LETTERS: DERON BENNETT
EDITOR: MOLLY MAHAN

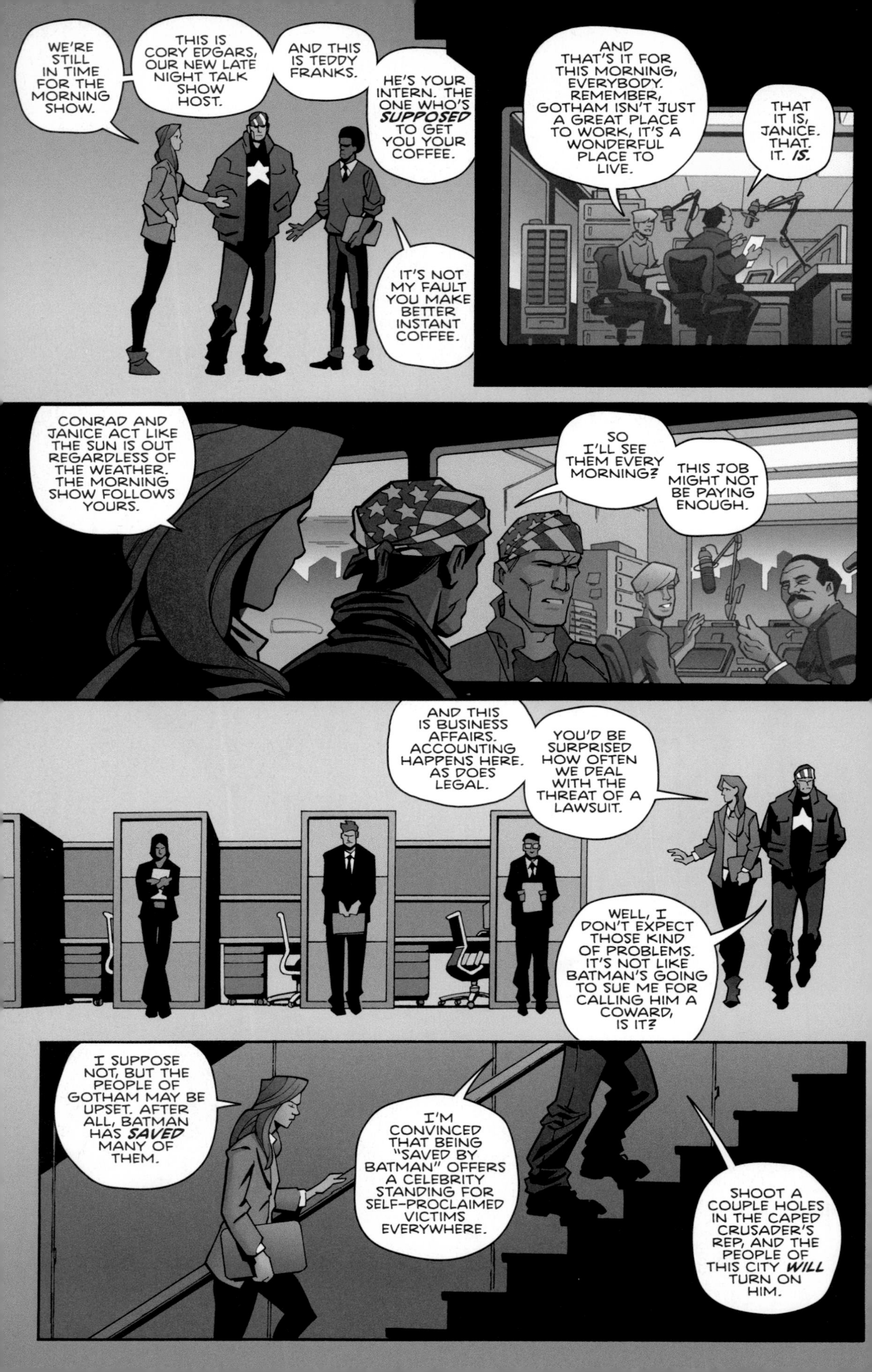

WE'RE STILL IN TIME FOR THE MORNING SHOW.
THIS IS CORY EDGARS, OUR NEW LATE NIGHT TALK SHOW HOST.
AND THIS IS TEDDY FRANKS.
HE'S YOUR INTERN. THE ONE WHO'S SUPPOSED TO GET YOU YOUR COFFEE.
IT'S NOT MY FAULT YOU MAKE BETTER INSTANT COFFEE.
AND THAT'S IT FOR THIS MORNING, EVERYBODY. REMEMBER, GOTHAM ISN'T JUST A GREAT PLACE TO WORK, IT'S A WONDERFUL PLACE TO LIVE.
THAT IT IS, JANICE. THAT. IT. IS.
CONRAD AND JANICE ACT LIKE THE SUN IS OUT REGARDLESS OF THE WEATHER. THE MORNING SHOW FOLLOWS YOURS.
SO I'LL SEE THEM EVERY MORNING?
THIS JOB MIGHT NOT BE PAYING ENOUGH.
AND THIS IS BUSINESS AFFAIRS. ACCOUNTING HAPPENS HERE. AS DOES LEGAL.
YOU'D BE SURPRISED HOW OFTEN WE DEAL WITH THE THREAT OF A LAWSUIT.
WELL, I DON'T EXPECT THOSE KIND OF PROBLEMS. IT'S NOT LIKE BATMAN'S GOING TO SUE ME FOR CALLING HIM A COWARD, IS IT?
I SUPPOSE NOT, BUT THE PEOPLE OF GOTHAM MAY BE UPSET. AFTER ALL, BATMAN HAS SAVED MANY OF THEM.
I'M CONVINCED THAT BEING "SAVED BY BATMAN" OFFERS A CELEBRITY STANDING FOR SELF-PROCLAIMED VICTIMS EVERYWHERE.
SHOOT A COUPLE HOLES IN THE CAPED CRUSADER'S REP, AND THE PEOPLE OF THIS CITY WILL TURN ON HIM.

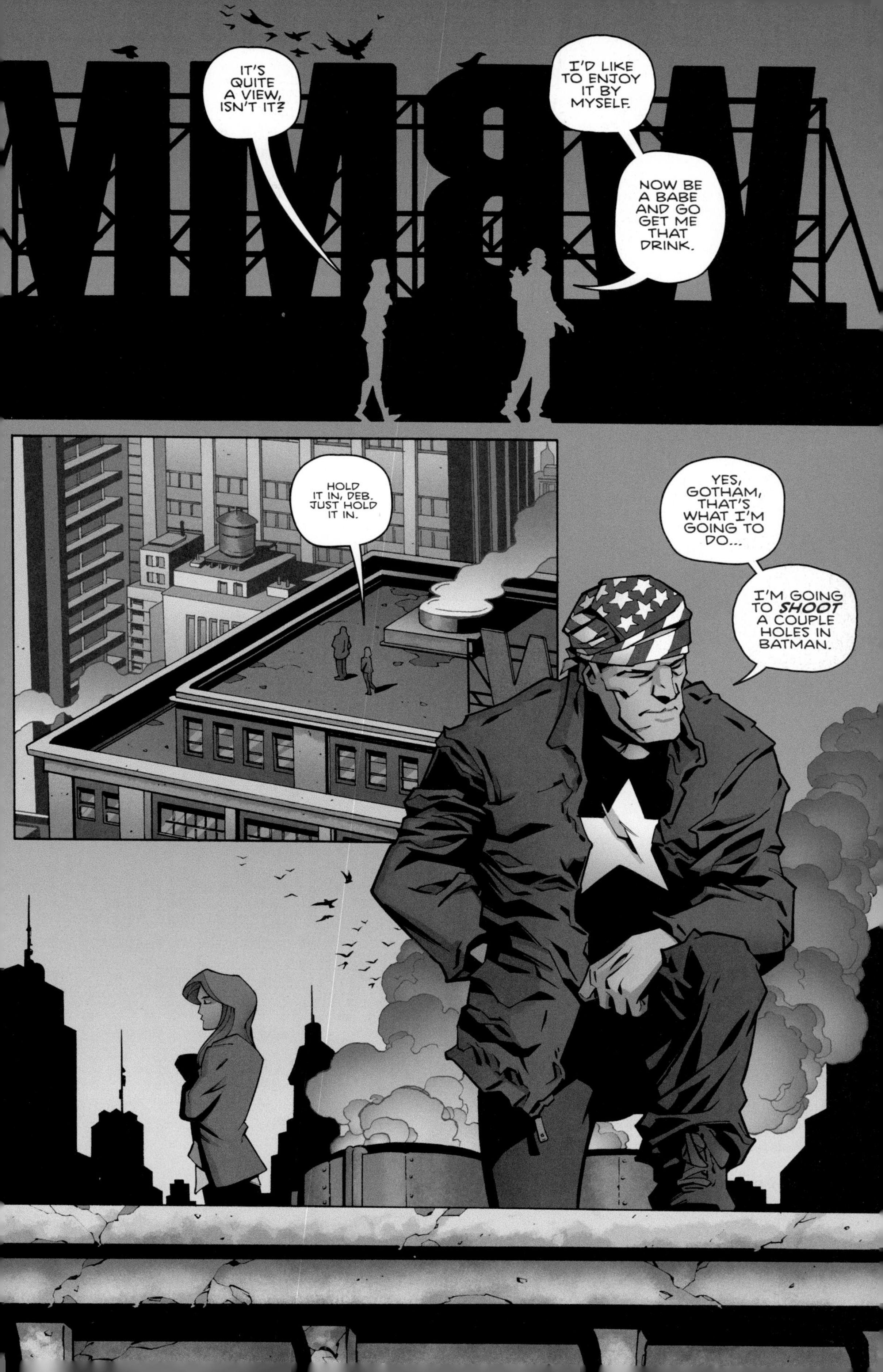
IT'S QUITE A VIEW, ISN'T IT?
I'D LIKE TO ENJOY IT BY MYSELF.
NOW BE A BABE AND GO GET ME THAT DRINK.
HOLD IT IN, DEB. JUST HOLD IT IN.
YES, GOTHAM, THAT'S WHAT I'M GOING TO DO...
I'M GOING TO SHOOT A COUPLE HOLES IN BATMAN.

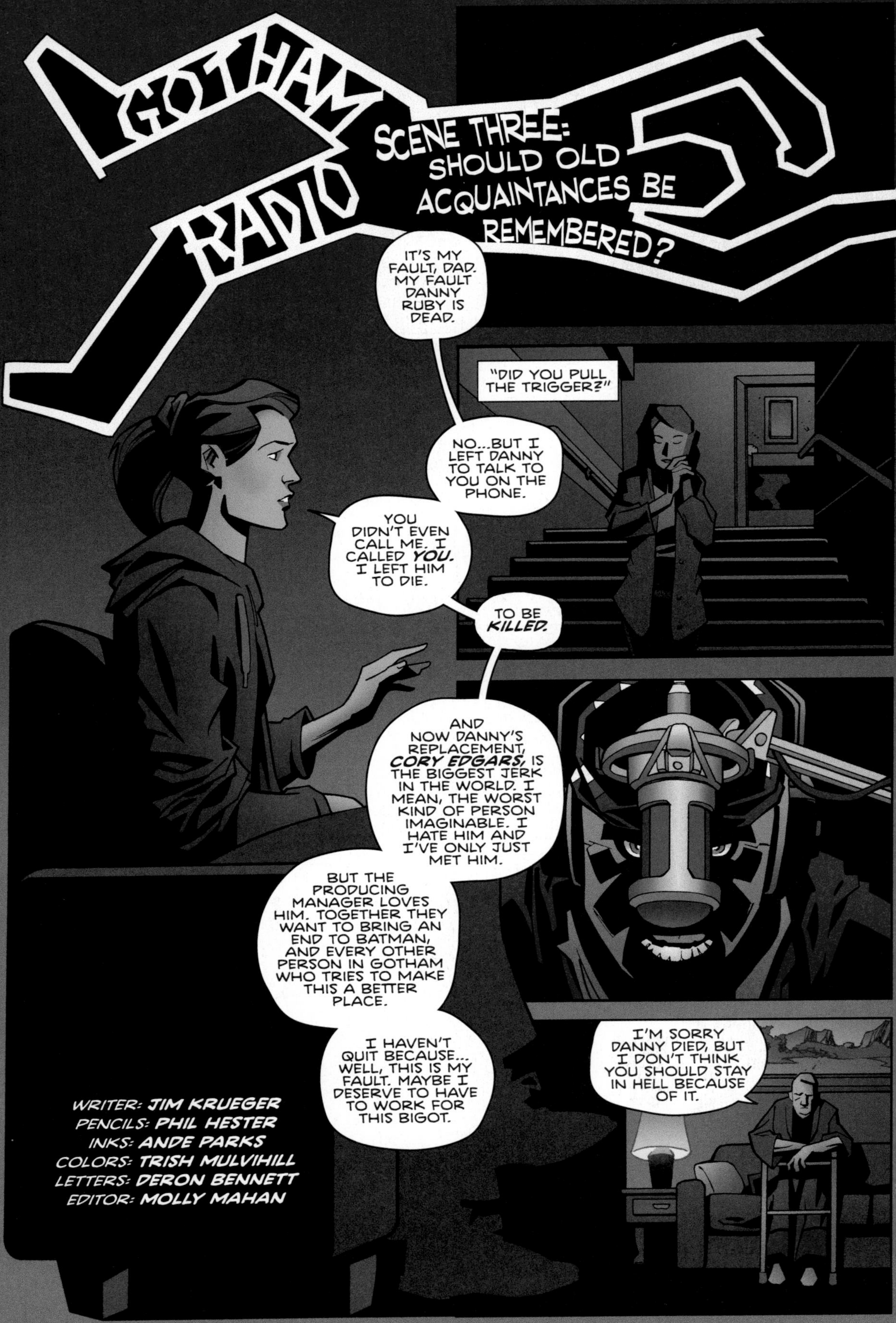
GOTHAM RADIO
SCENE THREE: SHOULD OLD ACQUAINTANCES BE REMEMBERED?
IT'S MY FAULT, DAD. MY FAULT DANNY RUBY IS DEAD.
"DID YOU PULL THE TRIGGER?"
NO...BUT I LEFT DANNY TO TALK TO YOU ON THE PHONE.
YOU DIDN'T EVEN CALL ME. I CALLED YOU. I LEFT HIM TO DIE.
TO BE KILLED.
AND NOW DANNY'S REPLACEMENT, CORY EDGARS, IS THE BIGGEST JERK IN THE WORLD. I MEAN, THE WORST KIND OF PERSON IMAGINABLE. I HATE HIM AND I'VE ONLY JUST MET HIM.
BUT THE PRODUCING MANAGER LOVES HIM. TOGETHER THEY WANT TO BRING AN END TO BATMAN, AND EVERY OTHER PERSON IN GOTHAM WHO TRIES TO MAKE THIS A BETTER PLACE.
I HAVEN'T QUIT BECAUSE... WELL, THIS IS MY FAULT. MAYBE I DESERVE TO HAVE TO WORK FOR THIS BIGOT.
I'M SORRY DANNY DIED, BUT I DON'T THINK YOU SHOULD STAY IN HELL BECAUSE OF IT.
WRITER: JIM KRUEGER
PENCILS: PHIL HESTER
INKS: ANDE PARKS
COLORS: TRISH MULVIHILL
LETTERS: DERON BENNETT
EDITOR: MOLLY MAHAN

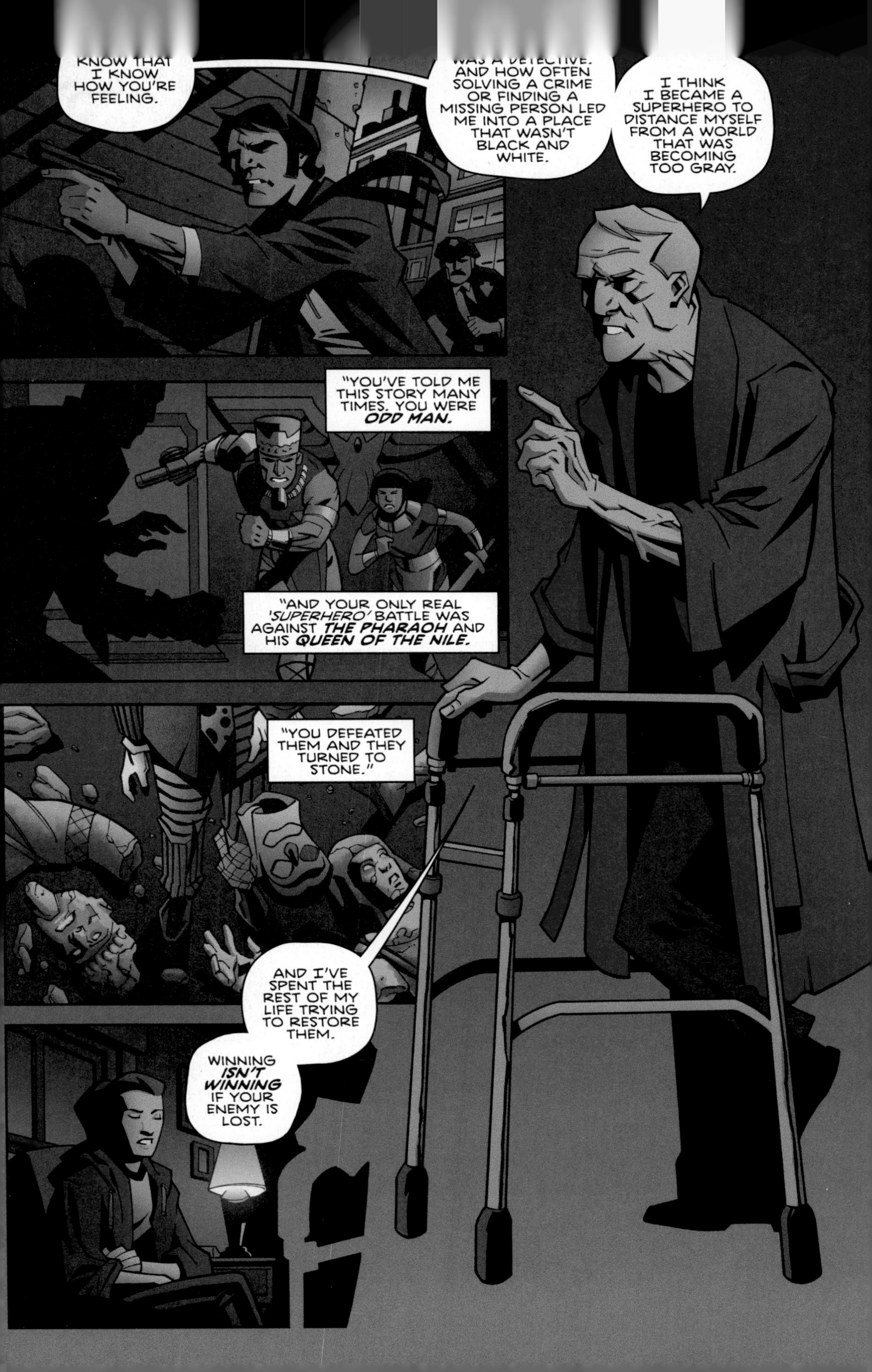
KNOW THAT I KNOW HOW YOU'RE FEELING.
WAS A DETECTIVE. AND HOW OFTEN SOLVING A CRIME OR FINDING A MISSING PERSON LED ME INTO A PLACE THAT WASN'T BLACK AND WHITE.
I THINK I BECAME A SUPERHERO TO DISTANCE MYSELF FROM A WORLD THAT WAS BECOMING TOO GRAY.
"YOU'VE TOLD ME THIS STORY MANY TIMES. YOU WERE ***ODD MAN.***
"AND YOUR ONLY REAL *'SUPERHERO'* BATTLE WAS AGAINST ***THE PHARAOH*** AND HIS ***QUEEN OF THE NILE.***
"YOU DEFEATED THEM AND THEY TURNED TO STONE."
AND I'VE SPENT THE REST OF MY LIFE TRYING TO RESTORE THEM.
WINNING ***ISN'T WINNING*** IF YOUR ENEMY IS LOST.

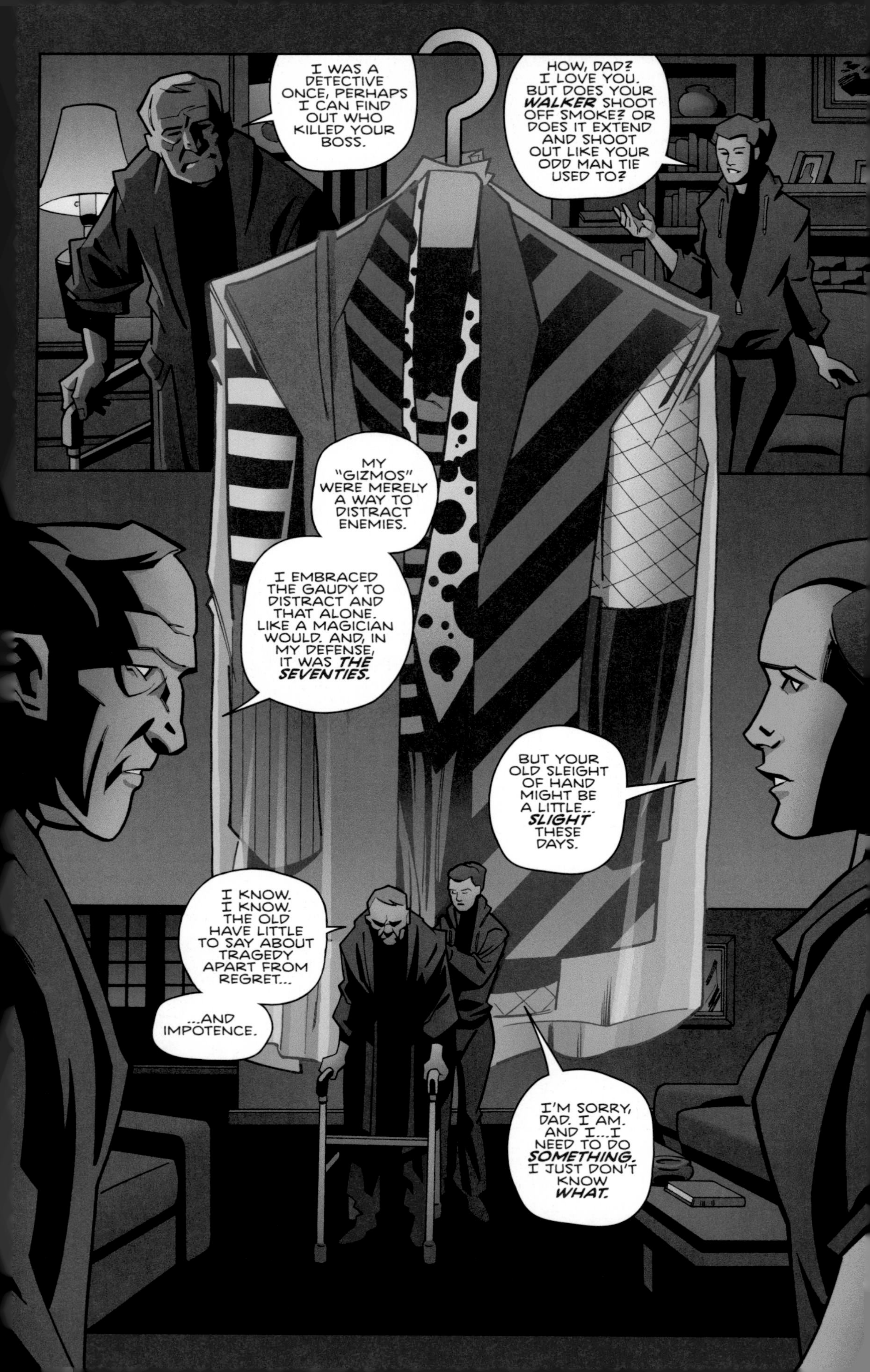

I WAS A DETECTIVE ONCE, PERHAPS I CAN FIND OUT WHO KILLED YOUR BOSS.
HOW, DAD? I LOVE YOU. BUT DOES YOUR **WALKER** SHOOT OFF SMOKE? OR DOES IT EXTEND AND SHOOT OUT LIKE YOUR ODD MAN TIE USED TO?
MY "GIZMOS" WERE MERELY A WAY TO DISTRACT ENEMIES.
I EMBRACED THE GAUDY TO DISTRACT AND THAT ALONE. LIKE A MAGICIAN WOULD. AND, IN MY DEFENSE, IT WAS ***THE SEVENTIES.***
BUT YOUR OLD SLEIGHT OF HAND MIGHT BE A LITTLE... ***SLIGHT*** THESE DAYS.
I KNOW. I KNOW. THE OLD HAVE LITTLE TO SAY ABOUT TRAGEDY APART FROM REGRET...
...AND IMPOTENCE.
I'M SORRY, DAD. I AM. AND I...I NEED TO DO ***SOMETHING.*** I JUST DON'T KNOW ***WHAT.***

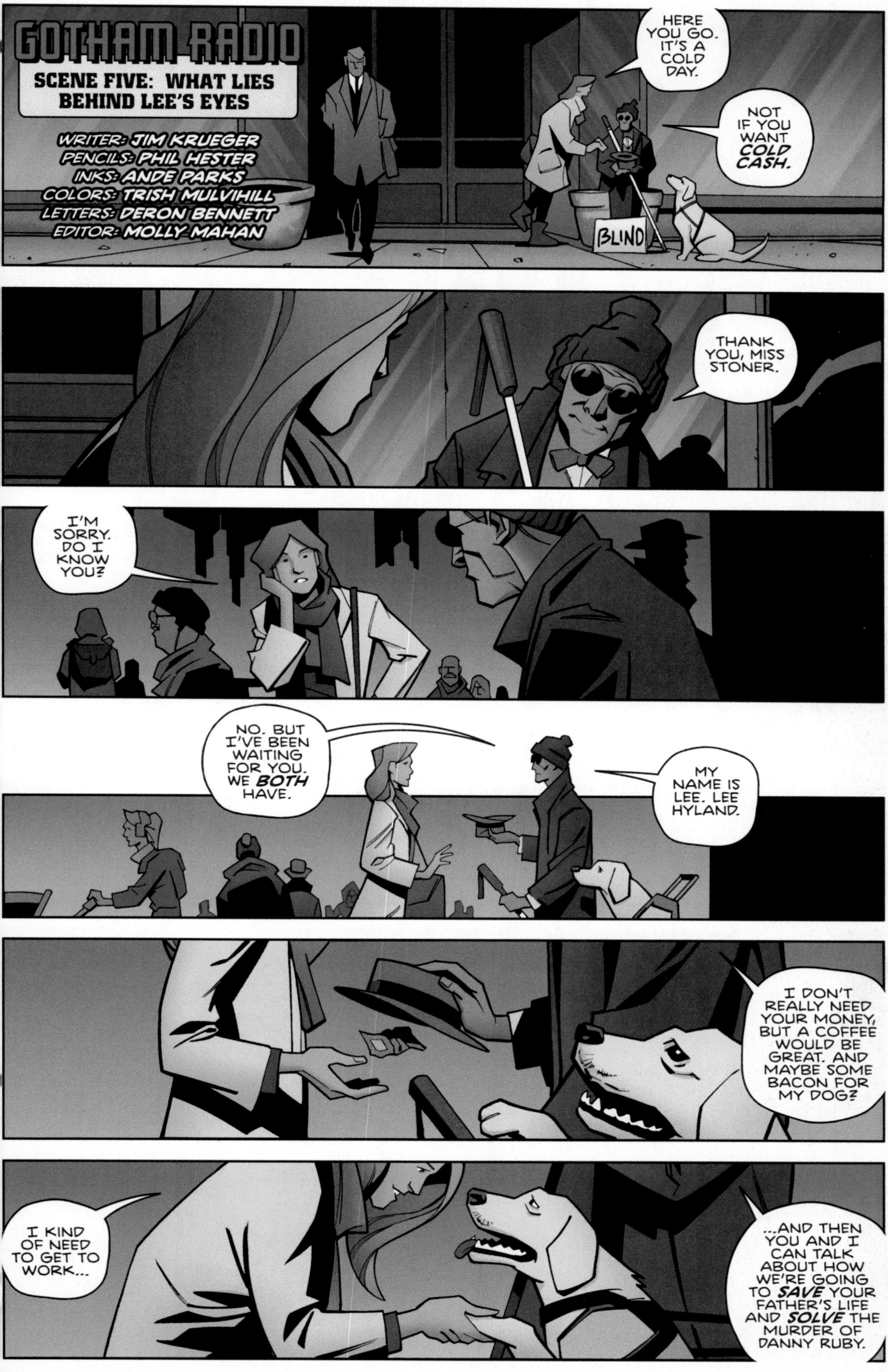
GOTHAM RADIO
SCENE FIVE: WHAT LIES BEHIND LEE'S EYES
WRITER: JIM KRUEGER
PENCILS: PHIL HESTER
INKS: ANDE PARKS
COLORS: TRISH MULVIHILL
LETTERS: DERON BENNETT
EDITOR: MOLLY MAHAN
HERE YOU GO. IT'S A COLD DAY.
NOT IF YOU WANT COLD CASH.
BLIND
THANK YOU, MISS STONER.
I'M SORRY. DO I KNOW YOU?
NO. BUT I'VE BEEN WAITING FOR YOU. WE BOTH HAVE.
MY NAME IS LEE. LEE HYLAND.
I DON'T REALLY NEED YOUR MONEY, BUT A COFFEE WOULD BE GREAT. AND MAYBE SOME BACON FOR MY DOG?
I KIND OF NEED TO GET TO WORK...
...AND THEN YOU AND I CAN TALK ABOUT HOW WE'RE GOING TO SAVE YOUR FATHER'S LIFE AND SOLVE THE MURDER OF DANNY RUBY.

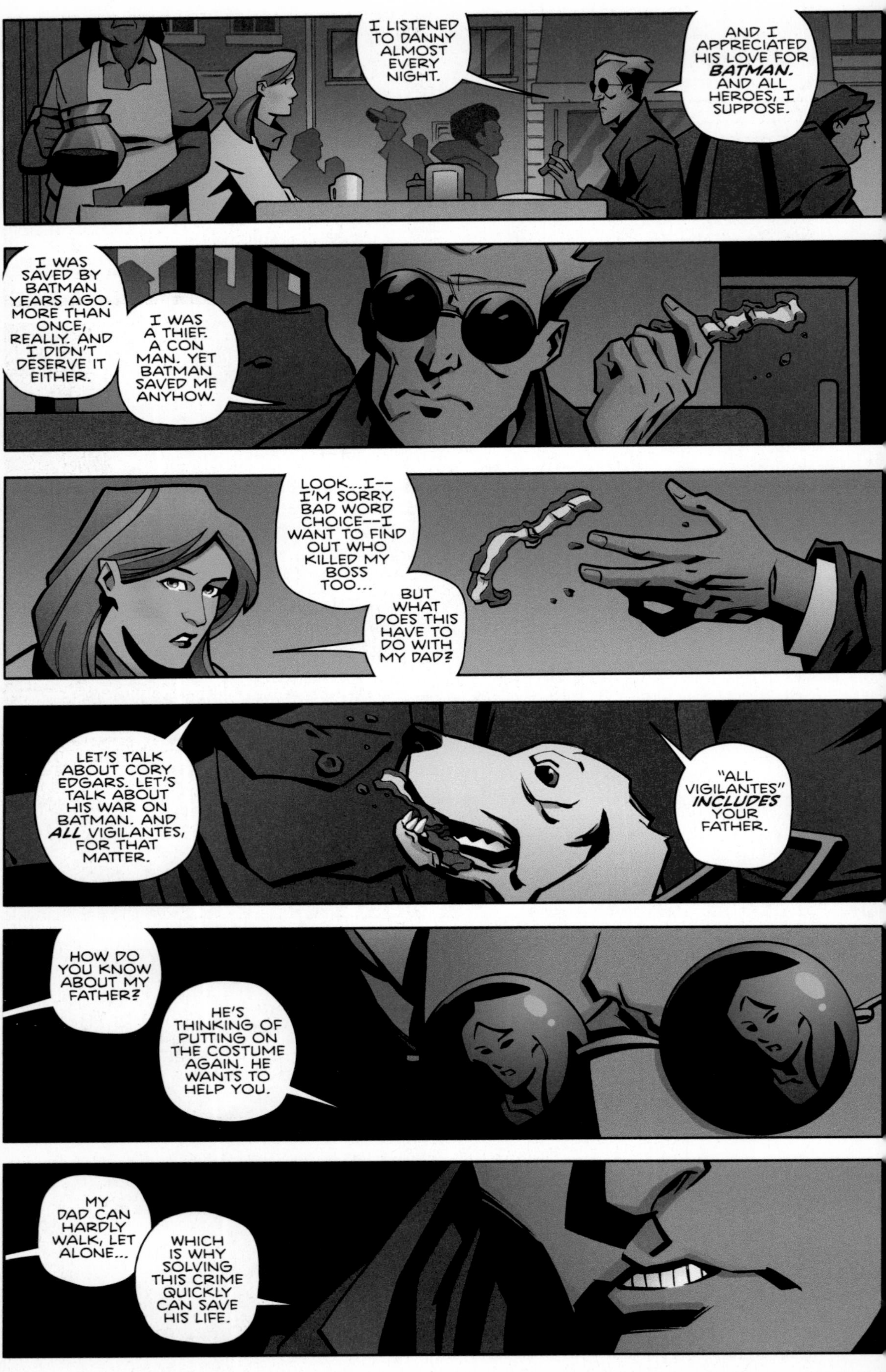
I LISTENED TO DANNY ALMOST EVERY NIGHT.
AND I APPRECIATED HIS LOVE FOR BATMAN. AND ALL HEROES, I SUPPOSE.
I WAS SAVED BY BATMAN YEARS AGO. MORE THAN ONCE, REALLY. AND I DIDN'T DESERVE IT EITHER.
I WAS A THIEF. A CON MAN. YET BATMAN SAVED ME ANYHOW.
LOOK...I-- I'M SORRY. BAD WORD CHOICE--I WANT TO FIND OUT WHO KILLED MY BOSS TOO...
BUT WHAT DOES THIS HAVE TO DO WITH MY DAD?
LET'S TALK ABOUT CORY EDGARS. LET'S TALK ABOUT HIS WAR ON BATMAN. AND ALL VIGILANTES, FOR THAT MATTER.
"ALL VIGILANTES" INCLUDES YOUR FATHER.
HOW DO YOU KNOW ABOUT MY FATHER?
HE'S THINKING OF PUTTING ON THE COSTUME AGAIN. HE WANTS TO HELP YOU.
MY DAD CAN HARDLY WALK, LET ALONE...
WHICH IS WHY SOLVING THIS CRIME QUICKLY CAN SAVE HIS LIFE.

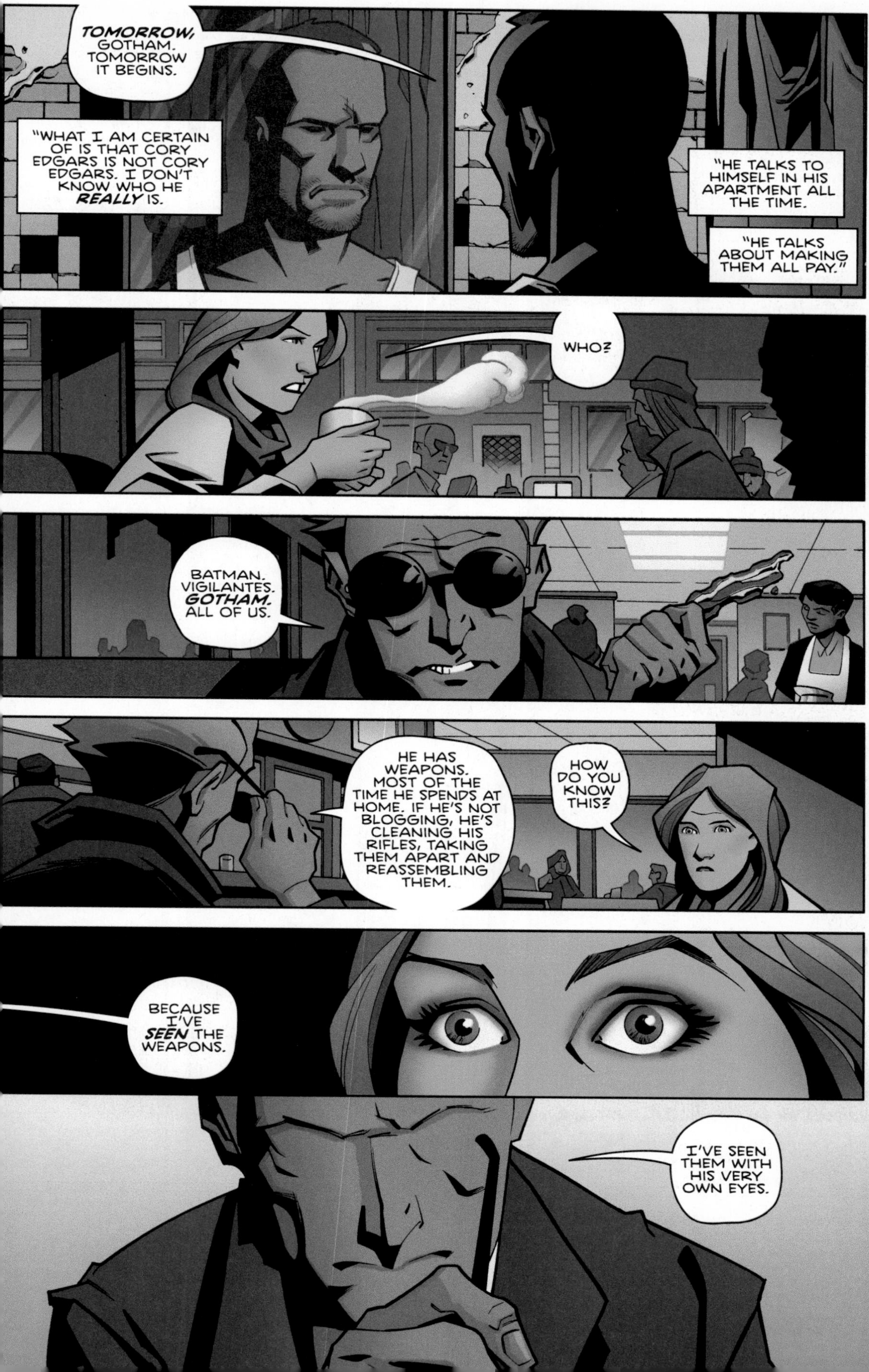
TOMORROW, GOTHAM. TOMORROW IT BEGINS.
"WHAT I AM CERTAIN OF IS THAT CORY EDGARS IS NOT CORY EDGARS. I DON'T KNOW WHO HE REALLY IS.
"HE TALKS TO HIMSELF IN HIS APARTMENT ALL THE TIME.
"HE TALKS ABOUT MAKING THEM ALL PAY."
WHO?
BATMAN. VIGILANTES. GOTHAM. ALL OF US.
HE HAS WEAPONS. MOST OF THE TIME HE SPENDS AT HOME. IF HE'S NOT BLOGGING, HE'S CLEANING HIS RIFLES, TAKING THEM APART AND REASSEMBLING THEM.
HOW DO YOU KNOW THIS?
BECAUSE I'VE SEEN THE WEAPONS.
I'VE SEEN THEM WITH HIS VERY OWN EYES.

# GOTHAM RADIO SCENE SIX: COLD AIR

WRITER: JIM KRUEGER PENCILS: PHIL HESTER INKS: ANDE PARKS COLORS: TRISH MULVIHILL LETTERS: DERON BENNETT EDITOR: MOLLY MAHAN

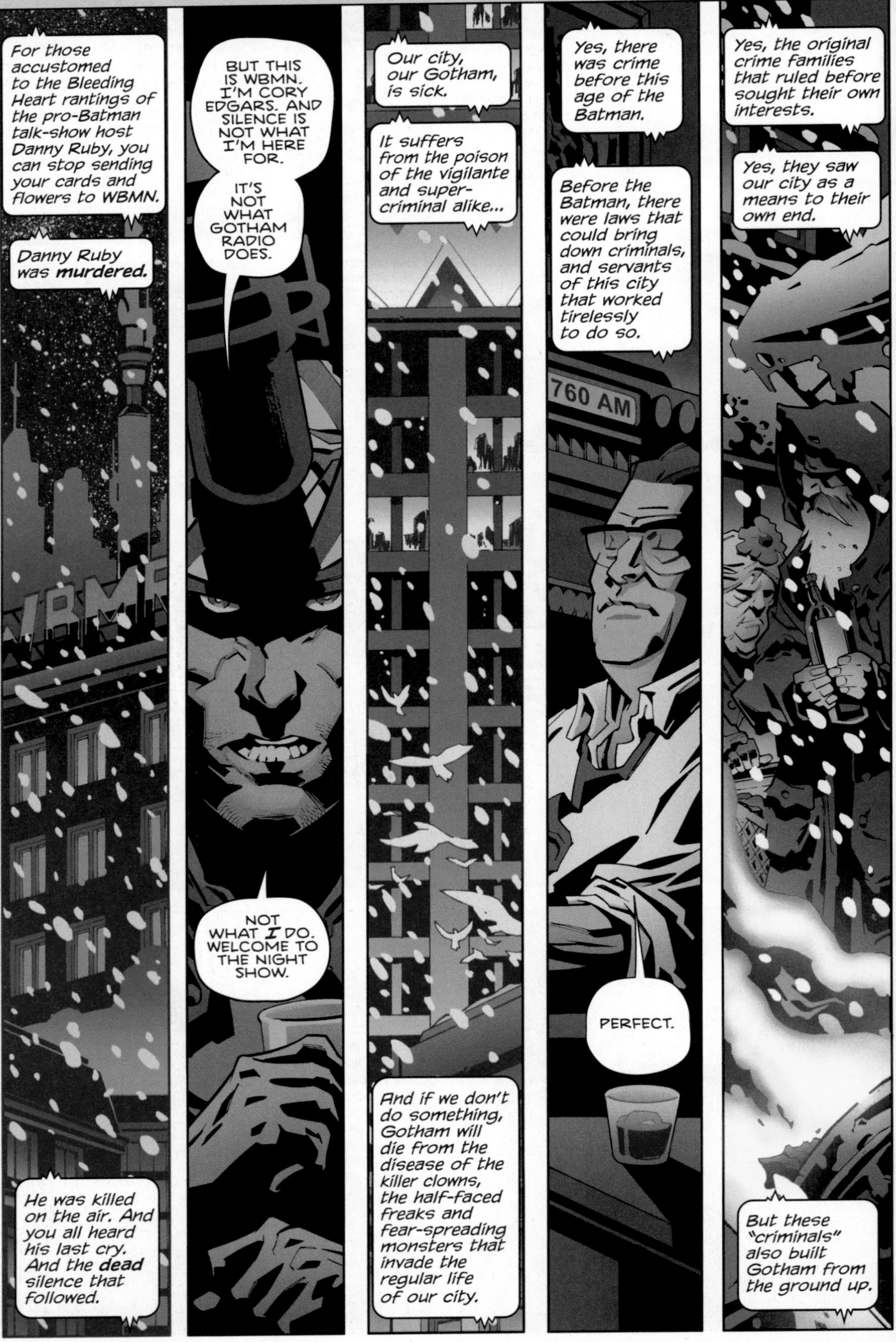

For those accustomed to the Bleeding Heart rantings of the pro-Batman talk-show host Danny Ruby, you can stop sending your cards and flowers to WBMN.
Danny Ruby was **murdered.**
He was killed on the air. And you all heard his last cry. And the **dead** silence that followed.
BUT THIS IS WBMN. I'M CORY EDGARS. AND SILENCE IS NOT WHAT I'M HERE FOR.
IT'S NOT WHAT GOTHAM RADIO DOES.
NOT WHAT *I* DO. WELCOME TO THE NIGHT SHOW.
Our city, our Gotham, is sick.
It suffers from the poison of the vigilante and super-criminal alike...
And if we don't do something, Gotham will die from the disease of the killer clowns, the half-faced freaks and fear-spreading monsters that invade the regular life of our city.
Yes, there was crime before this age of the Batman.
Before the Batman, there were laws that could bring down criminals, and servants of this city that worked tirelessly to do so.
760 AM
PERFECT.
Yes, the original crime families that ruled before sought their own interests.
Yes, they saw our city as a means to their own end.
But these "criminals" also built Gotham from the ground up.

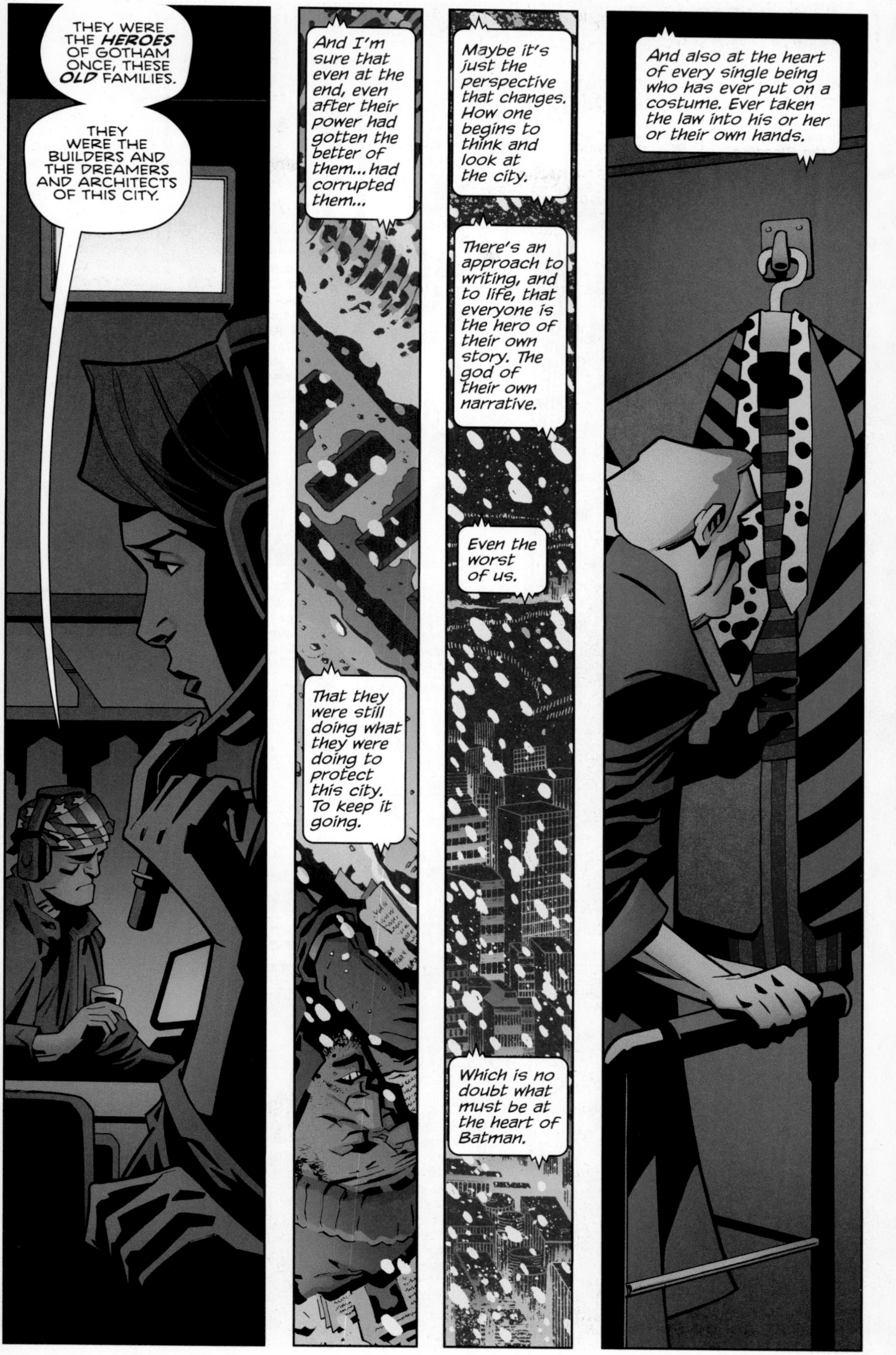
THEY WERE THE HEROES OF GOTHAM ONCE, THESE OLD FAMILIES.
THEY WERE THE BUILDERS AND THE DREAMERS AND ARCHITECTS OF THIS CITY.
And I'm sure that even at the end, even after their power had gotten the better of them... had corrupted them...
That they were still doing what they were doing to protect this city. To keep it going.
Maybe it's just the perspective that changes. How one begins to think and look at the city.
There's an approach to writing, and to life, that everyone is the hero of their own story. The god of their own narrative.
Even the worst of us.
Which is no doubt what must be at the heart of Batman.
And also at the heart of every single being who has ever put on a costume. Ever taken the law into his or her or their own hands.

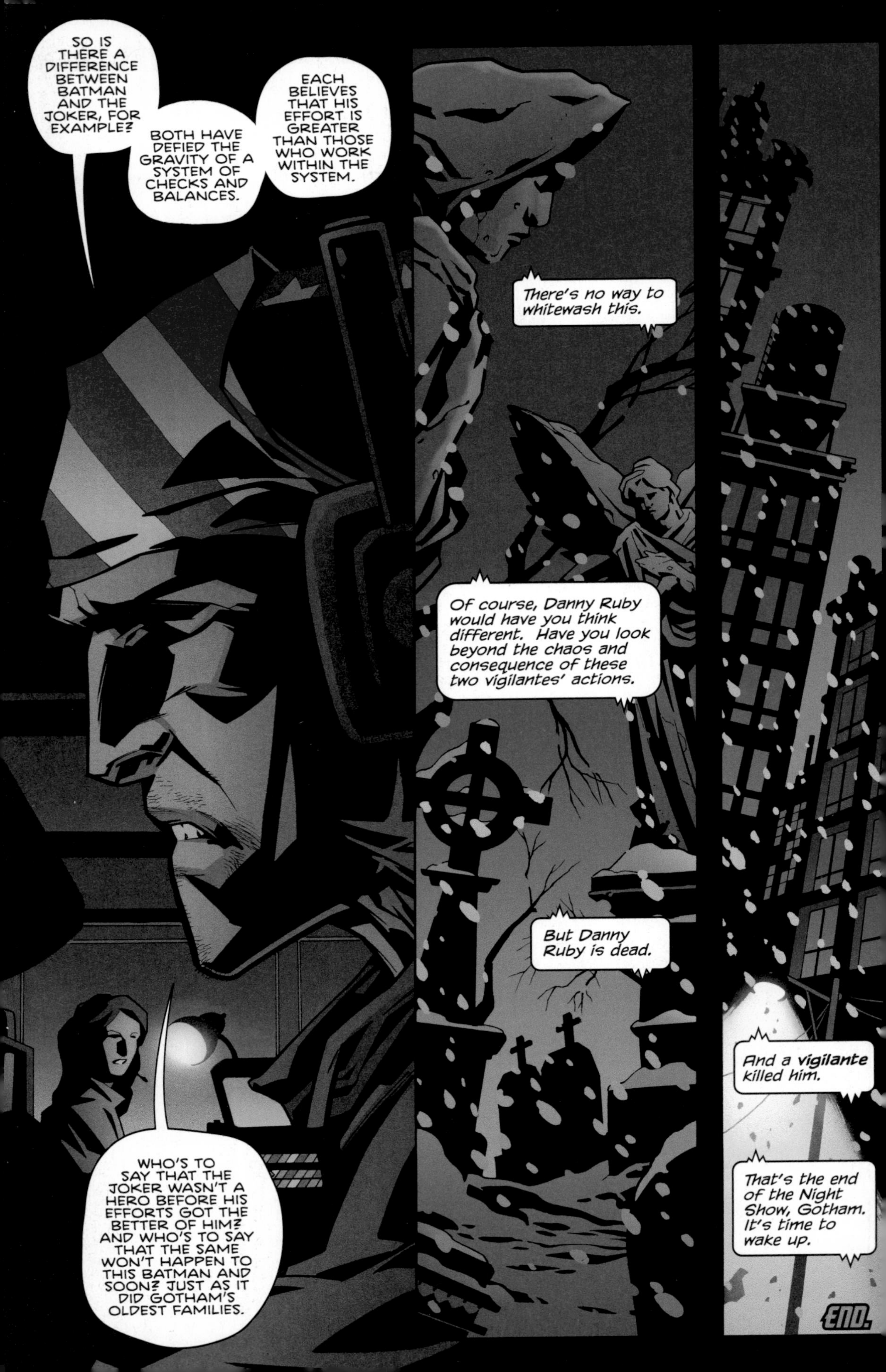
SO IS THERE A DIFFERENCE BETWEEN BATMAN AND THE JOKER, FOR EXAMPLE?
BOTH HAVE DEFIED THE GRAVITY OF A SYSTEM OF CHECKS AND BALANCES.
EACH BELIEVES THAT HIS EFFORT IS GREATER THAN THOSE WHO WORK WITHIN THE SYSTEM.
WHO'S TO SAY THAT THE JOKER WASN'T A HERO BEFORE HIS EFFORTS GOT THE BETTER OF HIM? AND WHO'S TO SAY THAT THE SAME WON'T HAPPEN TO THIS BATMAN AND SOON? JUST AS IT DID GOTHAM'S OLDEST FAMILIES.
There's no way to whitewash this.
Of course, Danny Ruby would have you think different. Have you look beyond the chaos and consequence of these two vigilantes' actions.
But Danny Ruby is dead.
And a vigilante killed him.
That's the end of the Night Show, Gotham. It's time to wake up.
END.